Politics and Psychology

Contemporary Psychodynamic Perspectives

Edited by
Joan Offerman-Zuckerberg

Brooklyn, New York

Plenum Press • New York and London

Library of Congress Cataloging-in-Publication Data

Politics and psychology : contemporary psychodynamic perspectives /
  edited by Joan Offerman-Zuckerberg.
      p.   cm.
   Includes bibliographical references and index.
   ISBN 0-306-43864-X
   1. Political psychology.   I. Offerman-Zuckerberg, Joan.
 JA74.5.P643   1991
 320'.01'9--dc20   91-28033
                                                             CIP

ISBN 0-306-43864-X

© 1991 Plenum Press, New York
A Division of Plenum Publishing Corporation
233 Spring Street, New York, N.Y. 10013

Printed in the United States of America

To my father

BERNARD OFFERMAN

a traditional man with a heart of gold

In memoriam

Contributors

HERBERT BARRY III, Ph.D., Professor of Pharmacology and Physiology, University of Pittsburgh School of Dental Medicine, Pittsburgh, Pennsylvania 15261; President of the International Psychohistorical Association (1991-).

LLOYD DEMAUSE, Director, The Institute for Psychohistory, New York, New York; editor, *Journal of Psychohistory*; author, *Foundations of Psychohistory* and *Reagan's America*.

LEANNE DOMASH, Ph.D., Clinical Assistant Professor of Educational Psychology, New York University, New York, New York 10003; Private Practice, 12 East 10th Street, New York, New York 10003.

PAUL H. ELOVITZ, Ph.D., Former President of the International Psychohistorical Association (1988-1990); Founder and Director of the Psychohistory Forum (1983-); a founding faculty member at Ramapo College in New Jersey; a psychotherapist in private practice; editor of *Historical and Psychological Inquiry* (1990).

BETTY GLAD, Ph.D., Professor of Political Science, Department of Government and International Studies, University of South Carolina, Columbia, South Carolina 29208.

GLEN JEANSONNE, Ph.D., Professor of History, University of Wisconsin, Milwaukee, Wisconsin 53201; currently a recipient of a MacArthur Foundation grant to write *Women of the Far Right: The Mother's Movement in World War II*; author of *Leander Perez: Boss of the Delta* (1977), *Gerald L. K. Smith: Minister of Hate* (1988), and *Messiah of the Masses: Huey P. Long, An American Dissenter* (forthcoming).

OLGA MARLIN, Ph.D., Supervisor, William Alanson White Institute, New York, New York; Faculty, Postgraduate Center for Mental Health, New York, New York; Faculty, Brooklyn Institute for Psychotherapy and Psychoanalysis, Brooklyn, New York; Private Practice, 110 East End Avenue, New York, New York 10028.

DOMENICO ARTURO NESCI, M.D., Associate Member of the Italian Psychoanalytic Society and of the International Psychoanalytic Association; Researcher for the Department of Psychiatry and Psychology, Catholic University of the Sacred Heart, Rome, Italy.

JOAN OFFERMAN-ZUCKERBERG, Ph.D., Member, Psychoanalytic Society of the Postdoctoral Program, Inc., New York, New York; Faculty and Supervisor, Brooklyn Institute for Psychotherapy and Psychoanalysis, Brooklyn, New York; Supervisor, Yeshiva University Clinical Program and National Institute for the Psychotherapies, New York, New York 10033.

SAMUEL P. OLINER, Ph.D., Professor of Sociology; Project Director, Altruistic Personality and Prosocial Behavior Institute, Humboldt State University, Arcata, California 95521.

SPYROS D. ORFANOS, Ph.D., Faculty and Supervisor, New York University School of Medicine, New York, New York 10016; Co-Director, Greek American Research Project, Center for Byzantine and Modern Greek Studies of Queens College, City University of New York, Queens, New York 11367.

RITA R. ROGERS, M.D., Clinical Professor of Psychiatry, University of California at Los Angeles, Los Angeles, California 90024; Private Practice, 36 Malaga Cove, Suite 203, Palos Verdes Estates, California 90274.

LOWELL J. RUBIN, M.D., Faculty, The Boston Psychoanalytic Institute, Boston, Massachusetts; Assistant Clinical Professor of Psychiatry, Brown University, Providence, Rhode Island 02912.

MOHAMMED SHAALAN, M.D., Professor of Psychiatry, Al Azhar University, Cairo, Egypt; Private Practice, 10 Abdel Hamid Lotfi Street, Dokki, Cairo, Egypt.

NANCY SMITH, Author, 271 East 78th Street, New York, New York 10021.

MARTIN WANGH, M.D., Training and Supervising Analyst, New York, New York; Professor Emeritus, Clinical Psychiatry, Albert Einstein College of Medicine, Bronx, New York 10461; Training Analyst, Israel Psychoanalytical Institute, Jerusalem, Israel; Scholar, Freud Center, Hebrew University of Jerusalem, Jerusalem 91905, Israel.

BRIAN WHITMORE, Ph.D. Candidate, Department of Government and International Studies, University of South Carolina, Columbia, South Carolina 29208.

THEODORE OTTO WINDT, JR., Ph.D., Professor of Political Rhetoric, University of Pittsburgh, Pittsburgh, Pennsylvania 15260.

LUITGARD N. WUNDHEILER, Ph.D., Faculty and Supervisor, Brooklyn Institute for Psychotherapy and Psychoanalysis, Brooklyn, New York; Private Practice, 925 Union Street, Brooklyn, New York 11215.

RICHARD M. ZUCKERBERG, Ph.D., Cofounder, Chairperson of the Board of Directors, Brooklyn Institute for Psychotherapy and Psychoanalysis, Brooklyn, New York; Coordinator, Mental Health Clinic, Kingsbrook Jewish Medical Center, Brooklyn, New York.

Preface

The world is a different place today.* Much of this has to do with the increasing volume and clarity of the people's collective voice. The power and pressing desire in man for autonomy, self-determination, and change are emerging as a demand. As a consequence, Communist governments are giving way to democratic restructuring, Europe is being recrafted, and the Cold War is slowly thawing. Simultaneously, back home, our government is becoming increasingly bogged down by media-created political images and psychodramas lacking in substance and value—the degree of exposure somehow determined more by commercial appeal (inherent sensationalism) than merit. The newborn child (i.e., the budding democracies) is looking eagerly to Uncle Sam as a role model: throughout the world, people are quoting our political scriptures, our proclamations, our Bill of Rights, and yet as models we seem sorely lacking.

Given this climate, this book intends to address a number of contemporary themes: the role of the media—symbolization, idealization, and projection—on political choice; the roles of group fantasy; and the more rational force of "group governance" on political elections; the personalities of our presidents and leaders, their psychic vulnerabilities, their public versus private personas and how this division interacts with the complex unraveling of historical events (for example, Jimmy Carter's response to crises in Afghanistan and Iran, Michael Dukakis and the 1988 campaign, George Bush's emergence as president, John F. Kennedy and his private versus public personas, Anwar Sadat as myth and symbol).

We look to the heart of darkness and try to explore and explicate the dynamics of a very primitive form of leadership in Jim Jones. We look at childhood

*Today refers to the world before the Gulf war, 1990—a time of great hope.

ix

patterns and extrapolate possible sources of influence: growing up in Nazi Germany, changing Soviet child-rearing practices, and the current "gentle revolution." We turn to the impact of growing up in Czechoslovakia, a totalitarian regime, on an analyst's perception of current realities. Finally, we look at the ingredients that go into making war and making peace. The forces of altruism and common security are counterbalanced by the voices of adolescents, yesterday and today, and the politics of peace and war—the reality of what we might still call a death drive—are explored.

This is a book of many voices. What is particularly rich are the diverse backgrounds represented. We have three psychoanalysts who grew up in totalitarian regimes and who examine the impact of this shared history on their responses to and understanding of the world today (Romanian-born Rita Rogers, Czechoslovakian-born Olga Marlin, and German-born Luitgard Wundheiler). Different parts of the globe are further represented by Martin Wangh of Israel, Domenico Nesci of Italy, Mohammed Shaalan of Egypt, and Spyros Orfanos, whose roots are Greek. Clearly, in each chapter, the impact of one's ethnicity and homeland is felt, perceptions and understandings ultimately being derived from a highly personal base. Lloyd deMause, Paul Elovitz, and Glen Jeansonne are recognized psychohistorians/historians and add insight and knowledge to the integration and application of psychological concepts to our understanding of history. Herbert Barry and Theodore Windt contribute a scholarly, more rationalist explanation of psychopolitical events. Richard and Joan Zuckerberg, Leanne Domash, and Lowell Rubin come from a psychoanalytic tradition and seek to apply psychoanalytic understandings to this increasingly complex world. And Samuel Oliner and Betty Glad have done extensive empirical research in their areas and lend further depth to this collection.

As psychoanalysts, psychologists, psychohistorians, political scientists, historians, and psychiatrists, we are sharing our views on topics not necessarily or traditionally belonging to the scope of our daily work. Regardless of our differences in approach and expression (academic versus clinical, research-oriented versus personal commentary), we share a common need to step out of the consulting room and become more actively involved in the real world around us. We realize that the world is going through a global identity change: we need to raise awareness within ourselves, tuning in to the inevitable psychological "fallout" attending such global changes. Our thinking must shift and direction is needed. From vast emotional investments in cold war, enemy-oriented attitudes, images, and actions, we must turn our energy inward toward solving our own problems. We are not lacking in enemies; they are just being redefined. Clearly, the enemy is us—our shameful homelessness, our saturation in drugs, our damaged environment, our indefensible illiteracy and poverty. Acknowledging this is the first step.

In compiling these chapters, and in constructing the ideas and organization of this book, I would like to thank Leanne Domash, who shared enthusiastically and quite actively in the original and then changing conceptions of this book and who continued to be a truly supportive colleague; Paul Elovitz, whose passion for psychohistory and many contacts proved invaluable; and my 20-year-old son Joshua Zuckerberg, whose recent immersion in political activism as it relates to racism reminded me of a too-dormant, yet preserved part of myself: the part that wants to care beyond oneself, parents, family, children, students, and patients, to the world at large. Many thanks to the staff at Plenum Press as well for its patience. In the few years since the conception of this book, the world has changed and it took some significant updating to be current and relevant.

Contents

III. A GLOBAL VILLAGE? CHILDHOOD ROOTS, REFLECTIONS, AND HOPES

IV. MAKING WAR, MAKING PEACE

I

Political Leadership
Myth and Reality

This process of election affords a moral certainty that the office of President
will seldom fall to . . . any man who is not in an eminent degree endowed with
the requisite qualifications. Talents for low intrigue, and the little arts of
popularity, may . . . suffice to elevate a man to [the governorship of a state]; but
it will require other talents, and a different kind of merit, to establish him in
the esteem and confidence of the whole Union. It will not be too strong to say
that there will be a constant probability of seeing the station filled by characters
preeminent for ability and virtue.

ALEXANDER HAMILTON, *The Federalist (no. 68)*

How we come to choose our leaders is a complex phenomenon. Motives both
conscious (Barry) and unconscious (R. Zuckerberg, J. Zuckerberg, Domash) in-
terweave. Political image crafted in part by projection and idealization is in
perpetual motion, politics being clearly fueled by both fact and fantasy. Given
this, we look further. The Jonestown "collective suicide" illustrates a catastrophic
form of submission to leadership that is at best disquieting, shedding some light
on our deepest and darkest urges—that is, the wish to merge with something
magical and powerful, to surrender self, to return to a state of protection and
symbiosis.

1

1

Shifting Images in Politics

Leanne Domash and Joan Offerman-Zuckerberg

During the 1988 presidential campaign[1] the American people sat and listened. At first many of us were pro-Dukakis, admiring his independence, his intelligence, his egalitarian marriage, his substance. Bush seemed boring and a "wimp," his marriage from another era. Sheehy's (1988) analysis, in *Character,* of Bush as a hopeless follower and a sycophant of Reagan's seemed apt. Then, slowly, over the course of several months, Bush looked better and better. He emerged from under the domination of Reagan. He shed that "deferential Episcopalian tilt" as one friend called the self-effacing manner he had assumed as vice president (Dowd, 1989b, p. 1). And he was a quiet man. He listened. He was from the eastern upper class but could stop and talk to a woman on the campaign trail about her particular concerns. He *seemed* to care, and more importantly appeared responsive.[2]

Dukakis, on the other hand, began to represent the "big chill." A short article in the *New York Times* (Campaign Trails, 1988) said it all. It reported how curiously reserved Dukakis was with Bentsen. Immediately after a photography session in which both men posed together, Dukakis spun around and left without a word to Mr. Bentsen. A senior Dukakis aide was asked if the relationship was stiff and formal. "That's Michael Dukakis you described," said the aide.

LEANNE DOMASH, Ph.D. • Clinical Assistant Professor of Educational Psychology, New York University, New York, New York 10003; Private Practice, 12 East 10th Street, New York, New York 10003. JOAN OFFERMAN-ZUCKERBERG, Ph.D. • Member, Psychoanalytic Society of the Postdoctoral Program, Inc., New York, New York; Faculty and Supervisor, Brooklyn Institute for Psychotherapy and Psychoanalysis, Brooklyn, New York; Supervisor, Yeshiva University Clinical Program and National Institute for the Psychotherapies, New York, New York 10033.

Politics and Psychology: Contemporary Psychodynamic Perspectives, edited by Joan Offerman-Zuckerberg. Plenum Press, New York, 1991.

If the Democrat Dukakis represents our need for change and the Republican Bush our need for conformity, familiarity, and predictability, Dukakis lost his appeal because intuitively we know that an inflexible, cold approach, one that does not reach out to us, cannot herald freshness, openness, and change. Bush, however, continued to convincingly represent conformity, plus he evidenced an ability to change and to be personal and warm. He managed to embody both sides of the universal struggle in all of us between continuity and change. In a quiet way, he seemed to give us a bit of everything, and perhaps as well retained a bit of Reagan's warmth and appeal (or was that transference, a carryover regarding our wish that he embody the good father without the actor's trappings?).

What happened? Are we simply being manipulated by the media or are we perceiving real traits in these people? Do the candidates themselves become transformed by the campaign? How come the Bush marriage, which initially seemed so antiquated, now appears warm and reassuring, a source of strength. Barbara Bush's image has changed from a somewhat cold and perhaps manipulative woman to one warm and irreverent. She is seen as "steadfast as Mother Courage and as spirited as Auntie Mame" (Weintraub, 1989, p. 1). She is a woman lacking in excessive personal narcissism, a welcome respite from Nancy Reagan, and from our culture's obsession with youth, appearance—the polished image. Barbara is real, wrinkled, white-haired, fully proportioned; she possibly embodies a new acceptance, a new self-image less perfectionistic for the American woman, and the American man for that matter. She does not hide her aging. She is not self-effacing about her weight. Her elegance is in her acceptance of who she is, her age, her lusty appetite; and this, in our youth-obsessed, narcissistically ridden culture, inspires. Shifting images: this is the woman a year ago we saw as archaic, maternal, unsexual, harsh. Now, when we compare her with Kitty Dukakis who required rehabilitation from diet pills and more recently alcoholism, we ask ourselves, who is a more worthy role model? Shifting images: the outer form, our initial image gets filled out and substance alters the original percept. This oscillating function of self-correcting perceptions seems a constant in how we understand the world.

We cannot make note of this phenomenon without extending our observation to another leader across the world, inextricably tied to us now and perhaps forever, namely, Gorbachev. For as long as we can remember the Soviets were the enemy and somewhere inside we needed that image, in fact, required this polarization of good and bad, rich and bereft, modern and archaic in our thinking. Reagan played to these images—and in fact romanticized them. They were the "barbarians." Now Gorbachev, a man of sensitivity, superior intelligence, and depth, visits our country and he becomes a star. We looked to our leaders, the Reagans then and the Bushes now, and they seemed even more clearly lacking. Here, we scream out, is an opportunity, unheralded! Yes, of course, we need to be cautious; yes, there is a history of distrust, but "seize the day," this may be a moment of hope—and somehow Reagan came around at the end. Was it for the record, was it political strategy, was it his increasing maturity?

In Bush, we have renewed hope that the outstretched hand will not be ignored. He still thinks in terms of arms control buildup and deterrence. He still assumes, "paranoid like," that "they are out to get us;" this paranoid thinking is the bedrock of most international political thinking, but *slowly*, very slowly the images may change. Does it not seem in this age of global democratization that Shiite terrorists are more the enemy these days; that like the Soviets of the 1950s and 1960s, *they* are playing with a whole new deck, the observers of an unfamiliar religion that makes them (we think) relatively immune to the fear of death. We wonder—shifting images.

At the start of the campaign, when we know the least about the candidates, their "symbolic" value is highest; that, based on only a hint or suggestion (Bush's wealth and conservatism or Dukakis's independence and immigrant background), we project certain ideas and ideals of our own into their image. We embellish what we see and like or dislike it according to our value system. Zuckerberg (1987) advanced this hypothesis to help explain the original appeal of Gary Hart. Much like the Rorschach inkblots, we project much of what we need, or wish for, in response to these relatively unstructured and ambiguous forms.

As the campaign proceeds, however, more of the *reality* of the candidates takes hold as interpreted, portrayed, and controlled by complex media intervention. The task of finding out how much is the candidate and how much is media fantasy is formidable (like the dream, there is both manifest and latent content). Most probably a really excellent media campaign takes the best actual qualities of the candidates and transforms them into appealing concepts to the public. An interview with Peggy Noonan, speechwriter for Presidents Reagan and Bush, reveals just that (Dowd, 1989c). During the campaign, Noonan traveled with Bush. She ate with him and watched him with his children and grandchildren. She interviewed him like a reporter. She compared the people's response to him with their response to Reagan. Then she interpreted him in his speeches, finding the "quiet man" who was "kinder and gentler."

In short, she looked and found the best in him and transformed this into poetic, moving words that inspired the public. This connects us to the candidate. We can look up to him, thereby gaining hope[3] and reducing our isolation. In Noonan's words, a great political speech "makes people less lonely. It connects strangers with simple truths" (Dowd, 1989c, p. 10). So the answer to the question: are we seeing something real in the candidates or are we being manipulated by the media; the answer is, both. And the picture we saw of Bush was preferable to that of Dukakis to the majority of Americans. (Other reality factors of course play a role in political choice, but our emphasis here is on the psychological.)

Bush, in his effort and wish to redeem, in his speech punctured by hesitances and slips, in his at times awkward availability and responsiveness, contrasts with Reagan's polish and well-practiced reserve—Reagan, the epitome of the "scripted man," the political actor, is now upstaged by a "real" person—a person who makes no greater appeal than to "roll up your sleeves and get the job done." Bush lacks an "image" and this in a way is reassuring. The campaign of 1988 soured us in unpredictable ways. We became agitated with the political gamesmanship. From farmer to businessman, from stockbroker to housewife, we interviewed people on their sentiments, feelings, and thoughts regarding the campaign. People uniformly spoke of feeling tired of being "told what the politician thought they wanted to hear." Where is the real Dukakis? If he is a liberal, say it!

An intriguing question is why Bush became so positively transformed by the campaign—it appeared to have a generally therapeutic effect on him: he became his own man (see Chapter 7, this volume). It is possible that what Sheehy (1988) described in George Bush was an Oedipal inhibition (a wish to and fear of surpassing the father and an assumption of a chronically self-effacing stance). However, both the push of the campaign and the endorsement of the good "father" (Reagan) helped Bush break through his inhibition and assume a successfully authoritative stance. "It's as though a great shadow has been lifted," said one of the men chosen for the Bush Cabinet (Sheehy, 1988). Perhaps Bush's conflict was resolved with the help of the campaign. Given an opportunity to grow, one can seize it, if intrapsychic conflicts do not shackle or constrain. Bush was given this opportunity and in seizing the role, he is working through the developmental issues.

Dukakis, on the other hand, seemed to suffer from character issues of stubbornness, arrogance, and inflexibility (see Chapter 5, this volume). These intensified during the campaign with the public perceiving him as cold and detached, and with his being unable to listen even to his media advisors. The public needs a hero they can admire both as a political figure and one who will listen. Dukakis wasn't listening, and if he was, seemed to go only halfway.

Bush also may be appealing to the hero or heroine in each one of us as he attacks selfishness in people and calls for civic pride and morality. His "thousand points of light" are the conservative version of Kennedy's "Ask not what your country can do for you, ask what you can do for your country." In this way, Bush is calling for us to reach for something ideal or heroic within ourselves. As Campbell (1973) states,

> The end of the hero's journey is not the aggrandizement of the hero. The ultimate aim of the quest must be neither release nor ecstacy for oneself, but the wisdom and power to serve others. The celebrity lives only for the self. The hero acts to redeem society. (p. 340)

More recently, Bush's genuineness and altruism were commented on by Maureen Dowd (1989a) in the *New York Times*. She states:

> Although Mr. Reagan made family values the touchstone of his political career, he has often been publicly estranged from family members during his tenure in Washington. It is the Bush White House that will bustle with family, and it is Mr. Bush who can spend a couple of hours showing his granddaughter, Ellie, the contents of his tackle box, or a day floating in a boat with his grandson, George, casting their lines and watching for starfish. Mr. Reagan talks a lot about the importance of religious values.
>
> It is Mr. Bush who goes to church. Mr. Reagan has the romantic, rugged image of an American cowboy and tells sentimental war stories better than anyone, and yet Mr. Bush was the decorated war hero. Mr. Reagan exudes a manly bonhomie, but it is Mr. Bush who has the wide circle of pals. The President has few close friends and does not keep in close phone contact with old cronies.

The 1988 campaign, unlike the preceding others, seemed to herald a new era, one marked by massive media manipulation, interpretation, and control; a control that seemed to feel strangely natural given the scripted actor–president we knew, given the continuous media inoculation of antibodies to knowledge, substance, issues, and facts to which we had become accustomed (perhaps a "cultural addiction"). Steven Roberts (1988), a former White House correspondent for the *New York Times* and currently a senior writer for *U.S. News and World Report,* describes the 1988 campaign as

> The Year of the Handler, a campaign waged "between high-tech button-pushers unburdened by contending visions or issues."
> The Dukakis camp is described as practicing "microwave politics, cold image in, warm image out" and Senator Paul Simon is described at one point as having "a great face for radio." (p. 6)

Given this addiction to a quick high-tech media fix, it is interesting to note how much we really want or need to know about a particular candidate or official. What is "knowing" about a public official? There is the role, the protection of "the presidency," which offers protection to the people. The office transcends any one particular person. Too much protection, however, is a collusion with infantile wishes. Too little protection overwhelms the public with unnecessary trivia and irrelevant sensationalism. This was in the recent Abernathy book on Martin Luther King, which discussed King's sexual liaisons the night he was assassinated. For a person in authority, there needs to be a balance between the image and the real object. Some optimal distance must be kept.

The constant tension between our wish to know and the media's wish for us not to know certain things is reflected in the bizarre fact that numerous polls indicate that the electorate wants substance, not gossip, image, and manipulation (see Chapter 2, this volume). However, when this information is presented to media moguls, they deny it and offer sensationalism instead. Or when a complaint is offered to government, for example, that Bush is not sufficiently assertive, government officials say the public is misperceiving, then offer still more powerful media manipulation to correct this "misperception." If a child were treated in this way, we would say he is being robbed of his feelings and perceptions and perhaps being made to feel "crazy." This is precisely how the public is being treated by the media/government. We want to judge on issues and not personalities. Yet certain character traits may imply certain behaviors and therefore should not be ignored. In our frustration over any "real knowing" about the candidates in order to make decisions about leadership ability, we sometimes settle for mere gossip and needless intrusion into private lives. This is a perversion of real knowing and allows us to abdicate responsibility for real knowledge as the electorate. Our "need to know" personal trivia is a misconception of genuine knowing and represents our collusion to remain infantile.

The massive extent of government manipulation of image and media bombardment has left us physically numb. When real issues and real emotions are so removed from us, we cease to feel. This trauma of manipulation leads to detachment and a political schizoidism. We turn to private lives for meaning because we feel so impotent in the larger arena. Just as a child turns away from a parent who is only image, lacking in guidance and substance, so the electorate tends to turn away. This, of course, leaves us even more open to corruption and/or media manipulation. We become vulnerable to projection and idealization. We become easy targets for those who gain power and abuse it. Knowing so many people have become cynical, they feel no one is watching or caring. This collection of chapters is in part to invite the psychological community to open up the political arena to their insights and to bring their creativity to this vitally important area.[4]

In a sense, the trauma of government and media manipulation produces defenses such as splitting and idealization. The world gets divided into good guys and bad guys and we have an illusion of knowledge. The psychic numbing exacerbates our own inner ambivalence about knowing, about giving up our tendencies toward splitting and projection. Then, in our need to externalize "bad," in our need for enemies, we search for new opposition: the Mideast and Central America have upstaged the Soviet Union, and terrorism has upstaged communism. In a recent article, Landan (1989) discusses the universal and unconscious need of people to split, project, and externalize. Both our wish to love and our wish to destroy contribute to this. This is partly the reason, of course, for the power of psychoanalysis, in that these universal needs can be worked with, that is, clarified and analyzed. However, when these needs are projected onto society in general, with no reliable correction of distortions, there ensues a need to see others as bad and a concomitant wish, although often denied, for war.

Landan speaks of our internal war that we attempt to solve by projecting part of the badness onto others. For example, in our wish to achieve a perfect relationship, one in which there is no hostility or rivalry, only love, we need to project our destructive anger onto others—for example, the Russians or the Shiites. We retain the ideal of perfect union (originally with the mother or mother figure). Then the bad anger belongs not to us, but to the other (see Chapter 12, this volume). Similarly, it could be said that the stability of the groups we form depends in great part on the degree to which we succeed in projecting our feelings of hatred. Projection remains one of the most important ways of handling primitive impulses. The question is whether we as adults can recognize these projections and take them back. Otherwise, of course, these projections may eventually lead to war where even members of our group get destroyed. The important test ahead is what we do without "familiar enemies." What do we do with budding democracies? In psychoanalytic treatment, we often deal with conflict resolution. A couple comes to mind.

Bill and Sandra are married but for the most part remain separate. Sandra had two children in the first 4 years of this marriage. She had some difficulty separating from them, for the most part a natural difficulty that attends the intense bonding and attachment that is part of the nursing and early infancy experience. She experiences Bill as remote, aloof, married to his computer and house. Bill rejects her sexual entreaties, and she feels unimportant and inconsequential. Bill experiences Sandra as "bitchy" and tough on him, critical but "a wonderful mother." Bill, now 55, says he's been burned too many times by women. Now he cannot trust. He is withholding and he is scared to let down his defenses; he is avoiding intimacy consciously and unconsciously. His mother was abusive physically and emotionally and women thereafter have been as well. Sandra experienced her family as emotionally negligent, and what is being played out here is more of the same. She says she is distrustful. Does he really love me? And why?

It is not always justified to extrapolate from the individual to a group then to a nation, though striking parallels remain. It is untrue to assert that group/societal behavior follows individual dynamics without modification, for the group has dynamics that are more than just the "sum of the parts." The group is different. Nevertheless, parallels remain.

Couples exemplify all too often the complexity of interpersonal compatibility, the shifting differences in image and perception, in experience and feelings that can emerge as irreconcilable realities. Often in our work we are faced with a difficult paradox. How do we forge a new *trust* in two distrusting individuals who collectively have had a troublesome history and who as individuals have had emotional problems dating back to early childhood?

Such is the task ahead for the Soviet Union and the United States, for Israel and Palestine, for South Africa. Trust does *not* spring naturally unless there is benevolent historical experience to feed its growth. Lacking that, trust requires the *gradual* build up of good and shared experiences over time and perhaps additionally a "leap of faith." So it seems there is today around the world a gradual "global warming" not belonging solely to climatic conditions. There will be inevitably, with the hopeful dissolution of external nationwide tensions, a turning inward, a "national introspection" if you will. When conflicts get deeply resolved, on an unconscious level defenses get restructured, and what is freed is energy for ego to function more effectively and more pervasively.

The task at hand, then, is to find a means of communication that is substantial and constant and that does not depend on "splitting" our emotions and thoughts into good and bad. To accomplish this, we need to recognize and resolve our internal wars, as well as fight against government or media manipulation in healthy ways, without resorting to costly, and possibly deadly, defenses.

America may slowly be giving up its "war neurosis"; with the iron curtain melting, and with the cold war warming, we will hopefully look to our own garden, a garden both ugly and beautiful, cultured and raw. The eradication of homelessness, hunger, hopelessness-fed addiction, rage-filled child abuse, and illiteracy; these are the wars ahead, wherein the only enemy to be found is ourselves.

The challenge is formidable. Enemies are changing. Images are kaleidoscopic in their shifting reconstitutions. With the collapse of the Berlin Wall, there has been a feeling among young Germans of absolution. The wall was a symbol of punishment, division, and distrust. The wall comes down as repression is lifted. Now what we see is an unprecedented rush of creative wishes and demands for freedom, self-expression, participation, and protests all over the globe. In this regard, Nelson Mandela's eloquence serves here:

> And so we have come to Washington ... not as pretenders to greatness but as a particle of a people whom we know to be noble and heroic, enduring, multiplying, permanent, rejoicing in the expectations and knowledge that their humanity will be reaffirmed and enlarged by open and unfettered communion with the world. (Speech to joint meeting of Congress June 26, 1990)

What we have to be cautious about is reactionary forces seeking to suppress these frightening new voices (already in evidence are more overt forms of anti-Semitism and more violent pro-apartheid factions, etc.). As Americans, our leadership has to meet this new age with "new thinking," renewed hope, and trust. It is imperative. What we stand to lose is nothing less than peace.

NOTES

1. This chapter was written over the span of a year-and-a-half, beginning with the presidential campaign through Bush's first six months in office.

2. Our comments are necessarily psychological in orientation. Our interest is in exploring unconscious motives and conflicts. The rationalist viewpoint of political life is omitted here for the sake of emphasis, but certainly understood to play a significant role in the dynamic complex interplay of forces that constitute political choice, movement, and outcome.

3. Hope alters perception. Even now, in reading this chapter, perceptions have changed. When leaders are new, there *is* great hope that he/she will be different somehow; this raises our expectations and colors our views.

4. Even more relevant now, given the urgent need for us to respond in an "enlightened" way to the global forces of democratization currently unleashed.

REFERENCES

Campaign trails: Big chill in evidence at top of the tickets. (1988) *New York Times,* September 12.

Campbell, J. (1973). *The myth of the hero with a thousand faces,* Princeton, NJ: Princeton University Press.

Dowd, M. (1989a). *New York Times,* January 15.

Dowd, M. (1989b). Transformation of Bush: His own man. *New York Times,* January 21, p. 1.

Dowd, M. (1989c). A stirring breeze sparks feelings, then words for a president's vision. *New York Times,* January 21, p. 10.

Ladan, A. (1989). The wish for war. *International Review of Psychoanalysis, 16* (3), 331–337.

Roberts, S. V. (1988). *New York Times,* January, p. 6.

Sheehy, G. (1988). *Character: America's search for leadership.* pp. 154–187, New York: William Morrow.

Weintraub, B. (1989). A Down-to-earth tenant for an exclusive address. *New York Times,* January 15, p. 1.

Zuckerberg, R. (1987). *Why Gary Hart's fans don't know why they are.* Unpublished manuscript.

2

Some Reflections on Political Choice in America

Symbol and Substance

Richard M. Zuckerberg

In an unpublished paper written in 1984, soon after the Democratic primary of that presidential election year, I mused on one aspect of the character of the relationship between the populace and its leaders, namely, the decision making that went into choosing political candidates for office. The idea of choice is an interesting one for a psychoanalytic psychologist, since much of my understanding and assumptions of human nature tie me to a vision of man as being moved by unconscious and unforeseen motives. So, my interest is more in the interface of the unconscious with a realm of experience we consider to be very conscious, that is, reality. Freud originally delineated the notion of secondary process, as opposed to primary process, to describe that part of man that was engaged in finding out about reality in an effort to maintain one's own survival. He even referred to the development of certain reality-oriented mental structures (i.e., thought, perception, memory, judgment, etc.) as so crucial to the survival of the individual and the race that he considered the source of their development as belonging to the self-preservative *instincts*. These instincts were different from the

RICHARD M. ZUCKERBERG, Ph.D. • Cofounder, Chairperson of the Board of Directors, Brooklyn Institute for Psychotherapy and Psychoanalysis, Brooklyn, New York; Coordinator, Mental Health Clinic, Kingsbrook Jewish Medical Center, Brooklyn, New York.   Editor's Note: This chapter with the comments was originally presented at the 12th Annual Scientific Meeting of the International Society for Political Psychology in Tel Aviv. It was intended to reach the audience on a number of levels—ideational, conceptual, as well as more personal and emotive. It is for this reason that we kept to the format and retained the brief commentary.

Politics and Psychology: Contemporary Psychodynamic Perspectives, edited by Joan Offerman-Zuckerberg. Plenum Press, New York, 1991.

libidinal instincts, which were more unconscious and unknowable and involved with the dynamics of pleasure and pain. The former set of instincts apparently developed for us to use in the service of judging how we could negotiate reality to keep ourselves alive (and in some complementary way, the libidinal instincts used the ego instincts for their own purposes, i.e., to find in the world that which would be gratifying, which is always that which has *been* gratifying).

As is usual for man, we would like to think that we are in control and that our decisions and decision making are derived from a knowledge of those factors that would best serve our needs. We would like to think that this is true even in no less an important process as that of choosing our leaders. Should it not be that we are choosing the best person for the job, at least as we each define this, that this choice is governed by reasoned and knowledgeable judgment, and that we choose people who express in some representative way those ideas and values we ourselves hold as important.

Some anecdotal remarks by the people and the leaders in 1984 underscored just how vague and ill-defined is this process. What touched off my thinking, in particular, was an article in the *New York Times* in March 1984, entitled "Gary Hart's Fans Don't Know Why They Are." In this article it was pointed out that just following the New Hampshire primary Hart's voters were not able to describe his ideas or positions on important topics affecting their lives. And yet they expressed deep conviction that he was their man. Similar patterns were found in other states that had conducted primaries and caucuses. Why then this dramatic shift to Hart and a parallel rejection of the other Democratic hopefuls at that time?

The thesis that I offered then was that most of us are caught up in the political selection process, more than we know (or would dare to admit), not so much in rationally selecting candidates in terms of the positions they hold on important issues, but of what we would like them to be for us.[1] It was particularly interesting that Hart himself appears to be aware that his popularity had less to do with his political positions than it did with what people may have wanted him to be for them, or what he seemed to promise. In this same article he is quoted as remarking, "I've been talking about a lot of issues for a long time, and no one knows it. There is a lot of tabula rasa here" (p. 41). It seemed that Gary Hart, at the time, had some inkling that the source of his popularity had less to do with voter knowledge of his positions than it did with some kind of "projection" upon him, or perception of him, of another kind. This idea of the political candidate as a "blank slate," of course, has a familiar psychological ring to it, calling up what we know of the relationship of perception and projection. It suggests that the people's response to a candidates's political slate may be intermingled with an unconscious use of him for their own purposes (i.e., seeing their own purposes reflected in him), and/or perceiving something about him which suggests that they need him, in some survival-linked way. Mirroring this process in the people is the leader's conscious or intuitive sense of this dynamic, which serves as a bridge to gain access to the voters' trust.

But Mr. Hart's use of the tabula rasa metaphor to indicate an awareness of these themes may be an oversimplification. In fact, accepted psychological belief suggests that whenever there is projection of some kind operating between the perceiver and the perceived, there are always some qualities of a perceptual (and apperceptual) kind operating, that is, there is always a "hook to hang one's coat upon." It is not so much that there is projection of meaning out of thin air, but there is some "seeing into," or the embellishment with meaning, to some perceptual properties that are given in the basic act of perception. It is not so much that people's perceptions are wrong or right; it is that out of their need to see things a certain way, out of wishes perhaps for a leader to be a certain way for them, or in relationship to them (an apperceptive ideational package of attributes that each of us formulates about what we want a leader to be for us), they may well unconsciously and intuitively "rediscover" perceptual properties that they are so vigilant in seeing and "wanting" to perceive in their potential leaders. (This notion of "rediscovering" is what Freud had in mind when he assumed this tendency to find again in the present what once was satisfying, in a transferential sense.)

So, at that time Gary Hart may have possessed some basic properties that were immediately perceivable in perception. One must keep in mind that people were inferring these aspects of leadership not from what they read about him or knew about him in some considered way, but what they thought they knew about him from what they saw or heard of him.[2] This is how perception and judgments about people are linked. We naturally move from the perceptual material to a more complex "intuitive understanding," if we can be so bold as to say that an intuition can reflect an understanding. That is, major inferences can be derived from very limited pieces of information because this is in the nature of intuition: that the whole is judged from some basic part of that whole, especially if there is a need, and therefore a readiness, to see it that way.

And so, Mr. Hart was not totally a blank form; people did see something in him. In fact, many people shared a common view of him as suggested by the wave of popular opinion and positive regard, and this perhaps arose out of some basic inner agenda of the people. But what were these qualities and what was that agenda? Among those interviewed, the perception of Hart kept focusing on his "youthfulness," "newness," "independence," and even "courage." People were obviously more drawn to him because of these perceived qualities than they were with the content of any of his "new ideas." In fact, one could argue that if these were the qualities they saw in him, and given our tendency to make inferential leaps, he might have been chosen as the leader to come to represent new ideas, or a man who would bring change.

But why was there this sudden wave of popularity for a leader who represented change, particularly, if people seemed unable to say anything about the kinds of changes he had in mind for them? One can at least suggest that there was then (perhaps always is) in the mood of people, as there is in the mood of any person, a wish for change and the move to Hart, at least by some, represented this prevailing feeling. But this is not all, because the wish for change and newness is not experienced without ambivalence. Typically, as individuals, and as a nation, we are constantly in a struggle between the wish for change (represented by Hart) and holding on to the familiar (as expressed in Mondale's or Reagan's image). (Remember that Mondale later failed not only because the people were holding on to the familiar, as expressed in Reagan, but because Mondale could not adequately separate himself from the perception that he would bring us back to the way it was under Carter. Not only the familiar was represented by Mondale, but a familiar unpleasant past.)

At least in this election, and it may well be that in each "election," there was a choice that came to be signified by those "running" for election. And this is a choice that represents some inner struggle within man and is personified by the candidates. Carter's campaign versus a Nixon-tarnished Ford certainly posed this in the issue of morality versus immorality, just as perhaps Reagan reflected our own struggle between our conservative and liberal tendencies, that is, the struggle between our self-interested motives and the altruistic side of ourselves. In this election there was clearly the wish for and resistance to change that was reflected in the choice of the leaders. With our political leaders and contests, as in our personal lives, we may have been viewing here the externalization of this perceptual conflict in ourselves, between the old and the new, between what is familiar and what might be different, between continuity or discovery. It may have been that we were witnessing here the people's effort at setting the stage for the presentation and embodiment of this conflict. It is not so much that people wanted Hart, but wanted to experience in themselves, and even among each other, the conflict between what has been given and a possibility for a chance at what could be new. New in this sense does not have to be something utterly new, but some aspect of ourselves that needs to be expressed as individuals or as a group or as a nation. So that, for example, "new" may well be a return to what has been, if what has been represents some aspect or aspects of ourselves that has not been used either through suppression or even repression, but which we feel is still of value to us individually or as a group. Reagan's, and later Bush's, use of the "L" word to associate *liberal* with a tabooed curse word that should not even be spoken aloud underscores the attempt to relegate a political tradition to the depths of the unconscious. Thus, one might say that the oppression of ideas that takes place at the cultural level can often result in repression of human attributes associated with those tabooed ideas.

There are some lessons that can be found in this and similar political events. One is that there is a tendency of the people to be swayed by impressions of candidates, to "see" truths "into" candidates' political ideas or character traits that may or may not be grounded in reality. There is a complementary tendency on the part of leaders to *use* this human tendency of the people for their own purposes; that is, to create and manipulate impressions of themselves or their interpretation of events that they think the people want to see of them or what they want to communicate to the people. This is successful because there is a tendency to infer meaning from dramatic images, to infer the character of a person from some piece of his behavior, and because there is an infantile place in each of us that wants to believe in our leaders. Of course, there are some dangers in all of this. These are that we may offer our trust to those who may not be deserving of it, and we remain susceptible to manipulation, persuasion, and even exploitation in creating ideas that may not be borne out or confirmed by reality.

Within this context, there are some disturbing signs of an increasing use of manipulation, a manipulation that is attempting to create powerful images to replace thought or to misrepresent reality. Image over substance has been the hallmark: image used to resolve ambiguity and complexity and to signal a people what it *should* want. There is a tendency in each of us that wishes we had no conflicts burdened by complex issues, and to have someone tell us it is alright to feel just one way about an issue—no abortion under any conditions, capital punishment will solve crime, no new taxes to burden the electorate, nuclear weapons to increase and preserve national security—simple messages to solve complex social issues. We wish to hear that this is true. Behind closed doors, this is the message to be sent out to the public. It is at the heart of advertising and marketing. The president has become a consumer product, and the presidential races have become no more than manipulation of images to convey who is the "better choice." The political war between Bush and Dukakis was strikingly similar to the battle between Coke and Pepsi, and the tactics to win over public opinion were frighteningly similar. One marketing executive sums up the soda pop wars by saying that the "Coke and Pepsi have run out of things to say about their products. They have to do it via image" ("Star Wars," 1989). In fact Coke regularly polls consumers to determine how closely they associate Coke with important attributes, including young, modern, warm, friendly, and so on. When a dip in one of those attributes is spotted, ads are created to reinforce it in the public mind through methods associating and linking Coke to the attributes they feel will improve the selling of their product. Thus, the use of certain "celebrities" in ads to help bolster the image of Coke as associated with "young" and "modern." This, of course, is not unlike what we see more and more in presidential politics, a kind of marketing of the president as consumer product. George Bush's advisors, worried that he was being linked with the personal attribute of "wimpish," which they felt was singularly "unpresidential," ran to the drafting desks to undo this public perception through the use of images creating the impression of a "real man." Soon, we were watching political ads with Mr. Bush standing in a speed boat traveling at high speeds over ocean waves, his hair blowing in the wind, smiling at the challenge. The idea of the wimpish president quickly dissolves into the perception of a real man challenging the elements in frontiersman-like fashion. Image over substance, image to convey meaning. In a similar vein, we saw the use of Bush ads to "inform us" of his opponent's stand on crime. Here we saw a revolving door attached to a prison entrance and, of course, the idea that follows is that the Governor of Massachusetts will let prisoners out as soon as they come in. This use of image to bolster one's own image and to slander the image of one's opponent is, of course, not new, but it does seem to be gaining in popularity and effectiveness with increasing use of sophisticated marketing techniques to sway public opinion. And, there appears to be an almost reflexive use of such techniques to change the public's beliefs and attitudes, not by appealing to one's own values and to offer these to an intelligent public, but to manipulate ideas through the perception of images. Thus, we have Dan Quayle struggling to "fix" an "image" that we have of him as youthful, inexperienced, and inarticulate by having his advisors "provide him with literate speeches intended to combat the idea that Mr. Quayle is less than cerebral" ("Quayle Campaigns," 1989). This, of course, avoids the issue of whether Mr. Quayle is or is not informed. On another front, we began to hear about the Republicans complaining of a perception that the Bush presidency was "adrift." As reported recently in the *New York Times* ("Bush Fights," 1989), one analyst conceded there is drifting but is irked about the "talk" of it:

> The perception of drift, the discussion and dissection of drift is worsening the drift that exists. It's focusing attention to it. It's helped turn the transition from the happy talk view of the new president to a cold-blooded assessment that they don't have an agenda. (p. 85)

This is a troublesome and almost frightening view of events. It is an attempt at turning the public's felt experience into something wrong, inaccurate, or incomplete. It is blaming the public for its faulty perception by implying "you're seeing things, you're crazy, the problem is in your perception, not the reality of events." Rather than use this real sense of public opinion to listen to what is out there as a legitimate concern of the people, the attempt is to deny and to blame this on faulty reality perception. Furthermore, the emphasis is on "fixing" the perception in support of the image of the president and the presidency, without responding directly to the reality from which these perceptions originate. This is the old authoritarian trick, in which failures in communication are blamed on the one of lesser power, where leverage is achieved through manipulation. And in so doing one fails to answer the questions of the public—real questions regarding the people's concerns of a "drifting" presidency and the implications of questionable leadership which it implies. Why does an elected administration not use this as a source of legitimate criticism, as a need of the people which is not being fulfilled? Is our perception real and justified? There are issues of the day that beg for leadership with substance, not denials through the manipulation of image.

This is one of the potential dangers of our infantile dispositions to sacrifice reality testing and give up our personal power to those who we feel will protect us. The origins of our openness to leaders, of course, lies in the original parent–child relationship in which we looked to those who were more powerful than us for our survival. The wish and tendency to trust is very powerful because of this early dependency, which is characterized by inequality of strength and is in the beginning very necessary for our survival. It is a dependency that tends to be aroused even in adulthood, when we feel ourselves in relationships that are characterized by unequal distributions of power, as in the relationship between the leader and the led. But this tendency to give ourselves over to the other is adaptive especially when the key to survival is to place one's trust in a person on whom one must depend for their survival. As adults, the nature of self–object relationships needs to change in the direction of mutual participation in order to insure one's own survival. The direction of change is from blind trust in an omnipotent good object (or, conversely, blind mistrust of a bad other) to the expectation of a trustworthy relationship based on mutuality of give and take and a constant measuring of the adequacy of the partnering in such a relationship.

The danger has always been, and today is no exception, that we are not only giving up ourselves to those of power, but through image manipulation we are no longer even certain of the character of those we are electing or the reality of the events of our times. Through the reliance on image to form our own opinions we cannot even be sure of the truth or reality of our own thoughts. Some try to convince themselves and to persuade us of their character and those ideas through the altering of self-perceptions (which the self can really begin to believe in if you say it enough) or manipulation of our perceptions (if we need to believe in them enough). This is why we rage so when the substance emerges to destroy the image; we feel betrayed and in some infantile way, with naivete, say "you didn't protect us, you let us down, you were out for yourself, not my interests." This is the price we pay for giving up our good reality testing under the influence of infantile dispositions. We give up government by the people for government by the leaders. This collusion between giving up our own power and assigning it to those who we "know" only from perceptions of reality that we have gained through the manipulation of idea-laden images naively trusted without testing reality is an ever present danger. As Mark Gerzon (1982) asks,

> What sort of leader do I want? Since the nod of his head can initiate Armageddon, I want him to be free of the unconscious desire to prove himself a man. I do not want him to dismiss as effeminate everyone who counsels caution or mediation or who favors nonmilitary responses to conflict. If he ever has to decide whether or not to "push the button" in a crisis, I want him to perceive that crisis accurately—to recognize it as the killing of America, civilization, and perhaps the planet, not as a presidential test of manhood. (p. 100)

The more that we are, the less we will need them to be for us. We can no longer afford to exist in a world of "omniscient experts and ignorant citizens" especially with the dangers nowadays of the meaning power has in the hands of the leaders. We must hold them accountable, but more importantly, we must hold ourselves accountable. If we avoid this, we may allow leaders of minimal substance to gain access to power, and we may evolve into a society of nonthinkers whose ideas about our leaders and our society are determined by pictorial images without bringing our intellect and our own values to bear on what we see. The abandonment of our own good judgment and values is tantamount to a return to childhood, to turn one's survival over to the other. In so doing, we then become either the beneficiaries of their goodness or the victims of their badness. In either case we remain children.

But there are some signs that suggest that both our values and our reality testing is still alive and well. These signs also point and suggest some direction for real leadership. For example, a recent article on Margaret Thatcher ("After a Decade," 1989), suggested that both her admirers and critics concede that the values of Thatcherism, with its emphasis on individual self-reliance and deregulated private enterprise, now dominate the political agenda. In fact, one might conclude that this is in the Zeitgeist of Western civilization in general. But this of course means that it has dominated the personal agenda as well and is reflected in what appears to be a striking cultural emphasis on personal gain and reward. In only a generation we have moved from the yippies of social unrest to the yuppies of self-involvement. In Britain, and no doubt in the United States, welfare state socialism or liberalism is often dismissed as a tired idea that has lost its vote-getting appeal. But the question that is being asked in Britain is how much have social and political attitudes really changed under the surface? A recent poll there found that seven people in ten thought Britain was Thatcherist (defined as a society where the individual is encouraged to look after himself and where the creation of wealth is more highly rewarded) rather than Socialist (defined as a society that emphasizes the social and collective provision of welfare, and in which the caring for others is more highly rewarded). Yet, of these same people polled, only four in ten thought that Britain ought to be this way. The researcher concluded that "if anything, she (Thatcher) has made no further inroads on the values that people hold" (p. A20). Similarly, Louis Harris (1989) reports on the results of a recent poll that uncovered some deeper truths regarding two persistent cultural myths. One is that middle-income people worry only about "making it" and feel no obligation to care for the less fortunate. The other is that the poor have lost hope of extricating themselves. His results showed, to the contrary, that "members of the underclass have not lost hope that life for themselves and their offspring can be better. And middle-class people expressed strong support for programs that would help those in the underclass achieve their ambitions" (p. A25). But Harris concludes by underscoring an irony and a question:

> The expressed needs of the underclass turn out to be precisely what society is willing to provide: education, job training, child care, etc. A central question remains: Why doesn't the establishment, public and private, move promptly to alleviate the lot of the underclass, which costs us so much and is so inhumane. (p. A25)[4]

And so, what it gets down to is this: that we must challenge ourselves and our leaders. Image manipulations, verbal and pictorial, will not create solutions to the desperate problems of our times. In fact, they only serve to hide them. In so doing, we are prevented from applying a fuller use of our intellect and values to the analysis of our problems and to potential solutions as well. On the other hand, what counters this susceptibility to exploitation and manipulation has a great deal to do with the character of the individuals in a society, both the leaders and the people. And an essential element of this character is our own capacity to test reality with all the means at our disposal to avoid the reliance on a trusting dependency of an infantile kind, to know what it is we want, and to choose leaders who can best represent and lead the way in bringing out what is best about all of us in the creation of a more just and humane society.

COMMENTS (by Joan Offerman-Zuckerberg)

In commenting on this chapter, I find myself asking some rather basic questions, pondering familiar issues anew. Is it Pollyannaish to expect that we can have a more real relationship (as opposed to more transferential) with our political leaders, given the wishful nature of man and the media-saturated world in which we live? As clinicians, we know that in psychoanalytic psychotherapy, as in life, all relationships contain both elements, that is, all relationships are composites of projections–idealizations–wishes shaped from our personal past history and also contain elements of reality—true and more accurate perceptions of salient traits. Human beings perceive in subjective ways, human nature distorts, and experience is always—to some extent—a Rorschach inkblot. What we see is in part who we are (our thoughts, our feelings, our drives, all pouring forth from a personal, private, psychohistorical source). Given this, and added to it, do we want to know more? The perceived power of the leader often rests in delicate balance between knowability, visibility, and the projected image. Too often today the exposure of the real person leaves us disappointed, disgruntled, and searching once again for an ideal (perhaps the good Oedipal father) to fill the void. Is it better not to know? Or can we know? (given the fact that mass media has come to play such a significant part in the social construction of reality).

In growth, we try to measure our expectations with reality; disappointments and disillusionment may lead to a loss of idealization, but hopefully what is restored are more "solid" aspirations and healthy self-esteem derived from a more measured and realistic source. We learn in life to *come to terms*—that goes with our leaders as well. Clearly, we have left the planet of giants long ago. America does not seem any more to clamor for a Jefferson, Washington, or Lincoln—or, in more modern times, a Roosevelt or Kennedy. Do we miss the hero? Have we empowered a Gorbachev, for instance, because he *reminded* us of an archetypically wise and compassionate lost hero? We can idealize him more readily given the greater psychological and physical distance between image and substance. (More recently, our passionate response to Mandela reflects our "hunger" for a *real* hero.) Whether we agree or not with Galbraith's observations that the presidency has become a "relatively unimportant job," it nevertheless remains a rather potent symbol to the world.

This fact, together with media and polling manipulation, is somewhat unsettling. Jan Margolis, in commenting on the 1988 campaign, complained in *The Chicago Tribune* that "professors who profess to be experts in the efficacy of television commercials" were being interviewed "more frequently than the experts on foreign policy" (Diamond, 1988, p. 26). As Reagan had stated in Alter's (1990) article, "the biggest of Big Brothers is helpless against the technology of the Information Age" (p. 25). More fascinating are Alter's comments:

> Ceausescu's security forces had to see their chief's body with their own eyes on television. If they had merely heard he was dead, more might have chose to fight on. (p. 25)

Some 15 years ago, I had the opportunity to learn the Rorschach under the tutelage of Gustave Gilbert, who had been an examining psychologist during the Nuremberg trials. During the seminar, we studied the Rorschach protocols of the Nazi war criminals. To our surprise, we learned that the most commonly reported animal percept given to the cards by these men was the chameleon, actually a rather unusual response when compared with normative data. A chameleon, as we all know, is noted for its ability to change its coloration so as to blend with the immediate environment. To extend the metaphor, its adaptability and survival rests on its psychopathy: its ability to change its colors with the situation at hand. The political character, the "scripted man," becomes the chameleon par excellence unless challenged by an informed electorate. This mixture of the political chameleon with a human environment, which is at best capricious, fickle, and media bound, represents to my mind an unfortunate—perhaps even, an incendiary—situation.

Today we are immersed in a thermonuclear world. This we cannot undo; this we cannot reverse. Man has gone beyond himself. His technological brilliance has far outstripped his emotional maturity. In 1918, Freud observed civilization and its discontents, and stated:

> Long ago he [man] formed an ideal conception of the omnipotence and omniscience which he embodied in his gods. To these gods he attributed everything that seemed unattainable to his wishes, or that was forbidden to him. One may say, therefore, that these gods were cultural ideals.
>
> Today, he has come very close to the attainment of this ideal, he has almost become a god himself. Only, it is true, in the fashion in which ideals are usually attained according to the general judgment of humanity; not completely, in some respects not at all, in others only half way. Man has, as it were, become a kind of *prosthetic god.*
>
> Future ages will bring with them new and probably unimaginably great advances in this field of civilization and will increase man's likeness to civilization and will increase man's likeness to God still more. But in the interests of our investigations, we will not forget that present day man does not feel happy in his Godlike character. (Freud, 1961, p. 64)

Yes, man still does feel uneasy about his newfound power—uneasy emotionally, ethically, morally, and intellectually. It is this—the juxtaposition of the sophistication of nuclear technology and the earth's vulnerability, together with the obvious weakening of leadership in America—that remains unsettling. Now more than ever, opportunities for total annihilation rub shoulders with renewed hope. In this "warmer" year of 1990, there have been unprecedented gains in world democracy. There exist unparalleled opportunities to engage in meaningful dialogue with the Soviet Union. There have been striking advances toward freedom and self-determination all over the globe: in Eastern Europe, in South Africa, in the Philippines, in the Republic of Korea, and in Latin America. We need, we must require, and we must demand, competent informed leaders, leaders of substance; and we, of course, must ask this of ourselves. As a psychoanalyst, I view the world in a certain way (the unconscious in large part shapes our motives). As a woman, my gender colors my perceptions and thoughts further (emotion and relatedness are critical factors in the interpersonal realm). As a person, I share common dreams (a better tomorrow). But allow me to end this brief commentary as a mother.

When children are exposed to trauma, they sometimes respond by growing up too fast. They become and look like old people before their time. Children of alcoholics, of crack abusers, children of incest, of sexual abuse, children of war-torn Europe, children of the Holocaust, and the orphaned children of our planet do not have to be reminded that this is a dangerous place, a dangerous time. The adolescents of today do not have to be reminded. Beginning now, in this time of renewed hope in the home, in our exchanges—personal, impersonal, professional, nonprofessional—we need to educate them and ourselves, to think more deeply, to think more critically—to question leaders, and to read between the lines. It is in the children, of course, that the planet's future resides. We must require them to be intelligent, curious individuals of character and compassion. And in so doing, we must remain competent models. This is difficult, given today's sociopolitical climate. As Walter Mondale emphatically states: "We've got a kind of politics in irrelevance, of obscurantism, that is more prevalent than in any time I can recall" (Walter Mondale, 1990, p. 1).

This takes strength. We must resist a powerful seduction—the media offers us a quick fix, the image is worth a thousand words. But unless we read those thousand words and ask our children to do the same, we are cooperating in a grand scheme—a political seduction of sizable scale. We become co-conspirators in the moral as well as in the political arena.

NOTES

1. "What we want them to be for us," is only one option in this interactional projective process. Other possibilities for projection include the use of others as extensions of ourselves, reflections and personifications of our views, or some vision, inarticulate as that may be, of some unconscious notion of leader, with whom we can feel safe, protected, cared about. The leaders's message that "I will be what you want me to be," or "You need what I have to offer," is a complement to the people's projections. After all, this is what reality testing was originally about; that is, judgments about the world are originally constructed out of gauging and measuring those aspects of reality that will help to satisfy our feelings and wishes for survival and well-being. But we measure what is "out there" by "turning to" what has been good (the good breast) and we reject and "turn away" from a bad reality (the bad breast). This is why it is said that the libidinal instincts "use" the self-preservative instincts for their own purpose. In the beginning what gratifies is experienced as self-preservative.

2. We make inferential leaps of all kinds. Hart was just as rewarded by this process in the beginning of his political career as he was later punished by his alleged "affair" that became public. In the first instance of public impressions he was intuited to be a man of "courage" and in the second to be a man with "questionable judgment" or "immoral." How inferences are made is a complex relationship that has a great deal to do with the leader's potential (promised) relationship to the people and the actual relationship. Without a "real" relationship, the public is perhaps more apt to make inferential leaps that result either in idealizations or devaluations. With a base of a "real" relationship between the leader and the led, "incidents" are seen more in the experienced context of that relationship. This has a great deal to do with our readiness to respond with different kinds of reactions, that is, "to forgive" (as it is with leaders who fall but who have been loved) or to feel "betrayed" or "enraged" (as it is with leaders with whom we have had relationships colored by suspicion or significant ambivalence).

3. Compelling attributes must be seen in the context of the "times" (i.e., the variations of the prevailing feeling that the "people" have regarding the wish for change) and in the context of other aspects of personality that we perceive about that person. For example, the perception of "youthfulness" was a signifier of very different meanings in the persons of Gary Hart, John Kennedy, and Dan Quayle. This was dramatically underscored in the now-famous "You're no John Kennedy" remark leveled at Dan Quayle by his opponent. Quayle was obviously trying to exploit the similarity between himself and John Kennedy by using this shared perceptual image

of their "youth," while Senator Bentsen's remark was intended to remind people not to make inferential leaps about similarities of character based on a single attribute.

4. Harris found that "when asked to name the most important changes that might improve their lives, members of the underclass offered these top choices: better job opportunities, more schooling available, more job training" p. 25. More direct help from government, including handouts, was far down the list. He also found that while the underclass is clearly willing to work to improve their lives, the question of whether society is willing to help them was found to be overwhelmingly affirmative. For example, more than nine in ten Americans would support special school programs for children or locate workplaces in areas where the underclass live, and sizable majorities support building new parks, expanding rehabilitation facilities, and helping in child care.

REFERENCES

After a decade of Thatcher, are her ideals now Britain's? (1989). *New York Times,* May, p. A20.
Alter, J. (1990). Prime time revolution. *Newsweek,* January 8, p. 25.
Bush fights perception that he is adrift. (1989). *New York Times,* March 12, p. B5.
Diamond, E. (November 21, 1988). *Too much, too soon. New York Magazine,* p. 26.
Freud, S. (1961). *Civilization and its discontents* (Vol. 21, pp. 64–193). London: Hogarth.
Gary Hart's fans don't know why they are. (1984). *New York Times,* March 20, p. 41.
Gerzon, M. (1982). *A Choice of heroes: The changing face of American manhood.* New York: Houghton Mifflin.
Harris, L. (1989). Examine these myths of the 80's. *New York Times,* November 30, p. A25.
Quayle campaigns for respect. (1989). *New York Times,* March 12, p. B5.
Star Wars in cola advertising. (1989). *New York Times,* March 12, p. B1.
Walter Mondale Speech. (1990). *New York Times,* March 18, p. 1.

3

National Group Governance in Presidential Elections

Fact and Fantasy

Herbert Barry III

This chapter describes a shared social purpose that is designated as national group governance. This shared purpose develops from social communications about the election by many people, including those who do not vote. Each person who talks to a friend about the forthcoming election contributes to the national group governance and thereby influences the choices by the voters.

This chapter identifies three national group preferences in presidential elections: the voters desire an American prototype president, a strong president, and an alternation between continuity and change. These preferences are expressions of national group governance.

One of the shared purposes in U.S. presidential elections is the competition between two major political parties. This chapter describes four stages in the identity and status of the two major parties. In spite of conspicuous changes from one stage to another, the national group governance has remained remarkably consistent throughout.

National group governance thus far has had predominantly constructive effects on the presidential elections in the United States. These effects throughout the prior history of this country provide useful information for predictions about the presidential election of 1992 and subsequent elections. The example of national group governance in the United States has inspired expressions of similar

HERBERT BARRY III, Ph.D. • Professor of Pharmacology and Physiology, University of Pittsburgh School of Dental Medicine, Pittsburgh, Pennsylvania 15261; President of the International Psychohistorical Association (1991-).

Politics and Psychology: Contemporary Psychodynamic Perspectives, edited by Joan Offerman-Zuckerberg. Plenum Press, New York, 1991.

shared purposes in foreign countries, notably the former Communist regimes of Eastern Europe. The experiences in the United States offer guidance and predictions for strengthening national group governance in other countries and for developing international group governance by human beings everywhere in the world.

SHARED PURPOSES

Human beings are highly social. Most behavior occurs in a variety of groups such as the family, the school, the workplace, and social clubs. Political activities are intensely social because their purpose is to influence the sentiments and actions of other people.

National Group Governance

Presidential campaigns are recurrent events that are shaped by the rules and traditions of the federal government of the United States. Each new campaign induces extensive communications of candidates with people, of people with candidates, and of people with each other. These influences all contribute to a national shared purpose, designated as national group governance.

This shared purpose has four components: (1) national group identity, (2) national group rivalry, (3) national group cooperation, and (4) national group individualism. Each of these components is necessary to maintain the tradition of a strong, stable government that preserves individual liberties and control of the government by the voters.

National Group Identity

This is a feeling of affiliation with the other people who are members of the same nation. The existence of a national group requires patriotic loyalty to the group by its members. This by itself, however, is not sufficient for national group governance.

The declaration of independence from England in 1776 by the 13 colonies in North America marked the beginning of this shared identity, which paved the way for inclusion of immigrants from other countries. After an interval of many years, this shared identity added the surviving American Indians and the former slaves captured in Africa. In 1789, the Constitution of the United States of America established an adequately strong union of the states. This began a gradual process of transferring people's principal affiliation from their state to the nation.

National Group Rivalry

This refers to the development of two major parties, both representing diverse adherents with the aim of attracting the majority of the votes in national elections. Whichever party controls the government, the other party provides a strong opposition and an effective alternative. The nominees of the two parties for president permit the voters to choose between them. This competition between the two major parties is the most effective way to prevent one faction from perpetuating its control of the government.

England had a well-established group rivalry between the Tory and Whig parties, beginning long before the Declaration of Independence. The authors of the Constitution did not regard this as a model to imitate. They felt that the national unity was impaired by the partisan struggles, both parties struggling to win power rather than to govern for the benefit of all the people. The authors of the Constitution also did not trust the voters to make a wise choice of the president. Therefore, the voters in each state chose a group of electors, who in turn voted for the president. There were expected to be more than two qualified candidates for president, especially since the electors would tend to vote for a candidate from their state. If no candidate gained a majority of the vote of the electors, the House of Representatives would choose one of the three who obtained the most votes.

Contrary to the desires and expectations of the authors of the Constitution, two major political parties developed before the end of Washington's second term as president. The rivalry between two parties has remained a consistent component of national group governance.

National Group Cooperation

This refers to a peaceful and cooperative relationship that accompanies the competition between the two major parties. The loser of the election accepts the outcome and cooperates with the winner until the next election. National group identity should be regarded as including a combination of national group rivalry with national group cooperation.

In many countries, the losers of an election have destroyed national group governance by attempting to reverse the outcome by armed force. Whichever side wins the struggle, the conflict establishes a precedent for control of the government by military intervention rather than by the voters.

National Group Individualism

This refers to group protection of dissent against majority beliefs and customs. This tolerance of dissent broadens the national group identity so that it includes people with opposing doctrines. This helps to maintain the combination of group rivalry and group cooperation. Without the influence of national group individualism, the weaker political party is likely to be denounced and suppressed as being contrary to the national group identity. This is a path to establishment of an authoritarian government, which destroys national group governance.

Many of the American colonists left England or other European countries because of persecution of their religious beliefs. They included a wide variety of religious doctrines, including Catholic, Jewish, Protestant dissenters, pacifists, and freethinkers. Protection of national group individualism was an important component of the Declaration of Independence in 1776 and of the Constitution in 1787. The first ten amendments to the Constitution, called the Bill of Rights, were added because of fears that a strong federal government would suppress individual freedoms.

Communication of Group Purposes

The voter's choice of the president of the United States is an individual act. The secret ballot in the privacy of the voting booth is a crucial necessity for free elections. In contrast to the privacy of this final act of voting, the decisions by most voters are highly public. People discuss the candidates extensively prior to the election. Group sentiments thereby influence the choice of most voters. After casting the secret ballot, most voters divulge their choice to their family and friends.

Group sentiments are generated and spread by the extensive publicity that accompanies the campaign for president. The voters are the targets of campaign promises, other political propaganda, news stories, and comments in newspapers, magazines, by television, and by radio. Other communications are conversations by voters with each other. These are more influential because they are very numerous and important to the individuals. Most people are influenced by this group sentiment and most people contribute to it. Even those who do not vote may influence the votes of their friends and relatives.

National group governance in the choice between the nominees of the two major parties also influences the choices in earlier stages of political activity. The group sentiments of the members of the same party influence the choice of the nominees in the presidential primary elections in the states and in the national presidential nominating conventions. The people who do not participate in these party decisions nevertheless share and contribute to the national group governance that influences the choice of nominee.

The presidential election every four years in the United States enables the voters to choose between the nominees of the two major parties. The limitation of the choice to two major parties has important benefits. Each party unites members with diverse points of view. This diversity favors moderation and conciliation rather than extremism and militancy within the party. It also minimizes the ideological differences and antagonism between the two parties, which compete for the same voters.

Alternative Group Purposes

National group governance is a strong influence but there are many alternative group affiliations. The United States combines people from widely separated regions, representing various national and ethnic origins, religious beliefs, and racial categories.

Many important affiliations are not political. Such affiliations may be centered in families, neighborhoods, communities, social clubs, shared vocations, and hobbies. All of these groups generate shared purposes that may compete with national group governance.

Another competing loyalty is group internationalism, a feeling of affiliation with all other human beings. The world is becoming a global village. Television brings news of events in distant countries. Group internationalism is strengthened by organizations with international scope, such as the United Nations and its agencies, as well as Amnesty International, the Red Cross, and many other volunteer organizations.

Another alternative to national group governance is the type of patriotism that is expressed by one of the components—national group identity—without sufficient strength of the other components—national group rivalry, national group cooperation, and national group individualism. Recent world history includes many dismal examples of national group identity that supports authoritarian rule by a minority. Examples are Hitler's Germany, Mussolini's Italy, and Stalin's Russia. These governments were preceded by violence and discord within the country. Many people welcomed the suppression of national group governance as a method for enforcing public safety and national unity. This "escape from freedom" is described in a classic book by Erich Fromm (1941).

A different type of national shared purpose is group fantasy, described by deMause (1979). This emphasizes the irrational and maladaptive aspects of a national shared purpose. DeMause characterizes group fantasy as a displacement of the individual search for love onto the group, resulting in a group trance state that may require discharge in violent historical action. An example is the demand for war in response to a group fantasy of being suffocated, originating from the birth trauma of the individuals (deMause, 1975). Writings by deMause on this topic have been collected in a book (deMause, 1982). Literature on this concept is summarized and evaluated in a book by Lawton (1988).

Group fantasy is a shared sentiment that emphasizes irrational attributes and destructive consequences. It becomes manifest in times of national crisis. National group governance refers to the participation of shared purposes in the choice of national elected officials, especially in the election of the president every four years. Most voters are not consciously aware of the influence of national group governance on their choice of the president. This unconscious attribute of national group governance resembles the repression from conscious awareness of the destructive motivations that underlie group fantasy. In contrast to group fantasy, the shared purpose of national group governance is adaptive and constructive instead of irrational and destructive.

NATIONAL GROUP PREFERENCES

The authors of the Constitution were mainly afraid of authoritarian rule. Accordingly, powers of the federal government are divided among the executive, legislative, and judiciary branches. This implies the danger of insufficient presidential power. The federal government shares powers with the states and local governments. This implies the danger of insufficient federal power or destruction of the union due to secession of states, as in 1861.

National group governance has counteracted those dangers, thus protecting the effectiveness and integrity of the federal government. The shared purpose has induced the choice of presidents with characteristics that preserve the integrity and effectiveness of the government. One of these characteristics is a preference for American prototype presidents. A second characteristic is a preference for strong presidents. A third characteristic is a selective preference for continuity or change, depending on the situation. The incumbent president is usually reelected, but there has seldom been a lengthy succession of presidents of the same party.

American Prototype Presidents

The first president of the United States was an example of an approved American prototype. He was a prosperous landowner in the centrally located state of Virginia. His antecedents and cultural traditions were English, but he was an early supporter of the demand for political independence from England.

Most of the subsequent presidents, in common with Washington, have had family backgrounds that enabled voters to regard them as American prototypes. Their ancestries are predominantly English, Scotch, Irish, or Dutch. The surnames of the presidents, listed in Tables 1 through 4, are predominantly derived from the British Isles or the Netherlands. The only exception is the German name Eisenhower.

Most presidents have come from farms or the frontier or small towns. Kennedy and Ford are the only presidents to have grown up in a large urban environment.

Some prominent leaders of countries have come from peripheral or alien areas. Examples are Napoleon from Corsica, Hitler from Austria, and Stalin from Georgia in the Caucasus mountains. Many presidents of the United States migrated from one state to another in their childhood or adulthood, but their locations and travels did not deviate from the population norms.

Faber (1978) has documented well the childhood family environments of the presidents. Most presidents had parents who exemplified and taught virtues of diligence, dependability, and education. These characteristics are consistent with traditional American ideals. Wagner and Schubert (1977) reported that the majority of presidents grew up in unusually large families. This difference from the norm is consistent with American traditions, deriving from the large farm families of the colonies on the Atlantic coast. The only bachelors elected president were Buchanan and Cleveland. Only one president, Reagan, has had a marriage end in divorce.

With regard to policies and doctrines, most presidents have been moderates, not representing an extreme point of view. Their campaign statements as candidates were usually reassuring. People want a president they can trust.

Another bias favoring American prototypes is indicated by several presidents who had kinship connections with a former president. John Quincy Adams was the son of John Adams. Benjamin Harrison was the grandson of William Henry Harrison. Franklin D. Roosevelt was a cousin of Theodore Roosevelt. These connections with former presidents contributed to the attractiveness of these candidates for their party's nomination and in the election.

The shared preference for an American prototype president is partly motivated by fear of a candidate who is exotic or has unfamiliar attributes. This motivation was expressed well in a comment on voters by Nixon, quoted by Safire: "People react to fear, not love—they don't teach that in Sunday School, but it's true" (1977, p. 8).

Strong Presidents

The first president was a military hero who had been commander-in-chief of the Revolutionary army. His background of victorious military leadership was an important part of his suitability as the elected leader of the new government. Several of his successors also were military heroes. Most notable among these are Jackson, Taylor, Grant, and Eisenhower. Other presidents who were former generals are W. H. Harrison, Hayes, Garfield, and B. Harrison. Other presidents who were wartime officers in lower military ranks but also military heroes are Colonel Theodore Roosevelt and Navy Lieutenant John Kennedy.

National group governance has contributed to the selection of presidents with a record of impressive accomplishments in government or other vocations. Examples are J. Adams, Jefferson, Madison, J. Q. Adams, Cleveland, T. Roosevelt, Wilson, Hoover, F. D. Roosevelt, and L. B. Johnson. Most of the remaining presidents, who were not renowned as political or military leaders, or as outstanding achievers in other fields, had impressive vocational accomplishments that earned the respect of knowledgeable colleagues. Examples are Van Buren as the Democratic leader of the state of New York, Polk as Speaker of the House of Representatives, Lincoln as a lawyer and Whig politician in Illinois, Coolidge as Governor of Massachusetts, Truman as a Senator from Missouri, Nixon as a former vice president and nominee for president, Ford as Republican leader of the House of Representatives, Carter as a liberal Governor of Georgia, and Reagan as leader of the Screen Actors Guild, Governor of California, and public speaker.

In general, most of the presidents had an impressive attribute that was a necessary qualification for their nomination and election to that office. In addition to high intellectual or vocational stature, high physical stature shows evidence for contributing to the group choice of an impressive president. Most of the presidential elections have been won by the taller of the two major party nominees. The most recent exception was Carter's victory against Ford in a close election. The subsequent elections have been consistent with the prior trend, Reagan over Carter and over Mondale, and Bush over Dukakis.

Continuity and Change

National group governance, which favors a stable and effective government, also favors limitations on government power and reforms of the inevitable abuses of government power. Therefore, the shared purpose induces both continuity and change in government. The result has been an emphasis on continuity in the short-term sequence and change in a longer perspective.

The majority of incumbents who run for reelection are reelected. Tables 1 through 4 show that 13 presidents were reelected following their first term. The percentage of the vote increased greatly in the reelection of all except Washington, who was elected unanimously both times. The reelection of Wilson was an especially impressive achievement against the highly qualified nominee of a united Republican party, following his initial victory with 40 percent of the popular vote against two rival Republicans.

In comparison with these 13 presidents who were reelected, eight were defeated after nomination by their party for a second term. Unusual circumstances contributed to each of these eight defeats. Four of these one-term presidents—J. Adams, J. Q. Adams, Van Buren, and B. Harrison—were defeated by the same nominee of the rival party who had lost to them four years before. Cleveland was elected to a second term four years after his defeat by B. Harrison. Taft was a victim of the opposition of his predecessor and fellow Republican, T. Roosevelt. Hoover was a victim of the great depression. Carter was a victim of severe inflation and the American hostages in Iran.

Vice presidents who became president because of the death or resignation of their predecessor have also fared well as the nominee of their party for reelection. T. Roosevelt, Coolidge, Truman, and L. B. Johnson were elected. The only one defeated was Ford was in a close election under unusually adverse circumstances. Four vice presidents who became president because of the death of their predecessor were not nominated for president by their party. These are Tyler, who followed W. H. Harrison; Fillmore, who followed Taylor; A. Johnson, who followed Lincoln; and Arthur, who followed Garfield.

Contrary to the short-term continuity of frequent reelection of the incumbent, the same party usually does not elect many successive presidents. Tables 1 through 4 show a predominant transition to the rival party after a small number of successive presidents of the same party. Four consecutive presidents constitute the maximum succession of the same party this far. This occurred only in the first stage (Table 1) and in the third stage (Table 3).

The choice between the nominee of the incumbent party and the nominee of the rival party involves a choice between candidates with different personality characteristics. Presidents who are politically affiliated with their predecessor are more likely to be the first son and to have the paternal affiliation of sharing the same name as the father (Barry, 1979). These presidents also are more likely to have a long life span (Barry, 1984).

STAGES OF THE PRESIDENCY

The 51 presidential elections in the United States, 1789–1988, contribute much information on the influence of national group governance. This historical record is simplified by dividing the elections into four stages. Each stage began with a major change in the political alignments. These alignments thereafter remained constant until the next stage.

The first and third stages began with the dominance of the traditionalist party, influenced by a need for national strength and unity. Continuity predominated over change in the subsequent elections of these stages. This attribute of continuity was consistent with the conciliatory aim and general popularity of the presidents who initiated these stages: Washington in the first stage, Lincoln in the third stage.

The second and fourth stages began with a reformist victory over the traditionalist party. Change has predominated over continuity in the subsequent elections of these stages. This attribute of change is consistent with the militant, controversial role of the presidents who initiated these stages: Jackson in the second stage, Franklin D. Roosevelt in the fourth stage.

Federalist Founders

Many of the leaders of the new government owned land and slaves in the dominant state of Virginia. Beard (1913) emphasized their conservative views and financial interests. Protection for the privileged minority of the population was a shared purpose of the signers of the Constitution of the United States of America.

The establishment of a strong, stable government was helped greatly by the availability of George Washington as the first president. He was the military leader and generally acknowledged hero of the American Revolution, who had suppressed his personal ambitions to an extraordinary degree. His status and policy as the first president is summarized by Flexner (1972) as follows: "Madison wrote that Washington was the only part of the new political dispensation that really appealed to the people. . . . He enforced, as President, complete personal control in the executive, and with equal rigor, kept his hands off the other departments" (p. 497).

One of the early influences of national group governance was to enable the people to choose the president, contrary to the Constitution's provision that the president would be chosen by electors who had been selected by the voters. This important change was accomplished by the development of two major political parties. The voters choose between the nominees of the two parties.

The authors of the Constitution did not anticipate the development of political parties. They viewed the contemporary Tory and Whig parties in England as divisive, striving to defeat the rival party rather than to serve the welfare of the people. Nevertheless, two major parties developed rapidly because President Washington included in his Cabinet effective leaders of opposing points of view, especially Hamilton and Jefferson. During Washington's second term, Jefferson resigned from the Cabinet and founded the Democratic party as the opposition to the Federalist party.

Jefferson fulfilled the purposes of national group governance not only by founding a rival party but also by the nonviolent mode of his opposition. He accepted his defeat by Adams in the election of 1796 in spite of receiving more electoral votes. National group governance, favoring the previous loser, contributed to Jefferson's victory over Adams by a large margin four years later.

Table 1 shows a pattern of continuity in the elections of Jefferson and his two successors. This is noteworthy because it has not yet been repeated in the numerous presidential elections since then. Beginning with Jefferson, four successive presidents were elected as the nominees of the same party, the first three of them each serving two full terms.

Table 1.   First Stage of Presidential Elections, Dominated by the Federalist Founders[a]

Federalists	Jefferson Democrats
Washington, 1789, 1792	
Adams, 1796	Jefferson, 1800, 1804
	Madison, 1808, 1812
	Monroe, 1816, 1820
	Adams, 1824

[a] The name of each president is followed by the year or years he was elected. The presidents listed on the left were nominated by the traditionalist Federalist party. The presidents listed on the right were nominated by the reformist Democratic party.

The shared purposes of national group governance contributed to the stability of the presidency during this stage after the election of Jefferson. People wanted and needed a harmonious and constructive phase in the early years of the nation, especially following the acrimonious conflict in the elections of 1796 and 1800 and during the War of 1812 against England. The Federalist party rapidly became weak and ineffective. Monroe was reelected in 1820 without any organized opposition. National group identity became group affiliation also with what was called the Democratic–Republican party. The party became more traditionalist than reformist as it incorporated most of the former Federalists. This development of a single dominant party could have inaugurated authoritarian rule, with adverse effects that have been seen in many other countries, including Hitler's Germany and Stalin's Russia.

Populist Revolution

The competition between two major parties was renewed by Andrew Jackson of Tennessee. He was a member of the Democratic–Republican party but represented the underprivileged people, especially in the Western states. Each of the preceding presidents was from Virginia or Massachusetts. Jackson lost to John Quincy Adams in 1824, in spite of receiving more popular and electoral votes. He accepted this defeat peacefully in accordance with national group cooperation, and defeated the incumbent Adams four years later. Jackson's experiences in the elections of 1824 and 1828 thereby resembled Jefferson's experiences in the elections of 1796 and 1800.

Jackson formed the Jacksonian Democratic party. The Democratic–Republican opponents of Jackson, called Whigs, replaced the Federalists as the conservative party. Table 2 shows that the presidential elections after this populist revolution contrast with the succession of victories by the same party in the preceding stage of Federalist founders. Jackson was the only president in this second stage who was elected for a second term. The majority of presidents in this stage were Jacksonian Democrats, but there was a lack of continuity.

Table 2. Second Stage of Presidential Elections,
Initiated by Jackson's Populist Revolution[a]

Whigs	Jacksonian Democrats
	Jackson, 1828, 1832
	Van Buren, 1836
Harrison, 1840	Polk, 1844
Taylor, 1848	Pierce, 1852
	Buchanan, 1856

[a] The presidents listed on the left were nominated by the traditionalist Whig party. The presidents listed on the right were nominated by the reformist Democratic party.

The failure of Jackson's successors in this stage to be elected to a second term is partly attributable to greater strength of national group rivalry than of national group cooperation, initiated by Jackson's partisan, combative nature. National group governance counteracted the aggressiveness of the Democrats by the victory of two Whig opponents in the next four presidential elections after Jackson's two terms.

A profoundly divisive issue during this stage was slavery. National group governance was temporarily split into two rival countries during the Civil War, 1861–1865. Preceding this armed conflict, national group governance in both major parties sought to preserve the union by emphasizing the national scope of the parties. Although the Democratic party was strongest in the South, its presidential nominees after 1844 were all Northerners. These were Cass of Michigan in 1848, Pierce of New Hampshire in 1852, Buchanan of Pennsylvania in 1856, and Douglas of Illinois in 1860. The principal policies of Presidents Pierce and Buchanan were to conciliate the Southern Democrats, who were heavily represented in their cabinets. Meanwhile, the two Whig presidents had Southern affiliations. Harrison and Taylor both were born in Virginia, and President Taylor represented Louisiana. The members of their cabinets were predominantly Northerners.

National group governance was weakened by the disunity and decline of the Whig party. An adverse influence was the rivalry of their two dominant leaders, Henry Clay of Kentucky and Daniel Webster of Massachusetts. Another misfortune was the deaths while in office of both Whigs who were elected president, Harrison and Taylor. Their vice presidents, Tyler and Fillmore, were not able to gain their party's nomination for president. In the election of 1856, the Whig candidate received fewer votes for president than John C. Fremont, the candidate of the new Republican party, which represented Northern abolitionist sentiments.

Group nationalism was threatened by the abolitionist focus of the Republican party. The Democratic party was temporarily dominant over the fading Whigs and the newly established Republicans. Competition against a strong rival was thereby eliminated as an incentive for Democratic party unity. The demand for secession in Southern states was led by Democratic slave owners and their supporters who realized that their influence in the United States Congress was declining as the population of the Northern states increased and the new Western states were predominantly not slave states. The fear and desperation of these Southern Democrats overcame their participation in the shared purpose of national unity. The decline of the Whigs appeared to give these Democrats an opportunity to control their party and the federal government.

Republican Dominance

The Republican nominee for president in 1860, Abraham Lincoln of Illinois, was a prominent former Whig who was not an abolitionist. The Republican party served the purpose of group nationalism by selecting a candidate who could attract votes in addition to his Republican supporters because of his willingness to allow slavery to continue where it was already established. The Democrats split into two factions, each with a presidential nominee. Lincoln won the election with only 40 percent of the popular vote. The nominee of a united Democratic party would have won the election.

The ensuing secession of 10 of the 33 states led to the Civil War, in which the North had the difficult task of conquering zealous enemies who had good military leadership while the South needed only to persist until the North would abandon the effort. The uncertainty of the outcome throughout most of the four years, 1861–1865, indicates that the Confederate States of America would probably have won their independence if the war had occurred several years earlier, when the North was less overwhelmingly superior in population and in economic strength. Conciliation of the Southerners by the Democratic and Whig leaders delayed the onset of the war. This policy contributed to the preservation of the union, in accordance with the shared purpose of national group governance.

The victory of the North under the leadership of President Lincoln established the Republicans as the dominant party. Table 3 shows that they won 14 of the 18 presidential elections during 1860–1928. This third stage of the presidency constituted a resurgence of the traditionalist party, which had been fragile and only sporadically victorious following the election of Jefferson in 1800.

A detrimental and dangerous development in this stage was dominance of the Democratic party in the former Confederate States of America. This constituted rule by a single party in that region, contrary to the shared purpose of national group rivalry between two major parties in all regions. The dominance of the Democratic party in the Southern states contributed to the ability of the Republicans to maintain their dominance in the Northern and Western states and thereby to win most of the elections.

The regional bias in the competition between the two major parties intensified the antagonism between the regions and also prolonged the white supremacy that inflicted the whole country but was more blatant in the South. The Southerners justifiably felt underprivileged. For example, although they were the strongest component of the Democratic party, all the presidential nominees of the party in this stage were Northerners.

Table 3.   Third Stage of Presidential Elections,
Republican Dominance, beginning with the
Election of Lincoln and the Civil War[a]

Republicans	Democrats
Lincoln, 1860, 1864	
Grant, 1868, 1872	
Hayes, 1876	
Garfield, 1880	Cleveland, 1884, 1892
Harrison, 1888	
McKinley, 1896, 1900	
Roosevelt, 1904	
Taft, 1908	Wilson, 1912, 1916
Harding, 1920	
Coolidge, 1924	
Hoover, 1928	

[a] The presidents listed on the left were nominated by the traditionalist
Republican party. The presidents listed on the right were nominated
by the reformist Democratic party.

The shared purposes of national group governance were served well by the survival of the Democratic party in the Northern states as a rival against the Republican party. The Democrats increasingly obtained the allegiance of disadvantaged minority groups, including laborers, farmers, and Catholic immigrants from Europe. They became a majority of the population but remained a minority of the voters in the North. The Democratic party nominated highly qualified candidates for president, thereby attracting votes from many Republicans and forcing the Republican leaders to nominate attractive candidates also.

In the election of 1876, the Democratic nominee won the majority of the popular votes. His failure to win the majority of the electoral votes was due to controversial decisions concerning disputed counts in several Southern states. National group governance was served by the peaceful acceptance of this result by the loser, Tilden, and by the respected character and conciliatory policies of the winner, Hayes. A national shared desire to compensate for this shameful event probably contributed to the victory of the Democratic nominee eight years later. Cleveland in this election was supported by several prominent Republicans, called Mugwumps, who were repelled by evidence of politically corrupt actions of the Republican nominee, James G. Blaine.

The shared purpose of preventing prolonged control by the same party contributed to a more profound split in the Republican party that allowed election of the only other Democratic president in this stage. In 1912, Theodore Roosevelt, who had chosen Taft as his successor four years earlier, competed against him. When Taft won the Republican nomination, Roosevelt ran for president as nominee of the Progressive party. The winner was the Democratic nominee, Wilson, although he received only 40 percent of the votes cast for him, Roosevelt, and Taft. Either Republican would have won if the other had supported him.

Roosevelt's New Deal

The fourth stage of presidential elections was one of the consequences of the depression that began with the stock market crash in 1929. Franklin D. Roosevelt's New Deal began an era of prevalent Democratic majorities in Congress, persisting at least through the election of 1990. Contrary to this Democratic dominance, the Republican nominee for president has won 7 of the 11 elections during 1948–1988, after the death of Roosevelt (see Table 4).

A difference from previous stages of ascendancy by the reformist party, following the elections of Jefferson and of Jackson, is that the traditionalist party has not become weak or disorganized. National group governance has induced the Republican party to accept the most popular innovations of the New Deal, such as social security, more social services by the federal government, and increasing federal control over state and local governments. These accommodations, resisted by the conservative elements of the party, have enabled the Republicans to remain a strong rival in accordance with the shared purposes of national group governance.

A beneficial change from the prior stage of Republican dominance is that both major parties have become more truly national. The Republicans with their traditional, conservative ideology compete strongly in the former Confederate States of America. The Democrats compete strongly in all regions as the party of minority groups and disadvantaged people.

National group governance appears to have punished the Democratic party for Roosevelt's denunciations of the wealthy, his great expansion of federal and presidential power, and his unprecedented election to four terms. The constitutional amendment limiting presidents to two terms was ratified less than eight years after his death. No subsequent Democratic president has been elected for two terms. Meanwhile, the Republicans Eisenhower and Reagan both served two full terms.

Table 4.   Fourth Stage of Presidential Elections,
beginning with Roosevelt's New Deal[a]

Republicans	Democrats
	Roosevelt, 1932, 1936, 1940, 1944
	Truman, 1948
Eisenhower, 1952, 1956	Kennedy, 1960
	Johnson, 1964
Nixon, 1968, 1972	Carter, 1976
Reagan, 1980, 1984	
Bush, 1988	

[a] The presidents listed on the left were nominated by the traditionalist Republican party. The presidents listed on the right were nominated by the reformist Democratic party.

The shared purpose of national group cooperation contributed to the acceptance of defeat by the Republican nominee in the 1960 election of Kennedy, in spite of allegations that fraudulent counts produced slim majorities for Kennedy in Illinois and Texas and thereby his majority of the electoral votes. It is disputed to what extent this peaceful response was the decision of the Republican nominee, Nixon, or forced on him by the incumbent Republican president, Eisenhower. A national shared desire to compensate for this controversial defeat probably contributed to the election of Nixon eight years later.

The succession of Reagan by his vice president, Bush, in 1988 is a type of continuity that has been absent in recent presidential elections. Bush is the first president since Hayes, in 1876, to be elected president following two full terms by a predecessor of his party. Vice President Bush in 1988 was the first member of the administration of a predecessor serving his second full term to be elected president since Vice President Van Buren in 1836.

PREDICTIONS BASED ON NATIONAL GROUP GOVERNANCE

Several predictions can be made on the assumption that national group governance, which has influenced previous presidential elections, will continue to influence future elections in the same way.

Presidential Election of 1992

Bush has major advantages as the Republican candidate in 1992. He will be the elected incumbent, seeking his second term. He is a member of the traditionalist party, whose candidate has won the majority of presidential elections since 1860. He exemplifies national prototypes, such as American ancestry for many generations, an affluent family, education at an Ivy League college, and Protestant Episcopalian religious affiliation. The most recent prior president with these attributes was Franklin D. Roosevelt. The advantages of Bush's gregarious nature and long experience in Republican politics were underestimated by most commentators during the 1988 election.

An additional advantage for Bush in 1988, which may continue to benefit him in 1992, was a shared purpose of creating a more stable political succession: after the death of Roosevelt in 1945, the transition to a Republican president in 1952, to a Democratic president in 1960, the assassination of Kennedy in 1963, the transition to a Republican president in 1968, the assassinations of Martin Luther King and Robert F. Kennedy in the same year, the resignation of Nixon in 1974, the transition to a Democratic president in 1976, and the transition to a Republican president in 1980. If Bush is reelected in 1992, it will be the first election of two or more successive presidents of the same party for two full terms since early in our national history: Jefferson, Madison, and Monroe, during 1800–1824. Voters desire a repetition of this stability although most are not consciously aware of this specific precedent.

Contrary to these advantages, Bush has major disadvantages. The most important of these is that the massive federal deficits are likely to induce an economic crisis in the form of disastrous inflation or a business recession prior to 1992. This will turn the voters against the incumbent, as occurred with Carter in 1980 and Hoover in 1932.

Another disadvantage for Bush is that the Democratic party represents policies that agree with the majority group purposes. These include freedom for pregnant women to choose whether to abort their fetuses; more federal help for minorities, the unemployed, and homeless people; and willingness to increase federal spending to protect the environment. Accordingly, the Democratic party appears assured of retaining its majority control of both houses in Congress. One of the prevalent shared purposes is for control of the presidency and Congress by the same party. This is feasible in the election of 1992 only if the Democratic nominee wins the presidential election.

The present commentator therefore predicts that even without an acute national economic crisis, national group governance will induce election of the Democratic nominee in 1992. The type of Democrat most likely to be nominated and elected is a Southerner who is regarded as a moderate rather than a liberal and thus can gain votes from economic conservatives and others who usually vote for the Republican nominee. Examples are Senator Nunn of Georgia and Senator Gore of Tennessee, both of whom were potential Democratic nominees in 1988.

Subsequent Continuities and Changes

Some commentators have suggested that recent changes in the manner of campaigning for the presidency induce undesirable criteria for the selection. Modern candidates campaign strenuously, raise millions of dollars, and become known mainly by brief exposures on television. Campaigning and publicity are national rather than focused on particular states. The presidential nominees of the major parties were traditionally selected at their national conventions, but subsequent to 1952 these conventions have merely confirmed the choices previously made in the state primary elections.

Contrary to these fears, the changes do not constitute fundamental differences in national group governance. Indeed, the recent changes probably cause this shared purpose to function more efficiently and with broader public participation. The merits and weaknesses of the candidates are more effectively exposed to the voters during the prolonged presidential campaigns. National group governance is expressed more directly by the members of the party who vote in the presidential primary elections than when the nomination was determined by a few party leaders at the national convention.

Some changes are clearly beneficial. A high evaluation of education and compulsory schooling are American traditions that have strengthened national group governance. Education in recent years has improved in quality and has been extended to later ages for many people. People learn about political events by news broadcasts on television. For those who read newspapers and newsmagazines, the coverage of the campaigns and candidates has improved. Many people travel widely and communicate with others by phone. These changes result in voters who are better informed than in the past.

A danger is that some trends in modern society will weaken national group cooperation and national group individualism, which are important components of national group governance. People increasingly admire and act out violent and impulsive action. Restraint and respect for the rights of others are necessary conditions for national group governance, but these traits are not effectively trained.

Impulsive acting out also threatens the dominance of the two major parties, which enable all the voters to choose between two nominees for president. Some adherents of both major parties complained in 1968 that there was little difference between Nixon and Humphrey. They did not appreciate the fact that both parties compete for the same voters in their effort to win the majority of votes. Supporters of a policy that is rejected by both parties can be more effective by persuading one of the major parties instead of denouncing both parties.

Impulsive protest against both major parties can take the form of supporting small parties that fragment the choice. An example was the independent presidential candidacy of John B. Anderson in 1980. There have been minor party candidates throughout the history of presidential elections, and they should be permitted. One of these, the abolitionist Republicans, became the dominant party six years after it was founded in 1854. The norm, however, should be a choice between the nominees of two major parties.

Both major parties have extremists who try to commit their party to doctrines that are unpopular, thereby weakening the party and frustrating the shared purposes of national group governance. The Republicans have moralistic fanatics, libertarians, and opponents of the United Nations. The Democrats have socialists, opponents of world trade, and pacifists.

It is more likely that both major parties will choose adaptive policies to broaden their support and thus compete for support by the majority. The Democrats have a great advantage because they already have majority support in Congress.

The Democrats can broaden their appeal by accepting the Republican policy of lower income taxes. Heavy taxes on high incomes detract from the productivity that generates wealth for everybody. A preferable source of government revenue is the land value tax (George, 1879), which continues to be advocated by many economists (Andelson, 1979). The Democrats can propose higher taxes on the value of land accompanied by lower taxes on the products of human labor and enterprise, including income taxes, sales taxes, and taxes on the value of houses and on other improvements of property. This would obtain more revenue from large corporations and other wealthy landowners without impairing the incentives for individuals to maximize their earnings.

The Republicans can broaden their appeal by withdrawing party support from authoritarian doctrines that are contrary to the party's traditions of individual freedom. For example, the party favors laws to forbid or severely restrict abortions, although the right of a pregnant woman to choose between childbirth and abortion is accepted by the majority of Americans, including a substantial proportion of Republicans.

Elections in Other Countries

The economic and political systems established in the United States are useful models for other countries. There is considerable correspondence between the free market, where buyers choose between competing merchants, and the control of the government by the people, where the voters choose between competing candidates. People in many countries with Socialist or Communist economies and authoritarian governments are demanding this freedom, in both the economic and political institutions.

National group governance in the United States has stimulated the demand for similar shared purposes in other countries. The recent overthrow of Communist rulers by the people in countries in eastern Europe is evidence for successful development of national group governance. An especially encouraging event is the peaceful nature of this change in several countries, such as Poland, Czechoslovakia and Hungary.

Group nationalism requires effective communication among the people of the nation. This has been enhanced by the prevalence of education in the technologically developed countries. Even in the highly authoritarian regime of Stalinist Russia, education was widespread and encouraged. This has created people who are ready for the group nationalism that establishes and maintains selection of the political leaders by the voters.

National group governance in most countries is based on the English model of parliamentary rule. The voters choose one legislator who represents a district, similar to the division of the United States into districts for electing members of the House of Representatives. The legislators in turn select the leaders of the government. The voters thereby select their leaders indirectly rather than directly. The voters are further removed from the direct selection of leaders because in many countries the candidates in each district and the members of the legislature are divided among many political parties, none of which represents a majority of the voters or of the legislators. Governments consist of coalitions of several parties.

Coalition governments are usually unstable and change often. The extreme conservative and radical parties are disruptive influences. Effective change is impeded by the need to reconcile diverse parties, and the same people repeatedly serve in successive governments.

This type of legislative government by coalition was prevalent in western Europe following World War II. There has been a tendency for two principal parties to emerge in most of these countries during the several decades since then. The United States provides a model for the development of two major parties, both attempting to gain the support of the majority of voters. In some countries, such as France, this has been helped by a new constitution that establishes an independently elected president with substantial powers.

Some previous developments of group consensus have had international scope, spreading rapidly to all nations rather than being limited to the group nationalism of one country. An example is the rapid disintegration of colonial rule of other nations after World War II. Although Great Britain was one of the winners of World War II, its colonies rapidly became independent countries with the help of an international consensus. An earlier example of international group consensus was the worldwide disapproval of slavery, which developed during the nineteenth century.

National group governance in all countries has been aided by the expansion of international travel and communication. Airplanes, telephones, and television have increasingly international applications, so that the world becomes a community. People in each country are increasingly aware of events in other countries. Awareness provides the opportunity for group internationalism, making the world a global community.

These trends are likely to accelerate in the future years. This is an encouraging prospect for the future of the world. A group consensus will spread among the nations, encouraging communication and trade. The communication and economic interdependence among countries will be the most effective safeguard against the disastrous possibility of World War III.

REFERENCES

Andelson, R. V. (ed.) (1979). *Critics of Henry George: A centenary appraisal of their strictures on* Progress and Poverty. Cranbury, NJ: Associated University Presses.

Barry, H., III (1979). Birth order and paternal namesakes as predictors of affiliation with predecessor by presidents of the United States. *Political Psychology, 1*(2), 61–66.

Barry, H., III. (1984). Predictors of longevity of United States presidents. *Omega, 14,* 315–321.

Beard, C. A. (1913). *An economic interpretation of the Constitution.* New York: Macmillan.

deMause, L. (1975). The independence of psychohistory. *Journal of Psychohistory, 3,* 163–183.

deMause, L. (1979). Historical group-fantasies. *Journal of Psychohistory, 7,* 1–70.

deMause, L. (1982). *Foundations of psychohistory.* New York: Creative Roots.

Faber, D. (1978). *The presidents' mothers.* New York: St. Martin's Press.

Flexner, J. T. (1972). *George Washington: anguish and farewell (1793–1799).* Boston: Little, Brown.

Fromm, E. (1941). *Escape from freedom.* New York: Farrar and Rinehart.

George, H. (1879). *Progress and poverty.* New York: Robert Schalkenbach Foundation (Centenary Edition, 1979).

Lawton, H. (1988). *The psychohistorian's handbook.* New York: The Psychohistory Press.

Safire, William. (1977). *Before the fall.* New York: Ballantine Books.

Wagner, M. E., & Schubert, H. J. P. (1977). Sibship variables and United States presidents. *Journal of Individual Psychology, 33,* 78–85.

4

Collective Suicide at Jonestown

An Ethnopsychoanalytic Study of Leadership and Group Dynamics

Domenico Arturo Nesci

A LETTER

On September 25, 1978, Jim W. Jones, the pastor and leader of the Peoples Temple (affiliation of the Disciples of Christ) from the Agricultural Mission of Jonestown in the Guyana jungle sent a five-page typescript to President Carter:

> Dear Mr. President:
>   I write with extreme urgency. We have been victims of conspiracy for years. I have reiterated many times that, although we have reliable proof that there are elements of law enforcement involved in this, it in no way reflects on the administration of President Carter. It is for this reason that I am writing you to ask that you take some action on our behalf before our people are totally alienated. This would be a terrible thing. The schemes against us include some of the most devious stratagems imaginable. One of the principles told me, several years ago, in tears: "I have to quit my job. . . . I have to leave the church. My wife is going to leave me. But she is attracted to you. Will you please have sex with her?" I have never done that in my life—I have always been faithful to my wife of some 30 years of happy marriage. Well, I checked with my wife and the church board and they thought it would be alright if I went ahead to satisfy this desperate man's plea.

DOMENICO ARTURO NESCI, M.D. • Associate Member of the Italian Psychoanalytic Society and of the International Psychoanalytic Association; Researcher for the Department of Psychiatry and Psychology, Catholic University of the Sacred Heart, Rome, Italy.

Politics and Psychology: Contemporary Psychodynamic Perspectives, edited by Joan Offerman-Zuckerberg. Plenum Press, New York, 1991.

They reasoned that this woman was distraught or confused enough to tell all kind of lies about the church. Also that the man in question [. . .] would do likewise. I went into the relationship, and although I used preventatives, she got pregnant. And now, six years later, a big issue is being made over the child. I can prove paternity, and I ask that Mr. G. (who claims to be the child's father) take the latest tests at the University of California. The situation is distressing and cruel, since these people are attempting to use a child as a pawn in a plot to discredit and ruin my work. I do not feel good about it. But I also do not feel good about a child being delivered back to a woman who abandoned him to me and my wife, and now wants him back. Anyone who compares my childhood pictures with the boy's can see the striking resemblance. [. . .] We have taken children and seniors trapped in ghettos on trips all over the United States, to historical sites. [. . .] We have built a beautiful community that is showing a model of interracial harmony. We can develop it better without this harassment, and it would be a light to the cause of international co-operation that would be a credit to the American character, to the spirit of service and charity that we have seen exemplified in your life and work. Thank you very much, Mr. President, for your attention to this letter. I have written it hastily, and am dispatching it now from the jungles of Guyana, where a thousand Americans are living and building, and sending you their best wishes. In His Service. Sincerely, Rev. Jim Jones.

This disquieting letter deserves to be compared with another document from the Peoples Temple's files dated February 6, 1972, and delivered to the press by Jones some months before writing the letter to Carter.

I, hereby acknowledge that in April 1971, I entreated my beloved pastor, James W. Jones, to sire a child by my wife, who had previously, at my insistence, reluctantly but graciously consented thereto. James W. Jones agreed to do so, reluctantly, after I explained that I very much wished to raise a child, but was unable after extensive attempts, to sire one myself. My reason for requesting James W. Jones to do this is that I wanted a child to be fathered, if not by me, by the most compassionate, honest, and courageous human being the world contains. (Reiterman with Jacobs, 1982, p. 131)

The ambiguous message of these two documents reveals some elements that help understand why the Peoples Temple, in September 1977, had threatened plainly to commit collective suicide. Some events of that period should be remembered.

The child's mother, who had already left the Peoples Temple, sent a lawyer to file a suit in the Court of Georgetown (Guyana) in order to have back her son who was living at that time in Jonestown. The Court summoned Jones with the child requesting him to explain why the son should not be returned to his mother. Jones did not appear and he even pretended not to be in Jonestown when a Court Official went there to notify him. Then, the Court ruled that Jones be arrested for contempt. Jones panicked and declared a state of siege at Jonestown. For six days and nights, the whole community had formed a human circle to protect its boundaries, while Jones worked up to the climax, shouting continuously into the microphone from his cottage at the invisible (and nonexistent!) enemies who were supposed to beseige them. A loudspeaker system broadcast all around his persecutory anxiety, at Jonestown as well as in San Francisco, into the radio room of the Peoples Temple headquarters.

The tape recordings of those dramatic hours still prove that Jones and his followers would have even died together in order not to expose their leader to arrest, in order not to give the child back to his natural mother. For the group, that child was the son of Jones, of the "Father," and the Peoples Temple was his real family. For Jones that child "was much more than a son, he was a symbol of the future of his cause" (Feinsod, 1981, p. 106). But for the Jonestown commune, too, that child had become a living symbol.

The ambiguous status of the child, abandoned by/stolen from his legitimate parents, nonnatural/natural, and favorite son of the "Father," made him an object of collective identification. The child incorporated, in fact, one of the underlying unconscious fantasies of the Peoples Temple: all members are children of the "Father," no one has parents other than "Father" and the mother/group. For this reason, Jonestown was ready to die for him.

A SYMBOLIC CHILD

On November 18, 1977, shortly after the "September siege" (Reiterman with Jacobs, 1982), the child's legitimate father (who had also quit the Peoples Temple) appealed, with the child's mother, to the Court of San Francisco (California). The judge ruled that the child be returned by Jones. If he were not to comply with the court's order, Jones could never return to the United States without taking the chance of being arrested. In this way, holding the child as a hostage and rejecting the court's justice, Jones had been able to break off definitively with both America and Guyana.

My intention in this chapter is not to emphasize the instrumental use of the child. I would rather investigate Jones's decision to send President Carter a letter wherein such an uneasy issue was dealt with openly (and contradictorily, compared with the document previously given to the press by the Peoples Temple, following the same suicidal logic).

My hypothesis is that Jones was unconsciously challenging Carter to a paternity test over a symbolic child: the American people. In the letter, in fact, Jones claimed to have delivered a group of people, hostages (the Peoples Temple's "children") trapped in ghettos and rejected by their motherland (like the child of the letter), and to have guided them to a "Land of Promise." There, they would refind the roots of their American Dream; they would settle into a new motherland (the jungle) and regain the lost Paradise of intrauterine life. Jones claimed to be the deliverer of the oppressed American people, and while pretending to ask for help, he was indeed threatening. "Several nations have offered to take us in, even Russia has offered us money to speak out against human rights violations in the United States."

Jones hinted that he could give up his threats if the legitimate "Father of the Motherland" (the President) recognized him as father of the child and acknowledged his right to keep him against the will of his natural mother and legitimate father, an absurd request if we think of the child as such, a perverse challenge if we think of the child as a symbol of a people.

Actually, the letter hinted at a far more serious threat: the "terrible thing," the total alienation of the people of Jonestown; a threat that the September 1977 siege and the testimonies seeping out of Jonestown had definitely clarified—collective suicide. Would motherland America and its legitimate "Father" (President Carter) dare do something to save the lives of a thousand of their "children" held hostage in the ghetto of Jonestown? Or would they leave them at the mercy of their charismatic "Father"?

From a historical point of view, Jones had been able to disguise himself behind the mask of a request for help, simultaneously predicting the impending holocaust of Jonestown. This trapped Carter into the roles of a disabled husband, of a rejecting wife/mother (America), and/or of a legitimate father who had disavowed his own people/child.

The whole episode of Jones writing this letter to Carter could be interpreted in a limited way by linking it to what we know about Jones's life and particularly about his early childhood; a childhood spent with a rejecting mother and a disabled father. In turn, this may lead us to ponder a wider theoretical issue: the very nature of leadership itself. In fact, Jones tried to establish an ambiguous dual relationship with President Carter, addressing him as a thaumaturgist who is able to solve magically the evil that has been produced, but also inducing him to become a scapegoat of the catastrophe of Jonestown. The dual metaphor of the placental leadership then should be analyzed if we want to reach a deeper insight into Jim Jones and his Peoples Temple, if we want to go back to Jonestown and begin unveiling the mystery of its ordeal, an uncanny ritual whose unconscious dynamics are not alien to the basic themes of this book.

THE PLACENTAL LEADER

The placental leader acts as a filter between the community and the outside world: on the one hand, it allows "nutrients" from the environment (the motherland/body of the mother) into the community (the people/fetal–placental unit), and on the other hand, it expels the inner evil of the community, thus preventing the latter's endogenous poisoning.

Although they have not been recognized as placental, some of these functions have been described in detail in the literature on divine kings. The basic quality of these personages lies in their ability to ensure growth. Rain, fertility of land, bountiful crops, animals' reproduction, even people's lives depend on the king's activity. The therapeutic aspects of the divine king are known as well as the institution of temporary kings, who are mirrors of the leader, doomed periodically to die in his place as scapegoats of the group.

Therefore, the universal custom, according to which at the least sign of aging (particularly loss or whitening of hair), the divine king was instantly murdered, can be given a new interpretation. The divine king was "put to sleep," that is, poisoned or suffocated (typical intrauterine deaths) when the sign of aging revealed his secondary function: as a scapegoat. From beneficial filter for the fetal–placental unit, the king could be transformed, with a sudden turnabout and/or betrayal, into malevolent filter, polluting rather than purifying. By that time the king was no longer able to absorb and neutralize the inner evil of the community. The inner evil had already filled his body and threatened to spoil the valuable substance of growth contained in it (Frazer, 1922). The vital principle therefore had to be transferred somewhere else (into the successor); while the old king's body could only be used as a receptacle of the community's inner evil. In some cultures, he had to carry it away with him, just as a *pharmakos*, beyond the boundaries of kingdom and life.

This twofold function of the divine king (growth and delivery from inner evil) is embodied in the language of the unconscious, which is made up of mental representations of organs and functions of the body, by the placenta. Indeed, the placenta is the grower and *pharmakos* of mankind. I prefer to say *pharmakos* rather than scapegoat, for the Greek term has an important twofold meaning. In fact, it indicates not only the victim sacrificed for the delivery of the people, but also the drug. Furthermore, each of these terms is, in its turn, twofold in meaning. The purificatory victim can be either the most noble and holiest or the most evil and marginal person of the community. Similarly, the drug can be either a medicine or a poison. Moreover, the *pharmakos* is either the healer or the sorcerer, the poisoner.

The placenta is the organ/metaphor of these "double" functions. The placenta enables the fetus to develop, but at the same time can poison it. The placenta is the sacrificial victim, the scapegoat of any childbirth, but at the same time can transform itself into poisoner and poison, both mother and child. It is still used today in medicine as a panacea and in cosmetics as a rejuvenating substance. Furthermore, it has been considered universally as a double of the child (Davidson, 1985), which is in its turn a classic symbol of the people. For all these characteristics, the placenta suitably represents, in the language of the body, the organ/word/metaphor of the archaic leadership (Nesci, 1989).

Jim Jones as Placental Leader

One of Jones's typical miracles consisted of collecting money from his followers with the assurance that if they gave a certain amount, they would receive it multiplied according to their needs. Sometimes, in order to confirm this conviction, he himself used to perform the "miracle" by sending an unexpected check to the follower, whose special needs he knew. All this was then largely advertised in order to collect more money and bring about other miracles. For example, a leaflet/testimony shows the photograph of one of his followers smiling and holding fanwise a bundle of banknotes. "I gave $7.00 in an offering when Pastor Jones reminded us that those who gave with a cheerful heart would have their money multiplied. The very next day I received $1,738.87."

Despite some statements by Jones, who denied the importance that miracles might have for the success of his religiopolitical movement, miracles were one of the leading rites on which the Peoples Temple was based. "No halos please" (a long manuscript by several Peoples Temple members) bears this out in a straightforward manner, with its endlessly boring list of faith healings.

But where did all this evil go, after Jones had taken it out of his followers' bodies? The placental leader metaphor provides an answer to this question. In fact, his thaumaturgic (miracle working) function forced him to project elsewhere the evil he had absorbed—and precisely into the body of the mother (motherland America, and whole world) in the hope that it might metabolize and discard it.

These dynamics are clearly described in several versions in the front headlines of the *Peoples Forum* issues (the Peoples Temple's journal). Earthquake, global catastrophe, slaughters of baby seals, invasions of killer bees, famines, changes in climate, death penalty, pollution, torture epidemics—Jones returned to his followers the "Evil" he had taken from them in the form of an apocalyptic vision of the universe, thus nurturing their continuous need to be "saved."

This apocalyptic vision became an image in one of the leaflets that was handed out to advertise Jones's "Miracle Ministry of Christ" in the American cities, where he led his "Temple Crusaders" to drum up support and offerings. I will try to describe it.

The Knights of the Apocalypse, hooded and dressed in white like the Knights of the Ku Klux Klan, bring death and destruction throughout America, riding over a thick black and bloody cloud. To counter the threat, here comes "Jim Jones the One You've Been Waiting For," with a Hitlerian grim look and a parody of the Fascist salute: his body embraces, encompasses, and towers over the Greyhound fleet by which the Peoples Temple used to travel throughout the country. The message is repeated in the back of the leaflet: on one side, there is Jim Jones promising delivery from Evil, on the other side, there is America seeking refuge (Peoples Temple?) and a divine protection (Jim Jones?). The "Anointed Prayer Cloth," which is given to the believers in exchange for their "Full Measure offering," is the talisman that will protect them. Anointed and blessed by "Pastor Jones," it becomes the filter between a motherland/body of the mother increasingly poisoned (by pollution, illnesses, hunger, poverty, crime, racism, etc.) and its own people/child: the tangible sign of the placental leader.

It is through this apocalyptic fabrication that Jones will manage to lead a group, made up mainly of black people, out of a supposedly racist and Nazi America in order to stage the very genocide he accused the American Nazis and the KKK of planning to commit. Thus, the leaflet ends up by depicting what Jones had disavowed and repressed, what he hated and loved at the same time in an absolutely split way, what he was making with his right hand while pretending to unmake with his left hand, and vice versa.

DOUBLE-DEALING

Jim Jones not only held dual roles (placental leader–divine king/*pharmakos*), but also as a person he was equally split (and therefore absolutely unable to control his own unconscious aspects, violently disavowed and violently emerging in his behavior: hetero- and homosexual, uncompromising and transgressive, benevolent and ruthless, fond of his wife and an adulterer, atheist and believer, Communist and Fascist, always extremist and dual in any of his manifestations).

Carter was not the only victim of his double-dealing. During a dinner held in his honor (we are left with a videotape recording of it), an American politician urged the participants to join in the applause by giving him a presentation that clarifies a facet of Jones's leadership: "Let me present to you what you should see every day when you look into the mirror in the early morning hours. Let me present to you a combination of Martin King, Angela Davis, Albert Einstein, Chairman Mao" (Reiterman with Jacobs, 1982, p. 308).

Seen through the eyes of his admirers, Jones was their own idealized self. He was a mirror, reflecting instead of the drowsy and nonheroic image of their real faces, the ambiguous combination of all powers and qualities desired: male and female, white and black, politician and scientist, believer and atheist, everything and the opposite of everything—a perfect double.

According to Vernant (1970), in Greece during an archaic period the *pharmakos* was nothing but a double of the divine king, doomed to die in his place to purify the community, as is the case for the Carnival kings. Some aspects of the annual rite of the expulsion of evil in Athens in historical times become essential to better understand Jim Jones as a modern version of the twofold figure of the placental leader.

First of all, the Athenian scapegoat was dual: there were two *pharmakoi*, a man and a woman. They wore necklaces strung with dried figs, which were black or white depending on the sex they embodied; the couple was led around the town, their genitals beaten with green twigs by everyone as a good omen for fertility and prosperity, and finally they were driven out of the community. In ancient times, they were stoned, their bodies burned, and their ashes scattered to the wind. These *pharmakoi* were the most amorphous creatures (in the sense that they lacked a definite identity) that could be found in the community.

Reminded of this, it is now possible to go through the fundamental stages of the Athenian ritual in Jim Jones's story. I will at first discuss how, through "faith healings," Jones was firmly convinced that he absorbed the evil of his followers, and in the last period of his life he accused them of having caused him to fall ill. Jones felt overwhelmed by all the evil he had absorbed from the bodies and minds of his children. He felt that they were actually killing him; he felt that his body had been irremediably poisoned. Indeed, he was poisoning himself, by taking high and inappropriate doses of antibiotics and psychotropic drugs; but he felt he was a scapegoat. In his long career at the service of the poor and helpless, he had often collapsed under the excessive burden he had taken on. But this time it was different. This time there was no chance of recovery. Jim Jones had fled to Guyana, after having carefully planned the last exodus of the Peoples Temple. From there he was preparing to celebrate the last phase of his placental leadership, the last move to win the title of divine king: death as *pharmakos*.

The flight to Guyana was important because it aimed at ridding the American people of its evil. But at the same time, with the usual structural duality of character, Jones's move also helped carry out the developmental plan of the country he was in.

In the first July 1977 issue of the *Peoples Forum*, these dynamics can be read between the lines of one of the articles:

In recent months, we have come to devote more and more of our time to our efforts to get people rehabilitated from lives of crime, drug addiction, or antisocial behavior. We have been described as one of the most effective groups in San Francisco in fighting crime. Our efforts in providing structure for young people, and our emphasis on individual responsibility, combined with the healthy lifestyle of our mission abroad, has brought about marvelous transformations in many lives. We didn't begin the mission program for that purpose: our basic intention was (and still is) to feed, clothe, and house people, in accordance with the central teachings of the humanistic Christ.

The mission in Guyana, which started like any of the leader/grower's many projects ("To feed, clothe, and house people"), therefore became the leader's/*pharmakos*'s crucial commitment ("fighting crime"). A month later, after Jones had finally taken refuge in the commune deep inside the Guyana jungle, an article was published in the *Peoples Forum* (August, 1977) entitled, "Hunger in the U.S.A." (the leader/grower had left), and at the same time, in large print between two stripes of stars, "The Temple Is Saving Taxpayers Millions of Dollars by Providing an Answer to the Youth Crime Crisis" appeared. The *pharmakos* machine had been started and would not stop until Jones had definitely removed from motherland America all those whom he claimed to rehabilitate, the outcasts he collected in his trips throughout the country. And it was an obscure story of sexual practices and the ability to procreate (the child's double paternity) that determined the decisive decision to flee the United States.

All the elements of the Athenian ritual, even if confused and inverted or in metaphorical form, can therefore be found again in the story of the leader/*pharmakos* of the Peoples Temple: to collect the evils of his motherland, traveling throughout its territory, to receive blows/attacks regarding sexual practices and the ability to procreate, to carry all evil away, to be "stoned to death," to be burned and scattered—after being reduced to ashes—to the wind. Actually, this is what became of Jones's body in the end.

THE SYNCYTIAL GROUP

One of the most fundamental and startling differences between the mentality of primitive humanity and a more contemporary conception of human nature, is the degree, almost inconceivable to us, to which the notion of individuality is undeveloped in the primitive mind. A savage will not only identify himself with an animal, or a tree, or even a stone, he will say that his son or his brother is "himself"; he will tell you with no perception of inconsistency that he is here and that he is, at the same time, somewhere else. He quite seriously regards any detached portion of his body as a part of himself, his hair, nail-pairings, spittle are accounted parts of his person, and what befalls them after they are separated from the body affects him also. His clothes and his name are part of himself, and have to be protected from injury just as he desires to be protected. In the same way, an injury to a member of the group to which he belongs, to one who is one flesh with him, is an injury suffered by himself. He feels this way not by virtue of magnanimous sentiments, or elevated principles of honor, or sublime ethical faiths, but because of his hazy conception of individuality which permits of a complete identification with the group. He does not think in terms of his ego and its interests, but in terms of the group–individual. (Briffault, 1927, p. 499)

Briffault defines primordial human groups as psychologically syncytial, structures in which the individual boundaries (membranes) among single members (cells) tend to disappear in the attempt to reinforce the ability of implanting into and adjusting to the environment, as if an excess of individuation might threaten the survival of the human species during its first phases of ecological adaptation. But there is no such thing as perfect dynamic equilibrium. Alongside the evident advantages (such as the possibility of bringing up children collectively, making up for any individual disabilities of natural mothers), it is easy to detect the drawbacks of a syncytial organization. First, there is the risk that any inner evil wreaks havoc to the entire structure, rather than being limited to a single group member.

Anthropological literature seems to bear out this risk. Roheim (1945), for example, studying some funerary rites, formulated (and rejected) the "impossible" hypothesis that human groups were originally exposed to the risk of collective suicide for any single death within the community. I do not think that this hypothesis is impossible, but rather paradoxical, and therefore understandable through the full acceptance of unconscious mental processes (Freud, 1966).

An evolutionary hypothesis regarding the drama of the syncytial group and its connection with collective suicide rituals could be put forward by considering ancient funerary rites. In the Warramunga society, a dying member of the group is buried under the mass of the other members, who injure themselves. They mourn continuously while they crush him to death under their weight. After his death, the ritual is repeated before his body is taken from the village, which is then destroyed and deserted (Spencer & Gillen, 1904). The natural death of a single member is perceived as a collective catastrophe; a maiming wound is inflicted on the body of all members of the group who are not willing to be separated from him, but fear being dragged to death with him. The syncytial group both denies and works through death in their own way: it transforms death, from a natural and individual event passively endured, into a collective and cultural event controlled by ritual. The murder of the dying member prevents people from becoming aware of natural death as the inner limit of human life.

The death of a member is perceived as a mutilation inflicted on the self of all other members of the syncytial group, and as the end of their world (the exodus from their village, as if for a natural catastrophe urging them to flee). At this cultural level, in fact, motherland and people, group and individuals, still live at the mother–child symbiotic level: if a death occurs within the system, everything is in jeopardy because of the lack of limits/boundaries. The social body, symbolically destroyed (and partly also physically) can be born again elsewhere. The dead becomes the placenta of the group, its *pharmakos*, its purificatory reject, a tangible sign of the collective disavowal: of death (natural limit of life), of the individual (natural limit of the group), of ambivalence (the natural limit of human emotional life). The primordial group claims in fact to be an evil-free community, claims to love the man it kills while mourning.

A slightly more developed pattern, for it is based on an oral incorporative dynamic rather than on an "imitative" or a "contact" one (Gaddini, 1969) (as is the case in Warramunga society) is shown by Normanby Island's Duau people.

> In Duau society we have the susu (breast), the group of those who are descended
> from the same uterine ancestor, as the social unit. The members of this fictive unity
> have "one body" and are supposed never to harbor any hostility against each
> other. But after each death, that is, whenever the mother–child unity is disrupted,
> they are tested by eating bwabware which will automatically kill them for any
> hostile emotions against the members for their own susu. (Roheim, 1945, p. 87)

The poison ordeal was not a unique feature of this people. It was so wide-spread in Africa, during the period of the slave trade, as to cause a sharp decrease in the population. Yet it was performed until suppression by European colonizers. People, in fact, submitted to it willingly, as they wanted to prove their own innocence toward the dead and their own group, and to demonstrate their imperviousness to individual death, perceived as murder by magic, a sign of hostility within the group, and therefore a risk of death for the whole community due to endogenous poisoning. Those peoples believed that the innocents would vomit up the poison, while the guilty would die.

It becomes therefore possible to hypothesize that primordial human groups have sought to limit the experience of mourning for the death of every single member of their syncytial group by establishing the figure of the divine king, that is, by setting up a subgroup (the divine king and his court—the placental leader and his own syncytial group) that took upon itself the handling of the group's inner evil: the individual death fantasized and emotionally experienced as death of the whole group, as total catastrophe.

The establishment of a dual institution (placental leader and his own syncytial group) as a filter of exchanges (the placenta) between motherland/body of the mother and people/fetal–placental unit had an important function. It prevented the catastrophic consequences of each death within the community. In fact, thanks to it, the only death that was really catastrophic was the sacred king's and the only persons who were really affected by his death were the members of his own syncytial group (his court, his closest relatives, his slaves, all those who were to die with him).

The Peoples Temple as Syncytial Group

My assumption is that the unconscious fantasy of the placental leader and his own syncytial group dates back to one of the most ancient human social organizations, an organization that originated in order to limit the self-destructive risks of the first human groups, exposed to collective suicide because of their excessive syncytiality.

This assumption is derived from Briffault's hypothesis (1927) of the precedence of basically female groups (mothers with their children at the center of the community, fathers and young adults in a marginal position and forced into exogamy) and of "collective clan relationships" as compared with any "family system of relationships." The institution of the placental leader and his own syncytial group (the divine king and his court) marks an evolutionary stage of the primordial human group through which it starts detaching itself from "the mothers" (Briffault, 1927). An important characteristic of this passage (from the syncytial maternal primordial human group to the one in which placental leader and his own syncytial group have become separated, as a subgroup from the community as a whole) is that the introjective patterns (the poison ordeal) of catastrophic mourning (i.e., of the natural individual death experienced as total collective death) were limited to a circle of a few (the sacred king and his court), whereas the rest of the community could resort to more cathartic defenses—war, for example, as a paranoid working through of death, according to Strehlow (1915–1920), Roheim (1945), and Fornari (1966). Collective suicide could then be interpreted as the oldest aspect of the war ritual (Nesci, 1985).

If this hypothesis were true, it would follow that any community can regress to this suicidal stage when it is exposed, or feels exposed, to the risk of a catastrophe, involving the fantasy of death or collective annihilation (the end of its own world, of its own people). The risk of collective suicide could then be anticipated and evaluated because its enactment would imply the creation of a syncytial structure governed by a placental leader.

Jim Jones and his Peoples Temple were such a group. The placental leader served as a model, whereby any member could overcome the feeling of being an individual, of living a limited life apart from the rest. Jones maintained that he was the reincarnation of Lenin and Christ, that he had lived in different ages, that he could communicate with the spirits of the dead through the ether, and that he was feeling the sufferings of mankind and animals as if they were his own. Furthermore, he attributed changing identities and roles to various members of his group. For example, when he decided to break up the marriage between two members of the Peoples Temple, he claimed that the woman (who had become his lover) was the reincarnation of Inessa Armand (one of Lenin's lovers). Thus, his followers might believe that Jones was invaded by other lives, and that all those who came into contact with him were automatically put into contact with other souls, regardless of time and space limits.

In this way, the group formed a syncytial structure based on the fusionality of relations and the disavowal of individual limits and death (as in primordial human groups). One of the letters sent out to potential new members, together with cakes, ends with the following words: "There is no sickness here, no hunger and no death. In fact, this church is the closest thing to paradise on earth" (Mills, 1979, p. 126).

Individual death could not be accepted by the Peoples Temple, as it brought back the anxiety of total annihilation. It was on the basis of an alleged vision of salvation from a nuclear holocaust that Jones guided his people from Indiana to California in 1965, and then to Guyana in order to save them from racist genocide.

The Peoples Temple sought to defend itself from these primitive anxieties by escaping regressively into the archaic syncytial matrix of the primordial human communities. Its regressive nature made this escape paradoxical: to reenact the syncytial structure meant exposure to the risk of annihilation each time evil appeared within the group. And even if the placental leader, organizer of the defenses against the evil, had been able to filter it, sooner or later the aging or weakening of Jones would have entailed the acting out of the archaic ritual of syncytial groups, that is, collective suicide.

An example of a syncytial group that clarifies the relationship between placental leadership, syncytial membership, and collective suicide is provided by a Bantu legend. Two Ba-ila clans competed for the right to bestow the leadership. When one of the two clans lost this privilege, all members decided to commit suicide. They intertwined a long rope and tied it around their necks. They gathered on the shore of a lake and drowned themselves (Smith & Dale, 1920).

Within a syncytial group (the suicidal clan) the loss of the leadership privilege corresponds to the aging of a divine king. It is as if all members of the clan turn white-haired and impotent. Therefore, the only way to regain their own social identity (the leadership privilege) is to sacrifice themselves (literally: make themselves sacred) according to the second aspect of the placental leader: mold themselves as his own syncytial group, dying together as *pharmakoi*.

From this point of view, the Jonestown's commune would have sought to recover, regressively, the old pattern of collective clan relationships, thus enabling its members to regain some archaic gratifications (the illusion of having overcome the limits, ranging from the individual limits to the extreme limit of death), but also exposing them to the risk of reenacting the collective suicide, that is, a ritual typical of syncytial social structure. Inside the Peoples Temple, the family system of relationships had been broken down into a system quite similar to the one that Briffault ascribed to the "primitive" human group. Due to a systematic breaking up of marriages and to a massive use of adoptions, the Jonestown's community was basically made up of mothers and children (and elderly as well). Young men were an outcast minority (actually, they let themselves out of Jonestown in the crucial days that led to the holocaust, so that they could do nothing to prevent it). The Peoples Temple's decision-making group was made up of women (like the female leadership of another sect that committed collective suicide in South Korea in August, 1987), and these women showed an ability to foster-mother, as Briffault hypothesized.

It was not by chance that the Ba-ila events were reenacted on the Jonestown stage: the last one in the human chain was a woman who was married to a man of a third clan, who rescued her from death by cutting the rope and bringing her safely to dry land. At Jonestown, it was only thanks to the arrival of a third (Congressman Ryan and his party) that twenty-odd persons, by defeating the suggestion of dying together, were able to detach themselves from the syncytial group and the placental leader.

Like the Ba-ila clan, the Peoples Temple members (unable to accept the fall of Jones's leadership, disrupted by the intrusion of Ryan and the defection of a small number of believers, i.e., by two events that proved the failure of the placental filter and the nonsyncytiality of the group) formed a human mass of intertwined bodies (a "placental" disk rather than an "umbilical cord") and poisoned themselves as a protest against the world—extreme sacrifice to a culture (syncytial) that is still far from having been desecrated (Nesci, 1989).

NOT RUNNING

In the February 2, 1977 issue of the *Peoples Forum,* Jones denied wanting to run for any political office. As in all assertions of a double, it was neither true nor false. It was true insomuch as he would never allow a free electorate to evaluate him. It was false in that he did not nurture political ambitions. Jones pursued them in a regressive and perverse way that can be explained only from an ethnopsychoanalytic point of view.

For example, his insistence on being seated next to Mrs. Carter (on the speakers' platform, during the presidential election campaign) and on being given the chance to meet her privately (before her departure from San Francisco) cannot be explained just rationally, that is, as a means to promote his image and increase his power. To the free-floating attention of a psychoanalyst, his gestures would rather evoke his past attempts to gain leadership of the Divine Peace Mission. In 1971, Jones tried to be recognized by Mother Divine as Father Divine's reincarnation. He claimed that the soul of Father Divine was living in his body. The point of contact between these two episodes, although they differ greatly, lies in the fact that Jones tried to win a power by relating himself to a maternal figure. Actually, these were the usual rules governing the passage of leadership in most archaic cultures, where the king's power (short-lived reincarnation of the lunar god) actually came from his spouse. The fact that almost all of Jones's lovers were daughters of ministers of cults would thus acquire a new meaning. Whether political or religious, he always tried to draw his power from female figures.

In the same way, Jones's (disavowed) desire to become President of the United States did not involve any evolved legal considerations, but the primitive one of the charismatic power which rests on ordeals. The succession to leadership in an archaic culture takes place by ritual murder or judgment of God. The allegations that Jones made against former members of the Peoples Temple (he accused them of having plotted the President's murder and the poisoning of water in Washington, D.C.) now become clearer. They were nothing but the projections of his own fantasies (regicide or poison ordeal) on how to ascend to the White House throne. With regard to this, it is worth noting that the photograph of Jones and Mrs. Carter, published twice by the *Peoples Forum,* hangs over a sinister "Death Penalty."

All this would have been irrelevant (and could also be considered unfounded) if Jones had not rediscovered and reenacted at Jonestown the archaic antecedent of the death penalty (the poison ordeal) and if he had not sentenced to death, instead of the President, a U.S. congressman. As he failed to convince the American people of an impending "global catastrophe" and of the need to induct him into the White House, the only chance he had to gain his leadership was to revive, in a regressive acting out, the archaic figure of the divine king.

Again, the pages of the *Peoples Forum* (February, 1977) provide evidence, for those who know how to read them from an ethnopsychoanalytic point of view, of Jones's regressive reengulfment into the kingdom of the Mothers.

Under the heading, "Not Running" (that in the ambiguous language of the Peoples Temple referred to Jones's next flight from America), his ambitions emerge from the words. Above it there is the text of a poem by Lynetta Jones (the mother of the Peoples Temple's leader) in which she tells of molding her only son as with clay and attributes to him a "godlike nature." In the left upper portion there is a photograph of Jones speaking into a microphone. A double image of Martin Luther King stands out behind him as the caption reads: "Rev. Jim Jones receives award in recognition of his outstanding efforts to further ideals of civil rights and civil liberties championed by Dr. King." To the left there is a text, reading, "Let us work together, and exemplify our common principles so that the seeds of a new society can find receptive ground, and flourish in the hearts of men and women throughout our nation." In the left lower corner, an editor's note explains how "the ideas that appear in the *Peoples Forum* are suggested by Rev. Jim Jones" and it depicts him in his continuous wandering "throughout the nation." Under the article, the filtering function, typical of the placental leader and his syncytial group, is described:

> Because of threats of violence and assassination from a lunatic fringe, we are being a bit more careful these days about giving out information on our programs and service schedules over the phone. We suggest that if you call inquiring about the *Peoples Forum,* or our church services, you leave a phone number, and your call will be returned.

The text of the article, enclosed in its frame, is therefore much clearer, and less innocent:

> There is a rumor circulating that Jim Jones would consider running for mayor in the next election. Some people have suggested and even encouraged him to become a candidate. His unqualified response was, "It is ludicrous. Some need to be on the outside of political institutions so they can form non-partisan judgments." The Temple's purpose has always been to unify to combat social problems common to all.

This text outlines the double (the two images) portrayal of the divine king/*pharmakos* (Dr. King, Jones's "godlike nature"), with its dual functions: growth ("further the ideals of civil rights and civil liberties," "the seeds of a new society can find receptive ground, and flourish in the hearts of men and women throughout our nation") and delivery from evil ("to combat social problems common to all").

The tragedy of Jonestown was allowed to take place because no one in the pragmatic and modern culture of today's America would believe that what Jones said and threatened to do was possible; that is a bizarre, but understandable, unconscious reenactment of the most ancient human ritual.

THE POISON ORDEAL

This death rite interests us for two fundamental reasons: its structure, very similar to the Peoples Temple's poisoning rite (the "White Night"), which I have described elsewhere (Nesci, 1985, 1988), and its frightening scope as a phenomenon of collective suicide. Just to give an idea, in Madagascar alone during the last century an estimated 3,000 persons died every year, and in the Ivory Coast the French government blamed the steady drop in population on the poison ordeal, even after the slave trade had been abolished (Frazer, 1922).

Frazer (1919) devotes a long chapter in his book to this ritual, which was widespread in most of tropical Africa. It is worth noting that the poison ordeal was transformed into a real self-administered genocide only in those areas most devastated by the slave trade. This was not only due to economic reasons (the relatives of the ordeal victims were often sold as slaves), but also to a particular modification of the leadership following the European colonization. According to Frazer, in such areas the figure of the fetish king and of the administrative king (distinct and separate before the white colonization) fused into a single person, in whom resided both the political and religious power. In this way a very dangerous situation developed. On the one hand, the fertility and the prosperity of the earth, animals, and people were believed to depend on the health and welfare of the fetish king; on the other hand, the relationships with the colonizers and the neighboring tribes depended on the energy of the administrative king. Sickness or death of a king who embodied both powers were catastrophic events indeed (Frazer, 1922). The poison trial was the ritual through which such catastrophes, like all others, were to be resolved.

It is necessary at this point to remember at least one of the collective suicides that shows the connection between the crisis of leadership and the poison ordeal. Goldie (1901) gives this example:

> Uwet, a small tribe from the hill-country, had settled on the left branch of the river, where it narrows into a rivulet. When we first visited the place, a considerable population, divided into three villages, occupied the settlement. Since that time it has almost swept itself off the face of the earth, by the constant use of *esere* [the native word for poison]. At one time two headmen contended for the kingship. He who succeeded in gaining it fell sick, and of course accused his opponents of seeking to destroy him, and insisted that his competitor and his adherents should test their innocence by the ordeal. A number died, and the sickness of the successful candidate also issued in death. The one disappointed now attained the coveted honour, and in retaliation subjected those of the opposite party to the test, and a number more perished. On one occasion the whole population took the *esere*, to prove themselves pure, as they said; about half were thus self-destroyed, and the remnant, still continuing their superstitious practice, must soon become extinct. (p. 38)

In his regressive flight into the jungle, into the village of Jonestown, Jones incarnated a modern version of the ancient figure of the fetish king. In a shocking videotape, we can still participate "live" in one of Jim Jones's religious services, and we easily become aware of the disturbing reappearance of this primordial figure in the leader of the suicide group. The main part of the rite is marked by the entrance of Jones, accompanied by the music of the International anthem, which reaches its climax in the exclamation: "I come as god socialist!" and, later, "I am god!" Political and religious power were so deeply confused in the leader of the Peoples Temple that his performance passed from a miracle to a political statement without any attempt at continuity (Nesci, 1986).

Regarding Jones as a sacred king allows us to better understand the fatal crisis of the Peoples Temple. After the exodus to Guyana in 1977, the physical and mental health of the leader rapidly deteriorated, creating a dangerous situation for the very survival of the commune. A succession was unthinkable, and only two possible alternatives remained: the dismemberment of the group or its consecration in death as a rebirth in another dimension, in a hereafter where the group would be eternally reunited.

A third alternative was also possible and apparently was thought of, according to the most accurate reconstruction of the tragedy (Reiterman with Jacobs, 1982): to follow the classical succession of the divine kings. To kill Jones. The killer would incorporate the precious king's spirit, thus allowing all his people to continue to live and prosper. The spirit of a divine king, in fact, is a double of the spirit of the people. For this reason it is imperative not to run the risk of its weakening because of its stay in the body of a man who suffers a natural death. In that unfortunate event, the entire world would weaken to the point of extinction: it would be the end of the world.

Most probably Jones did not commit suicide. Like an African divine king he received a poison cup to drink, and only when he lost consciousness was he shot in the head. He was ritually murdered. But the Peoples Temple had already become Jones's own syncytial group: they had to "leave" with him, to poison themselves and follow him into the afterlife, just as the court of an archaic divine king (Nesci & Bersani, 1988).

CONCLUSIONS (JONESTOWN, NOVEMBER 18, 1978)

The difference between placental leadership, associated with the universe of syncytial culture (which dates back to the primordial human groups, unaware of war and exposed to the risk of collective suicide), and Oedipal leadership, associated with the universe of a later culture (where war tends to replace, progressively, the poison rite), provides an ethnopsychoanalytic insight to the last White Night of Jonestown.

Let us recall a fragment of the tragic end of the utopian commune, as in it the psychodynamic patterns of syncytial and Oedipal leadership face each other and provide mutual insights.

Congressman Ryan and his group were able to visit Jonestown, despite the actual difficulties in reaching the jungle commune and Jones's opposition to the visit. Although all dwellers had done everything to prove that they were happy and did not wish to go back to the United States, a small group of persons fled or expressed openly their resolute desire to leave with Ryan and his party. While the lawyers of the Peoples Temple maintained that it was an irrelevant incident compared with the positive fact that most people living in Jonestown seemed to be happy and united around their leader, Jones appeared wounded to death. His mood was shared by the members of the commune, as the following episode clearly shows.

When the journalists and the "traitors" (as those who were leaving Jonestown were called) got into the truck that was to bring them to the airstrip of Port Kaituma, a man with his children tried to join them. Then the omnipresent loudspeakers of Jonestown called the man's wife, who accused him of kidnapping her children and threatened to kill him. The whole population of Jonestown was on her side. The quarrel was temporarily settled by the lawyers of the Peoples Temple. When the attempt to bring his children with him failed, the man refused to leave. Then Ryan offered to stay in Jonestown to attend to the man's safety and to allow others to speak out and express their desire to leave. Before long, however, another member of the Peoples Temple tried to stab the congressman, yelling as he did so: "Congressman Ryan, you motherfucker ... " (Reiterman with Jacobs, 1982).

But his gesture was too late in coming. The lie of Jonestown had already been unmasked by the last scene of Ryan's visit: a husband who quarrels with his wife because he wants to leave and bring his children with him reaffirms, inevitably, the reality of the natural bonds (genital/Oedipal) and inflicts an incurable wound on the group's narcissism: It is not true that the "children"/members of Jonestown are generated in a pregenital magical manner ("although I used preventatives") by the "Father" and belong to the Peoples Temple (the mother), as it is not true that they live in harmony inside their maternal womb (unborn "children" of Jonestown) and wish to stay there forever.

With this in mind, it is easy to understand the reaction of rage and despair that the "traitors" leaving Jonestown aroused in those who chose to stay. Ryan had been sentenced to death and killed, while Jonestown was celebrating its last White Night, because he had "fucked" the pre-Oedipal group/mother, thus breaking their "group illusion" (Anzieu, 1971), that is, the climate of euphoria, of manic triumph, that characterized Jonestown's "happiness." The tape recording of the last White Night begins with Jones's voice accusing those who left of having committed "the betrayal of the century," of having triggered "a catastrophe" (Pozzi et al., 1988). With an abrupt betrayal/turnabout, they had chosen a traumatic delivery rather than a deadly illusory reimplantation; they had chosen to follow an Oedipal leader abandoning their old placental leader to his fate.

The divine king had grown old. The placenta had grown old. If this reality could not be disavowed, the dangerous metamorphosis of delivery/birth had to be faced: the end of the symbiotic organization and the beginning of a new life through the process of "separation–individuation" (Mahler, 1968) between mother and child and of the avowal of the Oedipal father's role. The utopian paradise of the mythical golden age had to be left to enter the transient, ephemeral, but real time–space of history. A mourning had to be experienced and suffered.

> Dozens stood stiff as cane stalks were placed around the playground perimeter, their attention fixed on Jones and some aides. The rank-and-file members standing by the truck [the truck with Ryan's group leaving Jonestown definitely] had turned their backs to us to watch and wait. They all looked as though there had been a death in the family. (Reiterman with Jacobs, 1982, p. 517)

In the perverse universe of Jonestown, this mourning (that is the inevitable catastrophe of any symbiotic organization) could not be avowed but only acted out by reenacting regressively the White Night ritual, a modern version of the archaic poison ordeal.

REFERENCES

Anzieu, D. (1971). L'illusion groupale. *Nouvelle Revue de Psychanalyse, 4,* 73–93.

Briffault, R. (1927). *The mothers.* London: Macmillan.

Davidson, J. R. (1985). The shadow of life: Psychosocial explanations for placenta rituals. *Culture, Medicine and Psychiatry, 9,* 93–96.

Feinsod, E. (1981). *Awake in a nightmare.* New York: Norton.

Fornari, U. (1966). *Psicoanalisi della guerra.* Milano: Feltrinelli. [American translation (1975), *Psychoanalysis of War.* Bloomington: Indiana University Press.]

Frazer, J. G. (1919). *Folk-lore in the Old Testament.* London: Macmillan.

Frazer, J. G. (1922). *The golden bough.* London: Macmillan.

Freud, S. (1966). *The standard edition of the complete psychological works of Sigmund Freud.* London: Hogarth.

Gaddini, E. (1969). On imitation. *International Journal of Psychoanalysis, 57,* 475–484.

Goldie, H. (1901). *Calabar and its mission.* Edinburgh & London: Oliphant.

Jones, J. (1978). Letter to President Carter, Archives of Charles Garry, San Francisco.

Mahler, M. S. (1968). *On human symbiosis and the vicissitudes of individuation.* New York: International Universities Press.

Mills, J. (1979). *Six years with God.* New York: A & W.

Nesci, D. A. (1985). Morte a Jonestown: La prova orale. *Proceedings of the Congress on: Le psicosi e la maschera,* pp. 229–238. Roma: IES Mercury.

Nesci, D. A. (1986). *Sounds and images from Utopia.* (An audio-video presentation, Children's Hospital, San Francisco; Dept. of Psychiatry, UCLA; Dept. of Psychiatry, Harbor-UCLA; unpublished manuscript.)

Nesci, D. A. (1988). An ethnopsychoanalytic insight into the holocaust of the Peoples Temple. *Acta Medica Roma, 26*(2), 249–259.

Nesci, D. A. (1989). Inner evil and collective suicide: An ethnopsychoanalytic interpretation of the Peoples Temple's Holocaust. *Acta Medica Roma, 27*(2), 201–209.

Nesci, D. A. (1990). *Redwater: An ethnopsychoanalytic study of the Peoples Temple's Ordeal (Jonestown, November 18, 1978).* Unpublished manuscript.

Nesci, D. A., & Bersani, G. (1988). The collective suicide of the Peoples Temple: A psychohistorical approach. *Acta Medica Roma, 26*(2), 176–189.

Pozzi, E., Nesci, D. A., & Bersani, G. (1988). The narrative of a mass suicide: The Peoples Temple's last tape. *Acta Medica Roma, 26*(2), 150–175.

Reiterman, T., with Jacobs, J. (1982). *Raven: The untold story of the Rev. Jim Jones and his people.* New York: Dutton.

Roheim, G. (1945). *War, crime, and the covenant.* Monticello, NY: Medical Journal Press.

Smith, E. W., & Dale, A. M. (1920). *The Ila-speaking people of Northern Rhodesia.* London: Macmillan.

Spencer, B., & Gillen, F. J. (1904). *The northern tribes of Central Australia.* London: Macmillan.

Strehlow, C. (1915–20). *Die Aranda und Loritja-Stamme in Zentral-Australien.* Frankfurt: Volker Museum.

Vernant, J. P. (1970). Ambiguité et renversement. Sur la structure énigmatique d'"Oedipe Roi." In J. P. Verant & P. Vidal-Naquet (Eds.), *Mythe et Tragédie en Grèce Ancienne* (pp. 101–131). Paris: Maspero.

II

Presidential Profiles

*Psychic Vulnerabilities
and Political Repercussions
(Both Catastrophic and Otherwise)*

As America's democratic visions and values seem to triumph around the
world, an unhappy consensus has emerged at home that domestic politics has
become so shallow, mean and even meaningless that it is failing to produce the
ideas and leadership needed to guide the United States in a rapidly changing
world.

MICHAEL ORESKES, *The New York Times*, March 18, 1990

In Part II we take a more personal, psychobiographical look at some twentieth-
century leaders and explore the complex interplay between the personality of the
leader, attending character strengths and weaknesses, and the impact of these
traits on political events. Greek hubris is examined as a critical dynamic in
Dukakis's nemesis (Orfanos). Carter's personality structure is evaluated in response to the Soviet invasion of Afghanistan (Glad and Whitmore). John F.
Kennedy's private persona is contrasted with his more "public" persona and
resultant rhetorical style (Windt). The masterful emergence of George Bush in the
1988 campaign, from wimp to patrician in politics, is explored psychohistorically
(Elovitz and Jeansonne). And Carter and Sadat are examined from two fascinating perspectives, one psychohistorical and psychobiographical in source and the
other more personal reflections coming from a fellow countryman (Elovitz and
Shaalan).

5

The Spelling and Seduction of Michael Dukakis

Spyros D. Orfanos

"We have not compromised our honor," said Euterpe Dukakis, the mother of Michael Dukakis, to the television reporter as she stepped down from the podium following the concession speech given by her son on election night, 1988. In an age when political analysts both admire and lament the importance of "political handlers," this comment by Euterpe Dukakis, literally the first handler of Michael Dukakis, may offer a clue to the personality of the Democratic party's presidential nominee of 1988 and his campaign behavior. This chapter will attempt to provide an understanding of the intersecting personal and political dreams and realities of the last presidential election. The emphasis will be on the self-proclaimed, "proud son of immigrants" and "product of the American dream," and his inability to confront George Bush, the Republican party's presidential nominee. By doing so, it is my hope that another view of mutually regulating aspects of the personal and the political will be established.

The days when psychoanalytic psychology was considered valuable only when it focused on the individual are over, as are the explanations that rely on reductionism and historism (Holt, 1989). Nevertheless, one is left with the awesome task, particularly when seeking to understand political leaders and phenomena, of trying to explain very complicated and interdependent dynamics in a manner that appears clear and self-evident. "Everything is related to everything

SPYROS D. ORFANOS, Ph.D. • Faculty and Supervisor, New York University School of Medicine, New York, New York 10016; Co-Director, Greek American Research Project, Center for Byzantine and Modern Greek Studies of Queens College, City University of New York, Queens, New York 11367.

Politics and Psychology: Contemporary Psychodynamic Perspectives, edited by Joan Offerman-Zuckerberg. Plenum Press, New York, 1991.

else," claimed Kurt Lewin, one of the first social psychologists to advocate a systems psychology in the 1930s. But this does not mean that everything should be studied at the same time. While I am aware that my understanding is an interpretation, that is, a personal statement that reaches beyond hard clinical and political data, I am also aware that an objective description of facts and developments does not sufficiently account or reveal aspects of personal and group conduct that are important and in need of explanation.

HONOR THY MOTHER OR FATHER?

To win the presidency in 1988, Dukakis and the Democrats had three different needs. They had to bring an end to the Reagan revolution, and according to Pomper (1989) they had to consolidate their base and extend beyond their base. Consolidation required the support and enthusiasm of liberals and blacks and extension required the return of moderates and Democrats who had voted for Reagan. How could Dukakis, an uncharismatic candidate of short physical stature, emphasizing competence over ideology, compete with the heritage of Reagan, an Ayn Rand superlibertarian and one who derived much of his voter appeal from the fact that he looked and "acted" the way Americans wanted a president to look and act? How could the party both promise the social programs and pluralism wanted by its left wing and avoid the tax increase opposed by most voters?

Dukakis started his presidential "marathon" with little recognition, and even during the first few days of the Democratic convention in Atlanta, Georgia, it was Jesse Jackson, his most serious ideological challenger, who was most visible. Jackson was making a serious bid for the vice-presidential slot, and had great popular appeal. But with skilled negotiating with the Jackson forces on such issues as strengthened condemnation of South African apartheid and adoption of platforms that called for "significantly increasing" federal spending on education, and most importantly the consideration for electoral victory, Dukakis won the nomination, chose his own vice-presidential candidate, Lloyd Bentsen, and was given the opportunity to display his personal leadership on the last night of the convention.

Dukakis brought the convention to its climax with his acceptance speech on the final night of the Democratic convention. Billed as a poor speaker, wearing a button-down shirt and business suit, the governor roused his audience with the best speech of his political career. Syndicated columnists Jack Germond and Jules Witcover (1989) wrote:

> Much of the speech was well-crafted but conventionally inspirational political rhetoric. "If anyone tells you," he said, "that the American dream belongs to the privileged few and not to all of us, you tell them that the Reagan era is over and a new era is about to begin ... Because it is time to raise our sights, to look beyond the cramped ideals and limited ambitions of the past eight years, to recapture the spirit of energy and confidence and of idealism that John Kennedy and Lyndon Johnson inspired a generation ago."

"This election," he said at another point, "is not about ideology, it's about competence."

But the passages that reached the delegates most obviously were those in which Dukakis seemed to reveal a little more of himself than he had exposed in his campaign for the nomination. "We're going to win," he said, "because we are the party that believes in the American dream, a dream so powerful that no distance of ground, no expanse of ocean, no barrier of language, no distinction of race or creed or color can weaken its hold on the human heart. And I know because, my friends, I'm a product of that dream and I'm proud of it, a dream that brought my father to this country seventy-six years ago, that brought my mother and her family here one year later; poor, unable to speak English, but with a burning desire to succeed in their new land of opportunity.

"And tonight, in the presence of that marvelous woman who is my mother and who came here seventy-five years ago, with the memory in my heart of the young man who arrived at Ellis Island with only twenty-five dollars in his pocket but with a burning desire and abiding faith in the promise of America—and how I wish he was here tonight. He'd be very proud of his adopted country, I can assure you." (p. 354)

What Germond and Witcover miss is the fact that Dukakis actually added the phrase, "He'd be very proud of his son," at the beginning of the last sentence to the paragraph they quote. No doubt that they were using the original text of the speech, but Dukakis, quite out of character, ad-libbed the phrase when he delivered the speech in Atlanta. John Chancellor (1988), the television broadcaster, speaking to his colleague, Tom Brokaw, and to the listening audience, said the speech was, "Delivered with extreme effectiveness, including, Tom, as you know, the ad-lib at the beginning of his acceptance speech about his father, which was quite moving and seemed very genuine."

It is very curious that on the night of the most important speech of his political life, Michael Dukakis, a man viewed as extremely unemotional, sidesteps his usual rigidity to the predetermined plan and makes a remark that refers to his personal achievement and to his father's pride in that achievement. Obviously, this phrase is not an unconscious slip-of-the-tongue along the lines that would strike a classical psychoanalyst as a critical piece of information perhaps suggesting some underlying conflictual feelings, probably along Oedipal themes. However, to assume that this spontaneous remark holds little psychic significance would be a serious mistake. Precisely what does Michael Dukakis's remark mean? And perhaps even more importantly for the present purpose of this chapter, what does it mean in the political context of the presidential election? For a possible answer to these questions, a look at the Greek and Greek American roots of this "son of immigrants" is in order.

GREEK ORIGINS

The sociologist and Greek American scholar, Charles C. Moskos (1989), has written extensively on the Greek roots of Michael Dukakis.[1] On his father's side, Michael Dukakis's roots extend to the island of Lesbos, known more commonly to Greeks as Mytilene. Mytilene, roughly 15 miles long and 30 miles wide, lies in the eastern Aegean, within sight of the coast of Turkey. The island has a population of about 100,000, but the Dukakis ancestral village in northeast Mytilene, Pelopi, has 614 people, somewhat fewer than at the turn of the century. Electricity and running water came to the village and the houses in the 1960s. Primarily an agricultural village, with men-only coffeehouses, the main road has been named Michael Doukakis Street with signs in both English and Greek that say, "Welcome to the home town of Michael Dukakis."

Michael's grandfather, Stylianos Dukakis (1866–1918), was born in Pelopi at a time when Mytilene was still part of the Ottoman Empire. The island did not become part of independent Greece until 1914. Travel and commerce were common between Mytilene and those parts of the empire that lay in nearby Asia Minor. When Stylianos was 12, he moved across the straits to Edremit in mainland Turkey to work in a general store owned by relatives, and subsequently he opened his own store. On one of his frequent returns to Pelopi he married a fellow villager, Olympia Georgiou (1866–1941), who had never left her home village. Stylianos took his bride back to Edremit where they had five children. Panos, the third eldest brother, would become the father of Michael Dukakis.

From an economic and educational standpoint, life as a Greek in Asia Minor at the turn of the century was relatively reasonable, but psychologically it was oppressive. The Young Turk's revolt of 1908 was at first welcomed, but their xenophobia soon became a much greater threat to the survival of the Greeks than the old Ottoman order. The political climate was tense and changing, and young Panos must have been witness to the increasing economic anxieties, distrust of rulers, and subsequent persecutions of the Greeks. Not seeking his father's approval, the eldest son, Athanasios, migrated to America in 1910. Once settled as a tailor in Manchester, New Hampshire, he sent for the family's second eldest, his brother George. George established himself in the restaurant business. In 1912, Arthur (the American name that Athanasios soon adopted) and George sent for Panos. By 1916, Olympia arrived with her youngest child, Constantine, and by 1918, Stylianos, the father, and Marina, the remaining sister, followed.

The first two decades of the century covered the period in American history that is known as the era of mass migration. Immigrants were arriving by the thousands, and they were coming to an America that had ambivalent feelings about the new arrivals. For example, American-owned restaurants would often display signs on their windows saying, "Pure American. No Rats, No Greeks." For the Dukakis parents and children, strong patriarchal and provincial values were not only being challenged by the totalitarian government in Asia Minor, but by the need to assimilate into the ways of their new American home. With the Dukakis children leading the way to America and its life, the hierarchial power of Stylianos was dealt a blow. We would be on solid ground to interpret his experience as being a humiliating and shameful one, both in having to give up his failing business in Asia Minor and in having to follow his children to America for a better life. To what extent he and his family mourned the loss of their original homeland and the rigid patriarchal family structure is unclear, but there had to be some sense of tragedy associated with the migration and transplant.

In Greek the family name is "Doukakis," but the "o" was dropped soon after the family arrived in America. The literal meaning of Doukakis is "son of a duke," and no doubt gave the family a sense of specialness. According to Dukakis biographers Charles Kenney and Robert Turner (1988), there was some talk about changing the family name to Duke, but it never happened. Omitting the "akis," which when applied to names means "son," surely did not go unnoticed by Stylianos.

Panos arrived in the United States at the age of 16 with $25 and a high school education, a rather reasonable head start for an immigrant of that time, despite the "poor and uneducated" label often used to describe him. He lived with the second eldest brother, George, and worked in mills, restaurants, and in Arthur's tailor shop. Holding higher aspirations right from the start, he attended school to learn English in Lowell, Massachusetts, and took premedical courses first at Boston College and then at Bates College in Maine, where he finished his studies in 1920. He applied for admission to the Harvard Medical School, but was refused by an admissions officer who disliked Panos's immigrant background (Kenney & Turner, 1988). But Harvard reversed itself and he was admitted after all: he graduated in 1924, becoming the first Greek to do so from that school. Arthur Dukakis proudly recalls that, "When Pan became a doctor, we all had to go to him. His prognosis was God. He knew all the answers" (Kenney & Turner, 1988, p. 7). Moskos (1989) writes that:

> Panos Dukakis, whose American friends called him Duke, practiced medicine almost until the end of his life in 1979. Because he spoke perfect English with only a trace of an accent and was relatively tall and fair, he would not have been taken for a Greek except for his name. Panos delivered over 3,000 babies in the Boston area ... Panos earned a good living from his profession and also invested wisely. When he died, he left trust funds totaling more than $1 million. By all accounts Panos was a political conservative. He shed his Republicanism grudgingly, only because of his son's advancement in the Democratic party. (p. 177)

The geographical origins of the family history of Michael Dukakis's mother, Euterpe, were different than that of his father, but the psychological experience of marginality and the immigration experience of America were somewhat similar. The rugged mountain ancestors of Michael Boukis (1857–1944), Euterpe's father, were called Vlachs. The Vlachs were a nomadic Balkan tribe of Romanian origins that settled in the northwest Epirus region of Greece. Like the Greeks in Asia Minor, the Vlachs in Greece had to negotiate ethnic identity issues and conflicts of being a people outside the mainstream culture. As an adolescent, Michael Boukis, whose father was a shepherd, moved eastward, eventually going to school in Smyrna in Asia Minor. This was rather unusual for a young man of his background, and reinforced an independence streak that was in line with his Vlach background. After completing a high school education, he moved to Larissa, one of the largest cities on mainland Greece's east coast. There he worked as a bookkeeper, and around 1888 married Chrysoula Kambourios. In Larissa, Michael and Chrysoula had six children, two boys followed by four girls, with Euterpe being the fifth child. Not unlike other families and groups, moving to America was an economic necessity for the Boukis family. In an interview with authors Kenney and Turner (1988), Euterpe Dukakis offered the following explanation for the migration, "In those days, you see, girls were really a burden. The family had to provide a dowry" (p. 3).

The two older brothers arrived first in the United States in the first decade of this century and worked in New England mills like so many thousands of immigrants of that time, and in 1913, Euterpe left Greece with her parents and sisters and arrived at Ellis Island in April. The family settled in Haverhill, Massachusetts, and Michael ran the family's boardinghouses. An expression of the cultural conflict of both Michael and Chrysoula was the fact that despite significant economic improvements in their adopted land, they never returned to visit the old country, and neither did they ever become U.S. citizens.

At the age of nine, Euterpe enrolled in the first grade in the Winter Street School in Haverhill, where she was to stand out academically. "It was my father who encouraged it," Euterpe says of her unusual chance to go to school, "because my father was an intellectual who had gone to school in Smyrna and been affected by very progressive people, and it made no difference to him whether it was a boy or girl, he encouraged it" (Balamaci, 1988, p. 7). But in addition to that paternal attitude, she attracted the attention of the Winter Street School principal, Stanley Gray, who became a mentor and friend to her until his death in 1938. With Gray's encouragement, she became the first girl among 3,000 Greek immigrants in Haverhill to go to college. It would be safe to assume that her actions caused a great deal of clucking among the Greek women in Haverhill, both for going to college and even more for leaving home. Of course, most of the men must have held their own traditional, negative attitudes about this also. Nevertheless, Euterpe graduated Phi Beta Kappa from Bates College in 1925. Later, when applying for teaching positions in Massachusetts and New Hampshire, she felt the sting of discrimination because of her foreign name. Kenney and Turner (1988) quote her as saying, "It wasn't the first time I felt discrimination. It was really quite rampant, especially for Italians and Greeks and Jews" (p. 5).

At Bates College, Euterpe never dated ("not that there weren't plenty of opportunities"), because she felt that such behavior would betray her parents' "trust." Her first meeting with Panos Dukakis in 1920 at Bates gave her the impression that he was "stuck up."

> When Panos came courting in 1928, it was not unexpected. Although the two young people had not been in much contact, they remained aware of each other over the years. In some ways their marriage seemed predestined. Euterpe was the best-educated Greek American woman in New England; Panos was the most promising of the young Greek American professionals. (Moskos, 1989, p. 180)

Euterpe's marriage to Panos on September 3, 1929, may at first appear to be just another instance of one aspiring immigrant marrying her own kind, not unlike her two oldest sisters had done, but Euterpe's choice was entirely her own. It had none of the traditional "arranged" trappings that were so common at the time.

The picture that emerges from the above is that the parents of the 1988 Democratic presidential nominee were disciplined figures of high standards and with a grave sense of purpose. Yet, while they both achieved a great deal in this country, they also experienced their own parents, particularly their fathers, as falling from the hierarchical heights they dominated across the Atlantic. This experience, a frequently documented one for immigrant children, in which there is a reversal of roles with the authority and the ability to negotiate the system falling on the next generation, was probably a very significant one in the Dukakis and Boukis families. Euterpe and Panos learned both pride and shame from their families for having bettered their fathers. So as they went about creating their own family, the stage was set for a series of psychological dynamics ready to influence and be influenced by the children they bore.

HIS MOTHER'S DESIRE

Stelian Dukakis was born to Panos and Euterpe in 1930. Following Greek tradition, he was named after his father's father. According to the custom of Greek families, the second child would also be named after the father's side of the family, but when the second child came along in 1933, he was named Michael, after Euterpe's father. Further, he was given the middle name of Stanley, in memory of the man who had served as her mentor. It could be argued that Panos and Euterpe were well assimilated into American culture and therefore did not closely abide by the patriarchal customs of Greece. Even if this were the case, however, the psychological possibility that Stelian was primarily Panos's child and that Michael was Euterpe's is still a reasonable hypothesis. A Dukakis cousin saw the distinction as follows: "Stelian was more of a Dukakis, Michael is more like his mother" (Kenney & Turner, 1988, p. 22). Both, as it turned out, also took on the name of "Duke" during their adult years, thus unconsciously avoiding the "akis" or "son" ending, not unlike their own father's flirtation with the use of the name "Duke."

According to Kenney and Turner (1988), the goal for Panos and Euterpe in raising their children was not comfort, but character. While they provided their children with an upper-middle-class lifestyle in Brookline, Massachusetts, they exemplified the traits that brought them success: strict self-discipline, frugality, hard work, and an expectation for achievement. These are the values they transmitted to their children, values that fit in nicely with what they brought with them from Greece. But, like other Greek families, they also dealt with powerfully conflicting feelings about authority and independence (Papajohn & Spiegal, 1975).

According to his mother, the first words Michael Dukakis spoke were in Greek, "monos mou," meaning "by myself." "He was an independent fellow. He never wanted me to help him." In an interview in 1974, Euterpe Dukakis said that Michael was an unusually persistent child from the first. "He never gave up. He was terribly persevering," she said. "Our home was bilingual," she added, "and as a little fellow we would find him standing by himself, mouthing a word over and over until he got it right" (Kenney & Turner, 1988, p. 20). One has the sense that Michael was not a demanding young child for his mother. While Michael was eager, ambitious, and self-assured, Stelian had a softer and shy personality. "He needed lifting," says Euterpe Dukakis. In contrast to Michael, who may have been a relief, Stelian required his mother's attention and her involvement in a much more active way.

The relationship between the two brothers in the Dukakis household was one of both friendship and fierce rivalry, with Stelian at first, perhaps because of birth order and age, as the leader. Michael began to excel, often beyond Stelian's accomplishments. As adults, the friendship was pushed more into the background of their relationship. Michael, at the age of 17, ran the Boston marathon on April 19, 1951, and finished with a very respectful time of 3 hours, 31 minutes. This was capped with graduation with honors from high school.

> Then suddenly, with no warning, this glorious spring of achievement and happiness was smashed by family grief. Stelian, a junior at Bates College in Maine, had a severe attack of depression. He returned home and shortly thereafter tried to kill himself. Family members are extremely reluctant to discuss the incident, and usually refer to it as a "nervous breakdown." But Mrs. Dukakis confirms there was a suicide attempt .... Incredibly, Michael says he does not remember whether Stelian tried to kill himself. He remembers the breakdown, but recalls few details. (Kenney & Turner, 1988, p. 32)

Stelian Dukakis continued to have severe psychiatric difficulties (depression) throughout his life. He died in a reported hit-and-run accident in 1973, but without details, the possibility of suicide cannot be ruled out. Furthermore, the sequence of events leading up to his 1951 ingestion of pills in the home of his mother and father have to be viewed as telling, if not causal. The limelight was on Michael that spring, and while Stelian was attending the college of his parents, he could not compete with Michael and his Homeric achievements for their admiration and pride. A psychological insult made all the more painful because he was the firstborn son. Michael Dukakis's repression of the suicide attempt makes it all the more likely that he felt tremendous worry and anxiety over the attempt. But whether he experienced himself as guilty or as a winner in the family competition for the eyes and hearts of his parents, particularly his father, is open for question. The psychic likelihood is that he internalized both, and in a paradoxical way he now had his father practically all to himself. His mother was already his.

THE ALL-AMERICAN GREEK FAMILY

Growing up in Brookline, Michael Dukakis did not have a typical Greek American childhood. Unlike the working-class and lower-middle-class experiences of most Greek Americans in the 1950s and 1960s, the Dukakis family was exposed to an upper-middle-class mix of old Yankees, Irish, and Jews. While Panos and Euterpe emphasized their Greek roots, both Stelian and Michael were given the message that acculturation was something to be desired. It helped that when it came to certain values, such as individualism, the Greek position was one of high personal value (Papajohn & Spiegel, 1975). Thus, the past achievements of Greek heroes were a resource from which to draw in socializing Stelian and

Michael to the ways of American individualism. Accommodation to this aspect of American culture was relatively smooth.

Michael Dukakis excelled in school and in sports. He attended college at Swarthmore, an elite liberal arts college, where he became an accomplished campus politician. After graduating Phi Beta Kappa in 1955 from Swarthmore, he served in the U.S. Army in Korea and then enrolled in Harvard Law School, graduating with honors in 1960. But, before beginning his Massachusetts political rise as a reformer in 1962, he met Kitty (Katharine) Dickson, a divorcée with a 3-year-old boy named John. And it was at this point that Greek ways and American ways must have clashed. Based on his interview with Euterpe Dukakis, Moskos (1989) writes that Michael's parents, especially Panos, were not pleased about the impending marriage—not so much because of Kitty's Jewishness, but because she was a divorcée with a child. While this may have been the case, it is more likely that both factors (Kitty's Jewishness and divorce status) were making it difficult for Panos. Greek fathers expect their children to marry Greeks. Greek mothers have an advantage when their sons do not marry Greeks. They can, from an unconscious perspective, remain "the" woman in the lives of their sons.

Shortly after marrying Kitty in 1963 in a Unitarian service, Michael adopted John. They had two daughters, Andrea, born in 1965, and Kara, born in 1968. The children were not baptized. According to all accounts, their marriage is reported to be a happy one, despite personality differences. One high school friend who knew both commented, "She has what he doesn't—she exudes passion.... He feels it but doesn't show it, she acts out what he can't" (Kenney & Turner, 1988, p. 56). Kitty Dukakis's chronic addiction to diet pills began in 1956 shortly before her first marriage. Diet pills or "uppers" have long been known to mask depression, and it may not be farfetched to consider that Kitty's vivaciousness was in fact a cover for an underlying psychological vulnerability, perhaps not that different from Michael's brother Stelian's.

Panos Dukakis's initial doubts about the marriage may have been dispelled with Michael's political successes. Politics and success had been staples in the home of Panos and Euterpe Dukakis.

> Recounting his family story as a candidate for the presidency, Dukakis said he thought his commitment to public service was inherited from his father, while his identification with the Democrats had been passed down from his mother. Throughout his public career, he had often quoted his father: "Much has been given to you; much is expected of you." At many stops in his presidential campaign, he had drawn a laugh by conceding that his father was on the conservative side and usually voted Republican until 1962, when Dukakis first ran in a partisan election.... Panos changed his registration to Democratic to vote for his son. But Euterpe Dukakis was the family Democrat. (Kenney & Turner, 1988, pp. 45–46)

Politics were not only a constant theme in the Dukakis household, but they influenced Stelian as well as Michael. In 1960, Stelian was at the Democratic Convention in Los Angeles supporting Adlai Stevenson; Michael was there favoring John Kennedy. Later the sibling rivalry took a bizarre political turn. In one of Michael's early runs for elected office in Massachusetts in 1964, Stelian dropped off leaflets urging people to vote against his brother and suggesting that he intended to run against Michael himself (Nyhan, 1988; Kenney & Turner, 1988). Michael's campaign operatives went around frantically pulling them out of mailboxes. Neither the candidate nor his family ever publicly commented on this. In 1972, Stelian, now a registered Republican, ran for the state representative seat Michael had vacated. He won the nomination, but then came in last of six candidates in the general election. Both Panos and Euterpe changed their registration to vote Republican that year. Some hold that Stelian's switch to the Republican party may have been a way of forcing his parents to choose between their sons. The reality was such that he could not compete with Michael's record. The point was poetically made when seven years after Michael Dukakis had run the Boston Marathon, Stelian entered the race, but dropped out after 16 miles.

ZORBA THE GREEK OR THE CLERK?

Cerebral candidates have not run well for the presidency of the United States. The best example was Adlai Stevenson who was a man of sparkling wit and speech, but ran up against the war hero, Dwight D. Eisenhower. Dukakis offered the possibility of providing intellectual leadership, which had been conspicuously absent with Reagan in the White House even by conservative Republican standards, but he misunderstood the need for creative and transforming leadership and the need for communicating such to the nation with passion. In 1988, America was in need of a political leader who, like Roosevelt on the left and Reagan on the right, could merge movement leadership with party and electoral organization, in order to win and hold governmental power (Burns, 1989). While George Bush was not the person to meet this need, his watered-down version of Reaganism and his campaign tactics were sufficient to win him the election.

With a devotion to reason and a meticulous ability for details, Michael Dukakis can be understood as a politician with an attitude of great deliberateness. He is also a man that is threatened by emotions. His preference for competence over ideology fits well with his obsessional character structure, a structure that may be in the service of a more covert and central narcissism (Barnett, 1973). The symbolic nature of leadership, particularly its affective elements, is too far removed from what he sees to be the struggle to find the right and objective solutions. Spurning confrontations, perhaps as a fear of losing control over his own inhibited aggression and hostility, he sees issues as problems to be resolved by reason. George Bush's attack politics and the Pledge of Allegiance were tactics that the dignified Dukakis had difficulty believing were having an impact on the voters.

> The fall media campaign opened with Bush attacking Dukakis on the Pledge of Allegiance.... "I don't know what his problem is with the Pledge."
>
> Foreign observers might find it puzzling that the Pledge of Allegiance, so thoroughly accepted by Americans, could ever become a big issue in a presidential campaign. The Pledge falls into the category of "valence issues": those on which a great majority of citizens agree. To most politicians, the best way to deal with a

valence issue is to get on the right side of it, quickly and very publicly, and stay there.

But Dukakis was a lawyer, surrounded by lawyers, who were incredulous that any intelligent American would fall for such an appeal. (Hershey, 1989, pp. 85–86)

Michael Dukakis was born to be dignified. It was his parent's desire. He had to learn "philotimo," literally "love of honor." More precisely, philotimo is a way of being in the world that values self-esteem, obligation, and personal and family honor. This characteristic is central to the Greek subjective self (Lee, 1959; Triandis, 1987). This is a characteristic that does not easily assimilate. Steven Salamone (1988), a scholar on Greek cultural identity, writes that in Greece such a characteristic is critical for public office.[2] Men who assume highly dignified public positions must especially project an air of confidence and control. In this respect, Dukakis was true to his cultural heritage which is how he came to often quote a very popular peasant aphorism: "The fish begins to rot from the head down." It is meant to emphasize the importance of dignified, publicly responsible leadership. "When a leader, 'the head,' loses his sense of 'philotimo,' everything in turn starts rotting—and, well, things 'stink'" (p. 3). Perhaps like the stench in Shakespeare's Denmark, another fishing society.

It follows that the "philotimo" of the public servant variety is threatened by the irrational parts of the soul that are risky and unstable. Appetites, feelings, and emotions have to be suppressed for greater rational control and self-sufficiency. One of the problems with all this for Michael Dukakis in the campaign of 1988 is that it did not fit the American cultural stereotype of the passionate Greek with the larger-than-life Zorba of Anthony Quinn.[3] Even the usually savvy Phillip Roth (1988) is critical of Michael Dukakis on this matter:

The Democrats keep insisting their man is, at the core, a Greek American . . . but Dukakis comes off as the antithesis of America's all-time favorite stage Greek, Zorba . . . you can sell Jesse Jackson as Martin Luther King and Reggie Jackson all in one, but you can't sell Dukakis as related in any conceivable way to Anthony Quinn. (p. 23)

There is another and equally significant point to be made in this context. Dukakis's lack of response to the Pledge tactic may have to do with the fact that Bush, an obviously mainstream American, was symbolically saying that Dukakis was "out of the mainstream." Had Dukakis addressed it head on for the symbolic sucker-punch that it was, Bush would have had to back down. Why did Dukakis not counterpunch? While the answer has much to do with his own discomfort with emotional symbols and actions, I propose that it also has much to do with an unconscious belief that despite his own chosen personal values (he had married a Jew, influenced the multiethnic platform of his party, and often campaigned in fluent Spanish), he believed that George Bush was right—as a Greek ethnic in America he was not a mainstream American. It goes without saying that this was irrational, but then, the unconscious is by nature irrational. While it can be argued that with the votes received by Jackson in his bid for the Democratic nomination and with what Robert Christopher (1989) calls the "deWASPing of America's power elite," the American dream is still alive. But, even if this were true, he could still be subject to the underlying nagging feeling that he was not "The Duke" of the John Wayne variety.

THE "L" WORD AND THE LAST CHANCE

The highly respected historian James M. Burns (1989) has written that the grand experiment that transcended all others in American history was the effort to expand both individual liberty and real equality of opportunity for all. The political and intellectual vehicle for the ideology of these types of freedoms was called liberalism.

> So pervasive was this doctrine in American history, so comprehensive its reach in American politics, that liberalism and liberals seemed unassailable. During the 1980s, however, Reaganites converted this mild and venerable word into a hate object. Where in the old days conservatives had attacked communism and social- ism, now they were moving toward the heart of their target. At the same time, liberalism was ripe for a fall. Like some old mansion top-heavy with junk-filled attics and sagging excrescences but weak in its foundations, liberalism collapsed of overextension—its overemphasis on individualism and pluralism, its flabby appeal across the wide center of the political and intellectual spectrum that re- sulted in a lack of core values. (pp. 679–680)

The liberal label was pinned on Michael Dukakis by George Bush early in an effort to define him to the voters before he was able, or willing, to define himself. The idea was to label him an economic liberal in favor of higher taxes, bigger government, and murderers. With Dukakis desperately ducking the label, it looked as if he was a liberal who would not admit it. Others believed he was trying to secure a broader base of voter support. Of course, an additional factor in his nonassertive responses may have been an unconscious attitude that "lib- erals" were indeed not to be admired. An attitude very closely aligned with that of his father's political stance.

The opening minutes of the last debate before the election provided Michael Dukakis with the unexpected symbolic opportunity to demonstrate in front of a nationwide audience that he was a man not soft on crime. One of the most successful attacks in the campaign, and in the media on Dukakis, was the focus on the Democratic candidate's support for weekend furloughs for prison inmates, a program the Massachusetts governor had inherited from his predecessor. One beneficiary of this program, a black man named Willie Horton who had been convicted of first-degree murder, had escaped to Maryland while on weekend pass, where he brutalized a white man and raped his fiancee. Bush used Willie Horton as the symbol of his claim that Dukakis was not tough enough on crime. Despite an impressive record of reducing the crime rate in Massachusetts, by Election Day Willie Horton had become almost as much of a household name as Michael Dukakis (Hershey, 1989).

According to Germond and Witcover (1989), prior to the debate Dukakis had been drilled by his advisor Tom Dillion to think in terms of clusters of questions. No matter what the specific question was, Dillion told him—prison furlough, death penalty, victims of violence—"what he's saying to you is, 'you're soft on crime.'" And whatever the question, then, the answer should be carefully prepared and rehearsed.

> Yet when the question came from CNN anchorman Bernard Shaw opening the debate in Pauley that night—"Governor, if Kitty Dukakis were raped and murdered, would you favor an irrevocable death penalty for the killer?—he inexplicably did not use the answer that could have squelched Shaw and showed Dukakis to be tough, passionate and compassionate all the same time. Instead, his bland reply that "I've opposed the death penalty during all my life," then citing how crime was reduced in his state without it and finally going into a short monologue on the need to fight drug traffic, left the audience, and Dukakis' strategists, aghast and baffled. . . . Dukakis never seemed to recover from his first question and disappointing answer. . . . John Sasso speculated later that Dukakis' first answer so "gnawed on him" the rest of the way that he couldn't really get back on the track. (p. 446)

In contrast to Dukakis's response, Bush dealt with Shaw differently:

> The opening question to Bush from Shaw was also designed to be a shocker. "Now to you, Vice President Bush," he said, "I quote to you this from Article Three of the Twentieth Amendment to the Constitution: 'If, at the time fixed for the beginning of the term of the President, the President elect shall have died, the Vice President elect shall become President,' meaning, if you are elected and die before inauguration day—"
> Bush broke in, "Bernie!" he cried in mock offense, drawing laughter from the audience and deftly taking the edge off the question. (pp. 446–447)

Here was a golden opportunity for Dukakis to take a blunt question thrown at him by a black correspondent and to respond to it directly, forcefully, and to show the human side of himself to voters. The stage was set for the Democratic presidential nominee to symbolically deal with the Willie Horton controversy. True, Bernard Shaw was a respected broadcast journalist and far from the type of man Willie Horton was, and further it can be said that it was his job to ask politicians tough questions, even personal ones, but embedded in this interaction were the superficial outlines of what Bush's negative campaigning was about.

Why did not Dukakis respond to the question? Why did the question unnerve him so? Several reasons for this can be located in the personal and family psychology of Michael Dukakis. Shaw's question dramatically raised Dukakis's anxiety level because it was both about him and about his wife. Dukakis was in a better position than anyone else to understand Kitty's fragility. Even a hypothetically violent attack on her was too much of a psychological threat. Not only was he aware of her vulnerability, but he was also in great need of her. She acted as his emotional release. And as implied earlier in this chapter, Michael Dukakis's feelings about his wife may have been unconsciously influenced by his experiences with his brother, certainly with regard to issues of fragility and possibly guilt.

In 1987, just after her husband declared his candidacy for the presidency, Kitty Dukakis disclosed she had been addicted to diet pills for 26 years but had stopped taking them in 1982. Diet pills not only have the effect of suppressing hunger and being addictive, but they elevate mood. One has to wonder if for all those years Mrs. Dukakis was in some form of depression and had need for the pills beyond their stated intent. It is also noteworthy that a few months following the election loss, Michael Dukakis announced at a press conference that his wife had entered a treatment center for alcohol abuse. While he reported that his wife's alcohol problems began after he lost the November presidential election, the cause, he said, was "a combination of physical exhaustion, the stress of a campaign effort and the post election letdown" (Kantrowitz & Starr, 1989, p. 54). But, one year to the day after Michael Dukakis lost the election to George Bush, Kitty Dukakis was hospitalized again after drinking a small amount of rubbing alcohol. The hospital reported that she had consumed the alcohol amid depression, exhaustion, and an apparent case of the flu. "Kitty Dukakis has suffered from chemical dependency and struggled with depression for many years," the statement said. "Those two problems are often related" (Hays, 1989, p. 21).

Given Dukakis's tendency to control his emotions, it is easy to understand that his wife would often bear the emotional burden for the both of them. Asked about the "killer" question after the election, Bernard Shaw said that, ". . . his question provided Dukakis with a chance to shore up his image by demonstrating both backbone and ire . . . My intent was not rolling a grenade across the stage" (Germond & Witcover, 1989, p. 13). Bush, on the other hand, took what he later termed Shaw's "morbid" question and instead of being personally threatened by it used humor to defuse the tension. Again, symbolically, he emerged the victor.

Later, close to the end of the campaign, Dukakis found one more chance to answer the question, in only a marginally effective way—this time in an interview with the man who asked it, Bernard Shaw. Shaw opened the interview but before he could get started, Dukakis interrupted and brought up the matter himself. The exchange went as follows:

> Dukakis: "Lots of people have asked me about that question you asked me at the debate, and let me say that it was a fair question, a reasonable one. I think it took me aback a little bit. And in thinking about it, had I had a chance to answer it again, let me just say this: Kitty is probably the most—is the most precious thing, she and my family, that I have in this world. And obviously if what happened to her was the kind of thing you described, I would have the same feelings as any loving husband and father."
> Shaw: "Would you kill him?"
> Dukakis: "I think I would have that, that kind of emotion. On the other hand, this is not a country where we glorify vengeance. We're a country that believes in the law and I believe very strongly in the law." (p. 543)

The response was the one that had been so well rehearsed in Dukakis' debate preparations. While he got it right this time, it was unfortunately without the mass television audience that heard his bloodless reply at UCLA.

Conventional political wisdom claims that unless candidates are incumbents they tend not to be well known. As the primaries were coming to an end in May of 1988, public opinion trends showed that George Bush was not well liked and Michael Dukakis was largely unknown (Farah & Klein, 1989). "By Labor Day, George Bush had succeeded in getting people to like him and not to like Michael Dukakis . . . By the beginning of October, the Republican's verbal assaults on

Dukakis had hit their mark" (p. 127). George Bush had taken the initiative and defined his opponent as a wild-eyed liberal. Michael Dukakis did not find his voice until very late in the campaign, but by then the political hemorrhage was too great and the surge too small.

HOW TO ACT AS A PRESIDENT AND HOW TO RACE FOR THE PRESIDENCY

A psychological understanding of the results of the 1988 presidential elections would be misleading if it just focused on a few features of Michael Dukakis's personality and failings. One critical part of what happened in 1988 is the relationship between the group psychology of the nation and the leadership of Ronald Reagan. A serious case can even be made that Bush's election was predicated on the Reagan heritage and the overwhelming advantage of a "third-term election" following two terms of success for the incumbents and the main "understudy."

Ernest Becker (1973) asserts one of the most puzzling things that has to be explained in human relations is the "fascination of the person" who holds or symbolizes power. There is something about this person that seems to radiate out to others and to melt them into his aura, a "fascinating effect of the narcissistic personality." Of course, the fascination is in the one who experiences it. The mysterious and hypnotic power of this fascination and human slavishness was psychologically first addressed by Freud. Astutely capturing Freud's great theoretical contribution, Becker writes:

> Freud saw that a patient in analysis developed a peculiarly intense attachment to the person of the analyst. The analyst became literally the center of his world and life; he devoured him with his eyes, his heart swelled with joy at the sight of him; the analyst filled his thoughts even in his dreams. The whole fascination has the elements of an intense love affair, but is not limited to women. Men show the "same attachment to the physician" . . . Freud saw that this was an uncanny phenomena, and in order to explain it he called it "transference." The patient transfers the feelings he had towards his parents as a child to the person of the physician. He blows up the physician larger than life just as the child sees the parents. He becomes as dependent on him, draws protection and power from him just as the child merges his destiny with the parents, and so on. In the transference we see the grown person as a child who distorts the world to relieve his helplessness and fears, who sees things as he wishes them to be for his own safety, who acts automatically and uncritically. (pp. 128–129)

It is a relatively short step from the consulting room to the political arena for this concept. For Freud men became sheeplike when they functioned in groups simply because they followed the inner voice of their parents, which now came to them under the spell of the leader. They identified with his power and tried to function with him as an ideal. Eric Fromm (1964) extended Freud's work and considered the pathology of group narcissism and its eagerness to have a leader with whom it can identify itself. The fact that the leader's attributes may be an illusion is of minor importance. While Ronald Reagan may have been an "acting," narcissistic leader, his symbolic appeal was unprecedented in American politics except for possibly Franklin D. Roosevelt.

In a creative application of psychoanalytic theory to the large group, the political scientist, C. Fred Alford (1989) offers an exegesis of Reagan's appeal. Citing Reagan's autobiography, *Where's the Rest of Me?* an account is given of one of Reagan's first jobs, that of "re-creating" baseball games. Reagan was not present at the game but received brief coded messages by telephone of each play. Reagan's job was to give life to the game, to describe it as though he was actually there. Yet, no one was fooled; indeed, occasionally the public was invited into the studio to watch him "visualize" the game. One day the telegraph went dead in the middle of the game and Reagan was forced to improvise plays. He tells the readers of his autobiography that it was very important that the audience not know that the line went dead. Why, one may ask, since the audience was aware that Reagan was not out at the ballpark?

> Gary Wills suggests the answer in *Reagan's America*. Even though all knew that Reagan's presence at the game was an illusion, there was "complicity in make-believe." All—broadcaster and audience—knew it was vital that the illusion be maintained, that neither remind the other that it was all pretend, lest the pleasure in the performance be shattered. For many claimed that Reagan's re-creations were better, more dramatic, than the actual game. (Alford, 1989, p. 94)

Alford claims that Ronald Reagan addressed our anxieties, particularly those feelings having to do with helplessness and a sense that society is out of control, that Americans have lost control over their collective lives. Signs such as ungovernable cities, poor economic goods, a vulnerable national economy, declining student achievement scores, short-sighted and unethical Wall Street businessmen, and drugs and crime in schools, sports, and corporate suites are troublesome enough by themselves, but these signs share an even more alarming quality according to Alford. "None is simply the result of outside forces beyond America's control. Rather, they are the result of Americans' own greed, selfishness, and aggression" (pp. 94–95). His thesis is that many Americans fear that they have destroyed the good object (in individual psychology the good object might be mother) on which we all depend for our prosperity, even our lives: America. Many Americans also fear that if we continue to be so greedy and selfish, we cannot work together to repair America. In response to this depressive uncertainty, many Americans have turned away from public life to their own private affairs. This withdrawal, according to Alford's analysis, is accompanied by an unconscious fantasy, one of utter autonomy. Hence, the individual American needs no one, no group, not even his country. "It is in this psychological context that Reagan is so appealing, for he labels narcissistic retreat into phantasies of omnipotence a return to the traditional verities." The retreat from repairing America becomes a return to traditional values. "In so doing, Reagan translates manic denial into the language of the American dream" (p. 95).

> Reagan is a master at using American myths to reinforce group defenses. This is an active, creative process, not the project of a compliant personality. Reagan also seems to stand for something, to be stubborn in his commitment to his basic values, even when doing so is politically inexpedient. Yet, this sharply etched

aspect of Reagan's character is mostly confided to the realm of symbols and values. There is widespread agreement, even among his supporters, that Reagan is strikingly casual, even passive and withdrawn, in attending to the details of how symbols and values might be realized in practice. Perhaps this is because Reagan— and the remarkably tolerant voters—unconsciously realize that it is really the symbolism that counts. It is the symbolism that reinforces psychological defense, not reality (at least in the short run). In this sense there may be an element of complicity between Reagan and many voters—they both know it's really a game. In eagerly fostering and participating in this complicity (as Reagan did "re-creating" baseball games), while not mastering the details of what it would take to implement his policies, Reagan may be seen as a partially empty vessel . . . "Facts are stupid things," said Reagan (in a wonderful Freudian slip) in his valedictory address to the 1988 Republican National Convention. (Alford, 1989, pp. 100–101)

Of course, the problem is that facts are important, and Reagan as an empty vessel or a blank screen, perhaps not unlike that associated with the movies, allows the voters to project onto him their own anxieties. The social fantasy that Reagan promotes—that America and Americans need no one—is self-defeating because it is out of touch with reality. It is a distortion. It is pretend. Rugged individualism is not what brought down the Berlin Wall.

Ironically, Michael Dukakis also was seduced by the illusion of autonomy. First, as a little child telling his mother that he wanted to do things by himself, and then later as a self-contained, dignified, and honorable Democratic nominee for the presidency of the United States. The problem with honor, as the Ancient Greeks warned, is that it can be the other side of hubris. In a recent speech delivered to the Civil Liberties Union of Hawaii (an obviously liberal organization), Dukakis said that he made a major mistake in the 1988 presidential race by underestimating the power of negative campaigning and the growing importance of the television "sound bite." "I made a lot of mistakes. . . . But none was as damaging as my failure to understand this phenomenon, and the need to respond immediately and effectively to distortions of one's record and one's position" (Butterfield, 1990, p. 16). Most political analysts seem to agree, at least partially, with this assessment.

This chapter has attempted to show some of the intersections between personality and politics. I have noted the Dukakis family's immigrant experience and the transplanting of certain Greek values of individualism and achievement and codes of behavior such as honor and a dignified posture, and how such values easily fit into the American value system. The Dukakis family dynamics, as manifested in child-rearing and sibling rivalry, led to a range of feelings about autonomy and competition. It was Michael Dukakis who emerged the undisputed winner in the struggle with his older brother. The victory could not come without feelings of denial and guilt. Further, I have outlined how Michael Dukakis's obsessional personality and his style of campaigning hampered him in the aggressive American political arena. The stereotypes held of all Greeks as passionate and all presidents as performers with uncomplicated patriotic policies also played a role in the 1988 presidential campaign. While the disavowal of a liberal identity may have been a tactical error, there was a personal dimension to that error, namely, the fact that Michael Dukakis, clearly his mother's one and only, was also unconsciously motivated to seek the approval of his father, a conservative patriarch. His cool, technocrat image could not withstand the American public's desire to deny hard facts, something that George Bush, with Ronald Reagan as the perfect model, learned quickly to do. Dukakis wanted to be president, but he behaved as if fighting the "good" fight was enough, and that "dirty, sweaty" politics were not in his repertoire. What Michael Dukakis forgot is that while honor got him to the start of the marathon race, no one, not even the winner, finishes a twenty-six-mile 385-yard race looking dignified—proud yes, dignified hardly.

NOTES

1. I follow Charles C. Moskos's treatment of Dukakis's life as found in his *Greek Americans: Struggle and Success* (1989) quite closely at several points in this section.

2. The fact that contemporary Greek politicians, like former Prime Minister Andreas Papandreou, have moved away from this dignified public posture and now flaunt adulterous liaisons, reportedly embezzle funds, and engage in theatrical, negative campaigning does not negate the argument. Panos and Euterpe Dukakis left Greece at the start of this century and hence brought with them values that were important for their time and place in Greece, and it was these time-bound values that were transmitted to their son. Of course, even in those early days the dignified behavior of Greek politicians probably left a great deal to be desired, but that was certainly the "philotimo" mythology of the day.

3. Anthony Quinn is of Mexican origin although he played the film role of Alexis Zorba in Michael Cacoyianis's *Zorba the Greek*. Related to the question of Greekness is the fact that the marvelous intricate dance performed by Zorba in the film was a cinematic "sleight-of-foot." The dance was actually performed by Michael Cacoyianis, the director. Michael Dukakis knows Greek dances and was often seen engaging in such during his campaigning in Greek sections of cities, such as Astoria, New York.

REFERENCES

Alford, C. F. (1989). *Melanie Klein and critical social theory*. New Haven, CT: Yale University.

Balamaci, N. S. (1988). Ethnic identities: Euterpe Dukakis' Vlach and Greek background. *The Greek American*, November 12, pp. 6–7.

Barnett, J. (1973). On ideology and the psychodynamics of the ideologue. *The Journal of the American Academy of Psychoanalysis, 1*, 381–395.

Becker, E. (1973). *The denial of death*. New York: Free Press.

Burns, J. M. (1989). *The crosswinds of freedom*. New York: Knopf.

Butterfield, F. (1990). Dukakis says race was harmed by TV. *New York Times*, April 22, p. 16.

Chancellor, J. (Commentator). (1988). *NBC News Decision 88: Coverage of the Democratic National Convention* (videotape recording). Atlanta, GA: National Broadcast Company.

Christopher, R. (1989). *Crashing the gates: The deWASPing of America's power elite*. New York: Simon & Schuster.

Farah, B. G., & Klein, E. (1989). Public opinion trends. In G. M. Pomper (Ed.), *The election of 1988: Reports and interpretations*, pp. 103–128. Chatman, NJ: Chatman House.

Fromm, E. (1964). *The heart of man*. New York: Harper & Row.

Germond J. W., & Witcover, J. (1989). *Whose broad stripes and bright stars? The trivial pursuit of the presidency 1988*. New York: Warner Books.

Hays, C. (1989). Kitty Dukakis's illness tied to rubbing alcohol. *New York Times*, November 9, p. 21.

Hershey, M. R. (1989). The campaign and the media. In G. M. Pomper (Ed.), *The election of 1988: Reports and interpretations*, pp. 73–102. Chatman, NJ: Chatman House.

Holt, R. R. (1989). *Freud reappraised*. New York: Guilford.

Kantrowitz, B., & Starr, M. (1989). She clearly recognizes she has a sickness. *Newsweek*, February, 20, pp. 54–55.

Kenney, C., & Turner, R. L. (1988). *Dukakis: An American odyssey*. Boston: Houghton Mifflin.

Lee, D. (1959). *Freedom and culture*. New York: Spectrum.

Moskos, C. C. (1989). *Greek Americans: Struggle and success*, 2nd ed. New Brunswick, NJ: Transaction.

Nyhan, D. (1988). *The Duke: The inside story of a political phenomenon*. New York: Warner Books.

Papajohn, J., & Spiegel, J. (1975). *Transaction in families*. San Francisco: Jossey-Bass.

Pomper, G. M. (1989). The presidential election. In G. M. Pomper (Ed.), *The Election of 1988: Reports and interpretations*, pp. 129–152. Chatman, NJ: Chatman House.

Roth, P. (1988). Ethnic pop and native corn. *New York Times*, September 19, p. 23.

Salamone, S. (1988). Michael Dukakis [Letter to the editor]. *Hellenic Chronicle*, September 23, p. 3.

Triandis, H. J. (1987). Educating Greek Americans for a pluralistic society. In S. D. Orfanos, H. J. Psomiades, & J. Spiridakis, (Eds.), *Education and Greek Americans*, pp. 19–34. New York: Pella.

6

The Public Presidency
A Psychological Inquiry
into John F. Kennedy

Theodore Otto Windt, Jr.

In his book, *George Washington: The Making of an American Symbol,* Barry Schwartz (1987) noted:

> It is the range and significance of Washington's shortcomings that make it difficult to understand his veneration on the basis of personal qualities alone. By any standard, Washington was an intelligent and accomplished man, but he was neither brilliant nor self-confident, and his experience ... was not precisely suited to the needs of his time. (p. 6)

Despite his shortcomings, Washington became an icon for an age, an American symbol venerated not only in his time, but for all times to come. Schwartz tells the story of that transformation with great care and with attention to the politics, culture, and art of the times that made it possible. And it was the public Washington who united the nation and gave legitimacy to the new federal government. But "transformation" is not exactly the right word to describe this development. Always there were private doubts in Washington even as there was the public show of confidence. The point is that there were two Washingtons: the private man and the public man. And it was the public Washington who led the nation. So, for the most part, has it been with all presidents.

American presidents, especially modern presidents who live or have lived in the television age, have dual selves. They have a private self molded by heredity and by environment, much of that formed during their early years. But they also

THEODORE OTTO WINDT, JR., Ph.D. • Professor of Political Rhetoric, University of Pittsburgh, Pittsburgh, Pennsylvania 15260.
Politics and Psychology: Contemporary Psychodynamic Perspectives, edited by Joan Offerman-Zuckerberg. Plenum Press, New York, 1991.

have a public character, much of it created as they enter public life and then developed and refined by political opportunities, by the media of their era, by events, and by history. The two personas may be closely aligned, the public self being only a sanitized version of the private self; or they may be widely divergent. But it is the public persona that is central to presidential leadership.

The primary writings on the psychohistory of presidential leadership have focused on the private character of various presidents—especially as it was developed in their infant and childhood years—as the key to understanding their public lives (Abrahamsen, 1967; Brodie, 1983; deMause and Ebel, 1977; Freud & Bullit, 1966; Mazlish, 1972). As important as these studies are, they explain only one part of the leadership style that presidents adopt when they enter office. Such analyses assume that private life explains public life, that the early personality and character structure is the dominant influence on the public personality and public character of presidents. But such an explanation is inadequate to explain the differences between the private Washington, described by Schwartz, and the public Washington, revered by Americans. They may help us understand why a person would choose to enter public life, but they do not explain the psychology of that public persona. Thus, an additional approach to the psychological study of presidents is needed if we are to understand more fully political leadership. Therefore, it may be advisable to make a clear distinction. We may say that "image" is the projected version of presidents as they are performing duties not connected with their official roles, whereas the "public persona" is the public self as defined by the typical ways in which they perform their public functions (Nimmo & Combs, 1983).

The thesis of this chapter is that the public persona is more important than the private persona in determining and understanding political behavior. The public character is the basic orientation of presidents to their public responsibilities, and it is the persistent patterns of thinking about problems that create a fundamental style of leadership, often a predictable style. This persona is revealed through the rhetoric of presidents. Thus, the principal way to understand this style of leadership is through a study of the public rhetoric of particular presidents: from its creation, through its development and refinement (Windt, 1990). It is the rhetoric that presents these persistent patterns of thinking to Americans which in turn gives the public a sense and knowledge of the public persona of a president. Each presidential style is unique because the office is unique.

The American presidency is a personal office. Unlike the Supreme Court with its nine justices and unlike Congress with its 535 members, the presidency is occupied by a single person. It not only is one that a president can mold, but one that molds the person who holds it. In the course of their duties, presidents play many public roles. Among those they must assume are: chief executive, chief of state, primary formulator of foreign policy, principal diplomat of the United States, leader of their party, symbolic leader of the United States, and a host of other roles as circumstances dictate. These are public roles that raise public expectations about the person who occupies the White House. How effectively particular presidents manage these roles determines how effective they are as presidents. The people around Ronald Reagan recognized this power immediately. During the transition period to the first administration, David Gergen, soon to be director of communications for the president, put together a thick volume entitled *The First 100 Days* in which he concluded that these 100 days were the time in which the "president establishes his presidential persona" (Blumenthal, 1982, p. 286).

The rise of television as a pervasive and preeminent force in American politics has made the public persona even more important to presidential leadership. Quite simply, presidents are the "star" actors in the great drama of American politics and history. The word, "actor," is deliberately chosen. Television is a dramatic medium. It dramatizes and personalizes issues. It makes people into symbols, as Nimmo and Combs (1983) noted. On the presidential level, television magnifies the acting, the personalization, and the symbolism. Every public event is dutifully recorded by the ever-present television camera, and even small incidents assume importance as symbolic of the type and quality of a particular president's leadership. In writing about the contemporary "rhetorical presidency," James Caesar and his co-authors (1987) noted:

> The media and the modern presidency feed on each other. The media found in the presidency a focal point on which to concentrate its peculiarly simplistic and dramatic interpretation of events; and the presidency has found a vehicle in the media that allows it to win public attention and with that attention the reality, but more often the pretense, of enhanced power. (p. 12)

The statement "pretense of enhanced power" is misleading. Gaining and maintaining public support is essential to the other powers that presidents wield. Diminution of support from the electorate diminishes presidents' ability to exercise even their constitutional powers. But the fact remains that television has become a formidable force in modern politics, and one of its major influences has been to focus attention on the public personas of political leaders, especially presidents.

Instead of concentrating on the development of the private character of presidents, my intent is to examine the development of the public character of one president—John Kennedy—through an examination of the development of his rhetoric and to demonstrate that his persona had a psychology of its own that created his distinctive style of leadership. The important word here is *public*. This persona was developed with the purpose of appearing before the public in official roles. Thus, to determine how the individual public character was created, one has to note how the president saw himself in relation to the public. Three different areas need to be examined: the prepresidential years when the contours of the public persona were created; the ways in which presidents choose to use the press conference or formal speeches to relate to the public; and the psychology inherent in the major speeches of presidents. It is here that we begin before going to the case study of John Kennedy.

PREPRESIDENTIAL YEARS

James David Barber (1972) was the first to stress the importance of the prepresidential years in the psychology of leadership. In young adulthood the

ways in which the child and adolescent has learned to orient to the world create
the themes for later life. But Barber went on to write:

> These themes come together in early adulthood, when the person moves from
> contemplation to responsible action and adopts a style. In most biographical ac-
> counts [of presidents] this period stands out in stark clarity—the time of emer-
> gence, the time the young man found himself. I call it his first independent political
> success. It was then he moved beyond the detailed guidance of his family; then his
> self-esteem was dramatically boosted; then he came forth as a person to be reck-
> oned with by other people. The *way* he did that is profoundly important to him.
> Typically he grasps that style and hangs onto it. Much later, coming into the
> Presidency, something in him remembers this earlier victory and re-emphasizes
> the style that made it happen. (p. 10)

This transformation from private person to public citizen is profound. In its
formation it can be deliberately chosen, unlike a child's early character formation.
In the creation of the public persona, environment plays a much larger role than
it does in infant and adolescent character formation. In fact, the political environment in which one begins to assume public responsibilities may create one's
persistent image of the political world. Take, for instance, those young people of
the Great Depression who were so profoundly affected by it that they spent the
rest of their lives preparing for another Great Depression. Or, to use another
example, remember those young men who went off to World War II to defend
their country and were forever scarred by that experience, so much so that they
had no way of understanding the young people of a generation later who refused
to support or serve in the Vietnam War.

The public persona has its roots in the events of one's early adulthood. Just
as a child is born and has experiences that shape character and personality, so too
a politician is "born" with the first entry into public life and then has political
experiences that create the public persona: a second childhood and adolescence,
perhaps a second identity crisis. The new persona may be so important (after all,
one's career and livelihood are dependent on maintaining it) that the private self
may be subsumed into it or separated from it (Jamieson, 1988). Political figures
have to determine their place in the contemporary context and history of their
political party. They have to respond to events as they occur. As they respond and
act, they begin to shape their political character. Some events may be as traumatic
in shaping their public perceptions of the political world as their childhood
experiences have been in determining their private world. In sum, it is during
these prepresidential years, as Barber pointed out, that the public character of
presidents is created, formed, and refined.

PRESS CONFERENCES AND MAJOR SPEECHES

Once elected, presidents have two major ways of reaching the public with
their policies and programs: the press conference and major televised speeches.
The relative emphasis presidents give to these two opportunities tells us much
about the public persona of the president.

The press conference came into being during Theodore Roosevelt's administration (Cornwell, 1979). Before the development of radio and television, the press conference was a president's principal means for getting the administration's message to the public. A comparison of one president from the pretelevision years with another from the television age may demonstrate how much the press conference has changed as a presidential vehicle. Although Franklin Roosevelt is justly remembered for his "fireside chats" over radio, he only gave eight of these during his entire first term (four of them in the first year) and even fewer in subsequent years. On the other hand, Roosevelt held 998 press conferences during his 13 years in office. But by the time of Richard Nixon, much had changed. Nixon delivered 37 nationally televised addresses to the American people, but held only 39 press conferences during his presidency. Clearly, the shift in ratio between reaching the public through press conferences and through major speeches had changed, and the reason for this change was not solely that better technological instruments were available.

There are significant differences between the presidential press conference and a presidential speech. One should begin with distinctions between major televised addresses to the American people and other kinds of speeches presidents deliver. Presidents give all kinds of speeches to all kinds of audiences, from the brief ceremonial address to the long partisan harangue. The choice to use television for a major address is a critical choice. Speeches that are not televised usually reach the public only in bits and pieces of "sound bites" that journalists consider newsworthy. The televised address in prime time, however, allows the public to hear the complete message of the president on a major topic. The decision to take up valuable television time with such a speech is not a decision made lightly. And such a decision usually means that the administration has decided that some issue requires an official, fully publicized statement from the White House. It is here that the public persona the administration wishes to project becomes most evident.

With the televised speech, presidents are in complete control. They choose the time and topic for the speech. They can limit the subject to one issue or present a broad vision of the administration's policies and how the future will be affected by the issue or the vision. Speeches can be carefully prepared with words deliberately chosen so presidents say no more or no less than they want to say. And they can do so without fear of immediate interruption or questioning.

The press conference is quite different. Presidents and the press share control of the event. Although most recent presidents have attempted to direct the questioning by opening these meetings with a brief statement, they have learned that such statements only guide the first few questions from journalists. After that, all topics are fair game. Unlike the carefully prepared speeches, the answers are extemporaneous, even though presidents are briefed in preparation for specific questions. In addition, journalists often word their questions so as to elicit responses or answers that they might not get in other circumstances. These questions are sometimes ingenious. Often they present an opposing point of view. Usually, journalists are specific, trying to pin presidents to specific answers about specific policies, programs, or goals (Smith, 1990).

The choice to rely on the press conference or on televised speeches as the primary means for reaching the public is revealing of the psychology of presidential leadership. Presidents who use speeches as the principal platform for presenting their ideas usually are presidents with clear goals for their administration, with a developed philosophy of the relationship between the presidency and Congress, and with definite ideas about how one policy or program relates to others. An astute student of the presidency, James MacGregor Burns (1978), described such presidents as *transforming* leaders:

> The transforming leader recognizes and exploits an existing need or demand of a potential follower. But, beyond that, the transforming leaders looks for potential motives in followers, seeks to satisfy high needs, and engages the full person of the follower. The result of transforming leadership is a relationship of mutual stimulation and elevation that converts followers into leaders and may convert leaders into moral agents. (p. 4)

Above all, they call upon the public to join them in remaking the country in lines laid out by the president. Recent presidents who have taken this rhetorical route have been Johnson, Nixon, and Reagan, although Nixon seemed to have only a clear view of what he wanted to do in foreign affairs.

Those presidents who choose the press conference are usually presidents who feel comfortable in the give-and-take of meetings with journalists. They feel satisfied enough with themselves in their public roles that being questioned about their administrations is an opportunity rather than an ordeal. Such presidents generally feel more at ease discussing details of legislative proposals than with broad policy goals. They are what Burns calls *transactional* leaders:

> [transactional] leaders approach followers with an eye to exchanging one thing for another: jobs for votes, or subsidies for campaign contributions. Such transactions comprise the bulk of the relationships among leaders and followers, especially in groups, legislatures, and parties. (p. 4)

Such leaders tend to see themselves as part of the overall processes of government rather than as imperial monarchs presiding over the processes. Gerald Ford and Jimmy Carter relied more heavily on this form of leadership, even as Carter sought to be transforming as well.

The other side of the coin is that presidents often choose the formal speech because they are uncomfortable at being questioned by others about the direction they have chosen for the country, or may be so rigid in their beliefs that they cannot tolerate questions. Johnson and Nixon were examples of this type to the point that each sought various ways for avoiding questioning. So, too, presidents who rely on the press conference find themselves chided for not giving a "vision" of the future to the public because they get bogged down so easily in answering questions about the details of politics and particular policies, issues that work-a-day Washington journalists find more interesting and productive, but which the general public may find confusing and without clear direction.

Ideally, all presidents should be able to handle both these rhetorical activities with political dexterity. But that is rarely the case (Kennedy being a notable exception). Presidents may find themselves more comfortable with the formal speech rather than meeting others in the "give-and-take" of news conferences, or vice versa. The choice of which format to use in "going public" is usually made at the beginning of an administration. But more important is the decision about which format best serves a president's goals in making an administration work effectively. That choice is influenced by a plethora of political concerns: the president's own inclinations; the goals of the administration; the success of a previous president with either format; and a variety of other concerns that are brought to bear on the decision. Whichever choice is made, it begins to create the public persona of each president and the patterns that they use to present themselves as worthy leaders of the country.

Presidents must give major speeches to the public. In this media age, such speeches have become commonplace and expected. All of the preparation of the prepresidential years, as well as the choice of whether to rely on press conferences or speeches as a means of public leadership, pale in understanding public leadership when compared with the formal televised speeches. It is here that presidents can express themselves cogently on issues and can present themselves as they want themselves to be seen.

Most analyses of these speeches concentrate on the logical (or illogical) arguments presented in speeches; less attention has been paid to the psychology of the arguments. By "psychology of arguments," I mean the persistent patterns that various presidents have chosen to present their policies and programs to the public. Their patterns are superimposed on issues—sometimes regardless of differences among issues—and create the psychological style of presidential leadership. It is this dimension and analysis that gives insight into the public personas of presidents. Recent presidents have had individual patterns that when analyzed reveal the psychology of their thinking, and thus their leadership of the public. We may turn to the example of John Kennedy to examine how this style of leadership developed and how it was expressed in his administration.

JOHN F. KENNEDY

There were two John Kennedys. There was first the cool pragmatic existential Kennedy so celebrated by his biographers, the one who hated pomposity and clinically sought out the "best and the brightest" cost-effective managers to manage his administration. This laconic Kennedy coldly surveyed the political scene for opportunities and pitfalls. His biographers repeatedly refer to his calculated precision in the face of difficult decisions—the Cuban missile crisis being the most prominent—carefully weighing the possible responses precise actions might cause.

The second was the oratorical Kennedy given to grandiose rhetorical glitterings, to apocalyptic fears, and to crisis after crisis after crisis. This Kennedy created a "crisis" presidency. In fact, Theodore Sorensen lists no less than 15 "crises" the Kennedy administration faced in the first eight months it was in office (Sorensen, 1965). In his first State of the Union address, Kennedy warned

Congress that the nation was entering a period of prolonged crises, especially in international relations: "Each day the crises multiply. Each day their solution grows more difficult. Each day we draw nearer the hour of maximum danger, as weapons spread and hostile forces grow stronger" (Kennedy, 1962, p. 22). Crisis—both domestic and foreign—was the theme of the Kennedy administration and set the tone for his leadership. These two versions of John Kennedy have long mystified observers and scholars of his presidency. Henry Fairlie (1974) wrote:

> We must believe, for the evidence is ample, that in private John Kennedy was laconic and contained, cool and dry in his utterance. But what then happened when he rose to his feet? Where came the magniloquence? His speeches are not spattered with the popular idiom that, even after the loftiest passages, brought Winston Churchill down to earth. John Kennedy spoke in public as Byzantine emperors appeared on occasions: sheathed in gold, suspended between earth and heaven. One must find an explanation. (p. 73)

How, indeed, to explain these two different expressions of Kennedy as leader, and equally important, how did he use them once he achieved the presidency? For the first question we turn to the prepresidential years and then follow it with an understanding of his presidential leadership.

Prepresidential Years

Prior to the 1960 election, John Kennedy's reputation rested on his war record as hero of PT boat 109, his family's prominence and fortune, his unsuccessful bid for the Democratic vice presidential nomination in 1956, and his literary accomplishments. During his years as congressman (1947–1952) and as senator (1953–1960), he displayed little more than a traditional Democratic attitude toward issues. He was not known for initiating legislation, but rather for going along with the Democratic leadership in both the House and Senate. It might be said, as Justice William O. Douglas said, that Kennedy was disinterested and bored by Washington (Parmet, 1980). He was equally known, at least in his Senate years, for his absenteeism. Part of the reason for this was the recurrent illnesses that he suffered, part from his social life, and part (especially between 1956 and 1960) from his campaigning efforts to gain the presidential nomination. Indeed, his political persona was indistinct as he approached the 1960 presidential campaign. The problem was so politically potent during the campaign that Arthur Schlesinger, Jr., an adviser in the Kennedy campaign, churned out a slim volume for the campaign entitled, *Kennedy or Nixon: Does It Make Any Difference?* But it seemed to make such a slight difference that Kennedy only won the presidency by one tenth of 1 percent of the popular vote. Despite these concerns, a political and rhetorical style had been developing. It had its roots in his early adulthood, and its sources were in literature rather than oratory. [Indeed, Burns (1978) noted that his prepresidential speeches were "fact-filled, logical; his numbered arguments were well marshaled, but his speech had little of Wilson's golden rhetoric" p. xii.] Two of the books he published exemplify these two aspects of Kennedy's public persona.

John Kennedy came of age when the world was on the brink of World War II. It was a time of severe crisis to which Kennedy responded in two ways. As everyone knows, he served in the war and earned his reputation for heroism during it. It takes no great ability at analysis to see that his later penchant for "crises" had its roots in these traumatic events. But he also analyzed that crisis or, to be more precise, a major reason for the unpreparedness of the West to face the crisis. It is with this analysis that a part of the Kennedy style had its beginning.

In 1940 Kennedy revised his senior thesis and with the help of various people, not the least of whom were his father and Arthur Krock, published it under the title, *Why England Slept*. Although hardly a complete scholarly analysis of British unpreparedness, it was—given the circumstances of his youth and the closeness of events—a remarkable achievement. The book sold well and brought the 23-year-old Kennedy his first public recognition. But two things about it—one substance, the other style—should be noted.

Kennedy concluded the volume by noting the advantages totalitarian governments have other liberal democracies:

> It may be a great system of government to live in internally but it's [sic] weaknesses are great. We wish to preserve it here. If we are to do so, we must take advantages. We must keep from being placed on an equal keel with the dictators because then we will lose. We can't afford to misjudge situations as we misjudged Munich. We must use every effort to form accurate judgments—and even then our task is going to be a difficult one. (Parmet, 1980, p. 71)

Although his prescriptions for making "accurate judgments" are intellectually naive, Kennedy struck a note here that must have affected him deeply: "We must keep from being placed on an equal keel with the dictators because then we will lose." In his study of British unpreparedness, he described the disunity that led to that condition and contrasted it with the unity that totalitarian governments can enforce upon their people. Such a disadvantage had to be overcome if liberal democracies were to survive. Undoubtedly, his experiences in World War II, not only personal but all those around him as well, reinforced this theme in his political consciousness. How could liberal democracies coalesce their citizenry to meet the unity totalitarian governments insist upon from their peoples? One of the principal arguments of the book was that the English people were more to blame than their leaders, and thus the problem was how to make citizens tough enough to meet the challenges of hostile forces. This challenge later became a major theme of his administration, and its roots are found not so much in his personal life, but in his first book, his first foray into the public arena.

The second thing to be noted about *Why England Slept* is its style. There is little in the writing style to suggest the later grand style of Kennedy. It does not rely on the famous antitheses of his presidential speeches, nor does it have the internal rhythms and alliterations that stand out in his more prominent later addresses. It is instead aloof and detached, laconic and brisk. As Barber (1972) observed: "The world was falling apart and there was Jack Kennedy coolly surveying the dynamics thereof" (pp. 305–307). This clinical coolness and detachment were qualities that people recognized as characteristic of the private Kennedy then and later. The public would get glimpses of this side of Kennedy in his press conferences, but not in his prepared speeches or very many other public appearances.

If *Why England Slept* contains one part of the Kennedy persona, *Profiles in Courage* contains another part, the one most familiar to Americans. The theme of the book is political integrity, which Kennedy called "courage," at moments of great crises. These were stories of eight prominent American politicians who stood by their beliefs of what was in the national interest despite public pressures to the contrary, and these stories exemplify a corollary theme to the earlier book. This time, Kennedy used the examples to point to what he believed was necessary to unify people in working toward the common good. The choice he made for achieving unity is instructive. People were to unite not on the basis of a coherent set of political principles, but rather on the basis of the personal or psychological quality of courage. This quality transcended political beliefs, as Kennedy made clear by reluctance to criticize the specific political beliefs of the men whose stories he told. Instead, it is the public once again that he chastises for not appreciating "the art of politics, of the nature and necessity for compromise and balance," and he concluded that "if the American people more fully comprehended the terrible pressures which discourage acts of political courage . . . they might be less critical of those who take the easier road—and more appreciative of those still able to follow the path of courage" (Kennedy, 1964, pp. 3–4). The theme of courage needed an elevated style appropriate to such a lofty virtue. Thus, one notes in *Profiles* the emergence of the rhetorical style that was to become so familiar to Americans, especially the occasional use of balanced sentences and antitheses ["Surely in the United States of America, where brother once fought against brother, we did not judge bravery under fire by examining the banner under which he fought" (Kennedy, 1964, p. 211)].

In these prepresidential years, three themes emerged in Kennedy's public writing and speaking that were to define his leadership: "crisis" (the war in Europe and the great moments of decision by prominent American figures); courage (the defining mark of leadership and political integrity); and the disunity of the public (caused by the weaknesses of a democratic society in contrast to a totalitarian society as well as by its ignorance of how politics functions). All three came together in his inaugural address. In it he defined the new era of the 1960s as a "time of maximum danger" in which the new generation of leaders would "bear any burden, pay any price, meet any hardship, support any friend, oppose any foe to assure the survival and success of liberty." In his most famous statement, he called upon the public to sacrifice private interests for the national interest: "And so, my fellow Americans: ask not what your country can do for you—ask what you can do for your country" (as quoted in Windt, 1987, pp. 9–11). Once the words had been spoken, the task remained to put words into action and effective leadership.

Kennedy's Style of Leadership

When John Kennedy became president, he was still an indistinct public figure. His political persona was so indistinct that James MacGregor Burns (1961), most certainly a sympathetic biographer, noted on the eve of his presidency:

"What great idea does Kennedy personify? In what way is he a leader of thought? How could he supply moral leadership at a time when new paths before the nation need discovering? To these questions Kennedy's friends offer no certain answer (p. 277). Although he presented Congress with a long laundry list of proposals in his first State of the Union address in 1961, he would not lead through legislation. In fact, Kennedy is hardly remembered for major legislative proposals.* And in foreign affairs, he is more remembered for the "crises" he faced than for the limited nuclear test ban treaty he negotiated. The slender record, of course, can be accounted for by the Bay of Pigs disaster that damaged his presidency during the first two years and by the fact that his administration was cut tragically short by the assassination. He would not rule by legislation, but by personality. It was Kennedy the man and the Kennedy style that dominated his administration. Indeed, public admiration for Kennedy often exceeded public support for his policies. And it was the two different rhetorical patterns that came together in his administration that created that Kennedy style.

Upon entering the presidency Kennedy saw a world in crisis—"a time of maximum danger." His first book on the impending crisis of World War II, his experiences in that war, and his cold war mentality honed during his years in Congress impressed this view of the world upon him. At the same time he had written about political courage in the face of crisis in *Profiles in Courage*. This literary rhetoric and existential experience converged to create his style of leadership.

Kennedy saw crises everywhere (Windt, 1990). If one reads Sorensen's or Schlesinger's account of the administration, one will read about the Berlin crisis, the Laos crisis, the balance of payments crisis, the steel crisis, and, of course, the Cuban missile crisis. "Crisis" was a way of viewing the world for Kennedy.

But at the same time he saw disunity in the public. This problem came home to him directly in the aftermath of the Bay of Pigs disaster. Kennedy found himself attacked both at home and abroad for his leadership and decision that had created this fiasco. In defending himself before the American Society of Newspaper Editors, he voiced his concern about the democratic public:

> [I]t is clear that the forces of communism are not to be underestimated, in Cuba or anywhere else in the world. The advantages of a police state—its use of mass terror and arrests to prevent the spread of free dissent—cannot be overlooked by those who expect the fall of every fanatic tyrant. If the self-discipline of the free cannot match the iron discipline of the nailed fist—in economic, political, scientific and all the other kinds of struggles as well as the military—then the peril to freedom will continue to rise. (Kennedy, 1983a, p. 13)

Thus, the two-edged problem for the Kennedy administration: how to orient Americans to see the problems facing the country as the President saw them, and how to unify the public behind his leadership?

In his leadership of the public, Kennedy deliberately chose to use the presidential news conference as his principal vehicle rather than major addresses. Sorensen (1965) remarked: "John Kennedy saw no sense in dividing the country,

---

*The exceptions, of course, are the Peace Corps, the proposed tax cuts, and civil rights bills passed under Lyndon Johnson ofter Kennedy's assassination.

or alienating the Congress, or wearing out his welcome and credibility, by making major appeals for public support on too many hopeless or meaningless causes" (p. 329). During his administration, he would give only nine televised speeches, or "reports to the nation" as he preferred to call them. Instead, he instituted a major innovation by having his news conferences televised live so that the American people could see their President in action.

It seemed as if everyone watched Kennedy's press conferences. The Russians broadcasted excerpts (French, 1982). Given usually at 4 PM, they were a showy appetizer before dinner for the many people who watched them. Kennedy became the star performer. Although the news conferences were not unnewsworthy, the focus was clearly on the President. As French (1982) noted:

> Correspondents had never before been reduced to such a prop-like role. No matter how much respect or authority other presidents had commanded or enjoyed, they still had to rely on the reporters to perform the role of an intermediary. With Kennedy, the presidential press conference became drama, and he was the star. The public got "the scoop" simultaneously with the press. The latter could no longer lay claim to the unique advantage of having been personally present. (p. 32)

Kennedy sought to use the press conference to educate and unify the public, a problem he deemed imperative to his administration and to a democracy facing terrible challenges at home and abroad. These meetings with reporters gave him the opportunity to go over the heads of what he commonly called the "hostile press" and speak directly to the American people. Each news conference began with a brief statement by the president on some single issue he wished to put in presidential perspective and to discuss. It might be the "Berlin crisis" (June 28, 1961) or the crisis foisted upon him by the increase in steel prices (June 11, 1962). After "educating" the public on the issue, he submitted to questions which he answered with precision when he needed to and with evasion when he wanted to. What the public saw was the Kennedy of *Why England Slept,* except that he enlivened the meetings with a ready wit and quick tongue. Few viewers paid attention to what he said, but people who would never read a complete transcript of a press conference were able to watch their President handle the press. In those innocent times, it was the drama of Kennedy facing reporters. His mastery of them produced more drama than "hard news." Early in his administration he so dominated news conferences that a reporter was moved to make the following statement as preface to his begging the President to go easy on the press:

> Q: I am sure you are aware, sir, of the tremendous mail response that your news conferences on television and radio have produced. *There are many Americans who believe that in our manner of questioning or seeking your attention that we are subjecting you to some abuse or a lack of respect.* I wonder, sir, in this light, could you tell us generally your feelings about your press conferences to date and your feelings about how they are conducted? (Kennedy, 1965a, p. 41)

In such a rancorous environment, Kennedy appeared relaxed, alert, precise, unruffled—in sum, calmly courageous.

Kennedy's major addresses to the American people were quite different. They were "crisis" speeches (Windt, 1990). Of all the descriptions Kennedy could have chosen to depict certain situations he confronted (from Berlin to Cuba, from steel price increases to civil rights), he chose "crisis." But "crisis" is only a word, a rhetorical description. If one examines each of the incidents Kennedy deemed critical, one would be hard-pressed to see more than one or two (the Cuban missile crisis being the most notable) as a crisis, that is, a decisive moment in history. Kennedy chose to view events as critical because his entire political background predisposed him to see them that way.

Kennedy's crisis rhetoric deserves attention for what it projected about him and the effect it had on the public. Kennedy's crisis speeches began with a narration of events or incidents that created the "crisis." He would then shift the specific issue from its political context to a moral context by dividing the protagonists and antagonists into moral and immoral agents. On issues involving foreign policy, it was a contest between the "free world" and the "Communist world" in which the latter was contemplating some aggression against the United States. On domestic issues it was a contest between the altruistic president with the support of a sacrificing public and a small minority who would subvert the public interest, which his policies determined. His opening statement denouncing the price increases in the steel industry illustrates this moral dialectic:

> Simultaneous and identical actions of United States Steel and other leading steel corporations increasing steel prices by some $6.00 a ton constitute a wholly unjustifiable defiance of the public interest. In this serious hour in our Nation's history, when we are confronted with grave crises in Berlin and Southeast Asia, when we are devoting our energies to economic recovery and stability, when we are asking reservists to leave their homes and families for months on end and servicemen to risk their lives—and four were killed in the last two days in Vietnam—and asking union members to hold down their wage requests at a time when restraint and sacrifice are being asked of every citizen, the American people will find it hard, as I do, to accept a situation in which a tiny handful of steel executives whose pursuit of private power and profit exceeds their sense of public responsibility can show such utter contempt for the interests of 185 million Americans. (Kennedy, 1965b, p. 223)

Thus, the choice was between the "tiny handful" of executives seeking "power and profit" and the president seeking to defend the public interest of 185 million citizens of the United States: a classic confrontation for a courageous hero.

Kennedy usually concluded such addresses with a direct appeal for Americans to live up to their public responsibilities. The conclusion to the speech announcing the blockade of Cuba in October, 1962 provides an excellent example:

> The path we have chosen for the present is full of hazards, as all paths are—but it is the one most consistent with our character and courage as a nation and our commitments around the world. The cost of freedom is always high—but Americans have always paid it. (Kennedy, 1983b, p. 40)

Thus, Kennedy's policy became a "test of American character and will," a unifying principle for the American people. And unify it did. In his study of public opinion John Mueller (1970, p. 21) pointed out that when presidents declare a "crisis," public support dramatically increases, if only momentarily. Actions always seem more important when taken in moments of crisis than in times of tranquility or "politics as usual." Kennedy's rhetoric created the crises. His rhetoric excited a courageous spirit in the American people because he asked for personal dedication to causes that transcended private concerns. But these were not merely advantageous ploys. These exclamations of crisis were genuine expressions of Kennedy's own view of the world, "a time of maximum danger."

In terms of Kennedy's persona, the crisis speeches presented a much different Kennedy. Here was the risk taker, the bold leader of the free world, the fearless defender of the public interest: extravagant, adventuresome, exciting. In this sense, he made politics intensely personal, turning the impersonal forces of history into a moral dramaturgy in which he was star performer.

But how is one to reconcile these two Kennedy personas? In terms of presidential leadership, they were not contradictory, but complementary. And both served to confront public attitudes that Kennedy believed undermined a democratic society's attempts to deal with severe challenges.

Kennedy was both a transactional leader and a transforming leader. In terms of domestic policy initiatives, especially during his first two years, he was cautious and generally unsuccessful. He did not even consider the civil rights issue to be a major one on his agenda. It was not until the final year of his administration that he proposed a limited civil rights bill to Congress. In fact, it seemed as if he had no real agenda for the domestic problems facing the United States, but instead dealt with them on a pragmatic basis, one at a time. He was as cautious and precise in his approach to Congress as he was in his answers in news conferences.

On the other hand, in foreign policy he took risks from the threats of Khrushchev over Berlin to the ultimate threat over the missiles in Cuba. In this he was transforming, calling upon the American people to support him in his moments of crisis. He sought to unite Americans against a common enemy, transforming their usual diffidence into courageous assent to his policies. His "crisis" rhetoric achieved this goal with its emphasis on moral dramaturgy and its clarion call for citizens to test their character and will.

Kennedy's style of leadership was immensely personal. In his press conferences, he was the star performer facing the hostile and arrogant questions from reporters. In his speeches, he described crises and insisted upon support from the public. As he said in his inaugural address: "In the long history of the world, only a few generations have been granted the role of defending freedom in its hour of maximum danger. I do not shrink from this responsibility—I welcome it." (Kennedy, 1983a, p. 11)

But, as I said, the two personas of Kennedy were complementary, not contradictory. The rhetorical Kennedy of major speeches created an era of crisis, thus a time of unity, in which the courageous president would lead the people to their destiny as energetic defenders of national security and the public interest. The "crisis" Kennedy united Americans, if only momentarily, in risks and challenges. But when the chips were down, as they were over Cuba, there was the precise and pragmatic Kennedy cautiously weighing every move with exactitude and with concern for the reactions his actions might prompt. Thus, the public could rally behind the bravado Kennedy who indulged in rhetorical extravaganzas; and at the same time, it could find solace in knowing that the political Kennedy would act with prudence and care. His willingness to engage in questions and answers with reporters projected a president at ease with himself and willing to submit to examination by others. His speeches dramatized a bold leader willing to take risks (sometimes unnecessarily, critics would say) when he believed American interests were challenged. In either case, Kennedy emerged as a heroic leader, but with quite different qualities attached to each. And in such ways did the two Kennedy personas complement each other, respond to the problems he saw inherent in a democracy, and then finally blend together to create his unique brand of presidential leadership.

CONCLUSION

In his book on the Carter administration, *Jimmy Carter as President: Leadership and The Politics of the Public Good,* Edwin C. Hargrove (1988) described Carter as a "man without a mask." Carter, Hargrove contended, presented the public with a warts-and-all human being, and that caused many of his problems in leading the country. He was a mere person, not a public persona.

Politics, especially in this age of media politics, demands a public character that is more than a private person writ large. And in presidential politics, what with all the roles presidents have to play, the public persona must be written even larger. My purpose in this analysis has been to point to the ways in which that persona is created, developed, and used. John Kennedy understood the requirements of presidential leadership, and television—at the time of his presidency— was emerging to dramatize his form of leadership. Kennedy's ability to merge two different personas to match the different public opportunities he confronted, presented the public with a dynamic leader who could lead through "crises" but also manage those crises with political precision.

The presidency is a very personal office. If one is to understand the unique leadership each president brings to the office, one would do well to study the public persona that presidents have created in order to lead. The structure of that leadership lies in the public experiences and public persona presidents have created over the years from their young adulthood to the time they assume the presidency. It is within this structure that an understanding of their political psychologies lies.

REFERENCES

Abrahamsen, D. (1967). *Nixon vs. Nixon: An emotional tragedy.* New York: Farrar, Straus and Giroux.

Barber, J. D. (1972). *The presidential character: Predicting performance in the White House.* Englewood Cliffs, NJ: Prentice-Hall.

Blumenthal, S. (1982). *The permanent campaign.* New York: Touchstone.

Brodie, F. (1983). *Richard Nixon: The shaping of his character.* Cambridge, MA: Harvard University Press.

Burns, J. M. (1961). *John Kennedy: A Political Profile.* New York: Harcourt, Brace, & World.

Burns, J. M. (1978). *Leadership.* New York: Harper & Row.

Caesar, J. W. *et al* (1987). The rise of the rhetorical presidency. In T. Windt & B. Ingold (Eds.), *Essays in Presidential Rhetoric,* 2nd ed., pp. 3–22. Dubuque, IA: Kendall/Hunt.

Cornwell, Jr., E. E. (1979). *Presidential leadership of public opinion.* Westport, CT: Greenwood.

deMause, L., & Ebel, H. (Eds.) (1977). *Jimmy Carter and American fantasy: Psychohistorical Explorations.* New York: Two Continents/Psychohistory Press.

Fairlie, H. (1974). *The Kennedy promise.* New York: Dell.

French, B. A. (1982). *The presidential press conference: Its history and role in the American political system.* Lanham, MD: University Press of America.

Freud, S., & Bullit, W. C. (1966). *Thomas Woodrow Wilson: A psychological study.* Boston: Houghton Mifflin.

Hargrove, E. C. (1988). *Jimmy Carter as president: Leadership and the politics of the public good.* Baton Rouge: Louisiana State University Press.

Jamieson, K. (1988). *Eloquence in the electronic age.* New York: Oxford University Press.

Kennedy, J. F. (1962). Annual message to Congress on the State of the Union, January 30, 1961. *Public Papers of the Presidents: John F. Kennedy 1961,* pp. 19–28. Washington, DC: Government Printing Office.

Kennedy, J. F. (1964). *Profiles in courage.* Memorial edition. New York: Perennial Library.

Kennedy, J.F. (1965a). News conference of March 8, 1961. In H. W. Chase & A. H. Lerman (Eds.), *Kennedy and the Press: The News Conferences,* pp. 39–45. New York: Thomas Y. Crowell.

Kennedy, J. F. (1965b). News Conference of April 11, 1962. In H. W. Chase & A. H. Lerman (Eds.), *Kennedy and the Press: The News Conferences,* pp. 223–228. New York: Thomas Y. Crowell.

Kennedy, J. F. (1983a). Inaugural address. In T. Windt (Ed.), *Presidential Rhetoric: 1961 to the Present,* 3rd ed., pp 9–11. Dubuque, IA: Kendall/Hunt.

Kennedy, J. F. (1983b). The Cuban missile crisis. In T. Windt (Ed.), *Presidential Rhetoric: 1961 to the Present,* 3rd ed., pp. 36–40. Dubuque, IA: Kendall/Hunt.

Mazlish, B. (1972). *In search of Nixon: A psychohistorical inquiry.* Baltimore: Penguin.

Mueller, J. (1970). Presidential Popularity from Truman to Johnson. *American Political Science Review 41,* pp. 18–34.

Nimmo, D., & Combs, J. E. (1983). *Mediated political realities.* New York: Longman.

Parmet, H. S. (1980). *Jack: The struggles of John F. Kennedy.* New York: Dial.

Schwartz, B. (1987). *George Washington: The making of an American symbol.* New York: Free Press.

Smith, C. (1990). *Presidential press conferences: A critical approach.* New York: Praeger.

Sorensen, T. C. (1965). *Kennedy.* New York: Harper & Row.

Windt, T. (1990). *Presidents and protesters: Political rhetoric in the 1960s.* Tuscaloosa: University of Alabama Press.

Windt, T., & Ingold, B. (Eds.) (1987). *Essays in presidential rhetoric,* 2nd ed. Dubuque, IA: Kendall/Hunt.

7

George Bush

From Wimp to President

Paul H. Elovitz and Glen Jeansonne

Who is the real George Herbert Walker Bush? How did he overcome the psychological and political barriers that had prevented five vice presidents since 1837 from stepping directly into the presidency? How did he overcome the "wimp factor" and win the 1988 election?

The image that Bush and his writers have put forth in his campaign autobiographies (Bush with Gold, 1988; Bush with Wead, 1988) and in the first biography available to the public (King, 1980) can be summed up as follows. Even-tempered, open, and moderate, Bush is neither neurotic nor compulsive. While ambitious, he is not obsessed with power; while hardworking, he is not a workaholic; while confident, he recognizes his own flaws and fallibility. Broadly experienced, he has been successful in many fields, yet he is neither vain nor arrogant. Like most, he embodies contradictions; competitive but compassionate; driven to excel but not tormented by failure; cautious yet willing to take appropriate risks. This chapter will take a closer look at his background, personality, and the campaign of 1988.

PAUL H. ELOVITZ, Ph.D. • Former President of the International Psychohistorical Association (1988–1990); Founder and Director of the Psychohistory Forum (1983–   ); a founding faculty member at Ramapo College in New Jersey; a psychotherapist in private practice; editor of *Historical and Psychological Inquiry* (1990).   GLEN JEANSONNE, Ph.D. • Professor of History, University of Wisconsin, Milwaukee, Wisconsin 53201; currently a recipient of a MacArthur Foundation grant to write *Women of the Far Right: The Mother's Movement in World War II;* author of *Leander Perez: Boss of the Delta* (1977), *Gerald L. K. Smith: Minister of Hate* (1988), and *Messiah of the Masses: Huey P. Long, An American Dissenter* (forthcoming).

Politics and Psychology: Contemporary Psychodynamic Perspectives, edited by Joan Offerman-Zuckerberg. Plenum Press, New York, 1991.

Born in Massachusetts, raised in Connecticut, his affluent family included an older brother, a younger sister, and two younger brothers. At their summer home in Maine he sailed, fished, and played tennis and baseball. Bush became an alumnus of the same exclusive prep school (Andover) and Ivy League university (Yale) his father attended, and he competed in the same sports. His parents expected their children to succeed and taught them to compete, like the Kennedys (King, 1980, p. 10).

Bush's father, Prescott Bush, Sr., was an industrial organizer and financier who turned failing businesses into profitable ones. After earning a fortune in business he entered politics at fifty-five, but like his son would after him, lost his initial race for the United States Senate. Appointed to a vacant Senate seat in 1952, he won election in 1956 and served one full term before retiring due to ill health. His widow's declaration that he would have been the president of the United States if he had gone into politics earlier (Buchman, 1989, p. 8) perhaps offers a hint as to why her son would go into politics at a younger age. An internationalist, he supported Eisenhower rather than Taft for the 1952 Republican presidential nomination.

Prescott Bush set high standards and dominated his children (Sweeney, 1988). George told David Frost that "my Dad spoke loudly and carried the same big stick (as Teddy Roosevelt). He got our attention pretty quick" and "was really scary" (Sheehy, 1988, pp. 161–162). Pres, his older brother, would argue with the father (whose loud voice sometimes frightened the children) and even ran away several times. Jonathan Bush said that "as children we were all afraid of Dad" (Sheehy, 1988, p. 161) and in their early years some of the children were "terrified of their father" (Buchman, 1989, p. 7). George, who was small for his age until the ninth or tenth grade, was the most submissive of the four sons according to Sheehy, but his behavior may be interpreted as identification with his father's values rather than "submissiveness." As a second son with younger brothers he might easily have been overshadowed by his older and younger siblings, yet this was not the case. Poppy, a nickname reflecting a strong identification with his beloved maternal grandfather after whom he was named, "was earmarked by the family as a tremendous winner" according to his cousin George Herbert Walker III (Buchman, 1989, p. 10).

Some early incidents of his childhood help us to understand his personality development. At just over two years of age, he received a pedal car which was the first toy that he ever had that was not a hand-me-down from his 21-month older brother, Pres. As Dorothy Bush recounts the story,

> Pres knew just how to work it, and George came running over and grabbed the wheel and told Pres he should "have half," meaning half of his new possession. "Have half, have half," he kept repeating, and for a while around the house we called him Have Half. (King, 1980, p. 14)

Though his mother says that he "was a most unselfish child" (King, 1980, p. 14), it is not immediately clear if he was trying to limit his brother's use of the toy to only half the time or to more generously share it as she prefers to remember it. It is clear that he had to get along with an older, larger, more-in-control-of-the-wheel brother and that he would become a master of both pushing himself forward and also waiting his turn to be in the driver's seat. Sometimes Pres would become upset by his kid brother's "tweaky . . . verbal barbs" and "want to pound him" (Green, 1989, p. 12).

George was brighter, more coordinated and athletic than Prescott, one of whose eyes had been injured by the forceps at birth, which caused him to have a harder time in school, at home, and in sports. According to their sister, Nancy Bush Ellis, Presy was a "squarer" child without George's "grace." In this situation, parental hopes for a son who would be an outstanding achiever obviously shifted from the firstborn son to the second. It should be noted that as adults all the Bush children appear to be leading productive and successful lives.

The male teachers at the prestigious all-boys Greenwich Country Day School (Elia, 1986), where all the Bush sons were sent, recognized his brightness and soon skipped George a grade so that he was only one grade behind his brother, who was two years older. His younger brother Jonathan remembers him as being "a real, real teacher's pet" (Sheehy, 1988, p. 162), though his older brother depicts him as popular among the teachers, "though never a teacher's pet" (Green, 1989, p. 12). In the report to Andover on June 7, 1937 by the English headmaster he was described as being in the first quarter of his class of thirteen and as "a boy of excellent character, conspicuously straightforward and reliable. Good all-around abilities both in studies and athletics. Consistently industrious in school work. Attractive personality. Well-adjusted socially" (Meadows, 1937). George got in the habit of quietly competing with older boys. He also knew how to get on well with the boys, including his older brother, who he had in some sense displaced, but who he would "not tread on" (Ellis, personal communication, April 16, 1990). The two enjoyed sharing a large bedroom and when separated in a new home requested that they be allowed to sleep together as their Christmas present (King, 1980). At age thirteen, George followed Pres to Andover and after the war to Yale. Later in life they would marry within one week of each other and be each other's best man.

In his relations with others he played it safe by not seizing the initiative: he avoided criticism and also the limelight among the children. He also genuinely wanted to share with them. He was a generous child who would clean a fish before giving it away. He is remembered as wanting to share everything with his siblings. As previously noted, his family often called him "Have Half" because he offered half of the first toy that was not a hand-me-down from his older brother (King, 1980). His humor was a great asset. At church his mother once giggled so at his antics that the whole family had to leave. Humor was a way of stirring things up without having to take full responsibility since it was the others who were laughing. His humor is so self-effacing that he often puts the punch line in the other person's mouth.

"Play," according to his sister Nancy, "was an important element in the Bush household." A Ping-Pong table occupied the front hall even on at least one occasion when there was a dinner party. "Pres and Poppy would play baseball on their knees using a rolled up pair of Dad's socks and their arms for bats," scampering (or perhaps waddling is a better word) around the bases. Their mother would walk by and say, "boys, how many times have I told you not to play on your knees in your school corduroys?" As she passed into the other room, the game would resume on the school corduroys. Hockey was played using the arches of the dining room. "When it rained during the long summers at Kennebunkport, Mom could not abide children saying that they were bored. 'There is always something to do, go and walk in the rain,'" is what Nancy recalls her saying. George, like his father, was and is an excellent mimic. He also is remembered by his sister as quite a tease. When things were boring, "he'd tease just to stir things up" (Ellis, personal communication, April 16, 1990).

Prescott Bush was seldom there at playtime and is remembered for the difficult standards that he set. He seemed to instill in his second son a desire both to please and surpass him. Prescott nourished his son's sense of adventure and George also developed a desire to prove himself worthy of his family. He wanted to make money to demonstrate his independence. He did not want it given to him, lest he remain in his father's shadow. He learned to succeed through self-discipline and occasional ruthlessness, as he demonstrated in the presidential campaign of 1988. Yet this was accompanied by ambivalence and perhaps even guilt, because Bush also has a gentle side. Like John Kennedy, he was initially thrust into competition with an older brother and competing became second nature. But throughout his career, success brought only temporary satisfaction. He was driven to move on to another contest, another enterprise. Politics became his ultimate field of competition.

Dorothy Bush, who came from a Midwestern family "of power and distinction," taught competition in sports and for Poppy to put other people first (King, 1980, p. 15). She made a warm home for the children and their numerous friends. The family remembers her as a "star mother at Greenwich Country Day School" who called out directions to the whole team during the mothers versus boys softball game (Ellis, personal communication, April 16, 1990). George sees her as having been the family's inspiration. She had and still has high expectations for her second son, perhaps even before he was born. A great deal of thought went into deciding which of her father's names he would take, but that he would be named for her father seems never to have been in doubt. George Herbert Walker was quite successful in business as well as dearly loved and greatly respected within the family. With Dorothy's high expectations also came high standards (William Bush, personal communication, April 23, 1990). When recently asked why he did not change his crablike tennis serve, George answered, "Well, you know I am naturally a southpaw, but my mother insisted that I play tennis right-handed" (Green, 1989, p. 213). She stressed that her son should not claim too much attention, and as a child the family joked that the second son was best in "claims no more." Indeed, when he was running for president she called and said: "You're talking about yourself too much George." When her son the presidential candidate pointed out that talking about oneself is essential in a campaign, his mother reluctantly conceded the point, but admonished "but try and restrain yourself" (Bush with Gold, 1988, pp. 26–27).

In conclusion, while both parents were firm disciplinarians who emphasized competition, Bush gives the impression that they were more loving than stern and neither arbitrary nor authoritarian. Moreover, despite goading his children, Prescott Bush seemed happy when they surpassed him.

Before discussing Bush's own family, a brief analysis of the sources of information on his aspirations, childhood, family, personality, emotions, and life crises is in order. As with all people, we are primarily dependent on the materials that they and those close to them make available. These are relatively few and not very revealing. The title, *Looking Forward: An Autobiography,* epitomizes the psychobiographer's problem. Though an autobiography is by its very nature about the past, Bush and Gold have oriented his toward the future and provided relatively little of a personal nature. The reason for writing it is quite obviously that Bush wanted to be president and Carter and Reagan had demonstrated that an autobiography was virtually essential for a presidential candidate. Still, he resisted the idea. In 1980 he ran with only a biography (King) by a reporter and aide and without a political autobiography, and lost. In the 1988 campaign he had two autobiographical statements. *Looking Forward* (with Gold) was followed at the beginning of the primary season by *George Bush: Man of Integrity* (with Wead), which combines statements on political issues with autobiographical materials.

Since political autobiographies are aimed at putting candidates before the public in the most favorable light, they are seldom, like Carter's *Why Not the Best?* (1976), both written by the candidate and revealing. Though it is unclear just how much of these two documents was the work of Gold and Wead and how much that of Bush, there is an internal consistency in these as well as in the materials that Bush has given to reporters throughout the years. The problem is that he is simply not a very introspective or revealing man. The quote with which he introduces his autobiography, "Look up and not down; *look out and not in: look forward and not back* [italics added]; and lend a hand" (Bush with Gold, 1988, p. xix), illustrates this characteristic. He explicitly told reporters interested in his childhood: "Don't stretch me out on the couch" (Dowd & Friedman, 1990, p. 58). When we complained about the paucity of sources to a helpful official at the Greenwich Country Day School, she said that the Bushes are like her New England mother, who believes that a person's name should show up in the newspaper at birth, marriage, and death—period. Despite these difficulties, Gail Sheehy (1988) in *Character* probed more deeply and interviewed Bush and 40 people for her chapter on him. Unfortunately, her lack of empathy, the primary attribute of the psychobiographer, marred her study, which depicts her subject as a weak puppet whose strings are pulled by others. She also is careless in her treatment of some facts, such as when she writes of George being "the most submissive of the three sons" when in fact there were four Bush sons. More recently, Fitzhugh Green (1989), who claims to have been a school pal of Barbara Bush, interviewed 400 individuals to write *George Bush: An Intimate Portrait,* which provides more detail on Bush's life. A scholarly, full-length study of Bush the man remains to be written.

Bush's own wife and children (Adams, 1986), like his parents and siblings, are enormously important to him. Bush said that having his plane shot down during World War II and facing death in a raft on the Pacific, made him realize the importance of his family. "One of the things I realized out there all alone was how much family meant to me. Having faced death and been given another chance to live, I could see just how important those values were that my parents had instilled in me, and of course how much I loved Barbara, the girl I knew I would marry" (Bush with Wead, 1988, p. 8).

Barbara is an anchor in George's life and "he counts on her enormously" (Ellis, personal communication, April 16, 1990). They became engaged just before he went off to war, when he was 18 and she was 17. They were living "on the edge," their awareness accentuated by the imminence of war and likelihood of death. Barbara is not merely an extension of her husband, like Lady Bird Johnson, nor is she an alter ego, like Nancy Reagan. Nor is the Bush marriage the tyranny that the Johnson's was (Caro, 1982). Bush talks about his work with Barbara, but it is not their sole topic of conversation, as with the Johnsons. She has her independent interests. Like George, she is reserved, but more spontaneous with humor, an unpretentious first lady. Unlike Nancy Reagan and Jacqueline Kennedy, she is not vain about her appearance or preoccupied with haute couture. She is not as sensitive to criticism of her husband as Rosalynn Carter or Nancy Reagan and nourishes his gentler side. A kind woman, she does not seek attention, but accepts it. Although George makes the political decisions, their marriage is a partnership. The Bushes are sufficiently confident of their love to occasionally disagree, which is healthy for a presidential family (Bush with Wead, 1988; Bush with Gold, 1988). And their marriage has survived despite 29 moves in 46 years.

Bush is happiest with his family. His greatest personal trial was the death of his daughter, Robin, of leukemia, at the age of three years and ten months. He and Barbara attempted every known treatment, but Robin was incurably ill. He says he turned to prayer and to faith in God, but it remained a mystery to him why his daughter had to die. He does not seem to have drawn philosophical or religious implications from her death, but simply to have accepted it as one of life's tragedies. There is a certain stoicism to Bush, and it is reflected in his reaction to Robin's death. He was saddened but not incapacitated. He resumed his work and his life without much alteration or extended reflection (Bush with Gold, 1988).

Bush's hobbies are simple and family oriented: boating, horseshoes, baseball, and country music. He does not have sophisticated tastes in food, clothes, or entertainment. In Texas, his favorite diversion was a hamburger cookout with his family and others. "There was a unique warmth and camaraderie to the friendships Barbara and I made in those years, a lot like the attachment I felt to my shipmates and the members of my squadron during the war—except that it now extended to families" (Bush with Gold, 1988, p. 39).

War impressed Bush with the irony of chance and providence: Some live, some die, seemingly at random. Shot down in 1943 while on a bombing run, he was the only member of his three-man crew to survive. He could as easily have perished. "War," he wrote, "has a perverse logic all its own" (Bush with Gold, 1988, p. 34).

Bush was saved by an American submarine, the *S. S. Finback*. Grateful for being rescued, his reaction was muted. In a month aboard the *Finback*, he feared the depth charges it dodged more than the flak he tried to evade as a pilot. He writes that he did not mind the cramped quarters of the submarine because they necessitated close human contact, "I made friendships that have lasted a lifetime," (Bush with Gold, 1988, p. 39). To George Bush, war was the rite of passage marking his giant step from adolescence to adulthood. The camaraderie of war was most enjoyable as well. Since he has chosen war twice in the first two and a half years of his presidency, one wonders if he is predisposed to try and recapture the feelings associated with his proving his manhood a half century before. Failing health may both impede his judgment and give him an incentive to prove his vitality at the risk of the lives of younger men.

Highly sociable, Bush enjoys people and has an unusual number of close friends. Of his many jobs, he liked diplomacy best. He reports that he enjoyed the United Nations and China because they afforded opportunities to meet others. Whereas Jimmy Carter and John Kennedy were intellectually curious and loved to read, Bush is curious about people. Problems seem more tangible in a human context. He thinks in terms of people more than abstract ideas and hates to hurt individuals. While it is possible to deny welfare appropriations to construct shelters for the anonymous homeless, the poverty of one specific individual, conveyed in human terms, moves him.

Although Bush craves human contact and is repelled by individual suffering, he thrives on competition, pitting himself against others under controlled conditions. Tennis, a competitive sport, is his favorite participant activity. His passion for winning extends even to horseshoes. This competitive spirit reminds one of Theodore Roosevelt, or more recently, of Jimmy Carter. Both Carter and Bush are dedicated joggers who pride themselves on their lean, fit bodies, self-discipline, and endurance. On the other hand, Bush contrasts distinctly with Ronald Reagan, who rarely pushed himself, had things done for him, and liked to talk about competition more than engage in it. Reagan did not continue competitive athletics after college; he exercised by riding horses and clearing brush. Nor did Reagan seek political competition; he had to be talked into it. Carter and Bush both push themselves quite hard. Each had to please a domineering but loving father who appeared to overshadow them and each wanted to surpass his father. To be loved, they had to be successful; the love of their fathers was not unconditional. The combination of identification with a tough, competitive father and gentle, loving mother caused them to develop ambivalent personalities—in order to please both.

All successful politicians, even those as mild mannered as George Bush and Jimmy Carter, will sometimes take strong action. At Andover, where Bush captained several athletic teams, and at Yale, where he captained the baseball team, Bush's competitive spirit was more responsible for his success than were his inherent gifts. While agile and intelligent, Bush thrived on effort. As an athlete who lacked superior physical skills, he was opportunistic, alert, and quick to exploit the weaknesses of his opponents.

Bush's aggressiveness when cornered was demonstrated when he was appointed to the United Nations in 1970. He knew his confirmation might encounter opposition because he was a partisan politician with no diplomatic experience. The fact that the *New York Times* and other newspapers thought him unqualified aroused his anger. "They laid down a challenge," Bush writes. "I was determined to prove them wrong" (Bush with Gold, 1988, p. 108).

Bush, an assertive ambassador, was particularly provoked by the Russians. "They test the newcomer, sometimes deliberately provoking a confrontation to see what reaction they'll get," he writes of the Soviets (Bush with Gold, 1988, p. 109). President Bush responded cautiously to the Soviet arms control proposals because he thought they were meant to test him. He feels the United States competes with the Soviet Union for military supremacy and with Japan and Europe for economic supremacy. He believes the growing economic strength of Japan and Europe in the 1990s will "test our competitive mettle" (p. xv). He speaks of "stripping away corporate fat in our industrial community—creating companies that are lean, trim, and ready to compete" (p. xvi). Yet, he fails to launch an industrial policy that will meet this challenge. Assertiveness in domestic policy is much tougher to establish than assertiveness in foreign policy.

Bush's aggressive side surfaced in his invasion of Panama and liberation of Kuwait. Bush knows that decisive military action is usually popular with the American public. He felt himself personally challenged by both dictators. When General Manuel Noriega, the Panamanian dictator, induced his compliant assembly to declare war on the United States, the president took action. Against Saddam Hussein he took military action despite the advice of restraint urged by his generals. While Bush usually exercises restraint in diplomacy, he sometimes responds aggressively when challenged. His personality is one that responds to direct challenge assertively. Ironically, the end of the Cold War has freed the president to take military risks that the threat of Russian response had previously deterred.

Bush is far more disciplined than Ronald Reagan, though less so than Jimmy Carter. Less tense and nervous than Carter, he worries less, having learned to channel his energies. However, his discipline is more physical than mental. He retains an element of intellectual laziness and fuzzy thinking that Carter lacks and slogs through problems with a stoicism that minimizes creative thinking.

Though often depicted as a cautious man, Bush is willing to take calculated risks, including the uncertainty of war. Like Eisenhower, he deplores futility, but is willing to take chances if the stakes are sufficient. He married early and enlisted in the navy rather than enroll in college. He picked the most dangerous (and glamorous) job in the navy—pilot. Every landing was an adventure. After college, invited to join his father's old firm, he was drawn instead to the frontier—Texas—and the riskiest occupation there: oil. Moving west to build a business meant escaping the influence of his father. Bush did not move to lush East Texas but to arid Midland and Odessa, in the Permian Basin, where the opportunities were greatest. After two years' work for a company that sold oil equipment, he accepted an offer to create a company. Bush speculated in royalty percentages and bought mineral rights, competed for leases, and took risks that big corporations avoided. He not only entered a speculative field, but later moved into its riskiest aspect, offshore drilling. One of the first to realize its possibilities, he invested in an unproven design for offshore rigs (Bush with Gold, 1988; King, 1980).

Bush's life had been apolitical and he had no intention of entering politics when he went west, but opportunities abounded in Texas for an aggressive young businessman. However, seeking office in Texas as a Republican in the early 1960s was audacious. In 1964, Bush ran for the U.S. Senate against incumbent liberal Democrat Ralph Yarborough. Losing, Bush could have returned to his oil business and become a multimillionaire, but in 1966, he sold his company and ran for Congress in a Houston district that had never elected a Republican. He could not adequately explain to either his wife or his business associates why he was giving up the business he had labored so hard to build for a chance at an $18,000 job as representative (Bush with Gold, 1988). He defeated the Democratic incumbent, and due to effective work for constituents was reelected unopposed in 1968.

Bush's seat appeared safe and he advanced in seniority. But in 1970, he surrendered it to run for the U.S. Senate a second time. He was correct in perceiving that Senator Yarborough was vulnerable from the right, but a Democratic conservative, Lloyd Bentsen, won the seat. Bush was philosophical when some men would have been crushed, rationalizing that some things simply were not meant to be (Bush with Gold, 1988; King, 1980).

To reward his sacrifice, President Nixon appointed Bush United Nations ambassador. After serving less than two years, he resigned to take an unappealing job, chair of the Republican National Committee—unappealing because the appointment came at the height of Watergate. Bush writes that he accepted out of loyalty to Richard Nixon. He has a patrician's sense of duty and will do an unpleasant task if no one else is willing. He also has great faith in institutions and felt that he should defend his party (King, 1980).

Bush reprints in his autobiography his letter urging Nixon to resign in 1973 (Bush with Gold, 1988), a move calculated to free him from the taint of Watergate. But Bush, a Nixon loyalist, stuck with him longer than many Republicans. He says: "People who really care are with you when you're up and are with you when you're getting kicked" (Bush with Wead, 1988, p. 28). Bush is likely to support his own appointees who encounter trouble. He stuck with John Tower long after the political cost had become excessive. There is danger that his loyalty to friends, usually an asset, will be a liability if as president he tolerates mistakes.

Gerald Ford offered to reward Bush for his service to the party by appointing him ambassador to Great Britain or France, but Bush asked to become envoy to China. He perceived that China would loom large in the future of American foreign policy and wanted to be on the cutting edge of the power. "Beijing was a challenge, a journey into the unknown," he explains (Bush with Gold, 1988, p. 128; see also King, 1980, pp. 91–96). It is worth noting that he was following in the footsteps of his mentor, Richard Nixon, who had made contact with the Chinese acceptable. Bush was willing to risk political isolation in China to gain more foreign policy credentials.

Bush's statements that he did not want to surrender his post in China to become CIA director should not be accepted at face value. It is unlikely that he was comfortable in personal and political isolation in China especially since Kissinger did not want him to play an active role and had warned him "that he would be bored out of his mind by the inactivity" (Green, 1989, p. 144). Was it not sufficient to be able to list this foreign policy experience on his resume and to quickly return home? Nicholas Brady recalls receiving a note from Bush in China asking him to visit him since "I'm sitting out here trying to figure out what to do with my life" (Sheehy, 1988, p. 176). Sheehy notes that the envoy wrote President Ford asking to come home. In 1975 the CIA was in chaos as a result of post-Watergate hysteria over covert activities. The political price Bush paid for returning to the United States as CIA director was being excluded in advance from consideration for the Republican ticket in 1976 (King, 1980). Yet, without a strong political base in the United States, he was in the political wilderness and had no real hope of the presidency in that year. At the CIA he was considered a political director who had little impact.

Bush valued his relationship with Ford, though Ford was a rival for the nomination and though some thought Ford was eliminating a challenger. Bush cherishes friendships. He has sought to develop close relationships with such foreign leaders as Helmut Kohl, Margaret Thatcher, and even Mikhail Gorbachev, though not to the extent of ignoring realities as Reagan did.

In 1980 Bush made a serious bid for the presidency. He did well in several early primaries and for a brief time he posed a threat to Reagan. The turning point came in what was slated to be a two-man radio debate in Nashua, New Hampshire. On ethical grounds, as well as to keep his position as major contender to Reagan, he awkwardly resisted the gate-crashing efforts of the other contenders (Anderson, Baker, Crane, and Dole) to be included. Governor Reagan resolved the issue by declaring, "I paid for this microphone" and the others gave in (Bush with Gold, 1988, p. 199). In an unclear reference to their father his sister said "I thought I saw the ghost of our father that night" (Nancy Ellis in Bush with Wead, 1988, p. 116). Reagan established his dominance over Bush, who lost his confidence and momentum and soon bowed out of the race with the fatherly Californian. His subsequent win in Massachusetts was hardly noticed in the press as his presidential bid faded away.

He had not been Reagan's first choice for vice president in 1980—Gerald Ford had been. After this "dream ticket" fell apart, Bush accepted second place eagerly, though he did not openly campaign for it. He simply waited. Bush understands that patience is the essence of virtue for a politician. But when opportunity knocks he is ready. His aide and first biographer wrote "ever since he announced that he was a presidential candidate more than a year ago, Bush has lived, and not too painfully, with the idea of ending up in the number two slot" (King, 1980, p. 4). He was willing to "see himself as the back-up machinery" because he knew how to wait better than most of his political rivals (Rockefeller in Bush with Gold, 1988, p. 6).

Let us look carefully at what in his past made it possible to make the transition from the presidency to the vice presidency. As the second son, he was accustomed to deferring to his older brother, sharing his toys. Though he was brighter and more athletic than Pres, he had learned how to both put himself forward and maintain a close relationship with his older brother. When it came to the presidency, "Have Half" settled for the vice presidency in 1980.

Bush's connection with Reagan was his strongest political asset in the 1988 presidential campaign. He was a most successful vice president in that he demonstrated his competence, but not his ambition. His first principle in his new job was that he owed Reagan his "loyalty and support" (Bush with Gold, 1988, p. 225). His great test as vice president came with the Hinckley assassination attempt. Bush immediately flew back to Washington to do his job, but did not land on the south lawn of the White House (where only the president's helicopter lands) and reassured the nation by his competence and concern for Reagan. It was "instinctive" for him not to sit in the President's seat and to say a public prayer for an injured president. At a time when the evident power hunger of the secretary of state spelled the end to his career, Bush's tact brought him closer to the inner circle of the Reagan presidency. The President eventually came to feel that he was the suitable bearer of the Reagan banner in 1988. Yet deference to Reagan would be a liability if perceived as weakness.

Some journalists and politicians thought that Bush was deferential to Reagan beyond what a vice president need be. Such loyalty might mask an absence of independence. Journalists labeled him as a lapdog with a "thin tinny arf" and a wimp and polls showed that the public questioned his strength (George Will quoted in Sheehy, 1988, p. 156). Some thought him too nice to be strong. His bearing, background, and good manners made him seem wimpish. He also had awkward body motions, a weak speaking voice, and used phrases that seemed out of place. One could not imagine the Kennedys saying "heck" or "deep doo-doo," asking a waitress for "a splash" of coffee, or charging that an opponent was saying "naughty" things about them (Drew, 1989, p. 45–46, 201, 274).

During the campaign of 1988, however, Bush not only overcame the wimp image, he transferred it to his Democratic opponent, Michael Dukakis. The wimp issue is ironic in retrospect. A famous *Newsweek* cover heralded a series of articles asking whether Bush was tough enough to be president. The early reports on the primaries contrasted the snarling Bob Dole and hard-shell conservative Jack Kemp with the wimpish Bush. When Bush lost the Iowa caucuses to Dole and Pat Robertson, the media seemed prescient.

The wimp image consisted of a series of stereotypes. Bush was an Easterner who had attended an Ivy League institution and played the more dignified sport of college baseball rather than rough-and-tumble football or basketball. He dressed and spoke like a preppie. A man of inherited wealth, he owned a summer home in Maine. He had a weak voice, unlike Ronald Reagan, the cowboy, the tough Westerner. Reagan rode horses; Bush just pitched horseshoes. Bush had an impressive resume, but he owed his positions to others. He had never challenged the policies of the presidents he served. Some found it difficult to imagine Bush as his own boss. He seemed to have no ideas of his own. Who would give him orders if he were president?

With Bush's comeback in New Hampshire, the media saw a new toughness. Then he swept the South on Super Tuesday. He became a hard-boiled realist. Commentators discovered Bush the pragmatist, a capable planner. The wimp issue did not disappear entirely until the general election. The keynote speaker at the Democratic national convention ridiculed Bush's wealth and his tendency to mangle diction. Then Edward Kennedy recited mistakes of the Reagan administration and got the Democratic delegates and galleries to repeat with him: "Where was George?" He implied only a wimp would endure so much without objecting (Drew, 1989, p. 227).

In the general election campaign Republican strategists transferred the wimp image to Bush's opponent, Michael Dukakis. Dukakis seemed to fit the stereotype. He had no foreign policy experience and would be a patsy for the Russians; he wanted to limit nuclear weapons and reduce the military budget. Republican charges that Dukakis was soft on crime and drugs hurt even more than his alleged military weakness. The Republicans utilized Willie Horton, a prisoner who had committed rape and other crimes while on furlough to charge Dukakis with coddling criminals. It mattered little that the policy had been developed by a previous governor, that the federal government had a similar program, and that Ronald Reagan had supported a generous furlough program while governor of California. Bush's strategists exploited white fear of black criminals such as Horton and implied that the liberal Dukakis encouraged crime by opposing capital punishment. The impact of the racial issue was heightened by the unwillingness of the politicians and most of the public to openly discuss it.

Bush took the issue of environmentalism from Dukakis and turned what was expected to be a liability into an asset. The Reagan/Bush administration had a deplorable environmental record, but each time the environment was mentioned, Bush aggressively denounced the pollution of Boston harbor. It did not seem to matter that the problem had developed over many years or that Dukakis had begun to clean it up.

Bush also exploited the fact that Dukakis had once vetoed a bill requiring Massachusetts children to recite the Pledge of Allegiance, implicitly questioning his patriotism. Bush managed to completely reverse the wimp issue. He seemed strong and assertive and his Democratic opponent weak and vacillating, a stereotypical wimp. He was small, short, not as athletic as Bush. He had attended Harvard, which many westerners and southerners detested. More significantly, he seemed inhibited and unemotional. The press aided the Bush strategy by presenting Dukakis as cowardly for not counterattacking and by focusing on the race rather than exploring the issues. As Dukakis declined in the polls, Democratic defeatism fed on itself.

Bush managed to project his own perceived weaknesses onto Dukakis and Dukakis became a scapegoat for what had once seemed wrong with Bush. Bush became tough; Dukakis weak. Now it was Dukakis who was too nice or too inhibited to become president. There was a wimp in the race, but it was not Bush.

When we look more closely we discover that the election ended with two wimps. In the reversal of the "wimp" identification, Dan Quayle played a crucial role as the lightning rod for negative feelings about Bush. This is what psychotherapists call splitting. That is the tendency to divide things into good and bad, black and white. It serves as a denial of the profound ambivalence that is so much a part of the thinking of virtually all people. Since the days of the founding fathers, the public has split off some of its negative feelings onto the man who is one heartbeat away from the presidency. This is why vice presidents are not easily elected as presidents immediately after the retirement of the president they have served, the so-called "Van Buren Hex" (Bush with Gold, 1988).

The split is between the "good president" who protects the nation in a dangerous world and the "bad vice president" who benefits from the president's death and is waiting in the wings to take his place. Angry, disappointed feelings that the electorate has for the president end up displaced onto his next-in-line. The voters are torn between thinking that a vice president is the understudy who is best qualified for the job and fantasizing that he is a man so weak and depraved that he did nothing for four or eight years but wait for the president to die. Reagan was an extremely popular, idealized president who worked hard to keep himself on a pedestal. The campaign was being conducted during the last year of his presidency when the presidential team and country had to deal with the feelings of being abandoned by the leader who had led them out of the emotional quagmire of the Iran hostage crisis. One indication of the sense of abandonment was the willingness of people close to the president to write "kiss-and-tell" books about their years in the White House, portraying the less than idealized side of Reagan and those close to him. For seven years, the nation did not want to know that Reagan was a relatively inactive president, who spent a large amount of time on vacation, who slumbered, as one would expect from a man his age, at Cabinet meetings, and whose wife consulted astrologers. When it became clear that another man had won the nomination and there would soon be another president, even Republicans began to have doubts.

Bush's challenge was to prove that he was strong enough to stand alone by distancing himself from the enormously popular President Reagan and at the same time not offend the loyal supporters of the president. As a vice president campaigning for the presidency, like all his predecessors in this uncomfortable situation, he had to walk a tightrope. Bush was under enormous pressure to both be highly critical of Reagan and never utter a word of criticism. Selecting Quayle helped him in this process, because the senator from Indiana gave the electorate an individual toward whom they could quite openly express their contempt. Quayle was a tabula rasa—a blank slate without any notable accomplishments who soon became the butt of the criticisms of the media and the American public. Compared to Dukakis and Quayle, Bush seemed strong and presidential. He concentrated on emotional issues such as the flag, abortion, crime, and gun control rather than policy issues that were more within the control of a president.

Bush also emphasized the manly side of his character, a side exemplified by his interest in such masculine pursuits as hunting. He always has been more comfortable in male than female company, and like Reagan attracts more male votes. This is partly due to their stand on issues such as abortion and equal rights, but not entirely. Bush even exaggerated his manhood by commenting before his debate with Geraldine Ferraro in 1984 that he was going to "kick ass." Despite this aberrant crudeness, Bush is more popular with women than Reagan because he is more contemporary. Moreover, Bush has a happier family than Reagan. His adult children visit their parents and appear to love them, while some of Reagan's offspring are estranged.

Bush's personality thus exhibits some ambivalence; he is alternately tough and gentle. He manifests macho aggression, then wonders if he has gone too far. His invasion of Panama and use of the CIA for unpopular covert activities exemplify his aggressive side, as does his campaign statement: "As President, I will not leave the Contras twisting in the wind" (Drew, 1989, p. 52). As events worked out, it was in opposition to Iraqi aggression that he found his best opportunity to show his toughness.

Bush's aggressive tendencies may represent an identification with his sometimes terrifying father and a compensation for being stereotyped as weak. A malleable yet proud man, he resents being stereotyped as subservient. In his anxiety to prove he is tough and independent, he sometimes is uncharacteristically stubborn. For example, to assert his leadership, he kept to himself his vice presidential selection, then sprang Dan Quayle upon his advisers. More consultation might have revealed Quayle's limitations, resulting in a more qualified nominee. This surprise choice is reminiscent of Nixon's decision to pick Spiro Agnew in 1968. Both wanted someone without a strong political base who was dependent on them. Each in a sense recapitulated his own career by choosing a younger version of himself.

Bush's unequivocal refusal to consider raising taxes in the campaign and the first year of his presidency is another attempt to exaggerate his masculinity, though it is also clever politics. His "read my lips," there will be no new taxes statement was a deliberate reference to the masculinity of Clint Eastwood's violent characters. He promised to stand up to congressional liberals like Travis at the Alamo, refusing to surrender despite high odds. He wanted to demonstrate strength by his unyielding position but deprived himself of the flexibility he needed to reduce the deficit. Subsequently, when he did consider the possibility of raising taxes, he opened himself up to enormous ridicule, which perhaps prompted him to consider asserting his toughness once again.

Bush's alternation between submission and aggression was demonstrated during the campaign. He won because he was willing to do whatever was necessary, even though he found negative campaigning distasteful. In rough-and-tumble Texas politics, he had found "jugular politics—going for the opposition's throat—wasn't my style" (Bush with Gold, 1988, p. 86), but when paired with Dukakis he was the more rough-and-tumble candidate. His exploitation of Willie Horton could have backfired. Dukakis might have responded aggressively or the public might have expressed revulsion. His use of the Pledge of Allegiance to raise questions about Dukakis's patriotism was also a risk, but he recognized more clearly than Dukakis that politics is often about symbols. Ironically, it was the less articulate candidate who had the most impact with verbal and visual symbols. Bush accepted the irritating strategy pressed on him by his advisers because he wanted to win at all costs. He realized that to govern one must first get elected, while Dukakis avoided demagoguery. This does not mean that Bush is stronger than Dukakis; strength is not demonstrated by doing whatever one's advisers recommend. But Bush has superior political judgment and his flexibility is an asset.

Normally Bush listens and evaluates advice; he prides himself on being a good listener (Bush with Gold, 1988). As President, he has adjusted to public opinion, altering his positions on gun control and on conventional arms negotiations with the Soviet Union, and meeting Gorbachev at sea for an early summit conference and agreeing to marginally reduce defense spending because of a diminished Soviet threat. He has agreed to accept a position in the Cabinet for the Environmental Protection Agency after initially opposing it. On the other hand, the invasion of Panama, the war against Iraq, and his overtures to the Chinese government after the Tiananmen Square repression indicate that he remains willing to take calculated risks.

Bush's social welfare policies reflect his personal contradictions, exhibiting elements of social Darwinism, noblesse oblige, and compassion. A believer in limited government, self-help, and individual responsibility, he does not think that the federal government should help individuals beyond providing opportunity. He believes the fittest will prosper and speaks of "relying on the incentives of the free market—not the largess of the federal government" (Bush with Gold, 1988, p. xvi). However, he has a sense of responsibility something like the "gospel of wealth"—the duty of the prosperous to help the less fortunate. He realizes that in competition there are losers as well as winners and has lost enough in politics and athletics to appreciate disappointment. Thus, despite his belief in personal responsibility and individual attainment, he sympathizes with those who fail. His belief in Christian ethics further mitigates his predilection for unfettered competition, leading to a certain ambivalence about government programs. He wants government to leave people alone, but agonizes over human suffering. He thinks aid is salutary so long as it is voluntary. He dislikes weakness, but recognizes that all humans are weak, fallible, and mortal. On a human level, he wants to help people, but distrusts government intervention. This ambiguity creates tension; he could go either way on aid to needy children and money for research on AIDS.

Bush came to politics not from ideological passion, but rather from a sense of duty. In his youth he was apolitical. He was not politically involved at Yale or in the early years in business. He lacks the fervor of Goldwater and Reagan; his presidency is less passionate than Reagan's. Bush is not a crusader for ideas, but a conservative pragmatist who tries to solve specific problems. He is not inspirational because ideas do not inspire him. Though Bush has convictions, his temperament precludes zealotry.

Despite his ambivalence toward ideology, Bush is no technocrat, but a compassionate man. Yet, ironically, this warm, compassionate man opposes many of the programs for the poor and handicapped that the cool, detached Dukakis favors. People voted for him not because they favor his lean government over Dukakis's more generous one, but because they identify with Bush's warmth rather than Dukakis's detachment. Bush is a personally humane social Darwinist who wants to help people on an individual level, but does not believe government should do so. Reagan was similar. But Reagan's human compassion was more sentimental than genuine; Bush's is more genuine and the contradiction causes him to agonize. Mixed solutions to social questions may evolve, compromises between his social conscience and his preference for limited government.

People who know Bush recognize his compassion. Asked what principles she taught her children, Dorothy Bush said: "I taught them love. I taught them to love everybody, no matter what their background, and I taught them to be unselfish" (Bush with Wead, 1988, p. 134). Certainly Bush seems gentler and less openly power-hungry than Kennedy, Johnson, or Nixon. His mother says he never spoke of running for the presidency until he announced his candidacy in 1980. Asked his most striking characteristic, she stated: "The most consistent characteristic in his life, the characteristic I could see in him as a young child and that has stayed with him over the years, is his kindness to others. He has always worried about the other person" (Bush with Wead, 1988, p. 135). This is the candidate of "a thousand points of light."

For a politician Bush has few enemies; many who disagree with his policies like him personally. It is commonly charged, however, that he lacks the vision to articulate ideals. But people who agree with his view of limited government do not consider his failure to inspire a major handicap. Preaching limits is inherently difficult; it is easy to promise more, not less. Bush argues that a philosophy is not correct because it is expressed in sonorous phrases and that inspirational speeches cannot solve intractable problems. According to this argument, Lyndon Johnson's pragmatism was more effective than John Kennedy's idealistic speeches.

Bush tries to work with people rather than drive them. He said his relationship with Reagan was part of "my philosophy of being a team player" (Bush with Wead, 1988, p. 23). His war experience reinforces this predilection. Piloting his three-person fighter bomber and landing on an aircraft carrier required teamwork. They would live or die together. Bush sees no contradiction between cooperation and leadership. When risks are mutual risks, people benefit or suffer together.

Bush brought his concept of teamwork to the presidency; he assembled a staff of compatible individuals, but not clones, under a tough chief of staff, who can play the role of the heavy for the president. Bush delegates more than Carter but less than Reagan. He does not believe there is any single "correct" style of management; it must fit the personality of the president.

He concedes that he is not visionary. "I suppose, like all young men, I was a dreamer," he said. "But I never did set up a grand design for my life. I've always believed that you must do well whatever it is that you do" (Bush with Wead, 1988, p. 8). Bush's father emphasized self-discipline and success. But he was never specific about the accomplishments he desired for his children. Bush wants to be remembered as a successful president, but he has no overriding specific objectives. He enjoys politics for its own sake and derives satisfaction from winning elections and earning recognition. During the campaign he articulated no clear objective, only some very general things—he wants to be the "education" president and an environmentalist. His ambivalence toward the competition he was pushed into by his father led him to say he wanted to see a "kinder and gentler" nation, but he never defined this in terms of policy, other than to set an example and encourage voluntarism.

To better understand his behavior it is necessary to probe a bit more into the President's personality, background, and his relationship to the public. He is a man with enormous competitive spirit, drive, and ego strength as his accomplishments would indicate. He is also rather repressed in some ways. To quote him, "all my life I'd worked at channeling my emotions, trying not to let anger or frustration influence my thinking" (Bush with Gold, 1988, p. 12). Eventually this suppression of anger and frustration, emotions felt most keenly at times such as when it seemed that he would be bypassed for the vice presidential nomination, led to a bleeding ulcer. Bush's solution to the physical condition was to ease up on his work schedule while continuing to deny his own frustration. When certain feelings are denied to the extent that their very existence is lost sight of, this is an indication of repression. With his enormous emphasis on serving and giving back to society—his New England conscience—Bush is in some ways a repressed individual. This is to be expected in a man whose earliest nicknames reflect renunciation of his own desires (Have Half) and identification with a grandfather (Little Pop, Pop, Poppy), and whose mother emphasized that he should be a good boy who shared with others. He had to restrain himself in such a basic way as going against his normal reactions as a left-handed person and use his right hand and arm in golf and tennis in order to please his mother.

As a man "born to please" (Sheehy, 1988) others, George Bush has succeeded by being popular and identifying with the values of his parents, teachers, and other mentors and not directly challenging them. He only entered politics after he copied his father's educational, military, business, and political careers. Just as Prescott Bush, Sr. had moved to establish his own career, he left Connecticut and went to Texas to go into business so that he would neither be in his father's shadow nor in competition with him. He also chose the year that his father retired from politics to enter this difficult field. Throughout this part of his life and throughout others, he chose mentors who would help in the process both at the local level and at the presidential level with Richard Nixon being an important role model. Rather than challenge those close to him he took greater risks by establishing himself in relatively unchartered waters such as the offshore oil business and republicanism in Texas. He felt that he could run for president because there were no "Roosevelts or Eisenhowers running" (Bush with Gold, 1988, p. 191). He is a man of great achievement, but can he really stand alone?

Bush has sometimes been criticized as thin-skinned with reporters, but he also shows a willingness to confront uncomfortable facts from the so-called "Van Buren Hex," to the time he got drunk in Texas, to being rated one of the ten most overrated men in America. He invited the other nine to join him for lunch and had a wonderful time. If he is tempted to forget an unpleasant truth, one has the impression that Barbara will remind him of it. His considerable network of friends helps him to stay in touch with political and personal realities.

A truth of American politics is that the public is often unrealistic in its expectations of just what a president can and cannot accomplish. In good economic times, presidents are much more popular than in bad times. Decisive actions by presidents, such as the Panama invasion and the war against Iraq, are quite popular despite their questionable long-term consequences. One of the most important characteristics of a president is the ability to choose the time and place of his actions and inactions. In this he is much like the psychoanalyst who provides a safe holding environment for the patient precisely because he will not get involved carrying out the patient's desire for action. The public, like the patient, needs to become aware of its own fantasies and unrealistic expectations without acting upon them. Yet in this age of instant public opinion polls, the pressure to run away from uncomfortable feelings by an action is immense. President Bush has yet to demonstrate if he can withstand this pressure.

Bush is a pragmatist like Franklin Roosevelt rather than an idealist like Woodrow Wilson, but a conservative one. Like Roosevelt, he listens, then decides. He is capable of surprise and recognizes creativity. Bush is more at home in the 1990s than Ronald Reagan. It is not just his age. He has none of the romantic nostalgia of Reagan and is more comfortable in urban America. His values, while traditional, are less old-fashioned. Reagan's policies were sometimes predicated on the world as it once was, or as it should be. Bush is an optimist, but he is the product of a wider range of experiences than Reagan.

Bush's realism does not exclude emotion or intuition. His contradictions reflect his being sufficiently flexible to accommodate competing instincts. His passion for individual achievement tempered by compassion for the underdog makes him much like the nation that elected him.

REFERENCES

Adams, C. (1986). At home with George and Barbara Bush. *Ladies Home Journal,* July, pp. 103–131.

Buchman, D. D. (1989). *Our 41st president: George Bush.* New York: Scholastic Inc.

Bush, G., with Gold, V. (1988). *Looking forward: An autobiography.* New York: Bantam Books.

Bush, G., with Wead, D. (1988). *George Bush: Man of integrity.* Eugene, OR: Harvest House.

Bush, W. (1990). Telephone interview, April 23.

Carlson, M. (1988). A tale of two childhoods. *Time,* June 20, pp. 14–16.

Caro, R. A. (1982). *The years of Lyndon Johnson,* vol. I: *The Path to Power.* New York: Alfred A. Knopf.

Carter, J. (1976). *Why not the best?* New York: Bantam Books.

Dowd, M., & Friedman, T. (1990). The fabulous Bush and Baker boys. *New York Times Magazine,* May 6, pp. 34–37, 58, 62, 64, 67.

Drew, E. (1989). *Election Journal: Political events of 1987–88.* New York: William Morrow.

Elia, S., Seblatnigg, R., & Storms, V. (1988). *Greenwich Country Day: A history: 1926–1986.* Canaan, NH: Phoenix Publishing.

Ellis, N. B. (1990). Telephone interview, April 16.

Green, F. (1989). *George Bush: An intimate portrait.* New York: Hippocrene Books.

Holahan, D. (1988). A regular guy. *Connecticut,* August, pp. 53–59.

King, N. (1980). *George Bush: A biography.* New York: Dodd, Mead & Company.

Meadows, G. D. (1937). Greenwich Country Day School Headmaster's manuscript report to Andover, June 7.

Sheehy, G. (1988). George Bush: Born to please. In *Character: America's search for leadership,* pp. 154–187. New York: Morrow.

Sweeney, J. S. (1988). George Bush: The early years. *Greenwich Time,* March 13, pp. A1, A10, A12.

8

Jimmy Carter and the Soviet Invasion of Afghanistan

A Psychological Perspective

Betty Glad and Brian Whitmore

INTRODUCTION

Political scientists, when analyzing decision making at the highest levels of government in the area of foreign policy, usually emphasize rationally perceived national interests and domestic politics as the primary motivations. Obscured in such scholarship are the idiosyncratic personality traits of the decision makers themselves. A comprehensive explanation of high-level decision making, however, requires that scholars look below the surface to discern the particular worldviews and the psychological factors that interact with broader concerns of national interests and domestic politics to form governmental policies. These factors are most important for top decision makers in situations where they are facing crises (see Greenstein, 1967; Holsti, 1971). When major national and personal value are at stake, the ego defensive characteristic of those with the most responsibility for the national response are apt to be triggered and relevant to the policy response.

The Soviet invasion of Afghanistan in December 1979 was such an event. Jimmy Carter had entered office with a neo-Wilsonian view of the world and a stated desire to abandon the preoccupation with the Soviet Union and a containment policy that had driven U.S. foreign policy since World War II. The Soviet intervention in Afghanistan, however, marked a watershed in Soviet–American

BETTY GLAD, Ph.D. • Professor of Political Science, Department of Government and International Studies, University of South Carolina, Columbia, South Carolina 29208.   BRIAN WHITMORE, Ph.D. Candidate • Department of Government and International Studies, University of South Carolina, Columbia, South Carolina 29208.

Politics and Psychology: Contemporary Psychodynamic Perspectives, edited by Joan Offerman-Zuckerberg. Plenum Press, New York, 1991.

relations. Various possible interpretations of Soviet motives were discussed in American decision-making circles and several possible responses considered. Carter opted for the worst-case analysis of Soviet objectives and chose to use harsh rhetoric and policies that were reminiscent of the earliest days of the cold war. The whole interaction marked the end of the détente era and ushered in a new period of confrontation between Moscow and Washington.

Carter's choices, substantive and stylistic, as we shall show, were influenced by both his worldview and certain idiosyncratic personality traits evident in his earlier career.

BACKGROUND

The Soviet Invasion

On December 27, 1979, Hafizullah Amin, the President of Afghanistan, was overthrown in a bloody coup backed by Moscow. Shortly thereafter, thousands of Soviet troops were airlifted across the border, and Babrak Kamal was installed as the head of the Afghan government. By December 29, there were an estimated 30,000 Soviet troops in Afghanistan.

The Soviet Union had been involved in Afghanistan politics since the end of World War II, trying to draw that country into the Soviet sphere of influence and make it a showcase for Soviet aid projects in the Third World. From 1953 to 1978, non-Communist national leaders cooperated with Moscow in a variety of economic and political undertaking. When one of these nationalist leaders sought to steer a course of greater independence from Moscow, the Communist-oriented People's Democratic Party (PDP) took over the government in a coup. The new government, however, embraced radical policies that lost it the support of the traditional Moslem population, and the Mujahidin began a guerrilla war against the government. When this government proved incapable of restoring order, Amin, the leader of a pro-Soviet faction of the PDP, seized the government in yet another bloody coup. When Amin also provided unable to restore order, the Soviet Union opted for direct military intervention to install and support yet a new government and to put down the Mujahidin insurgency. Whether or not the Soviet leaders had broader geopolitical goals at that time was not completely clear.

The U.S. Response

Within American decision-making circles, the Soviet invasion was interpreted in several possible ways. Secretary of State Vance, in his memoirs, asserted that two main theories existed. One theory stated that the Soviet incursion was primarily local and defensive, an indication of their insecurity. The spread of fundamentalist Islamic movements in the region would undermine Soviet influence in the region and weaken the Soviet hold over its own Moslem population in Central Asia. Rather than risk this kind of contagion effect, the Soviet government had decided to replace Amin's regime with a more compliant and competent government and send in their troops to provide order and stability and push the insurgents back into more remote areas (Vance, 1983, pp. 387–388).

A second thesis stressed global geopolitics and Soviet offensive ambitions. The Soviet Union, seeing how bad their relations with the United States were going, simply decided that since they had nothing to lose they should try to liquidate the Afghan problem and improve their strategic position in Southwest Asia and the Persian Gulf. Control in Afghanistan would allow them to exert greater pressure on American allies such as Pakistan and to counter American strategic moves in the area in response to what the Kremlin perceived as a pro-China "tilt" by Washington (Vance, 1983, p. 388).

Secretary of State Vance, for his part, felt that both of these explanations were valid to a degree. The secretary of state rejected the notion that Moscow's policy was a monolithic decision as he recognized different positions within the Kremlin:

> My view was that Moscow acted as it did for a number of reasons. Its immediate aim was to protect Soviet political interests in Afghanistan which they saw endangered. Some Soviet leaders saw Amin as a national Communist who did not listen to Soviet advice and was stumbling into disaster. They feared that the regime would be replaced by a fundamentalist Islamic government that would, in turn, be followed by a spread of "Khomeini fever" to other nations along Russia's southern border. Other Soviets believed that they should position themselves more favorable with respect to China and Pakistan. Moreover, the downward spiral in U.S.–Soviet relations had released the breaks on Soviet international behavior. (Vance, 1983, p. 388)

National Security Advisor Brzezinski on the other hand viewed the Soviet move in older domino theory terms. He saw the Soviet move as an attempt to win dominance in the Middle East:

> It has eliminated a buffer between the Soviet Union and Pakistan and Iran, has brought the Soviet Union within striking distance of the Indian Ocean and even the Gulf of Hormuz and it places Soviet power on the edge of two highly exposed and in some respects vulnerable countries, Iran and Pakistan. These countries are now likely to be targets of Soviet political intimidation. (Brzezinski, 1980a, p. 2)

Moreover, as he saw it the Soviets had dared to take this action because the decline of American commitment to deterrence had given the Soviets a green light for their imperial ambitions. "The Soviets were becoming more assertive" he said, just at the time the United States was becoming "more acquiescent." The State Department, he felt, had through "inaction or opposition," diluted some of the President's decisions to demonstrate American firmness (Brzezinski, 1983, p. 428).

From a broader strategic perspective, Brzezinski argued that world peace and stability since World War II had depended on the United States and its allies successfully defending against aggressive Soviet probes in two central strategic zones—Europe and the Far East. With the new Soviet probe into the Middle East, the United States would now have to take a stand in this third strategic arena.

"We are, if you will, in the third phase of the great architectural response that the United States launched in the wake of World War II" (Brzezinski, 1980b, p. 5; see also Rosati, 1987, p. 87).

Though it may have been difficult at this time to know which interpretations were the correct ones, Jimmy Carter came down strongly on the side of the Brzezinski hard-line interpretation of Soviet motives. He characterized the event as a "clear threat" to the region, and deduced that a "successful take-over of Afghanistan would give the Soviets a deep penetration between Iran and Pakistan" and a dangerous footing in the Persian Gulf (Carter, 1982, pp. 471–472). Privately, the President sent Brezhnev a hot-line message that characterized the invasion as a "clear threat to peace" and an act that could "mark a fundamental and long lasting turning point in our relations" (Carter, 1982, p. 472). In a speech before the American Society of Newspaper Editors on April 10, 1980, the President embraced the notion that Soviet intervention in Afghanistan was a threat to the entire world political system:

> In this ever more interdependent world, to assume aggression need be met only when it occurs at one's own doorstep is to tempt new adventures and to risk new and very serious miscalculations. Our course is clear. By responding very firmly, we intend to halt aggression where it takes place and to deter it elsewhere. (Carter, 1980b, pp. 4–5)

To meet this Soviet threat, Carter also opted for the full panoply of political, economic, and cultural sanctions that various aides suggested to him. The United States proposed a resolution in the United Nation's Security Council condemning the invasion and calling for a Soviet pullout. When the measure was vetoed by the Soviet Union, it moved to the General Assembly where it was adopted on January 14 by a vote of 104 to 18, with 18 abstentions and 12 absent.

Economic and cultural sanctions included the suspension of the transfer of high technology such as computer hardware and oil drilling equipment, the curtailment of Soviet fishing rights in U.S. waters, and the suspension of Soviet–American cultural exchanges. Perhaps most important was the decision to impose an embargo on the shipment of American grain to the Soviet Union and the attempts to boycott the summer Olympic Games, scheduled for Moscow the following July. Seventeen million metric tons of American grown grain earmarked for Moscow would be halted, as well as all subsequent deliveries.

The President also redefined American vital interests to include maintenance of the status quo in the Persian Gulf and used rhetoric reminiscent of the earliest days of the cold war. Thus, in the State of the Union address before a joint session of Congress on January 23, 1980, he declared; "Let our position be absolutely clear: An attempt by any outside force to gain control of the Persian Gulf region will be regarded as an assault on the vital security interests of the United States of America, and such an assault will be repelled by any means necessary including military force" (Carter, 1982, p. 483).

To meet this broad commitment, Carter also opted for several measures to build up U.S. strength. These included the creation of the rapid deployment force, joint military maneuvers with Egypt, the ordering of amphibious forces into the Arabian Sea, and the sale of AWACS fighter planes. Carter also made the decision to provide military assistance to Pakistan, renewing a 1959 agreement. Reversing its previous policy denying Pakistan military assistance due to human rights abuses and suspicions about the Zia regime's development of nuclear weapons, the United States also offered Pakistan $400 million in military assistance over two years. Furthermore, the CIA engaged in covert operations to supply the Afghan rebels with arms (Brzezinski, 1983, p. 432; see also Rosati, 1987, p. 144).

Several other measures were undertaken to build up American military strength generally. These measures included the reinstitution of draft registration and a proposed 5 percent increase in the defense budget for fiscal 1981. Furthermore, the deployment of Pershing II and cruise missiles in Europe was planned by NATO, and the United States began to move into an even closer economic and strategic relationship with China (Rosati, 1987, pp. 144–145). These measures included Carter's acceptance of a proposal that Brzezinski had urged on him for some time, that the United States sell military equipment to the People's Republic of China. The sale of weapons, however, would be exempt.

CAUSAL FACTORS

Preliminary Considerations

Certain political factors tilted Carter in the direction of the some kind of hard-line response. This was the first overt Soviet military intervention since 1968 and the domestic political climate at the time had become so anti-Soviet that a negative response of some sort was perceived to be a political necessity. Carter himself would later suggest that the invasion has simply forced him to face up to external political realities. A few days after the invasion he told Frank Reynolds of ABC that "the Soviet action had made a more dramatic change in his opinion of what the Soviets ultimate goals are than anything they've done in the previous time I've been in office" (quoted in Glad, 1980, p, 481).

Yet, a closer look at Carter's prior dealings with the Soviet Union suggest that Carter's response at this time was not out of character. He had taken quite hard-line stances vis à vis the Soviet Union for some time and by his own statements and policies contributed to the anti-Soviet sentiment in the United States that now constrained his actions. Moreover, he had earlier in his career shown a tendency to overstatement, heroic responses, and the leading of crusades. He was also sensitive to frustrations or failures of any sort, and likely to respond to such frustrations with an aggressive response. These proclivities, as we shall argue, were based on certain basic personality and stylistic characteristics evident in his earlier political life and career. To show the influence of these characteristics on Carter's political role performance, we will backtrack at this point to his earlier life and political career. We will then show the particular ways in which these characteristics influenced his earlier approaches to the Soviet Union and contributed to both the political climate and the political frustrations he suffered at the time of the invasion of Afghanistan.[1]

Jimmy Carter's Personality

Karen Horney's work on the development of the neurotic personality provides valuable insights that appear to be relevant for our purposes. Horney asserts that in childhood an individual will develop internal conflicts within his or her psyche as a result of the perfectionist standards and conditional love he/she receives. As she notes:

> He may feel wanted, liked, and appreciated not for what he is but merely for satisfying his parents need for adoration, prestige, and power. A rigid regime of perfectionist standards may invoke in him a feeling of inferiority not for measuring up to such demands. Misdemeanors or bad marks at school may be severely reprimanded, while good behavior or good marks are taken for granted . . . . All these factors, in addition to a general lack of warmth and interest, give him the feeling of being unloved and unworthy—or at any rate of not being worth anything unless he is something he is not. (Horney, 1950, p. 87)

Carter seems to have been raised in such an emotional environment. His mother, Lillian, was clearly an intelligent, witty, and energetic woman. Yet, as one can see from interviews she gave during Jimmy Carter's campaign for the presidency, she held herself up as a person who met ideal standards. As she told her daughter Gloria in one interview, "I would like to be remembered as a person who loves everybody and everything" (quoted in Glad, 1980, p. 31). To another journalist she remarked, "I'm sure I'm not even bragging when I say that I never had anybody work for me who didn't love me . . . . Nowadays, I am supposed to be, and I think I am, the most liberal woman in the county, maybe the state" (Allen, 1976, p. 27). At times she portrayed herself as the lone proponent of virtue in the town. She would often note, for example, that she was the only white woman who attended the funeral of the black school principal. She and Jimmy were the only ones who stood up on matters of race in Plains (Allen, 1976, p. 30).

Moreover, Lillian Carter permitted no questioning of her self-portrait. When she heard during the 1976 presidential campaign that someone in a local variety story had questioned the sincerity of her commitment to civil rights, she tried to find out who had maligned her, querying the store owner and local blacks. They all assured her that they could not in the world figure out who had said a thing like that about her. She finally guessed that it must have been a "complete stranger." On another occasion, when asked if Jimmy could question her on any matters, she seemed perplexed and responded: "Criticize his momma?" (Safran, 1976, p. 84).

Not only did she present a tough model to live up to, she was tense and very strict in raising Jimmy, her first child. Jimmy had to be fed exactly so and on a precise schedule, as she later recalled (Glad, 1980, p. 32). When he was a bit older, she returned to her nursing profession, working from 12 to 20 hours a day, as Jimmy later recalled (Carter, 1976b, p. 13).

Black women took care of him in her absence. To some who later interviewed them, they seemed to be warm and caring individuals. But they also relied on physical punishments and fear to keep Jimmy in line. Rachel Clark spanked him as the situation required with "some branches from a peach tree . . . or an oak tree—whatever was necessary to do the job." Annie May Harvey controlled him by threatening to tell his daddy about his misbehavior, a threat which would immediately get him to behave. Annie May Holley told Jimmy and the other children about a boogie man who lived about a 100 yards from the house, so that there would never be any temptation to run away from home at night. She also told them an old bloody ghost walked the railroad track in front of the house as a means of keeping them off of the tracks (Glad, 1980, pp. 33–34).

Jimmy Carter, in his autobiography, does not really deal with these feminine influences in his life. The black nursemaids are not mentioned and Lillian is painted, in abstract terms, as an extroverted, dynamic, and compassionate parent. But Carter describes only one interaction with her in his whole book. One day, his hands and pockets full of rocks he had just collected for his slingshot, his mother appeared on the front porch. "Honey," she asked, "would you like some cookies?" The young boy stood there, as he later recalled, for "about fifteen or twenty seconds in honest doubt about whether I should drop those worthless rocks and take the cookies which Mother offered me with a heart full of love" (Carter, 1976b, p. 39). Using this story as a parable of how politically one should not hesitate to give up things of lesser worth for what is truly valuable, he never reveals whether or not he gave up his power to fight to receive the gift of love (Carter, 1976b, p. 39).

Earl Carter, Jimmy's father, seems to have been his main emotional provider. He was the one who helped him in his studies at school. He was the one who provided for the children's recreations—building a tennis court in their yard, teaching the boys how to fish and hunt (Glad, 1980, p. 34). He was also the one who took the children to church. Packing four Carter children into the car, he took them to their Sunday school classes while he went to the men's Bible class. Often he would skip the church service that followed to talk with his friends at the local drugstore, picking the children up later at the church. Occasionally, on what the children considered big occasions, the children were permitted to stay in the car and watch Earl and his friends visit at the drugstore (Glad, 1980, p. 38). Certainly Earl provided the model that Jimmy Carter would follow in his own life. His father, as he later recalled, was a "firm but understanding director of my life and habits . . . . Also, he was always my best friend" (Carter, 1976b, pp. 8–9). The idealization of his father is evident in his characterization of him. Earl was an "unusually hard worker," an "extremely competent farmer and a businessman," and an "aggressive and innovative" person in the area of selling. He was "scrupulously fair with all those who dealt with him," "extremely intelligent," "well read about current events," very popular, exuberant, a community leader, and a good athlete (Carter, 1976b, pp. 9–13).

Yet Earl's love could have been seen by Jimmy as a conditional love. His eldest son's misdoings were noted and severely punished while success and good behavior was not noted or rewarded. Jimmy Carter would later recall in detail each punishment he received. "From the time I was four years old until I was fifteen years old, he whipped me six times and I've never forgotten any of those impressive experiences. The punishment was administered with a small, long, flexible piece of peach tree switch" (Carter, 1976b, p. 12).

Perhaps, more important, was the fact that successes were not directly rewarded. One occasion along these lines is particularly revealing. Upon shooting his first quail, young Jimmy was so proud and happy that he dropped his gun and ran to find his father. Earl, rather than admiring or simply hugging his son, cut the young boy's excitement short with a critique. He should not have dropped his gun (Glad, 1980, p. 35). An emotionally wide-open Jimmy, in short, is admonished rather than simply admired and loved.

With a regimen emphasizing discipline more than love and parents who themselves seem to have achieved such high standards, it is not surprising to find that young Jimmy showed some signs of stress and anger. As an infant he cried a great deal more than normal. He was also often sick, suffering from colic at times and an attack of pneumonia. At the age of two he nearly died of bleeding colitis. He could also be very demanding. Once, after biting through his pacifier, he screamed and yelled until his Aunt Sissy walked to town and persuaded the local drugstore owner to open up his store so she could buy another one. When he was hospitalized for colitis, he cried for a goat—a common pet in the rural South—until the head nurse at the local Wise Hospital went out to buy him one and placed it beside his bed (Elovitz, 1977, p. 196).

When he was a little older, Jimmy tried to live up to standards set for him by his parents. He was for the most part a "good boy" who did what was expected of him. He did not cuss, or smoke, or fight with the other boys, though he sometimes teased his nursemaids and his sister, Gloria. Certainly he seemed determined, even as a boy, to be the very best. He got good grades in school, though he did not show the exuberance at this time that would make a natural leader. When he played ball he wanted to hit a home run every time, as his mother recalled. When he was on the debating team, he wanted to win. Or as one of his black playmates later noted, "Jimmy doesn't like to lose, but he always loved to be up front" (L. Carter, 1977, p. 36).

Carter's account of his interactions with the authorities he most admired later in his life suggest that he carried over even into his adult years this expectation that they would be extrademanding, searching for ways to find him short in some way. His recollection of his interview with Admiral Rickover is especially interesting along these lines. It is the source for the title of his autobiography, *Why Not the Best?* and suggests that harsh scrutiny, if in the service of perfection, is an appropriate way for an authority to relate to those in his charge:

> It was the first time I met Admiral Rickover, and we sat in a large room by ourselves for more than two hours, and he let me choose any subjects I wished to discuss. Very carefully, I chose those about which I knew the most at the time— current events, seamanship, music, literature, naval tactics, electronics, gunnery— and he began to ask me a series of questions of increasing difficulty. In each instance, he soon proved that I knew relatively little about the subject I had chosen.
>
> He always looked right into my eyes, and he never smiled. I was saturated with cold sweat. Finally, he asked me a question and I thought I could redeem myself. He said "How did you stand in your class at the Naval Academy?" Since I had completed my sophomore year at Georgia Tech before entering Annapolis as a plebe, I had done very well, and I swelled by chest with pride and answered, "Sir, I stood fifty-ninth in a class of 820!" I sat back to wait for the congratulations— which never came. Instead, the question: "Did you do your best?" I started to say "Yes, sir," but I remembered who this was and recalled several of the many times

at the Academy; when I could have learned more about our allies, or enemies, weapons, strategy and so forth. I was just human. I finally gulped and said "No Sir, I didn't always do my best."

He looked at me for a long time, and then turned his chair around to end the interview. He asked one final question, which I have never been able to forget—or to answer. He said, "Why not?" I just sat there for a while, shaken, and then slowly left the room." (Carter, 1976b, frontispiece)

Even as governor, Carter later recalled, he would break out into a cold sweat when Rickover called him on the phone—not sure whether the Admiral would consider his latest doing as worthy of blame or praise (Carter, 1976a, p. 136).

Children raised in regimes of the sort described above usually enter into a psychological "Faustian pact." Fearing that they may lose love, they create an idealized image of themselves, inflating those qualities that are admired by the authorities whose love and admiration they seek, suppressing all recognition of those which are despised. The result, as Karen Horney (1950) notes, is a loss of contact or alienation from one's real self and an intensification of an underlying fear that one is really not quite as good as one pretends to be. Horney delineates three major adaptations along these lines. For our purposes, the expansive–narcissistic solution is most relevant. The central feature of the expansive type is his identification with the values of mastery.

He has (consciously) no doubts; he is the anointed, the man of destiny, the prophet, the great giver, the benefactor of mankind. All of this contains a grain of truth. He is often gifted beyond average, early and easily won distinction, and sometimes was the favored and admired child . . . he may speak incessantly of his exploits or of his wonderful qualities and needs endless confirmation of his estimate of himself in the form of admiration and devotion. (Horney, 1950, p. 194)

Often expansive types will be gifted individuals who can achieve a degree of success either professionally or politically. The narcissistic subtype, that is, the individual who tends to so love his or her idealized image that they believe it is true, tends to achieve the highest success. They seem to possess an extraordinary degree of self-confidence, to be able to overlook flaws or turn them into virtues.

The expansive type . . . tends to identify himself with his inner dictates and, whether consciously or unconsciously, to be proud of his standards. He does not question their validity and tries to actualize them in one way or another. He may try to measure up to them in his actual behavior. He should be all things to all people; he should know everything better than anybody else; he should never err; he should never fail in anything he attempts to do. (Horney, 1950, p. 76)

Carter's embrace of an idealized self was evident even during his boyhood. He had to win, to be the best at the games he played. Later in his career, even in areas where his stardom in no ways seemed guaranteed, he saw himself as a winner who would go to the top. Certain very obvious virtues and accomplishments were exaggerated in ways that suggest he had accomplished more than he really had. As a college student at Georgia Southwestern, then Georgia Tech and Annapolis, he made good grades. But he never excelled in extracurricular activities or sports and was never seen as one most likely to win by his classmates (Glad, 1980, pp. 48, 49, 52–53). Yet, while at Georgia Southwestern College, he confided to a friend that he thought he would like to be governor of Georgia someday (Glad, 1980, p. 48). While at Annapolis, he expected to become Chief of Naval Operations and applied for a Rhodes scholarship (Glad, 1980, pp. 58–59). His later claims to be a nuclear physicist were based on one year as a naval officer in the nuclear submarine program and the two noncredit courses he had taken during this time at Union College (Glad, 1980, p. 64). During his presidential campaign in 1974–76, he sprinkled his speeches with quotes from Reinhold Niebuhr, Dylan Thomas, and Sören Kierkegaard, writers who had no apparent influence on his thinking in any way. He implied he had friendships with Golda Meir, Helmut Schmidt, and Bob Dylan, people whom he had met only once (Glad, 1980, p. 493). In his speeches he suggested that he had obtained qualities that are beyond most human beings: he could love individuals he met on the assembly lines, he would never tell a lie, he had never experienced fear—even of death— and he had no awe of the White House. Moreover, even when his candidacy was a long shot, he talked of what he wanted to do *when* he became president. The other contenders spoke of what they would do *if* they achieved the office (Glad, 1980, p. 493).

As president, he would see himself as the leader who would turn the United States toward a new mission—the attainment of a whole new kind of world order based on the peaceful resolution of conflicts and behavior (even toward one's own nationals) based on the recognition of certain universally recognized moral principles. The promotion of universal human rights, as he noted in his inaugural address, would be at the top of his foreign policy agenda. The U.S. role, as he further elaborated in his commencement address at Notre Dame University in May, 1977, was to take the lead in securing this new and moral order. "We can no longer separate the traditional issues of war and peace from the new global question of justice, equity and human rights . . . . It is a new world that calls for a new American foreign policy, a policy based on constant decency in its values and an optimism in its historical visions" (Carter, 1977c, pp. 773–779).

In line with this view, Carter saw himself as a great peacemaker in the tradition of Woodrow Wilson. His efforts on behalf of the Panama Canal treaties and his mediation of the Middle Eastern conflicts were several positive contributions along these lines. He was also committed to securing a nuclear arms control treaty with the Soviet Union, and he suggested in the early months of his administration that: "competition must be balanced by cooperation in preserving peace and thus our mutual survival. I will seek such cooperation with the Soviet Union earnestly, constantly and sincerely" (Carter, 1977a, pp. 397–402). Moreover, he noted on occasion the Soviet desire for peace. In a speech before the Southern Legislative Leadership Conference in Charleston, South Carolina in the summer of 1977, he said:

> Beyond all the disagreements between us—and all the cool calculations of mutual self-interest that our two countries bring to the negotiating table—is the inevitable human reality that must bring us closer together. I mean the yearning for peace, real peace, that is in the bones of us all . . . . Mr. Brezhnev said something very interesting recently, and I quote from his speech: "It is our belief, our firm belief" he said "that realism in politics and the will for detente will triumph and mankind

will be able to step into the 21st century in conditions of peace stable as never
before." I see no hidden meaning in that. I credit his sincerity. And I express the
same hope and belief that Mr. Brezhnev expressed. (Carter, 1977, pp. 1063–1069)

He was inclined, however, as his rhetoric suggests, to exaggerate the
significance of his very real accomplishments as a peacemaker. In his address
presenting the Camp David Accords to the Special Joint Session of Congress, for
example, Carter noted that it had been 2,000 years since there had been peace
between Egypt and a free Jewish nation, and that such a peace might be secured
"this year." The agreement, he proclaimed was "a chance for one of the bright
moments in history" (Glad, 1980, p. 433). Even his normalization agreements with
the People's Republic of China were interpreted as significant victories. After a
nationwide broadcast detailing the developing normalization process, Carter
leaned back in his chair and—unaware that his microphone was still on—noted
"massive applause—throughout the nation" (Glad, 1980, pp. 434–445). Not only
had Carter overplayed the importance of the event itself, the "massive applause"
from the American people never materialized.[2] The next month, shortly after
signing cooperation agreements on science, technology, space, and cultural exchanges with Deputy Prime Minister Teng Hsiao-Ping of the People's Republic of
China, Carter noted that they had just engaged in "one of the most historic events
in our nation's history" (Glad, 1980, p. 435).

Similarly, the threats he had to deal with as president were exaggerated into
heroic trials. Iran's capture and holding of American diplomatic hostages was
seen as an incident of such magnitude that the White House would not turn on
the Christmas lights until they were returned home. (That symbolic action had
not even been taken during World War II.) The Iran hostage and Afghan crises,
as he saw it, required his full time and attention in the White House and a
suspension of scheduled political debates as well as all criticism of his policies
and decisions. (The only president who had abstained from campaigning on such
grounds in the twentieth century was Roosevelt in the 1944 campaign.) Carter not
only relished these opportunities to show his dedication and his skills, he also
prided himself on how tough he could be. During the Iranian hostage crisis, for
example, against the advice of his secretary of state, he made the decision to go
for the very high-risk rescue operation (see Glad, 1989). When Colonel Beckwith,
the man who was in charge of the operation noted that Carter was "tough as
woodpecker's lips," Carter was delighted. It was the greatest compliment he had
received as president, as Carter later noted (Carter, 1982, p. 521).

This extraordinary show of self-confidence was an asset in many ways. His
drive for mastery and the feeling he was bound to win doubtlessly inspired others
around him and gave him the courage to take on long shots and difficult under-
takings. His intelligence and ability to work and his good luck meant that he often
did succeed. Certainly these qualities paid off in his campaign for the presidency.
As a governor from a smaller state with no major connection to the national
democratic party, he had to have extraordinary faith in himself to undertake such
a long-shot campaign and attract the staff people who were willing to commit
themselves to him even before he began to surface in the national polls as a real
contender.

As president, these same qualities contributed to his willingness to undertake politically risky peacemaking ventures, as well as his success in these ventures. Thus Carter had been willing to stake his personal reputation on the long-shot proposition that if he could get Sadat and Begin together at Camp David, he could get them to settle their differences concerning their mutual borders and the Palestinian question. His efforts at Camp David had been crucial to their success in developing a framework for peace. Later, when the subsequent talks seemed to be on the verge of failure, it was his decision to personally go to the Middle East that saved the day and led to the finalization of their agreements on these matters (Glad, 1980, pp. 435–460).

Adherence to an idealized self-image, however, can also create certain problems for the individual in its grip. The secret fear that one may not really be as extraordinary as one claims to be can lead to an individual with such an adaptation to be especially sensitive to any indication that he or she is falling short. As Horney (1950, p. 195) notes, he "can be quite tolerant, he does not expect others to be perfect; he can even stand jokes about himself, so long as they merely highlight an amiable peculiarity of his; *but he must never be questioned seriously*" (emphasis added).

Failures to accomplish major goals, given this adaptation, can leave the individual with a sense of great frustration and a proclivity to respond aggressively. As Horney notes:

> The greater the subjective importance, the more impelling is the need to attain the goal, and hence the more intense the reaction to the frustration. Although it is not always visible, the search for glory is a most powerful drive. It can be like a demonical obsession, almost like a monster swallowing up the individual who has created it. And so the reactions to frustration must be severe. They are indicated by the terror of doom and disgrace that for many people is spelled out in the idea of failure. Reactions of panic, depression, despair, rage at self and others to what is conceived as "failure" are frequent, and entirely out of proportion to the actual importance of the occasion. (Horney, 1950, p. 31)

Carter's sensitivities along these lines had been evident through his political career. When he failed to achieve his goals or was subject to criticism, his responses suggest that underneath his surface self-confidence he harbored a fear that he was not quite as good as he claimed to be. His failure in 1966 to win a long-shot try at the governorship led him into a depression, as he noted in *Why Not the Best?* (Carter, 1976b). During his campaign for the presidency, his eyes would freeze over and a vein in his temple visibly throb when he was confronted on some issue in a way he did not like (Glad, 1980, p. 501). Carter's displeasure at his ability being questioned is evident in his behavior immediately following his winning the White House. On the plane back to Plains the night after he won the election, Carter came back to the press section, "chortling, rubbing it in," as one observed noted. "You were wrong," he told them, "I won." Three weeks later he called Vernon Jordan, the civil rights leader in Georgia, to remind him that he was wrong when he advised Carter that he could not win the presidency (Glad, 1980, p. 594).

In office, Carter would become defensive when women's groups, labor, or black leaders would suggest he was not responding to their needs (Glad, 1980, p. 496). His need to win at everything and subsequent tendency to rationalize failure was evident in a footrace in the Catoctin Mountains, he persisted to the point where he collapsed and had to be carried off the course. "They had to drag me off," he later boasted (quoted in Glad, 1980, p. 501). The Iranian hostage issue, as he later admitted, became an obsession with him. He never could admit that the rescue operations was almost certain to become a fiasco, as one of the authors of this chapter has described in more detail elsewhere. The safety and freedom of the hostages were his paramount consideration, he later stated, but he also wanted "to have my decisions vindicated" (Carter, 1982, p. 594).

Another flaw that goes with the embrace of such an idealized self image, as Horney notes, is that such a person fails to see his or her limits. Often they attempt to do too much. "Assuming approximately equal gifts, he is the most productive among the expansive types. But he (the narcissistic individual) may run up against various difficulties. One of them is scattering interests and energies in many directions" (Horney, 1950, p. 312). A related problem, we suggest, is a failure to note the limits in the real world on what one can accomplish. Related to that proclivity is a tendency not to see how that world may force important trade-offs between the various important goals one embraces.

Carter's proclivities for scattering his interests were evident in his desire to master every detail in his presidency. As Rosati (1987, p. 104) notes: "During his first year as president he worked more than seventy hours per week, spending close to half that time reading and studying." Moreover, his wide agenda as president demonstrated his need to master a number of issues. Most presidents narrow their agenda of high-priority issues to relatively few items in which they have a high degree of interest. Carter, in contrast, focused his energy on a broad range of concerns ranging from human rights, nuclear proliferation, arms control, a Middle East peace plan, détente with the Soviet Union, and Third World development just to mention a few.

Most important for this discussion was Carter's inability to see the limits on what he could accomplish in his dealings with the Soviet Union. In pursuing values reflecting what Brzezinski called his "Wilsonian side"—that is, the attainment of world peace and the creation of a new international order based on universal respect for human rights—Carter did not clearly see how the interests and emotional responses of his adversary had to be taken into account, or how his own values might contradict each other. To secure world peace, one would have to show a certain moderation and prudence in dealing with the Soviet Union. As the other major power in the world, they would have to voluntarily come to any agreement to limit nuclear arms or settle other political disputes. An aggressive human rights campaign, however, could challenge the legitimacy of their regime, and his attempts to pressure them into accepting measures that threatened what they saw as legitimate national goals made it more difficult for them to come to terms with the United States. Carter's failure to see potential conflicts between his various goals, we suggest, contributed to his difficulties in dealing with the Soviet Union. An uneasy and unclear compromise between his conflicting values in the first 2½ years of his administration, we will now argue, eventually hardened into an anti-Soviet posture that had become quite clear even before the Russian intervention in Afghanistan.

Jimmy Carter's Conflicting Values: the Peacemaker versus the Anti-Soviet Crusader

Carter felt, as we have seen, that the Soviet Union desired peace and that on the basis of this common interest with the United States, a new nuclear arms control treaty could be obtained. At the same time, he harbored very negative views of Soviet motives and was inclined to take a harsh stance vis à vis them. His negative views of the Soviet Union had been evident even before attaining the presidency. In his initial draft announcing his candidacy for the presidency, he had referred to the Soviets as a "warlike power" and only pulled that phrase when Stuart Eizenstat, one of his campaign advisors, convinced him that it sounded too "Jacksonian" (Glad, 1980, p. 287). In the 1976 fall presidential campaign he had run television commercials in the South which targeted President Ford's "soft" dealings with the Soviets, and emphasized that Carter "had no illusions about Russia's intentions" (Glad, 1980, p. 393). Another set of commercials piggybacked on Ronald Reagan's critique of the Ford administration's détente policies, with Carter reaffirming Reagan's claims that "détente had been a one way street" in which the United States was always the loser (Glad, 1980, p. 393).

As President, he immediately undertook several steps that disturbed Soviet leaders. The Soviet Union was the first target of his human rights campaign.[3] On January 27, 1977, at Carter's direction, the State Department warned Moscow against violating the rights of the Soviet dissident and nuclear physicist, Andrei Sakharov. In this regard, Carter ignored State Department warnings that such activity by the United States would jeopardize arms control agreements (Glad, 1980, pp. 428–429). On February 17, the President sent Sakharov a letter stating that the United States would use its "good office" to seek the release of prisoners of conscience. It was the first direct communication between a Western leader and a Soviet dissident. On March 22, Carter personally announced his intention to increase expenditures for Radio Free Europe and Radio Liberty so that they could extend the range of their broadcasts into the Soviet Union (Glad, 1980, pp. 428–429).

Most important, Carter's first arms reduction proposals to the Soviet Union, presented in late March of 1977, were almost bound to provoke the Soviet leaders. The proposals not only departed quite drastically from the SALT II negotiations, which had been temporarily suspended during the 1976 presidential election, they cut deeply into land-based missiles in which the Soviet Union was particularly strong and would have curtailed modernization programs in which they the Soviets were already engaged. The United States, as Talbott (1980) has pointed out, was "seeking substantial reductions in existing Soviet systems in exchange for marginal cuts in future American ones" (pp. 60–61).

Carter, himself, had played a key role in the decision to move in this new direction. At a "principals only" meeting on March 12, at which the key decision were made, he expressed his desire for "real arms control" and his impatience with the "Vladivostok framework" (Talbott, 1980, p. 58). Secretary of Defense Harold Brown had originally presented this idea to Carter. But in the words of a person with first-hand knowledge of these events, it was like a "beautifully tied, juicy fly dropped right in front of a hungry trout's nose. The President bit and swallowed right away" (Talbott, 1980, p. 59).

In making this choice, Carter disregarded explicit Soviet warnings that they would oppose any major departures from the Vladivostok framework. Earlier, in response to Carter's suggestions that he was considering the possibility of deep nuclear cuts rather than the more modest limitation envisaged in the SALT II negotiations, Brezhnev had written the president that the whole approach was "deliberately unacceptable" (Carter, 1982, p. 218).

Carter's decision to go for this dramatic, new approach was partly motivated by his sense of competition with Henry Kissinger, as Talbott (1980, p. 79) has noted. Somewhat naively, given this orientation, Carter invited Henry Kissinger to a dinner at the White House and sought out his advice. Kissinger told Carter that the deep cut proposals had a good chance of being accepted by the Soviet Union, if they were sincere and desired real progress on disarmament (Carter, 1982). Carter never even considered the possibility that Kissinger might not wish to help a man who during the recent presidential campaign had undertaken a running attack on his détente policies, critiqued his "lone ranger" foreign policies, and now was trying to outdo him.

Given all the factors above, it is not surprising that the Soviet Union, on April 9, 1977, summarily rejected Carter's proposal "as a cheap and shady maneuver or unilateral advancement." Even the fallback proposal that Vance had managed to get the President to accept was ignored. Many Soviet specialists in Washington saw the blowup with the Kremlin as the "worst public turn in Soviet–American relations in five years of détente" and held Carter partly responsible for the debacle (Glad, 1980, p. 430).

The President, however, was surprised by their response. He was "angry" and "disappointed" that the timetable for an agreement had to be set back (Carter, 1982, p. 219). Certainly he did not seem himself as having any responsibility for the debacle, and he continued with his confrontational style. Thus on March 30, 1977, right after the American proposals had been rejected, Carter insisted that he would "hang tough" in pressing Soviet acceptance of his proposals. Should they not bargain in "good faith," he would have to "consider a much more deep commitment to the development and deployment of additional weapons" (Glad, 1980, p. 429).[4]

Yet Carter did want a nuclear arms treaty and by May he had somewhat reluctantly embraced a three-tier package, the first step of which was to secure cuts close to the old Vladivostok formula (Talbott, 1980, p. 85; Glad, 1980, p. 429). The road to the final signature of the treaty, however, was rocky, partly because of Carter's human rights crusade. Carter himself saw no relationship between the American human rights efforts and the SALT process, and even argued on occasion that despite many Soviet protests to the contrary, that there was really no "connection between the two in the minds of the Soviets" (Carter, 1977d, pp. 951–960). He was surprised, he admitted, by "the degree of disturbance by the Soviets" about what he considered to be "a routine and normal commitment to human rights" (Carter, 1977d, pp. 951–960). But he proposed that the Soviet response might be motivated by their desire, "for political reasons," to exaggerate the disagreements between the two countries (Carter, 1977e, pp. 985–993). He attributed the soured atmosphere between Washington and Moscow to the mistaken Soviet "belief that our concern for human rights is aimed specifically at them or is an attack on their vital interests." United States policy, he explained was directed at "all countries equally, including our own." To the extent that the Soviet criticisms of his policy are based on a misconception of American motives he vowed to redouble U.S. efforts to make them clear. But to the extent they are merely "designed as propaganda to put pressure on us, let no one doubt that we will persevere" (Carter, 1977e, pp. 985–993).

By 1978, Soviet human rights violations were being explicitly linked to possible U.S. punishments. On April 13, 1978, the U.S. ambassador to the Soviet Union, Malcolm Toon, issued an unusually blunt warning, suggesting that "U.S./Soviet relations would be adversely affected" should the Soviet Union proceed with their treason trial against the Soviet dissident, Anatoly Scharansky. When Scharansky and fellow dissident Alexander Ginzburg were sentenced for their supposedly treasonous activity, the White House canceled the sale of an advanced computer to Taas, the Soviet news agency, and ordered all sales of U.S. oil technology be placed under administration review.

The administration also suggested, at times, that the successful conclusion of the SALT talks were linked to Soviet political activities in the Horn of Africa. On March 1, 1978, Brzezinski suggested that Soviet involvements in that part of the world might have an adverse effect on the outcome of the SALT process. Though Carter denied the next day that the U.S. government sought to impose a linkage between Soviet actions in Africa and SALT, he stated that American public opinion would turn against SALT if the Soviet Union appeared unwilling to cooperate on other issues. At Wake Forest University later that month, Carter warned that a continued Soviet military buildup and the "projection of Soviet proxy forces into other lands and continents" could erode popular support in the United States for cooperation in any area (Carter, 1978a, pp. 529–538).

At the U.S. Naval Academy in Annapolis in June, 1978, Carter bluntly critiqued Soviet domestic failings and suggested that the Soviet Union was bent on aggression:

> To the Soviet Union, détente seems to mean a continuing aggressive struggle for political advantage and increased influence in a variety of ways. The Soviet Union apparently sees military power and military assistance as the best means of expanding its influence abroad. Obviously areas of instability in the world produce a tempting target for their attempt to export a totalitarian and repressive form of involvement. (Carter, 1978b, pp. 1052–1057)

In Korea, Angola, and Ethiopia, Carter continued in the same address, "the Soviets prefer to use proxy forces to achieve their purposes."

In the winter of 1978–79, Carter finally played the China card. In his earlier speech at Notre Dame in 1977, Carter had given the Soviets a glimpse of what he might do when he suggested that their Chinese rival was a "key force for global peace" and that the United States would work with "creative forces" in that country in the future (Carter, 1977c). Going beyond a mere normalization of relations with the Chinese, in January Carter signed a joint communique with the Chinese suggesting a common front against the Soviet Union. Condemned were efforts by any country "to establish hegemony or domination over others." It was a phrase the Chinese commonly used to characterize Soviet policies in the Far East (Glad, 1980, p. 435). This whole tilt toward the Chinese provoked severe consternation from Brezhnev and Dobrynin, both of whom asserted that the development would complicate the SALT process (Talbott, 1980, pp. 246–247).

The Crisis Before the Crisis: The Deterioration of Soviet-American Relations

Carter's inability to see trade-offs between his various values during this first 2½ years of his administration, in short, prolonged the negotiations leading to the final SALT treaty. At the Geneva talks in May, 1979, however, the negotiating team headed by Cyrus Vance downplayed claims of Soviet human rights violations and the next month, in a mood of quiet compromise, the SALT treaty was finally signed at Vienna. The domestic political climate at that time, however, was quite negative. If the Soviet Union were so aggressive and disrespectful of the rights and interest of others, as Carter's continuing discourse on Soviet misdoings suggested, what was the point of even making an arms limitation pact with them?

To change that political climate, the Carter administration undertook a major lobbying effort. Lloyd Cutler orchestrated the administration efforts to win Senate support for the SALT II treaty and hearings before the Senate Foreign Relations Committee generated wider understanding that the treaty would serve U.S. interests. Promises were even made to Sam Nunn, that if he did nothing to block the treaty, the President would later recommend greater increases in military expenditures (Brzezinski, 1983, pp. 336–337).

But then what appears to have been some behind the scenes politicking by Brzezinski got out of hand. In late July, Brzezinski informed the President that he had received a report suggesting that the Soviet Union might have a brigade in Cuba and that it could possibly harm arms control efforts. On August 14, he told the President that intelligence reports showed there *was* an actual Soviet brigade in Cuba and that this was an extremely serious development that could seriously jeopardize SALT II. Brzezinski, however, had not seen the whole issue as so pressing that he could not put it on hold over the Labor Day weekend, while he took a short vacation. While he was out of Washington, however, the whole affair spun out of control. Frank Church, the chairman of the Senate Foreign Relations Committee, was briefed by the State Department on the matter and he made the whole issue public, declaring in a rather bellicose press conference that the Soviet Union was testing U.S. resolve in Cuba. He was running for reelection in a heated contest in Idaho and this episode provided a means for him to correct his dovish image and make him more acceptable to conservative voters in Idaho (Brzezinski, 1983, pp. 347–348).

Carter's chief foreign policy advisors at this time suddenly took positions that were hard to understand, given their earlier and subsequent positions. Brzezinski had pushed for some time for Carter to put pressure on Cuba; he had obtained the President's permission for flights over Cuba to obtain hard evidence on Soviet activities there and had underscored the severity of the brigade issue. But now he advised the President that "in view of the possibility that the Soviet brigade might have been in Cuba for a number of years and in view of the fact that we had not contested it before, it seems hard to demand publicly that the Soviets all of a sudden withdraw the brigade." Vance, who had attempted to block most of Brzezinski's harder-line recommendations for dealing with the Soviet Union, took a harder line on this occasion, arguing that the United States had to demand the withdrawal of the brigade and note that the status quo was "unacceptable" (Brzezinski, 1983, p. 349).

In his first televised statement of the matter on September 7, Carter had not clearly decided on what stand he would take and he gave the American people a mixed message. The Soviet combat unit in Cuba, he noted, may have been in Cuba for quite a few years and it is not an assault force. Yet he went on to say other things that suggested these developments were nevertheless ominous. Its purposes are not yet clear, he said, and the status quo is "not acceptable." The issue, he suggested, revolved around the "stationing of Soviet combat troops here in the Western Hemisphere in a country which acts as a Soviet proxy in military adventure in other areas of the world like Africa" (Carter, 1979, pp. 1602–1603).

Meanwhile, behind the scenes, Carter's top advisors were fighting over the stance he should ultimately take. Cyrus Vance, Robert Culter, and Walter Mondale urged that the issue be confined to the Russian brigade in Cuba itself. Zbigniew Brzezinski and Harold Brown wanted to use the issue to emphasize the worldwide thrust of Soviet assertiveness. The latter secured the support of Jody Powell, Hamilton Jordan, and Rosalynn Carter along the way (Brzezinski, 1983, pp. 346–350).

Later that month, Brzezinski prepared a speech for the President on the subject that would have backed the Soviets completely in a corner. Special emphasis was placed on the wider "character of Soviet activities in the Third World, stressing that these were not compatible with a stable détente." Brzezinski also gave the President a memo urging him to stress the need for defense increases, the intensification of worldwide efforts to ostracize Cuba, the development of a dialogue with China on sensitive technology and military issues. No mention should be made of SALT in that speech, he suggested (Brzezinski, 1983, p. 350).

If Carter had followed this advice, he would have sunk SALT on the spot. But Brzezinski, knowing the President's commitment to the peace talks, argued that a tougher approach would place the United States "in a better position to argue that SALT should be ratified because it was confined to the strategic area and was not a symptom of broader U.S. weakness" (Brzezinski, 1983, p. 350).

Carter only saw the full implications of the Brzezinski stance for his SALT II proposals when he met with Senator Byrd in the White House on the evening of

September 23. Senator Byrd, who was accompanied by Cyrus Vance, told the President that the whole issue of the Soviet brigade was a phony one, and that he would have to find some way to get off it in order to save SALT. He expressed disagreement with the views expressed by the President, Vance, and Brzezinski. Administration leaders would have to cool their rhetoric (Brzezinski, 1983, p. 350).

The President, as Brzezinski noted, was deeply impressed by what Byrd had told him and it soon became clear that the wider attack on the Soviet Union that Brzezinski favored would not prevail (Brzezinski, 1983, p. 350). Yet, the President did not address the nation for yet another week, and when he did so, his message remained mixed. On one hand he was reassuring. He had received assurance from the highest levels of the Soviet government that the combat brigade did not pose a threat to U.S. security or interests in Latin America. The brigade issue, he said is not reason for a return to the Cold War. Yet he also declared the United States could not rely on Soviet assurances that their brigade intentions were nonbelligerent. Thus he would increase surveillance of Cuba through the creation of a Latin America military command (Brzezinski, 1983, p. 351). The speech seems not to have changed the opinion of many senators. Byrd noted that Carter's approach was "reasonable but firm." Senator Frank Church noted that the Soviet assurance on the brigade was "welcome but insufficient if the SALT II treaty is not to be rejected by the Senate." Robert Dole noted that "he's doing a lot of things for a non-threat."

The result of this whole crisis, as Brzezinski would later note, so shook public confidence in the administration and heightened hostility toward the Soviet Union that it checked the momentum on the SALT ratification process. "Approximately one month of time was lost, and it became increasingly clear that the ratification of SALT would have to slip until the end of the year or perhaps into early 1980" (Brzezinski, 1983, pp. 352–353).

Brzezinski's response to the whole affair, however, suggests that he had an agenda that differed from the President's. In attempting to disengage himself from the Cuban brigade issue, the President had given his national security advisor a severe disappointment. Even though Brzezinski realized that the Russian brigade was probably a phony issue, he thought Carter should "use the crisis to establish his credentials as a tough-minded Truman-type leader focussing the spotlight on the Soviet use of the Cuba to promote Soviet strategic interests in the Third World." Brzezinski went on to note that action along these lines could have further reduced the chances of SALT ratification. "But my feeling was that the Soviets were not giving us much choice" (Brzezinski, 1983, p. 352).

Brzezinski was so frustrated by Carter's decision not to use the Soviet brigade issue along the lines he recommended that he seriously considered resigning. On October 4, he made the "most disagreeable comment" he had ever made to the President. The United States had told the Russians on several different occasions that it took great exception to their action in Vietnam, the Middle East, and Africa and more recently in Cuba. "But then we do nothing about it." That could be dangerous, he argued for the future, because the Russians could miscalculate our responses. "The President looked quite furious" as Brzezinski told him that "he had no intention of going to war over the Soviet brigade in Cuba" (Brzezinski, 1983, p. 351).

Decision Making at the Crisis Point: Coalescence of Causal Factors

Carter, as we have seen in the foregoing discussion, saw himself as a peacemaker, one who would change the moral and political climate of the world. The ratification of SALT II, a centerpiece of his peacemaking agenda, had been in trouble before the Soviet invasion of Afghanistan, and Carter himself had contributed to these problems. The Soviet invasion of Afghanistan, however, administered the coup de grace to his project. The intensity of Carter's negative response to that setback, we suggest, was fueled by a subtle interplay of domestic political factors within the country and his own administration and his own psychological and stylistic proclivities. To these factors we now turn.

Domestic political forces—both within the country and his own administration—made some tilt in the direction of a worst-case analysis of Soviet motives likely and made a relatively strong negative response a political necessity. The Soviet intervention was their first obvious crossing of international boundaries since the 1968 invasion of Czechoslovakia and a public that had been forewarned of Soviet aggressive proclivities would demand action by the United Nations and some kind of economic and military follow-up. Certainly if Carter wished to win a second term of office, he had to take some strong steps along these lines. Ronald Reagan and other Republicans were suggesting that Carter's weakness and inconsistency had resulted in foreign policy disasters in Iran and Afghanistan, and that the country needed stronger and more decisive leadership. As Rosati (1987, p. 106) notes: "Nineteen eighty was . . . an election year, and the public agenda was basically defined by the political right. President Carter had to campaign for reelection in a domestic environment that was increasingly inhospitable to his earlier optimistic image of the international system."

Within his own administration, moreover, the intervention tipped the political cards toward the options Brzezinski and Brown had been pushing for some time. They had been arguing that the United States should redefine its vital national security interests to include the Middle East as central to U.S. security interests and they had pushed for a major arms buildup, including plans for a rapid deployment force as a means of backing that extended definition of American interests. Moreover, to enhance American capabilities vis à vis the Soviet Union, they had campaigned for a closer political and military relationship to China and the placement of the Pershing 2 missiles in Europe.

With the Soviet intervention in Afghanistan, Cyrus Vance and others who had opposed many of these policies were no longer in a position where they could or would advance their previous positions. At an NSC meeting on December 30, for example, the Secretary of State came out for reinstating the draft as well as substantial reductions in U.S. grain sales to Moscow (Brzezinski, 1983, p. 431).

Yet, it is not all clear that Carter had to respond as strongly as he did. Some of the language he used was especially hyperbolic. His proclivity for exaggeration is evident in the emotionally laden language he used to describe the source and the consequences of the Soviet action. In an exchange with Jordan, he suggested that *"the invasion had made the prospects for nuclear war more likely"* (Jordan, 1982, p. 99; emphasis added). In a speech on January 4, 1980, he saw the Soviet action as reflecting their lack of central moral values. The invasion, he said, was *"a deliberate effort by a powerful atheistic government to subjugate an independent Islamic people"* (Jordan, 1982, p. 100; emphasis added). In his January 23, 1980 State of the Union address before a joint session of Congress, Carter asserted that: *"The implications of the Soviet invasion of Afghanistan could pose the most serious threat to world peace since the Second World War"* (Carter, 1980a, A; emphasis added).

Indeed, the harshness of his rhetoric created some problems for him in his own fight for the Democratic presidential nomination. Carter was being challenged at this time by Ted Kennedy, who was doing well in the polls, and Kennedy proceeded to assault him from the left. In a speech at Georgetown University on January 28, 1980, Kennedy suggested that Carter had overreacted by characterizing the Soviet action as the greatest threat to peace since World War II. Certainly this action, Kennedy wryly suggested, did not overshadow the Berlin blockade, the Cuban missile crisis, and the Korean War. Furthermore, Kennedy warned that the United States should avoid a "rush into a helter-skelter militarism" (Glad, 1980, p. 465).

Moreover, some of the sanctions he chose were opposed by several of his top political advisors. Both Walter Mondale and Stu Eizenstat were opposed to the reinstitution of draft registration on the grounds that it was an overreaction and that it would be politically damaging. Vice-President Mondale strongly objected to the grain embargo on the grounds that it would harm the American farmers (Carter, 1982, p. 476). He also thought that the embargo would be "politically damaging" and that Carter was "overreacting to the Soviet invasion" (Carter, 1982, pp. 476, 482). Secretary of State Vance strongly opposed the Olympic boycott, when the issue was first raised by Mondale at a breakfast meeting on January 11 (Brzezinski, 1983, p. 433).

Both the grain embargo and the Olympic boycott also created serious political problems for Carter both at home and abroad. On the primary campaign trail, presidential aspirants from both parties lined up to take a shot at Carter for the grain embargo. Bob Dole commented that "Carter took a poke at the Soviet Bear and knocked out the American farmer." Ted Kennedy stated that a "weak foreign policy can't be redeemed by suddenly getting tough on farmers." The candidate with the strongest anti-Soviet proclivities, Ronald Reagan, quipped that "pigs, cows, and chickens" had not invaded Afghanistan. He offered the opinion that "no one segment of the economy should be asked to bear the brunt of American countermeasures" against the Soviets (Jordan, 1982, p. 101).

There were also serious problems in winning international support for the grain embargo. Canada, Australia, members of the European community, and Argentina and Brazil all refused to follow the U.S. lead in cutting off the grain sale. France even boycotted a proposed meeting of foreign ministers of the major Western Europe countries and the United States. As French Premier Barre said on February 7, France did not wish to contribute to any reawakening of the Cold War by adopting an extreme attitude. The West German leader, Helmut Schmidt, was also resistant to the effort. As Carter noted in a February 25, 1980 memo to Vance and Brzezinski: "Overall I see nothing encouraging here. F.R.G. opposes any sanctions against Iran or Soviets, are continuing business as usual with S.U., refuse to commit publicly to Olympic boycott, and privately are very critical of us" (quoted in Brzezinski, 1983, p. 462).

The Olympic boycott raised similar problems. The U.S. Olympic Committee (USOC) voted, initially, to "resist political intrusions into the Olympic games." A week later, Lord Killanin, president of the International Olympic Committee (IOC) noted that it would be physically impossible to move the Olympic Games at that stage. Killanin asserted that Carter's proposal was "inappropriate and gauche" and stated that he deplored "athletes being used as pawns in political problems that politicians cannot solve themselves" (Glad, 1980, pp. 461–462).

Despite this early opposition, however, Carter announced in an interview on "Meet the Press" on January 20, that the United States was proposing that the 1980 Summer Olympics be removed from Moscow—through postponement, cancellation, or a boycott—unless the Soviet Union withdrew its troops from Afghanistan within one month. There was an immediate "rally around the flag effect," and Carter won some immediate support for his position. In late January the House of Representatives and the Senate both passed resolutions backing Carter's Olympic stand, and the executive board of the USOC voted unanimously to ask the IOC to move, postpone, or cancel the 1980 Summer Olympics (Glad, 1980).

Yet, there was also considerable opposition at the international level from athletes and their organizations. On February 12, the IOC announced that the 1980 summer games would take place in Moscow as scheduled. In late March, the British, Canadian, and Norwegian Olympic committees voted to attend the Moscow Olympics. At a meeting in Brussels, representatives of the Olympic committee of 16 European nations voted against a boycott of the Moscow games. The British Olympic Association also voted to participate in the Moscow Olympics. After some of the governments had applied pressures, it is true, some of these national associations backed off from their original responses. But the British, French, Italian, Austrian, Belgian, Irish, Dutch, and Swedish committees did stick to their decision to attend the games.

The administration even had to bring out its big guns to bring about American compliance with the boycott. On March 21, meeting with several American athletes in the White House, Carter told them that they had no choice in the matter. They would not go to Moscow. "The decision had been made." USOC representatives were subsequently brought to Washington for top-level discussions with various administration officials who impressed upon them the seriousness of the Afghanistan situation. Corporations were encouraged to reduce or withhold contributions to the USOC unless the organization backed a boycott. Threats were even made to revoke the tax-exempt status of the USOC and to invoke the emergency power in the Amateur Sports Act of 1978 to block federal subsidies to the USOC. In early April, Carter brought out the heavy artillery, threatening to use the Emergency Powers Act to prevent U.S. athletes from traveling to Moscow. In these circumstances, the House of Delegates of the USOC finally voted 1,604 to 797 in favor of the Olympic boycott. Still, one of the two

Americans on the IOC called the USOC vote "disastrous" and accused the U.S. committee of knuckling under to "political pressure."

The intensity of Carter's response to the Soviet intervention in Afghanistan suggests that he took their intervention personally, and the extent of his emotional reaction was somewhat troubling to his Secretary of State, Cyrus Vance (Talbott, 1980, p. 290). The reasons for this reaction, we suggest, cannot be fully understood unless one takes into account the personality and stylistic proclivities described above.

The Soviet intervention was immensely frustrating to Carter. The SALT II treaty had been a centerpiece of his peacemaking and the Soviet intervention ended whatever small chances that treaty might have had of approval in the U.S. Senate. Given his need for accomplishment, and past responses to setbacks, it is not at all surprising to see him laying all responsibility for its demise at the door of Soviet Union and heaping all his frustrations on that country.

The level of his disappointment and frustration has been noted by people close to him. Rosalynn Carter notes in her memoirs that she had never seen "Jimmy more upset than he was the afternoon the Russian invasion was confirmed" (R. Carter, 1984, pp. 314–315). His immediate reaction to the intervention was to state: "There goes SALT II" (R. Carter, 1984, p. 315). In a sense it was a negation of one of the major missions of his presidency.

> He had worked hard for this treaty and had been sure it was gaining support in the Senate. Now the chance for ratifying it would be gone. Of all the goals Jimmy had as president, reducing the threat of nuclear war and preventing an expensive and dangerous arms race was the most important of all to him, and he had the sentiment of the people with him in his efforts for peace. There were no anti-nuclear demonstrations when Jimmy Carter was president. (R. Carter, 1984, pp. 314–315)

The strength of his frustration is also clearly evident in a phone conversation with his Chief of Staff Hamilton Jordan, who was in Atlanta at the time of the invasion. As Jordan later recalled their exchange:

> I put in a call to the President and asked simply if there was anything I could do. "No," he said, "unless you can get the Soviets out of Afghanistan." I thought for a second he was kidding, but his tone made it clear he was frustrated. I offered to go back to Washington immediately but he said no, it would take several days for the Afghanistan conflict to be clarified.
> "As if we didn't already have our hands full with the hostages," I said.
> "This is more serious, Hamilton. Capturing those Americans was an inhumane act committed by a bunch of radicals and condoned by a crazy old man. But this is deliberate aggression that calls into question détente and the way we have been doing business with the Soviets for the past decade. It raises grave questions about Soviet intentions and destroys any chance of getting the SALT Treaty through the Senate. *And that makes the prospects for nuclear war even greater.*
> I was chilled when I heard his analysis." (Jordan, 1982, 99; emphasis added)

Later, in his memoirs, Carter himself indicated his severe disappointment at the loss of SALT II. "Our failure to ratify the SALT II treaty and to secure even more far-reaching agreements on nuclear arms control was the most profound disappointment of my presidency." (Carter, 1982, p. 265)

The anger he felt at this frustration is evident in his commitment to make the Soviet Union pay for what it had done. Right after he was informed of the invasion, he told Rosalynn that "We will have to make sure that Afghanistan will be their Vietnam." He told Hamilton Jordan that "the world simply cannot stand by and permit the Soviet Union to commit this act with impunity. Neither the United States nor any other nation . . . can continue to do business as usual with the Soviet Union" (Jordan, 1982, p. 100). In his memoirs, the President asserts that: "The Soviet Union, like Iran, had acted outrageously, and at the same time had made a tragic miscalculation. I was determined to lead the rest of the world in making it as costly as possible" (Carter, 1982, p. 472).

He was able to adopt and follow through on the two sanctions that would create serious problems for him, because that response was fueled by several psychological needs. Through his commitments to those efforts, he could both demonstrate his toughness and take on the role of moral leader of the free world. Brzezinski, who certainly knew the man, even showed him how he could reconcile the apparently contradictory values of taking a tough stance against the Soviet Union and bringing peace to the world. As the National Security Advisor wrote in his memoirs:

> Knowing how deeply Carter felt about SALT, and sharing with him a genuine sense of regret about the way things had developed, I commented that I understood his desire to go down in history as a President Wilson but added that "before you are a President Wilson you have to be for a few years a President Truman." By that I meant that the President first had to convince the American public and the world of his toughness, and only then, during his second term, could he adopt a more Wilsonian approach. (Brzezinski, 1983, p. 432)

There are also indications that Carter welcomed these opportunities for sacrifice as a means of displaying his virtue. As he noted in his diary (Carter, 1982, p. 473), "some of these moves would require substantial sacrifice and would be very difficult to implement, but we would not flinch from any one of them." Regarding draft registration, he "listened to all the arguments they marshalled against the idea, but decided to proceed" (Carter, 1982, pp. 482–485). At the time he was considering the grain embargo, as Hamilton Jordan later recalled, Carter seemed to be aware of some of the political risks he was running." God knows . . . I have walked the fields of Iowa and know those farmers and realize that I promised them in the seventy-six campaign that I would never embargo grains except in the case of a national emergency! But this is an emergency and I'm going to have to impose the embargo and we'll just have to make the best of it. Farmers are patriotic people (quoted in Jordan, 1982, p. 100). With regard to the Olympic boycott, he later noted, "I did not want to damage the Olympic movement, but at the same time it seemed unconscionable to be guests of the Soviets while they were involved in a bloody suppression of the people of Afghanistan—an act condemned by an overwhelming majority of the nations of the world" (Carter, 1982, p. 481).

Carter himself drew attention to his ability to meet the difficulties he confronted during this period of time as an indication of his toughness. At one of his foreign policy breakfast meetings with advisers, the President asserted that: "There is a tendency on the frazzled edges of government to drift away from the tough decisions we made. I am not going to abide that. We cannot wince now or seem unsure of ourselves" (Jordan, 1982, p. 112). Later, he would even suggest in his diary that he was cooler about these matters than more ordinary men. On July 31, 1980, he wrote, "I have a lot of problems on my shoulders, but, strangely enough, I feel better as they pile up. My main concern is propping up the people around me who tend to panic (and who might possibly have a better picture of the situation than I do!)." (Carter, 1982, p. 524)

CONCLUSIONS

This chapter has attempted to demonstrate that Jimmy Carter's personality had a decisive impact on the style and substance of his decisions in response to the Afghanistan crisis. Carter's personality, with its grandiose and narcissistic elements, as well as his inability to understand the value trade-offs necessary to achieve his goals as president were instrumental in his response to the Soviet invasion of Afghanistan, as well as his dealings with Moscow throughout his administration.

This is not to suggest that personality variables alone can explain foreign policy behavior; these factors, nevertheless, neither can be ignored. Such factors, however, are most apt to be important in times of crisis, real or perceived, when leaders are under a great deal of stress. It is under such conditions that idiosyncratic personality characteristics become most decisive. Individuals, of course, always operate within an environment that gives them a menu of choices. But personality can to various degrees determine how one responds to that menu. Through an integrative approach that demonstrates how environmental factors such as domestic politics and national security considerations interact with personality, we are better able to comprehend foreign policy decision making and international behavior.

NOTES

1. Rosati (1987), in his rigorous and systematic study of the Carter administration's foreign policy, notes that Carter's image of the Soviet Union hardened over his four years in office, from a neo-Wilsonian position in the first year to a cold war orientation by the fourth. It is our contention that both the Wilsonian and the hard-line image were present throughout.

2. Public opinion polls in 1979 (see Gallup, 1979) showed a modest 57 percent approval for the normalization agreement with the People's Republic of China. Although this represents a respectable majority, it did not indicate a "massive applause" for the agreement.

3. The authors credit Jimmy Carter for his efforts at putting human rights on the U.S. foreign policy agenda. Our criticism stems from its inconsistent application. Carter was critical of Moscow while embracing, for example, the repressive regime of the Shah of Iran. Furthermore, Carter's style in addressing human rights questions was very troublesome to the Soviets. Finally, and most importantly, he failed to see the value trade-off between the goals of human rights and reaching arms control agreements with the Soviets.

4. In these respects, Carter was echoing Brzezinski's views that the United States should take the occasion to push the Soviet Union even harder.

REFERENCES

Allen, H. (1976). Just plain folks. *Washington Post/Potomac,* August 15, p. 28.

Brzezinski, Z. (1980a). Interview. *Wall Street Journal,* January 15, p. 2.

Brzezinski, Z. (1980b). Remarks before Woman's National Democratic Club in Washington D.C., *White House Press Release,* February 21.

Brzezinski, Z. (1983). *Power and principle: Memoirs of the national security advisor, 1977–1981.* New York: Farrar, Straus, Giroux.

Carter, J. (1976a). Speech to Georgia Association of Broadcasters. *Addresses,* June 13, p. 136.

Carter, J. (1976b). *Why not the best?* New York: Bantam Books.

Carter, J. (1977a). The President's address to the General Assembly, March 17. *Presidential Documents, 13,* 97–402.

Carter, J. (1977b). The President's remarks with reporters, March 30. *Presidential Documents, 13,* 469–473.

Carter, J. (1977c). The President's address at Commencement Exercises at the University [Notre Dame], May 22. *Presidential Documents, 13,* 773–779.

Carter, J. (1977d). The President's news conference, June 30. *Presidential Documents, 13,* 951–960.

Carter, J. (1977e). The President's news conference, July 12. *Presidential Documents, 13,* 985–993.

Carter, J. (1977f). Remarks at the 31st Annual Meeting of the Southern Legislative Conference, July 21. *Presidential Documents, 13,* 1063–1069.

Carter, J. (1978a). Address at Wake Forest University, March 17. *Presidential Documents, 14,* 529–538.

Carter, J. (1978b). Address at the Commencement Exercises [United States Naval Academy], June 7. *Presidential Documents, 14,*

Carter, J. (1979). Remarks to reporters, September 7. *Presidential Documents, 15,* 1602–1603.

Carter, J. (1980a). State of the Union Address, January 23. *State Department Bulletin,* February, pp. A–D.

Carter, J. (1980b). Address before the American Society of Newspaper Editors, April 10. *State Department Bulletin,* May, pp. 3–6.

Carter, J. (1982). *Keeping faith: Memoirs of a president.* New York: Bantam Books.

Carter, L. (1977). Miss Lillian: My two sons. *Ladies Home Journal,* August, pp. 36–37.

Carter, R. (1984). *The first lady from Plains.* Boston: Houghton Mifflin.

Elovitz, P. (1977). Three days in Plains. *Journal of Psychohistory, 5,* 175–200.

Gallup, G. (1979). *The Gallup Poll, Public Opinion 1979,* Wilmington, DE: Scholarly Resources.

Glad, B. (1980). *Jimmy Carter: In search of the great White House.* New York: Norton.

Glad, B. (1989). Personality, political and group process variables in foreign policy decision making: Jimmy Carter and the Iranian hostage crisis. *International Political Science Review,*35–61.

Greenstein, F. (1967). The impact of personality on politics: An attempt to clear away the underbrush. *American Political Science Review, 10,* 629–641.

Holsti, O. (1971). Crisis, stress, and decisionmaking. *International Journal of Social Science, 23,* 53–67.

Horney, K. (1950). *Neurosis and human growth: The struggle toward self-realization.* New York: Norton.

Jordan, H. (1982). *Crisis: The last year of the Carter presidency.* New York: Putnam.

Rosati, J. (1987). *The Carter Administration's quest for global community: The impact of beliefs on behavior.* Columbia: University of South Carolina Press.

Safran, C. (1976). The women in Jimmy Carter's life. *Redbook,* October, pp. 82–95.

Talbott, S. (1980). *Endgame: The inside story of SALT II.* New York: Harper & Row.

Vance, C. (1983). *Hard choices: Critical years in America's foreign policy.* New York: Simon and Schuster.

9

Presidents Carter and Sadat
The Repudiation of the Peacemakers

Paul H. Elovitz and Mohammed Shaalan

INTRODUCTION (Paul H. Elovitz)

Why Jimmy Carter and Anwar el Sadat? Why include an American and an Egyptian president in the same chapter? The answer to this question is that events brought them together as few leaders of a great power and a Third World country have ever come together. A strong personal connection was forged during the long peacemaking sessions at Camp David. Carter's feelings for Sadat were unambiguous. To the American, Sadat was "my wonderful friend" and "a great and good man" (Carter, 1982, p. 269). He was his "favorite person," "it was love at first sight and quite genuine," according to the American national security adviser who compares the "expansive, impetuous, and bold Egyptian" and the "highly controlled, precise Georgian with the computerlike mind" (Brzezinski, 1983, p. 24). When Sadat was worried at the Camp David negotiations, Carter's comments were, "I will represent your interests as if they were my own. You are my brother." He hoped he would "never let you down. You are probably the most admired statesman in the United States" (Brzezinski, 1983, p. 284). Sadat "was family" and Carter identified with him to an unusual degree bordering on "hero worship" (Brzezinski, 1983, p. 24). The Egyptian reciprocated with "my people

PAUL H. ELOVITZ, Ph.D. • Former President of the International Psychohistorical Association (1988–1990); Founder and Director of the Psychohistory Forum (1983–); a founding faculty member at Ramapo College in New Jersey; a psychotherapist in private practice; editor of *Historical and Psychological Inquiry* (1990). MOHAMMED SHAALAN, M.D. • Professor of Psychiatry, Al Azhar University, Cairo, Egypt; Private Practice, 10 Abdel Hamid Lotfi Street, Dokki, Cairo, Egypt.

Politics and Psychology: Contemporary Psychodynamic Perspectives, edited by Joan Offerman-Zuckerberg. Plenum Press, New York, 1991.

and I are grateful to you . . . I shall always be proud of our friendship" (Brze-zinski, 1983, p. 284). When his "wonderful friend" was assassinated, ex-President Carter was extremely upset. He wanted to attend the funeral as a private citizen rather than as the U.S. representative so that he could more privately mourn his friend (Carter, 1982).

There are many similarities between the two presidents. Each mingled with and identified strongly with the common people. Their autobiographies even begin with a similar tie both to the common people and history: "My life on the farm during the Great Depression more nearly resembles farm life of fully 2,000 years ago than farm life today," writes Carter (1976, p. 7); and "I, Anwar el Sadat, a peasant born and brought up on the banks of the Nile—where man first wit-nessed the dawn of time" (Sadat, 1979, p. 1). Each portrayed himself as less privileged in his childhood than in fact he was. Each had a military education, started his career as a soldier, and abruptly left the military. Each came from a small town and neither was viewed as presidential prior to assuming the highest office. Both saw themselves as peacemakers. Both men shared the persona of the messiah—the savior. Both felt for the Palestinian refugees, sought to improve their plight, and viewed the PLO as their legitimate representative (Carter, 1985). Both were repudiated by their constituents: Carter by the electorate and Sadat by bullets. Both men unconsciously sabotaged themselves: narcissistic issues were their downfall. Carter was stubborn and, at times, unresponsive. Sadat was self-involved and grandiose. The Achilles' heel of each was a psychic defense against deep-seated insecurities. Each man's vision was aborted prematurely.

Ironically, throughout their lives, both knew how to take negatives and turn them to positive advantage; specifically, each took certain humiliating expe-riences and situations and used them to transform his life. Carter felt utterly humiliated in his first encounter with Admiral Rickover and used it as a focal point for the development of his own ego ideal. Denigrated in 1976 as a Southern, small-town peanut farmer, he turned these negatives to advantage by successfully campaigning for the presidency as an outsider running against the establishment. He proudly used peanut power. Sadat was at a low point of his life in British-controlled Egypt in prison cell 54 as a suspected traitor in the post-World War II period when he declared that this is when his "self" became liberated. Though General Sharon's forces were within striking distance of Cairo at the end of the Yom Kippur (October) War and he was saved only by Russian and American diplomatic intervention, Sadat declared Egypt the victor, and thus was able to honorably enter into peace negotiations. Both showed resiliency in the face of most adversities.

Despite the similarities, the areas of contrast are also quite numerous. Carter was extremely controlled and Sadat quite impulsive. The inhibited, analytic American admired the Egyptian's ability to more freely express his emotions and to make the grand gesture for peace on the flight to Jerusalem. Carter revealed no signs of Sadat's grandiosity; any grandiose impulses that he had were probably displaced onto the people. Sadat's self-aggrandizement showed itself at times such as when he remembered himself, though a prisoner, as totally having the warden in his control and walking out of the prison at will (Sadat, 1978). The same type of self-serving reconstructing of events occurred in his recollection of the

Yom Kippur War. Sadat declared that he had defeated Israel and then, "for the previous ten days I had been fighting—entirely alone—against the Americans with their modern weapons" (Sadat, 1979, p. 263). Sadat's self-aggrandizement also took the form of a type of "presidential monarchy" (Hinnebusch, 1985, p. 78) that is unimaginable in Carter. The American president liked to be called by his informal name while the Egyptian preferred to be addressed in the style of a caliph. One carried his own bag and the other had the accoutrements of royalty: "pompous uniforms, the entourage, barber, masseur, valet that accompanied him, the numerous luxurious Presidential residences, the repossession of Farouk's Abdin palace." This was also in contrast to the austere simplicity of Sadat's predecessor (Hinnebusch, 1985, p. 84). Sadat gave away Egyptian antiquities to his foreign friends as if they were his own while his relatives looted the government (Heikel, 1983). Carter wanted to be "servant" rather than ruler of the people while Sadat saw himself as head of an authoritarian family and regularly referred to "my children" in his speeches in contrast to Nasser's "my brothers" (Hinnebusch, 1985, p. 84).

Carter was an eldest son while Sadat was almost denied an education because he was not. In their years out of government, Carter made his living as a peanut farmer and warehouseman and Sadat as a journalist. Carter maintained a close partnership with his wife Rosalynn while Sadat helped his political career by divorcing his peasant wife in favor of Jehan, a well-educated and sophisticated woman. Sadat took the vice-presidential route to power while Carter won the office as an outsider running against the establishment. While serving as an officer, the Egyptian was jailed as a traitor for being connected to an assassination plot. For the Georgian, that would have been unimaginable. Carter was most inhibited in his expression of aggression while Sadat "would make Theodore Roosevelt sound like a pacifist" (Brzezinski, 1983, p. 24). Each responded differently to falling out of favor with his constituency. Carter worked harder and suffered in silence while Sadat jailed dissidents and slept with a gun by his bed.

There are also contrasts in the approach of the two authors of this chapter. The American is an historian, psychotherapist, and Jew who emphasizes childhood and personality while the Egyptian is a Muslim psychiatrist who discusses group issues in a personal manner. They differ sharply in their views of Sadat. The chapter is all the richer for this diversity. In conclusion, with all of Jimmy Carter's and Anwar el Sadat's connections, similarities, and differences, each man has left his mark on the twentieth century.

JIMMY CARTER AND THE IRAN HOSTAGE CRISIS
(Paul H. Elovitz)

The Iran hostage crisis was Jimmy Carter's political downfall. The Carter presidency, which had made a giant step toward peace in the Middle East and dealt realistically and well with many of the country's challenges, floundered and became mired in the morass of the hostage crisis.

The scenario of events leading up to this turning point in the Carter administration is well documented. The crisis began a year before the election on

November 4, 1979, and was not a complete surprise to the State Department, the White House staff, or the President. The seizure of American embassy workers in Tehran prompted reporters, governmental officials, and the public to ask if the incident could have and should have been predicted and therefore prevented. The answer was yes. White House informants reported on page one of the *New York Times* on November 18, 1979 that President Carter was well aware of the dangers of letting the Shah of Iran into the United States for medical treatment. They divulged that his response to the advice to admit the Shah was, "when they [the revolutionaries in Tehran] seize our people [the embassy staff], what advice will you give me then?" (Gwertzman, 1979, p. 1) The adviser's answer is not recorded. In his memoirs, Carter (1982) gives a substantially similar account.

The President knew the situation in Iran was volatile under Khomeini and that there was a grave risk that hostages would be taken as they had been earlier in the year. Iranians were in the midst of a violent revolution and the most vilified person in the world was the Shah, who was forced into exile in January 1979. He had been a close ally of the United States who had known seven previous American presidents, but he had also helped engineer the oil crisis which hurt the U.S. economy.

The President and the leading advisers knew that there were dangerous political implications in letting the Shah into the United States for cancer treatment that he could get elsewhere. Giscard d'Estaing of France cautioned that it would be wiser for the deposed Iranian to stay in the Middle East (Brzezinski, 1983). When Mohammed Reza Pahlavi was allowed to come to the Cornell University Medical Center in New York, U.S. embassy workers in Tehran were seized as hostages. Carter's worst fears were realized.

As a result, Carter found himself in a most difficult situation because of the complexities of the relations between the two countries. In Iran, there recently had been American military advisers and over 50,000 U.S. workers drawing high salaries by aiding the process of Westernization. With the revolution most American workers had left because of terminated contracts and the intense anti-Western, anti-American feelings among the Muslim fundamentalists who now dominated the society. The diplomatic ramifications of Carter's decision were great, but so also were the economic investments of each country in the other as well as trade. There were complications such as a number of Iranians living in the United States and some intermarriages between the two peoples. It was too complicated a relationship to easily slam a door and have Americans on one side and Iranians on the other.

What options were open to the President at the beginning of his 14-month crisis? Diplomacy was the first option and the one pursued until the resolution of the crisis. When the hostages were seized, the United States protested strongly to Iran and the United Nations and sought diplomatic help from friendly governments. Waiting for an Iranian government more friendly to the United States to come to power and release the hostages was a fond hope in Washington. Economic sanctions were known to be slow but had the potential for success. The option of apologizing and handing over the Shah to Iran was never seriously considered because it would have been considered too humiliating for a great power. Letting the crisis blow over and quietly making a deal with the revolutionary government is the type of policy usually pursued in these situations. Massive military retaliation or the threat of it was tempting as frustration built up. One difficulty with this option was that the students who seized the American diplomats were not directly controlled by Khomeini. Less drastic alternatives were a naval blockade or an Entebbe-type rescue mission to quickly seize the hostages and fly them out before the Iranians knew what was happening. Diverting attention in a Grenada-type "feel-good" invasion as Reagan did after the humiliation of the slaughter of hundreds of marines in Lebanon was also a possibility. These were the difficult options that the President and the State Department had to face.

The crisis dominated the news. ABC News Nightline, initially a special program called "America Held Hostage," was a news program started specifically to keep track of the hostage crisis. Though there was nothing new about a diplomatic crisis dominating the headlines, it was unique that the news did not quickly switch to another issue. The lead story on today's news is usually quite different than that of a week or month ago. Though the intensity is often the same, the specific subject is different. The hostage crisis was the issue that simply did not go away for the remainder of the Carter presidency. Every morning, afternoon, and evening, television, radio, and newspapers unrelentingly brought it to mind. Average citizens tied yellow ribbons around the trees on their front lawns as a reminder. Carter was never able to escape from the Iranian albatross.

Politicians identify problems and promise solutions in neat packages. For example, Reagan promised a war on drugs and publicized a number of actions against the growing, transport, and use of controlled substances. Yet, the reality of politics is that problems are more often forgotten rather than solved. Carter, like every president before him, had issues that he wanted forgotten. Some issues were such that if he did something, he would make things worse. He expressed his concern and hoped that the public would turn its attention elsewhere. Why was the hostage situation not forgotten like most problems? Why did the American public not take President Carter off the hook? It mostly ignored the failure of Reagan's war on drugs and even elected its director as president in 1988. It was clear that if Carter used military force to attempt to get the hostages out of Tehran, they in all probability would be killed along with many other Americans in Iran, as well as innocent Iranians. Such action could also have ignited a much larger war that might involve the Soviet Union. Inaction might be frustrating, but the United States has had its citizens held as hostages at other times and places, ignoring their plight despite their families' appeals. American hostages had never before dominated the consciousness of the nation as in the Iran hostage crisis. It was as if the government itself was held hostage by the fear of the consequences of its own actions.

"America Held Hostage!" was the common headline that reflected the feelings of average people. Pierre Salinger (1981) used it as the title of a book describing the crisis. A few journalists explicitly began to write about Jimmy Carter as a wimp, breaking an unspoken prohibition against direct journalistic denigration of the president as a weakling. The idealization of the presidency began to crumble. By 1979, Carter appeared as all-too-human and vulnerable. The sense of

Carter, and ultimately America, as impotent began to dominate public conscious-ness. Subsequently, the crisis cost Carter reelection to the presidency.

The Iran hostage crisis made the "Reagan revolution" possible. Prior to this period, Ronald W. Reagan was viewed by most Americans as being much too radical, too extreme to be president. In 1978, Easterners were still making jokes about "Ronald McDonald." Political pundits were sure that a movie actor, a divorced man, and a man in his seventh decade of life could not possibly be elected president. The Iran crisis was so serious a blow to Americans' national identity that it played a crucial role in inducing the voters to elect a strong conservative as president, moving the country to a more right-wing position than had seemed possible a few years before. Post-World War II Americans who had seen their country as the most powerful, democratic, rich, and generous nation on earth now felt consumed by frustration and anger over the powerlessness of power—the impotence of power. Their government could move battle fleets and nuclear submarines around the world and send astronauts into space, but it could not change the nightly news reports. America's president could destroy the world with the press of a button, but he could not get 52 hostages out of Tehran. The pressure for action on the former peanut farmer from Georgia was enormous. Carter, even more than America itself, was obsessed by the Iran hostage crisis.

How could he get the hostages safely out? If he took military action, there was a likelihood that they would die in the attempt. Yet, until he succeeded in getting them out, it felt as if every finger in America was pointing at him through every media outlet. Intense public pressure spurred him to plan an Entebbe-type rescue attempt in late April of 1980, which was later aborted. Carter's attempts at diplomacy, economic sanctions, and rescue all failed, leaving him discredited before those he governed.

Americans felt as totally impotent as their president. But maybe it was this particular president who was impotent? Perhaps, a president representing older values could get the hostages' freedom and end the feeling of America held hostage? Enough voters thought that Ronald Reagan would not have allowed the mess in Tehran to happen and elected him to the presidency to replace Jimmy Carter. In fact, the hostages were released as the California conservative actually took the oath of office (Jordan, 1982). Why?

To start with, the Ayatollah now had more control over the revolutionary students and hostages than a year before. He freed the hostages because he thought Ronald Reagan might use massive military force against Iran. Under Carter, however, Khomeini had feared military intervention less than the domes-tic consequences of release. There is an irony in this situation in that Jimmy Carter had more military experience than all but a handful of his predecessors. After all, he was a career naval officer who was educated at Annapolis and who served in the nuclear fleet under Admiral Rickover. Unlike Reagan, who was in Hollywood making training movies in World War II, Carter was trained in the skills of war and crisis management and had hands-on experience in the clean up after a nuclear accident at Chalk River, Canada. Carter's failure had not come from a lack of military knowledge or experience. He knew much better than Reagan what the military could and could not do. Then why had Carter failed to extricate himself from the hostage crisis? A closer look at his personality, background, and need for popular approval will help us to understand this puzzle.

The man from Plains promised an open presidency. Immediately after his inauguration, as he strolled down Pennsylvania Avenue with a friendly smile, he inadvertently exposed his vulnerability along with his charm. As he walked with his family he announced in every gesture that he would forego the bullet-proof limousines, protocol, and pomp that protect and isolate the American president. Jimmy Carter would be the people's president. The eyes of the nation had not been so intensely focused on a slow procession down Pennsylvania Avenue since the funeral of President Kennedy. Yet even in his first year as president, Carter faced tremendous opposition to his policies and uneasiness over his personality. Why had Carter, who worked so hard to win popular favor and risked an assassin's bullet to make his walk, aroused such early opposition?

The answer may lie in part in unconscious desires within his personality that require opposition. The power of unconscious desires to thwart and undermine conscious intentions can make victims of presidents as they can of all human beings. The tragic careers of Woodrow Wilson and Richard Nixon illustrate how strong the will to self-defeat can be in powerful men. Wilson's uncompromising determination to have the League of Nations passed on his terms, or not at all, led his great opponent in the Senate, Henry Cabot Lodge, to comment that Wilson would be his chief ally in stopping the League. Wilson martyred himself in his attempt to preserve the League as God's sacred handiwork. In Nixon's case, a particularly striking example of how he unconsciously defeated himself occurred during the Watergate crisis. In the course of a major presidential address intended to prove to the nation that he was a strong and capable leader despite allegations of wrongdoing, Nixon stumbled and said, "Your thoroughly discredited president . . . I mean . . . " (personal observation, April, 1973). His one Freudian slip negated the rhetoric of the entire speech.

The reader may wonder how and why a president can culminate a successful political career by acting in a self-defeating way. One answer lies in the specific personality characteristics necessary for a person first to run successfully for the presidency and then to function effectively as president. In order to be elected, Jimmy Carter had to be immensely hardworking, attuned to the public mood, and sufficiently ambiguous so that people could project onto him their varied and contradictory needs and aspirations. But once into the office, the president must cope with new problems for which he is not adequately prepared. The loneliness of responsibility is compounded by the people's unrealistic expectation that he is an all-powerful parental figure who can somehow make all things right. The difference between the president-elect's expectations of power and his actual power once in office is immense. President Carter had difficulty ridding the Oval Office of mice because the Departments of Interior and Agriculture could not decide under whose jurisdiction the problem fell. The preceding anecdote illustrates this dilemma. Carter's reaction to these difficulties was to work all the harder and to place himself under tremendous strain. The intense public scrutiny of the White House denied him the privacy essential to rejuvenate himself in the warmth of family and friendship.

Jimmy's strengths and weaknesses in facing the enormous and often un-realistic pressures on a president can be understood in terms of his childhood experiences. There can be no doubt that he gained great sources of strength from Earl and Lillian Carter. Yet that same childhood also reflects clear indications of conflict and uncertainty. This characteristic combination of strengths and conflicts is revealed in Jimmy's seventh-grade health booklets, under the title, "Healthy Mental Habits." There he states:

> There are certain habits of thinking which have a good effect upon health. If you think in the right way, you'll develop: (1) The habit of expecting to accomplish what you attempt. (2) The habit of expecting to like other people and to [sic] have them like you. (3) The habit of deciding quickly what you want to do, and doing it. (4) The habit of "sticking to it." (5) The habit of welcoming *fearfully* [sic: italics added—he meant "fearlessly"], all wholesome ideas and experiences. (6) The person who wants to build up good mental habits should avoid the idle day-dreams; should give up worry and anger; hatred and envy; should neither fear nor be ashamed of anything that is honest and purposeful. (Carter, nd)

Twelve-year-old Jimmy Carter displays both a remarkable ability to enum-erate the habits that enabled him to be elected president at the age of fifty-two and the unconscious doubts that thwarted the implementation of his programs. He expected to do what was held to be impossible, namely, win the presidency as a Southerner. Friendliness, decisiveness, and stick-to-itiveness were key person-ality characteristics that enabled him to succeed in his campaigns. But what is most striking about this methodical school exercise in self-examination is the slip of "fearfully" for what was obviously intended to read "fearlessly." From the way that the letters are written over, it appears that Jimmy first wrote "fearlessly" and then changed it to "fearfully," disclosing his conflict in the very act of correcting himself. His error and the remainder of the passage reflect some profound doubts about himself and his behavior. By it, he is questioning the wholesomeness of his ideas and experiences. The feared unwholesomeness is included in the list of idle daydreams, worry, anger, hatred, envy, fear, and shame.

Carter's autobiography (1976) suggests that his anxieties about controlling his emotions had some real basis in his history. The father who beat him with a peach switch and shamed him was "fearful." A careful reading reveals that he was envious and angry toward his younger sisters and brother, whom he felt were favored over him. Would it not also be safe to assume that a boy who from the age of five wanted to go far away, to sea, was a daydreamer? But Jimmy wanted to be loved, and hatred and anger were emotions too frightening for him to acknowledge. This little boy, who struggles to be brave and to repudiate so many uncomfortable feelings, still lives in the man, though he cannot be seen beneath the Carter smile.

The Jimmy Carter who emerged from this childhood was a young man with a driving need for success and much ambivalence about authority. It is not difficult to see Jimmy's conflicts in later life as he contemplated the presidency. Although he had once looked on presidents and on the presidency with reverence and awe, his autobiography reveals that by 1972 he could no longer see either President Nixon or the Democratic contenders in these terms. He had to devalue authority, about which he was ambivalent, in order to see himself as a possible president. At the start of the 1976 campaign, he confessed that neither he nor his advisers could comfortably refer to him in terms of the phrase, "Mr. President."

Jimmy deals with his conflicts by going out into the world and proving himself in competition with others. He entered more primaries and worked harder than any of his competitors. Yet it was characteristic of him to begin his skillfully planned campaign by systematically and ruthlessly examining his assets and "shortcomings." It was, he admitted, "a time-consuming process," but he also declared it to be "one of the most enjoyable experiences for my staff, my friends, and my family" (Carter, 1976, p. 159). It is no accident that Jimmy Carter ran for president during a period of intense distrust of politicians and of the political structure. As a self-doubting man, Jimmy reflected the national mood. He seemed to recognize this and to capitalize on it. Rather than directly claiming to be the best hope for America's leadership, he let the title of his autobiography, *Why Not the Best?*, rhetorically imply it for him.

During Carter's campaign every potential liability was converted into an asset. He was, after all, only a small-town farmer, far from the centers of communication, finance, and power. But as an outsider, he could be perceived to be free from the taint of Watergate-stained Washington. He proudly acknowledged the "fault" of being "as stubborn as a South Georgia turtle" in his determination to serve the people (Carter, 1976, p. 91). "Peanut power," proclaimed by his neighbors who formed the Peanut Brigade, was his response to the denigration of him by many as a mere farmer. The message that he is the best only in connection with the goodness of the American people is successfully conveyed throughout his autobiography and his campaign. But he needed not only to have the people believe in his identity as one of them, he needed to believe it himself. When he writes about himself apart from the people, he comes across as small, lonely, and weak, which is why he struggles so to bridge the "chasm between people and government" (p. 168).

To be "a man of the people" is a political cliche, but in Jimmy Carter's case the idea is central to both his self-image and his political success. Running for president offered Jimmy the fantastic feeling of oneness with the American people, a feeling that he craved. The constant contact with the average citizen released his tremendous reserves of unconflicted energy. The exhausted reporters covering his grueling campaign marveled that this candidate could work continuously on long, turbulent flights, while they sipped martinis and complained about the miseries of campaigning.

Jimmy gained stamina from both the exaltation of touching and otherwise being in direct contact with the people and from identification with Earl Carter and Admiral Hyman Rickover, men whose leadership, energy, and capacity for innovation he emulated. It may seem paradoxical that Jimmy gained strength both as a representative of the people against the discredited fathers of Washington and by identification with the partially discredited father of his childhood and the father surrogate—Admiral Rickover. Since the unconscious mind can harbor many contradictory attitudes, it was not difficult for Jimmy to draw strength from such disparate sources. As a young naval lieutenant, Jimmy had vainly attempted to measure up to the standards of the hard-driving Rickover by working for the duration of a cross-country flight that they made together. His ability as a candidate to duplicate Rickover's feat was made possible by a feeling of oneness with both the people and his father surrogate. The campaign represented a unique opportunity to bask in a feeling of unity with the nation as both a man of the people and their perfect leader.

Jimmy Carter's ability to function as president was based on his perception of leaders and those whom they lead. One of the reasons that he went into politics was that he wanted to gain the love and admiration of the people. The other reason is that he identified with the men in charge. To Jimmy, concern for the people is associated with his mother, Lillian, while authority is associated with his father, Earl. In his boyhood fantasies, Jimmy could be both the perfect authority and the people's strongest advocate. Since his models of authority were respected but not loved, he became conflicted when he tried to be both the man of the people and the good daddy.

The stronger influence on Jimmy was clearly that of his mother Lillian, who nursed the poor blacks of Plains (Carter, 1976). At age sixty-eight, her devotion to helping poor black people was expressed by her going to India as a Peace Corps volunteer to work in a clinic. Her love and devotion to the needy was so great that her health was almost destroyed and her children insisted that she return home (Carter & Spann, 1977). Jimmy was also influenced by her interest in politics and by the Populist tradition supported by his maternal grandfather, Jim Jack Gordy.

In the neighborhood of Jimmy's childhood, "the common people" were black, and this automatic identification remains with him today. He identified with the aspirations of his black neighbors who rooted for Joe Louis in the second Louis–Schmeling fight, even though Earl Carter placed race above nationality and supported the fighter from Nazi Germany over the American. Jimmy, who had to prove himself to his father constantly, watched his black neighbors as they thanked "Mr. Earl" for the loan of his radio, which they then carried to a shantyhouse across the street. As they listened to the fight, they let out a tremendous cheer for Louis. Jimmy had to stay home under the close supervision of his father. It was painfully obvious to him that despite their poverty and subordinate position in Southern society, the blacks of the Archery section of Plains had more freedom than he to express openly their support for Joe Louis, the American victor. In the adult Carter, who was courageous enough to stand up to his racist neighbors for the rights of his black neighbors, one can sense the presence of the little boy who wanted to shout his delight in Louis's victory. He has had to contend with both redneck Georgia racists and the racist within himself who identified with the values of "Mr. Earl" and felt superior to the people on his plantation (Mazlish & Diamond, 1979).

The influence of a racist father and a more liberal mother helps to explain how Jimmy could be elected governor of Georgia with both the redneck and the black vote. Both of these groups responded to his energetic campaign, in which he reached out to hundreds of thousands of people. His ease at being among ordinary folk was evident when he moved his family into a low-cost housing project in Plains in 1953 at a time when it was not economically necessary to do so. After his unsuccessful campaign for governor in 1966, Jimmy used his vacation to work with the poor and spread the gospel among them. In running for president, he shook more hands than any other candidate, and even after the election he went to town meetings in Massachusetts and Mississippi to meet the people. In all these relationships, Jimmy has the ability to take the hands of both men and women and say "I love you" in the unself-conscious manner of the born-again fundamentalist Christian. The genuineness of this commitment is apparent in Carter, who is no longer running for office, continuing to donate vacation time to joining with poor people to build low-cost housing (Carter & Carter, 1987).

An incident a week before the 1976 election that occurred in the home of Billy Wise, a childhood schoolmate and friend of Jimmy Carter, comes to mind. At a kitchen-table discussion of the friendly childhood competition between Billy and Jimmy, an unspoken question hung in the air. Why was Jimmy about to become president, while Billy, who had defeated Jimmy in debating and other school activities, was still in the plumbing and heating business? Billy, who had become bogged down in such questions, looked across at his wife who was washing the dishes and said, "Of one thing I'm sure, even when he's president, when he meets Betty and me on the street it'll be Jimmy and Billy and Betty. And when he sees us, he'll come right up and give Betty a kiss and a hug, just like always" (personal communication, October 1976). The genuine conviction with which he said this, and his wife's smile, conveyed their satisfaction with the warm, human quality that Jimmy imparts and derives at such encounters.

The paradox is that when Jimmy's love for the people is spread too thinly, it becomes phony and meaningless. In the throes of campaigning, he once shook the hand of a store mannequin and thanked her for her support (Turner, 1976). People soon realize that to love everyone is in effect to love no one, and as a result they quickly become bored or disenchanted with those who profess love for everyone whom they meet.

Even if Jimmy could genuinely love everyone, it would have little bearing on the realities of leadership. A successful president recognizes the severe limits of his power and effects change only through his willingness to compromise. He must coordinate the demands of a vast governmental bureaucracy and a host of special-interest groups with the needs of the American people. The president is like a man riding on the back of a tiger in public. He must hold on, but remain calm and dignified, lest the onlookers panic and cause the tiger to run wild. To maintain the credibility of power, the president must preserve the fiction of being in control at all times.

A major problem for Carter was his contradictory vision of the role of the leader: the good president as extraordinarily powerful, knowledgeable, and decisive and at the same time as a compassionate man of the people waiting to greet them at the White House door (Turner, 1976). Jimmy Carter wanted to heal the rift between the goodness of the American people and the corruption of Watergate Washington by bringing integrity and competence to government. When, after the election, he said, "I am no big shot. I am not anybody's boss. I want to be everybody's servant," he was reflecting his own contradictory viewpoints, presenting a confusing message to the world (Adler, 1977, p. 119). Because "my strength comes directly from the populace," Jimmy was extraordinarily fearful of the detachment that is the fate of modern presidents (Adler, 1977, p. 120). Paradoxically, he presents both Earl Carter and Admiral Rickover as emotionally detached leaders. As America's leader he was unable to emulate their capacity for innovation and hard work without losing the contact with the people that was so necessary to his psychic well-being.

During the 1976 campaign, Jimmy offered himself as a political messiah—presenting himself as a humble man from the backwoods who had come to serve the people. It is no accident that fundamentalist Christian supporters began putting "J.C. Saves" bumper stickers on their cars. To the extent that Jimmy saw himself as a messiah, he was susceptible to politically self-destructive behavior, as well as to being perceived as being politically naive. As much as mankind longs for a savior, everyone knows that the fate of Christ and other messiahs is to be sacrificed. He clearly had some concern about living through his presidency, since he told students in 1976 "that if I am elected and *if I live*" (italics added; Turner, 1976, p. 10). In the Iran hostage crisis he chose to sacrifice his political future rather than the lives of others by not choosing popular military actions that would have resulted in many deaths. If there had been no other choices, then his self-sacrificing decision would have been most admirable. But in fact there were alternatives that would have been better both for America and for the president from Plains.

Carter always has had some awareness of the self-defeating tendencies that led him to look at the world "fearfully" at the age of twelve. Shortly before becoming president, he declared, "I relish open conflict a little too much. I don't know why I like it so much, but I do" (Carter, 1982). He then explained that he would attempt to involve the Congress in the legislative process to avoid the problems that open conflict brings. He did not involve Congress. When for his own political survival he should have done everything to discourage attention on Iran, he was determined that "I would always keep before the American people the plight of the hostages" (Carter, 1982, p. 525). He recognized that "the release of the American hostages had become almost an obsession with me" (Carter, 1982, p. 594). When things looked bleakest, he wrote, "I have a lot of problems on my shoulders but strangely enough, I feel better as they pile up" (Carter, 1982, p. 524). And pile up they did. It is regrettable but clear that Jimmy Carter's presidency was marred by his unconscious self-defeating tendency to engender conflict and opposition and therefore isolate himself from his beloved people, rather than by his conscious attempt at cooperation. There are elements of Greek tragedy in the Georgian's presidency.

It is important to look more deeply into President Carter's personality and background for the roots of the characteristics that would be crucial to his decisions in the hostage crisis and to America's assessment of him. What characteristic of Jimmy Carter was most outstanding during this 1976 campaign and throughout most of his presidency? When you think of him in this period and you look at his face, what stands out? His smile and his teeth. The cartoons of Jimmy Carter running for president showed smiling teeth that dominated his presence. Both pro-Carter and especially anti-Carter cartoons focused on gigantic smiling teeth.

His campaign staff talked of Jimmy's "good smiles" and "bad smiles". Why was there such a focus on this smile? What did it symbolize? A smile is usually a bridge that brings people together. But when a person smiles nervously or fearfully to discharge an uncomfortable feeling, no such connection is made. There are also sadistic smiles of dominance of one person over another. It became obvious at times that Carter smiled when he was angry and nervous. His smile thinly cloaked his aggressiveness—that he smiled when he would have like to bite. In the Iran hostage crisis the whole nation was looking to see if the president was going to smile or bite.

Southern men have had a reputation for being quick-tempered, pugilistic, and aggressive. The South, in war and peace, tended to be pro-military and pro-war. Lyndon Johnson, who sought to cover up his Southern background and be seen as a Westerner, had opted for war in Vietnam and been discredited by his choice. Carter would be the first avowed Southerner elected to the presidency since the Civil War. In 1976, Americans expected Carter, who had been a professional military man, to act aggressively. After impotently sitting in their cars in long gas lines during the gas crisis, suffering the humiliation of Watergate and the frustration of Vietnam, Americans wanted a president who would act decisively and aggressively if need be. Carter did not do what the people wanted. He told people to conserve energy. He tried to bring peace to the Middle East. In 1979 when military action against Iran would have felt good, he negotiated. The best estimates were that what the public wanted would have gotten most of the hostages and hundreds of other people killed. Eventually Carter gave in to the pressure and mounted a rescue operation which bogged down in a sand storm. Then he decided to cut American losses to eight, called it off, and took personal responsibility before the American people. American voters held him responsible in 1980.

Carter's response to a crisis is in sharp contrast to that of Ronald Reagan a few years later. Reagan made a terrible mistake when he sent American marines into the Lebanon quagmire in 1982. A number of experts warned that disaster was likely. Before long, terrorists drove a truck filled with explosives into the marine barracks and killed 241 young men. Reagan postured in an angry manner but found that he could do nothing effective against those who were responsible. What he did do was interesting and effective in relieving pent up frustration following the disaster. Within two months he invaded Grenada as a diversion. Grenada was safe. A quick military success was guaranteed. It did not matter to Reagan that there was no Communist threat, except in his mind, and that the American medical students at the college were not in danger. Some 7,000 soldiers were sent down to defeat 100 Cuban military advisers and over 8,000 medals were given out. After the invasion the American administrators and students mostly kept quiet about not needing to be saved (deMause, 1984). The reasons given for invading Grenada were illusory, but the good feelings Americans had afterward were real. America had a respite from feeling the impotence of power.

Reagan gloried in the good feelings and, unlike Carter, was not troubled by criticism of his aggressiveness. Nor did Reagan appear to feel personally responsible, as did Carter, for American servicemen killed abroad. A comparison of the relationship of each of these men with his father will help us to understand why they could act so differently. In his autobiography, Carter specifically remembers being switched six times by his father and presents a picture of Earl as so arbitrary, humiliating, and racist that his son was afraid to voice normal childhood complaints or laugh when his father's mail-order tailored shirt was comically large. Yet Jimmy bends over backward to praise "Daddy," and even declares that "he was always my best friend." Reagan's autobiography reflects no such ambivalence. He didn't respect his father. Jack Reagan is presented as an "unsuccessful first-generation 'black Irishman'" who would embarrass and mistreat his youngest son. Rather than say "my father was my best friend," he describes, with obvious disgust, having to drag his drunken father into bed and then go find the family car in the middle of the street with the engine running. All this in a small midwestern town where everyone knew everyone else's business (Reagan, 1965). Unlike Carter, he was not trying to convince himself that he really loved his father at a point when he was furious with him.

Reagan was more of a rebel against authority than was Carter. As a freshman at Eureka College, he led a successful strike against the president (Reagan, 1965). Carter was more in awe of authority as he also had been in awe of his father. When he felt humiliated by authority, he sought to prove himself to that authority rather than rebel. When Admiral Hyman Rickover coldly denigrated young Carter for not always having done his best at Annapolis, he became the future president's role model. Many other people simply viewed the Admiral as an impossibly demanding individual who should be avoided. Carter sought to control himself and his own environment at all costs as he had since he was a little child (Elovitz, 1977). This is one of the reasons why he went into the submarine fleet. On submarines in general, and on nuclear submarines in particular, the need for control is enormous. Throughout his life he struggled to bring more and more within his control.

Like all presidents, Carter would have enormous power, but his ability to control the environment was limited. Presidents act as if they are in control, while in fact they often are not. People come to the president with their biggest problems and ask for a solution. Many, if not most, of these problems are going to be unsolvable. And though the president really cannot solve the problems, he is held responsible. People simply want things that presidents cannot deliver. But one thing that presidents can do is to help people to deal with their emotions in this most dangerous, unpredictable world. Like good psychoanalysts, presidents can help the public sort out their fantasies from their realities and to act in a sensible manner. Carter, a more informed, hardworking president than Reagan, did a poorer job of staying in touch with the people. Surprisingly, Reagan, more as a cold war ideologue than a cool-headed psychoanalyst in a holding environment, kept more in touch with the emotional needs of the populace. This kept the ship of state in safer domestic and international waters.

Let us extend this comparison to the hostage crisis. The irony is that Carter worked so hard to do all the right things to lessen conflict during it. He cut off trade with Iran except for some items needed for humanitarian purposes. He seized Iranian assets in the United States until the hostages and American assets were out of Iran. He patiently negotiated through every possible channel before attempting military force. And he failed abysmally. Reagan succeeded partly by the threat of military force and partly by accepting Khomeini's proposal (Brzezinski, 1983). When he came to the presidency, the Iranians were given some assets back. He talked tough, but used the carrot as well as the stick. But there was such an extraordinary difference in the way they were perceived by both the American public and the Ayatollah Khomeini. Carter, who had the strength of character to resist movements to war, was seen as a weak president who need not be feared. The result was that day after day the Iranians could denounce the United States, and much more importantly, the American mass media people could denounce Carter and say, "Look how low he's bringing us." Carter became so glum that his nervous smiling even diminished. Let us look more closely at that smile which would be such a plus and such a minus for Jimmy Carter.

When Carter walked up to potential voters and smilingly said, "Hi, I'm Jimmy Carter," people responded positively. As previously mentioned, before the end of the campaign, his advisers were talking about Jimmy's "good smiles" and "bad smiles." The most damaging example of the latter was in the debate with President Ford when there was video but no audio for 27 minutes. The bulk of the voting nation was watching and waiting impatiently for the audio to be restored. It also was an unusual opportunity to assess the candidates' basic character without being distracted by a flood of words written by speech writers. Jerry Ford stood at the lectern looking annoyed as well he should have been at a technical foul up at a key moment in the campaign. Jimmy Carter was annoyed, frustrated, and eventually furious, and yet his smile got bigger. As soon as he was off camera, he chewed out his aides for leaving him out there with an inappropriate smile on his face. His anger at not being able to control his nervous smile was displaced onto his advisers. His aides came to know his "icy smiles" as did people he disliked such as Menachem Begin (Brzezinski, 1983).

That Carter smiled when he was furious and would have liked to have bitten off the head of whoever was responsible for the situation is an indication of a reaction formation. An involuntary part of his personality was showing itself in a most painful way. When Jimmy was a very small child he covered up many of his emotions. For example, he felt furious at his younger sister who was big for her age and pushy and who threw a wrench at him. He shot her in the backside with a BB gun. His punishment was a switching and a heavy dose of emphasis on loving his younger sister. The thought of wanting to hurt his sister became unacceptable to him as well as to his parents. But the repression of angry aggressive feelings did not eliminate the feelings; it simply drove them underground. Smiling when he wanted to fight or hurt somebody would become a lifelong trait. In grade school he wrote "good health is clean teeth." In high school he was so worried about his teeth that he went to the dentist three times a year and feared that malocclusion of his teeth would keep him from being accepted at the naval academy.

At Annapolis this cover-up of aggression would cause him great pain. Bullies among the upperclassmen hazed him unmercifully at mealtimes. They would order him to sing "Marching through Georgia," which glorifies the darkest period in Georgia history. As a loyal son of the Peach State he could not do this. To sadists, every nervous smile was an invitation. At mealtime, humiliation followed humiliation. His manuscript diaries reflect some of his sufferings. On two occasions he chose painful ways out by cutting himself, once on the gums. In the midst of this crisis, his handwriting, which was normal-sized, became very small, which was a sign of the extraordinary stress that he was under. His father came to visit him since he was obviously in severe distress. Carter survived the trauma of freshman hazing and set himself the goal of becoming chief of naval operations (Turner, 1976).

Defending America in the nuclear navy offered a socially acceptable outlet for his aggressive impulses. Yet even here he began to think that "you only have one life and I began to wonder if I should spend mine engaged in war, even if I could rationalize it as the prevention of war" (Turner, 1976, p. 23). Violence was hard for him to stomach. Upon his father's death he abruptly resigned his commission and returned home to Plains to his father's fertilizer and peanut business. He went through a period in which he seemed to do penance by living in low-cost housing and hauling cow manure. After building up the family business, he entered politics, which is what his father had done at the end of his life. Though success in the "combat" of politics came rapidly, it could not shield him from the conflicts that he had faced at Annapolis. When, in November 1976, he said "that the most difficult thing in my life is to admit lust, anger and hatred," the press concentrated on the "lust," but in several years it would turn to the "anger" (Adler, 1977, p. 60).

During Carter's presidency some people saw his nervous smiling as an opportunity for really giving him a tough time instead of feeling sorry for him in his pain. It was not the type of pain, like Jack Kennedy's loss of a child, that people could relate to and empathize with. There was a fundamental part of his personality that was quite vulnerable to ridicule, because of his own internal conflicts that are part of this reaction formation. In the Iran hostage crisis, the Annapolis situation was reenacted on a national scale. The public saw his nervousness and looked for more. It wanted him to go beneath the nervousness to the aggression that he could not quite get out.

Carter had wanted to be everyone's friend. When elected, he became President Jimmy Carter instead of President James Earl Carter II. He distanced himself from his father because Earl was a somewhat rigid man who people were afraid of as well as because he was a racist. Jimmy was afraid of being like his father, which is why he did not use his father's exact name. To be cut off from the common people was most upsetting to him, but what he feared most was what he ended up with. In the White House he became totally absorbed with the hostage crisis and cut off from the electorate. Ronald Reagan was chosen as Carter's successor precisely because he had few inhibitions about his aggressiveness and he would not let his personal pain show to the public. Even when shot, he joked instead of suffering in public. Unlike Carter, nothing seemed to get to him. Yet if you compare the accomplishments of these two presidents, Carter looks better as more distance is achieved from the painful emotions of his last year in office.

As the emotional fallout of the Iran Hostage Crisis recedes Carter's accomplishments are seen more clearly. He kept out of war, faced up to the energy crisis, deregulated the transportation industry, and began a Middle East peace process. Yet, people live in their feelings—individually and collectively. During the last year of his presidency, something went terribly wrong between the public and Jimmy Carter. There was a bad mix between public frustration over the use of American power and his personal conflicts. The president has to have the confidence of the public to govern effectively. People have to feel that he is doing his best and keeping the country strong. In 1979, the public lost that sense. Without it, it is hard to fall asleep peacefully at night. The situation is analogous to that of children who are trying to fall asleep while their parents are on the verge of a painful divorce and they are fighting quite openly. The populace, like the children, feel totally unprotected. The president plays an enormously powerful emotional role in offering a sense of security and protection that all need because it is hard enough to control an individual's small part of the world without thinking about how vulnerable the world is to earthquakes, hurricanes, tornados, global warming, as well as nuclear, bacteriological, and chemical destruction. Carter, for all his moral strength and effectiveness as a peacemaking president, could no longer fulfill this vital presidential function.

Historians and the public are viewing former President Carter more positively as emotional distance is gained. On July 4, 1990, he was awarded the second annual Philadelphia Liberty Medal for the human rights work of the Carter Center. Despite the tragic blow of the Iran hostage crisis to his presidency, a poll in April 1990 indicated that Jimmy Carter was held in higher regard than Ronald Reagan (DeFrank, 1990, *New York Times*, 1990).

PERSONAL REFLECTIONS ON SYMBOL AND MYTH
(Mohammed Shaalan)

The object of this section is not a psychobiographical profile of a leader's life history as such. Neither events nor facts are central except in so far as they are illustrative of a leadership style that may have influenced the social and historical conditions in which Sadat participated and lived.

There are two views that I would like to discuss that contribute to a leader's style: one is as an actor actively influencing his sociohistorical circumstance, and the other as a respondent reflecting and following the progress of his sociohistorical circumstances. An interactional model that can accommodate a mutual influence whereby each affects the other seems closer to a balanced view of reality. Bion's observations on leader–group interactions portray such an interrelationship (1975). A group may express a need to reaffirm its identity as a whole during a given stage. And an individual may, as well, possess a valency that is predominantly expressive of a given need. In that case, leadership naturally is relegated to him. If and when that need is transcended, the leader falls back and another individual comes to the fore. Nevertheless, the personality of the leader as proactive member is not without influence in shaping the group's personality as well as its individual members.

At another level certain individuals, which one might compare to a sensitive wireless receiver, may be receptive to the "soul" of the group, to the extent that what proceeds from them spreads with fervor and seems to actively influence the group. The Jungian archetypal dream, long known in Islamic Sufi and other traditions, may contain what is in form an individual vision, yet is in essence an expression and an inspiration for a massive historical change.

Muhammad expressed this complexity. The prophet Muhammad was a Bedouin Arab of the lesser elite of the Qurashis (tribe). While an elitist among the Arab tribes, he was a proletarian among the Qurashis; and his immediate kin were his first allies and supporters. But the tribe as a whole rejected and eventually evicted him. The state of decadence then and self-indulgence, conducive to self-destruction, was ripe for the coming of a savior who would restore this unending yearning for a state of utopian justice that the oppressed dream of and the oppressors claim they are providing. His arrival at that timely moment in history was not only welcome but necessary to save the warring Bedouins from self-destruction. Perhaps it reflects the critical turning point wherein a group is faced with a choice: its own demise or revitalization through rebirth.

The problem with such dramatic turns are their short duration and their equally dramatic relapses into the reverse phase of decline. Since early Islam, the Arabian peninsula has hardly lived up to, or anything close to, its original idealism. It is as if the hardship of Bedouin life can only produce extremes: either decadence or inspiration. Moderate perpetration of ideals, translated into a stable civilization, seems to be preserved in more settled societies (such as the Assyrian, the Egyptian, the Persian, the Andalusian). So that a prophet is not only least valued in this kind of society, but his values are least preserved and perpetrated there, except as rigid formats, no different from the idols that they came to pull down.

This introduction is not irrelevant to Sadat (or to Carter). Sadat was a genuine product of an Islamic value system, a devoutly religious person and also a fervent nationalist. He was an Egyptian to the core, brought up in the village of Mit abul Kom, Menofia, in the delta not far from Cairo. He was affected by the European Mediterranean influence that reached Cairo from British occupation, not to mention the various other foreign influences of the British occupation, the Napoleonic French expedition, and before that the Ottoman Turks and their many predecessors.

Finally, he was a Cairene who received his military education among the first group of middle-class Egyptians to be permitted entry into that academy. He did not last long in the army, having been incriminated in a plot to murder a prime minister who was accused of collaborating with the British occupiers (namely Amin Osman). His German sympathies were nationalistic rather than ideologic.

This was to his advantage as a politician. He remained in hiding among the populace, taking on odd jobs such as a truck driver. He developed sympathies and understanding for the true Egyptian, carrying and assimilating its long historical heritage into his psychic depths. In contrast to Nasser, who never freed himself from his middle-class constraints, namely, "I ally myself with the poor as their savior against the rich whom I resent and cannot forgive, though I cannot help looking up to." Sadat forgave the rich, looked up to them while never letting down the poor. If he was alienated from any class, it was probably the intelligentsia who spoke on behalf of the poor but would never really change their lifestyle or share it willingly. (One "socialist" candidate who was campaigning for elections always washed his hands with cologne after shaking the hands of his would-be supporters from the masses. Nasser himself never appeared in peasant clothes and could not hide his contempt for his lower-middle class relatives.) Sadat felt very much at home with the poor, as much as he impressed the world aristocracy and political elite. He felt most at home in his village wearing his peasant "gallabia" and sharing a meal with his poor relatives. This sheds further light on Sadat's character, which chameleon-like could take on any form and color to preserve his survival; perhaps more like Orpheus than Machiavelli.

No doubt Sadat was fond of acting, and practiced as well other forms of self-expression in his youth, especially journalistic writing. But these may be said to be two aspects of being an actor: one is the possible absence of a core personality, leading to the assumption of different roles to suit the needs of the circumstances; and another may be the presence of a collective kind of multipersonality, which is not restricted to one self with specific and fixed qualities. There is more evidence for the latter. The isolation of cell 54 was a turning point in Sadat's life:

> My biography is called *In Search of Identity*, but what I really mean by that is: in search of my own identity. I found it in a strange place: in cell 54, where I was kept in isolation after being suspected of conspiring to murder the politician Osman. I sat there in the dark: no books, no newspapers, no radio, alone. I had only myself to fall back on or I would break down. God helped me to discover my true self. Once I had discovered that, I knew that I had to devote my life to peace. That is what I always worked towards, and so I was surprised that outsiders regarded my journey to Jerusalem in 1977 as a surprise. It was a logical consequence of my way of thinking. (Sadat, 1977)

The experience of insignificance inspired by sensory isolation impressed him with its polar opposite; to be nothing is also to be everything. To be completely fused with the Divine Ground is also to be part of that Divine Ground. To be vulnerably human and insignificant is also to be all important. To be human is to be Divine. It is a point of intersection of the timeless with time; the center of the mandala where opposites meet.

Within such a selfless state, any qualities could be acquired without being restricted and possessed by oneself. He could be the person he is, and yet not attached to that person. I am I, but I am also not I. I am that. Tat twam Asi. (Sadat was fond of yoga and probably was inspired by such awareness of selflessness within self-centeredness—(Carter wanted to be loved by all and to love all.)

Sadat was therefore incomprehensible to intellectuals whose mental formation was based primarily on left-hemispheric, logical, rational, linear, analytic modes of thinking. He could be viewed as erratic, capricious, unpredictable, irrational, even insane. He followed and trusted his feelings and intuition rather than his rational modes (which were not absent but just nondominant).

It is this selflessness that provided him with the survival value that kept him from political elimination or arrest for years. It also kept him from being in competition with Nasser, who as a leader assumed a grandiose self both for the requirements of his role as "pharaoh" and by his own inaccessibility to the selfless state which he did not have a chance to experience (such as by the stress of sensory isolation accompanied by the mystical experience of union or grace).

The cynical perception of Sadat's relation with Nasser was that he was a nonentity who never opposed Nasser and was completely subservient to him; this is a rather unfair portrayal of a comradeship and friendship formed around a common national goal (unlike the less-balanced friendship that Nasser had with two others: Amer, his army commander-in-chief; and Heikal, his intellectual complement). In both cases there could be qualities of complementarity where both parties loved and respected each other, but were unable to keep a distance of sufficient separateness. They needed each other, and behind such a need was ambivalence, feelings of extreme admiration, love as well as their unconscious opposites. Sadat was probably more distant. He probably maintained an inner feeling of self-respect that might have been hidden behind a facade of self-abnegation and submission. No wonder the Nasserist devotees were deceived into thinking he was a nonentity who could not possibly initiate any policy of his own or form any following. On the other hand, Sadat had his following from his residue of deep empathy with the common people. He could revolt against the elite; he could easily and flexibly change allies, "betray" friends, and quickly make new ones. His orientation was objective, social, and essentially human and international.

Sadat was often criticized for such sudden turnabouts in his allegiances and friendships, including Sayed Marei, his daughter's father-in-law and close ally; Mamdouh Salem, who was instrumental in the May 15 palace coup; and Mansour Hassan, who he almost adopted as a political perpetrator of his strategic philosophy. Yet all this was understandable in that Sadat was not just a leader, a proacter, who manipulated people, but a representative who had to take into account their needs and yield to their pressures. He was not, as most of us like to think, the absolute dictator, pharaoh, half-human, half-divine who possessed omnipotent capabilities, a puppeteer. His survival was a function of his ability to be led by following his group as well as by leading them.

There were two kinds of groups that influenced Sadat: the professionals who sat near the throne, and the common people who showed their support or lack of it by passive noninvolvement, occasional disobedience, and even outright rebellion, or else by spontaneous shows of enthusiastic support. When he undertook the May 15 palace coup, he had no real support from other than a few key figures in the power elite. The rest, more numerous and powerful, assumed that their semipharaonic status was enough to deter him from taking any action against them that might incite public riots.

In this case, Sadat's intuition was correct. Despite the grief over Nasser's death, no one really cared for Nasser's instruments of oppression (despite their claim to be followers of Nasserist principles of Arab nationalism and socialism).

People were aware that these were merely iron fists that kept him in power while still allowing him the role of being the father–provider–protector.

Their overthrow, which could have been accomplished without even giving them the benefit of being heros, victims, or martyrs did not bring about any mass response; if any, it was one of relief. Sadat felt that people's hunger for freedom, food, and more important, restoration of national pride after the humiliating defeat of June 1967 (much like Carter after Watergate). Removal of army officers from political power coupled with installation of high-caliber professionals in military work, such as the late General Abdul Monem Riyad and General Gamasy, and installing professional and popular politicians including former opponents (e.g., a Marxist, Ismail Sabry Abdalla, and an Islamicist, Ahmed Kamal Abul Magd) were indicators of a fairer balance based on quality rather than favoritism and personal allegiance.

Sadat's faith in his own intuition against the advice of professional politicians and his trust in his empathy with the masses alienated many of his staff, especially in foreign affairs and diplomatic concerns. It also alienated many intellectuals and ideologues, especially leftists and Nasserists. Unfortunately, to counterbalance them he had to rely on their archenemies, the Moslem brothers and their more fanatic renegades. The latter, apart from the lack of depth in their understanding of religion, were more hungry for fascist-type power dependent on violence and secret organization. Ultimately, he helped arm them and they eventually killed him in a tragicomic and pathetic manner; Sadat was murdered by his own soldiers, on the anniversary of their military victory under his leadership.

Perhaps, part of Sadat's demise had to do with his premature responsiveness to the global situation. Several years before Gorbachev, he expressed similar global needs, though motivated by pragmatic local conditions; namely, that military solutions for international conflict were neither feasible nor necessary. Indeed, there was a dire need for a novel approach to international conflict management without resort to destructive military violence and waste through a futile arms race. Already after the discovery of nuclear destructive power, he realized that any win–lose postures between the major powers were bound to maintain conflict; for the loser would eventually return for his vendetta, and the winner would some day be blinded by his own pride, and the cycle would go on (perhaps a view more appreciated now than then).

Nevertheless, the surplus of arms and the need to dispose of them and to test new ones was then met by mass consumption. It was a world still deluded by the possibility that military power was an effective way of achieving peace and stability. The military-industrial complex in the West had its way, by continuing to invent, produce, and export weapons that resulted in: (1) the depletion of the national resources of the developing nations (e.g., the 8-year Iraq–Iran war which exhausted not only both parties but the whole Arab world and deflected their attention from their common goals, namely, cooperation for development and nonmilitary means of resolving conflict). Unfortunately, the world has not learned the lesson of the Palestinian uprising, the Iranian revolution, or the Afghan rebellion; namely, that superpowers cannot subjugate national aspirations by military force all the time, though perhaps partially for a period of time. (2) Postponement of the realization that cooperation between superpowers was possible without necessarily being played into the hands of irresponsible rival siblings who pitted the (parental) superpowers against each other (formerly successful as in the policy of Nasserism). (3) The use of folly and shortsightedness based on outmoded patterns of national liberation, national liberation being in the barrel of a gun; or the use of popular or guerilla warfare and violent revolution against superpower technology, including such primitive and essentially non-constructive means as terrorism and narcoterrorism, for example, exporting natural (plant) narcotics such as heroin from Asia, hashish from the Middle East, and cocaine from South America vis à vis the counterweapon of alcohol, tobacco, and synthetic tranquilizers, hypnotics, and analgesics from the West. Even some Americans feel that Panama's Noriega used his best available chemical weapon, cocaine, against American military might and there is still doubt about who won.

Despite this climate, Sadat, without the help of reasoning offered by the Soviet Communist party's philosophers, anticipated and initiated a novel approach to conflict management: unilateral renunciation of violence, strength based on principles of justice, and capacity for self-criticism and empathy with his enemy; addressing masses over their leaders' heads, directly risking vulnerability and expecting criticism from all sides; and recognition of the mutual benefits and dangers in conflict. When Sadat went to Jerusalem, there were no party philosophers; indeed, the professional diplomats were opposed and his foreign minister resigned. There were no preparations made as in the case in the current Soviet–American rapproachment.

To confirm this visionary quality, we can look back at Sadat's reforms in Egypt's Arab nationalist socialism, started in the early 1970s, without party philosophers and indeed under severe attack. At that early time, he was practicing perestroika and glasnost. It was no wonder that he was assassinated despite the lack of evidence of collusion between the many powers that were threatened by his approach. However, time has shown that superpowers are already following Sadat's principles without giving credit to his initiatives. Whether in Egypt or in the Arab world, Sadat is seldom, if ever, acknowledged as a creative or even a sincere politician. He has been showered with all sorts of accusations. In spite of current Egyptian and Arab policy that is in essence a continuation of what he proposed, hardly any overt credit is given to him.

Sadat was, therefore, an international rather than a merely national or regional leader; but it is difficult for the Western rational, pragmatic, scientific world to acknowledge the credit due an Egyptian, Arab, Moslem, Third World, Afro-Asian leader. The world follows and applies his principles. Verbally the Arabs glorify Nasser on the one hand or alternately or simultaneously dance to the Western tune; but hardly any acknowledge Sadat.

Sadat's Pitfalls

Obviously, though Sadat could be viewed by his admirers as a martyr, his downfall was welcomed nationally and internationally. Nationally there was no show of emotion as was demonstrated in Nasser's funeral. Internationally, the show was formal and ritualistic. Everybody was secretly glad that he was gone. There was no place for ideologues in a world that was still run by pragmatism, economic and military power, and technology as applied to moral power and principles of peaceful management of conflict. Even Sadat was aware of that. He never tried to impart his wisdom to his children or involve them in politics. But on such spiritual levels, a teacher's influence extends beyond blood relationship, and extends beyond those who have known him personally. Indeed, there might be some cynicism in saying that the less direct the contact, the greater the likelihood of a spiritual relationship. I, for one, never had a personal relationship with Sadat; and it is possible that had this been the case, my portrayal of him might have been less abstract and less spiritual, or the portrayal might have been concertized into defenses and attacks directed at specific qualities of character or politics. Volumes have pursued this course. In fact, my goal is to depict Sadat as a symbol and myth whose absence is responsible for our current stagnation. Myth can be more "real" than fact, and brevity more eloquent than lengthy and detailed descriptions. For Sufis, Muhammad is a symbol of the perfect man; but he is also perfect because of his imperfection. In his humanness lay also his prophecy, and in his corporality, his spiritualism. Moslems do not worship prophets, and do not need to idolize them; but they create poems, songs, and images with a mythical portrayal that inspires culture and moves history. It was important that Sadat's demise should have no ideological undertones. His assassins emphasized his tolerance of corruption and his "pharaonic" dictatorship, as well as his opening up to the Christian (rather than Zionist or Communist) world.

His faults were that he was portrayed as tolerating and covering up corruption, perhaps for reason of personal bias or fear of the power of the new corrupt elite. But, more importantly, the corruption he inherited from Nasser was covered up. Furthermore, the critics who emphasized his tolerance of corruption were not all that free from personal bias: either they were not able to get their share of the cake, or they lost the share they had, or they could not for ideological reasons ally themselves with the only allies Sadat had at the time (the rightists). His main faults from his assassins' point of view were not that he had made peace with Israel or allied himself with the U.S. and European block, which included encouraging their capitalistic open-door policy exploiting the Egyptian need for consumerism (facilitated by the surplus of petrodollars available to oil-rich countries), but that he allowed Western values and patterns of culture to corrupt traditions, and that he surrendered his democratic and tolerant policy to political opposition. For his assassins were neither leftists nor Nasserists, but the very Islamicists whom he protected and encouraged in order to counterbalance his verbose opponents. They were relieved at the replacement of a different regime. It is indeed baffling to see that the regime consolidated its stability, whether in policies or personalities, because of Sadat's demise rather than in spite of it. It is as though the corrupt elite decided to get rid of the symbol and hide behind apparently decent and noncorrupt, though nonadventurous, leaders such as Mubarak, thus maintaining a Sadat regime that has remained stable since Sadat's downfall. Indeed, corruption and inefficiency seem to have become so entrenched and accepted that they have almost ceased to be an object of criticism. It is as if we have all become partners in sin and dare not throw stones for fear of breaking our own glass houses.

Sadat could be accepted as an unacknowledged global leader but not as an ideologue, one who provided the world with a futuristic alternative: "No more war." The world was not about to give up its martial posture of equating might with right. It cannot therefore acknowledge Sadat's rightful position as world leader—perhaps as an attractive mass media figure, an elegant consumer of the latest fashion, a charismatic leader—but a national, regional, or global leader, not yet.

Sadat's Injured Self

In the beginning of this section, Sadat's strength was depicted by his self-lessness, even though this was mistaken for humility and opportunism. His real weakness was in his regression to self-involvement when the 1977 "food riots" took place. At that time he was intoxicated by the world mass media. All of a sudden he was shocked to realize that his own people were ready to dispense with him when they expressed their unplanned, unorganized, and spontaneous rejection of his austerity measures recommended by the International Monetary Fund.

For the first time his ego was hurt, and his selflessness was forgotten. Mansour Hassan was a naive politician who was to be downgraded until he could be educated into "dirty hands" by politicians. The ministry was reshuffled, coinciding with the arrest of all opponents who threatened Sadat's ego and ended up simply by excluding Mansour Hassan; he was able, by a diplomatic act of grace, to reject Sadat's reeducation into "dirty politics" by jumping off the bandwagon. He was disappointed, no doubt, but so were Egyptian counterparts who had hoped that Mansour would tilt the balance in favor of Sadat the visionary, selfless, global leader rather than Sadat with a hurt ego projecting his own sense of global rejection onto an essentially helpless opposition, arresting unnecessarily many verbose but harmless opponents.

Sadat felt let down by the world and condemned by those whom he supported most and ended by blaming them for his failure to be a real world leader. Sadat insisted that the world is in need of spiritual revival expressed in mutual support and win–win strategies rather than power politics or superpower win–lose competitiveness (not Khomeini Shiism or Saudi Wahhabism, not Dhia ul Haq or Numeiri legalism, and certainly not Lebanon and not Israeli exclusivism). Sadat's application of mutual acceptance and cooperation was the natural expression of these spiritual values. Sadat was devoutly religious and had very few worldly needs to which he was attached. He was in spite of that also spiritual; for often the two do not necessarily coexist. Although his religiosity was overt, it was not taken seriously but assumed to be a political tactic and a sham.

His spirituality was blurred by the requirements of political power, which took the form of qualities that appeared as ruthlessness, double-dealing, and deceit, the basis for the common disdainful remark that politics is "dirty business." From a psychiatrist's perspective and clinical experience, there is as much "dirty business" within the human psyche, between family members and friends as there is in politics. There are dozens of attempts to demonstrate the same "dirt" in Sadat's personal life past and present; but in my view, this is itself a "dirty" game. For a leader should not be judged by his public personality alone. After all, the prophet Muhammad acknowledged his human weaknesses and practiced them publicly and even gave them religious sanctity. He never hid his erotic attraction to his adopted son's wife; and his favorite wife, Aysha, never hid her joking but penetrating remark motivated by her jealousy that surely God sends him his verses to suit his liking. That is often taken as a critique of Islam's great prophet. Yet in Islam this is exactly the point. Muhammad always reminded us of his own humanness. ("I am but a man like yourself, but the inspiration has come, to me, that your God is one God: whoever expects to meet his Lord, let him work righteousness, and in the worship of his Lord, admit no one as partner.")

Muhammad never tried to display supernatural powers or miracles. He always emphasized thinking and reasoning as well as faith and intuition. He was self-critical and accepted criticism from others. The other source in Islam of the importance of not judging by appearances comes from the story of Al-Khidr when he was coaching the prophet Moses (on his insistence). (This illustration of a point using Sadat, a modern political controversial leader in juxtaposition with a historical figure of undisputed glory, Muhammad the prophet of Islam, could seem distasteful for Muslim moderates. My sincere intention, though, is neither to downgrade our prophet nor overidealize our former president.)

Iqbal, the great Islamic poet of the Indian Muslim nation (successfully divided and redivided by the British into Pakistan, Bangladesh, and Kashmir), interpreted the Muslim dictum "there is no prophet after Muhammad." Muhammad appealed to thought and reason, symbolizing an age where human evolution could permit faith in God through rational conviction or natural inspiration. In that sense, people did not need a particular prophet and could reach God without any human (or superhuman) mediator. In other words, "there is no prophet after Muhammad" could mean no particular prophet. There was no monopoly for any individual to claim prophethood and everybody was in a sense a carrier of the message. So that any insinuation or allusion to Sadat's "prophethood" could equally apply to you or me. This is an important essence in Islamic belief.

Sufi aspiration to communion with God, to the point of complete fusion, made Sufis subject to the "accusation" of pantheism, regarded by traditionalists as contrary to Islamic belief. However, the depiction of the anonymous wise teacher (generally recognized as Al-Khidr, the Qutb or pole, of Sufis), who coached the prophet Moses, as being wiser than the only prophet to whom God granted the request of appearing to him in visual form conveys the same message. Prophets are human; and all humans are in some way tentative, hidden, or partial prophets. At one level, God does not differentiate between his prophets:

> The apostle believeth, in what hath been revealed, to him from his Lord, as to the men of faith. Each one (of them) believeth, in God, His angels, His books, and His apostles. "We make no distinction (they say) between one and another of his

apostles." And they say "we hear, and we obey": (we seek) their forgiveness, our
Lord, and to thee is the end of all journeys.

On the other hand, God favors his latest messenger (who is uniquely described as such, namely, Rassoul or messenger and not just prophet. What is a
source of concern is the zealotry of the remnants of some of the modern substitutes for religion such as Socialism, Marxism, Arab nationalism, and the local
concoction of all those: Nasserism. The comparison between the two great leaders
displays the emotional nature of hero worship. Nasser was a leader who blew up
his nation's ego to near delusional grandeur and ended his career by leaving
Egypt in a state of near economic collapse, military defeat, and humiliation worse
than what he accused his great historical rival Muhammad Ali the Great of
leaving Egypt. Yet the Nasserists, until today and with generous support form
Nasser's former hostile Arab elites, continue to attack Sadat under a Nasserist
banner, almost bringing to mind the romanticism of King Arthur and his noble
knights; moreover denying that Sadat was one of the "round table," accepting
him merely as one who inherited Nasser by chance or even CIA manipulation.
Again, this is understandable since Arab regimes based on oligarchy and oppression fear a strong Egypt with an ideology that can have mass appeal. Those who
bitterly opposed Nasser during his life defend him now, only to downgrade Sadat
as a potential living leader. Luckily for Mubarak, he has not yet presented the
image of a potentially strong and dominant Egypt.

Such comparisons that depict leaders as dead mythological heroes and living
leaders as frail humans are not uncommon, for many reasons. This is an example
of racist imperialism, such as when some orientalists attempt to delineate true
prophets, citing Jesus, and mere social reformers or false prophets, citing Muhammad. Even for a young Muslim (the author) going through adolescent agnos-
ticism, this attempt at differentiation was flagrantly racist and a product of Western imperialism. Either they were all prophets or else social reformers, depending
on one's frame of reference.

For comparisons made between Sadat and Nasser, refer, for example, to
Sadat's 1973 successful destruction of the myth of the invincible Israeli army, as
a stage war and a pseudovictory, while Nasser's 1967 debacle is regarded as a
mere setback without Israeli victory simply because Nasser was not toppled; the
masses refused Nasser's resignation when he acted as an honest politician and
shouldered responsibility for the defeat. (There was an additional cynical aspect
here: you blew it, you stay and fix it.)

At best, Sadat's performance is ascribed to Nasser's leadership and reconstruction of the military and political structure' of the nation following the defeat
(partly true as shown in the war of attrition in 1967–69); though no one had the
audacity to retrospectively falsify reality to the point of blaming the 1967 defeat
on Sadat's having been vice president to Nasser at the time. Amer, the army
commander, was in fact already scapegoated by Nasser.

These comparisons between idealized father figures seem to reflect a subjective view on the part of analysts, who may have some unconscious (or even
conscious and possibly opportunistic motives). Such misconstructions of reality
are not new but have historical precedents. Prophets and leaders are mystified

usually after their death. Indeed, during their heydays they are often very controversial. Muhammad himself was and still is least mystified by his own people (the elite Quraish Arabs since early Islam until today among the Saudi-Wahabi elite). Islam was spread and preserved more by Indians, Egyptians, and to a lesser extent Persians than by its first recipients or their descendants.

Nasser had more enemies and critics among Egyptians with the exception of city-dwelling and landless peasants and among Arab elites during his heyday than he has now. Now Arab elites, such as those of Libya, Algeria, and Syria (who particularly gave him the greatest heartbreak of all) are paying handsomely to bring the myth of Nasserism to life to the spontaneous masses, whether Egyptian or Arab. The lifeless, uncreative Nasserists and other neoreligious substitutes derive their main strength from the present regime's repugnance of and resistance to such regressive solutions to our current problems, rather than any significant support. After all, the Soviet Marxists took the lead in evolving their beliefs, while local priests still cling to the "fundamentals."

The explanation for such a regressive solution could be based on a combination of factors: emotional and intellectual bankruptcy, or an inability to provide creative futuristic or even current solutions to our problems. This involves counting only on a retrospective falsification and mystification even of what is ironically recent history (apart from the neoreligious revivalists' regressive dreams). There is a reluctance to give up a familiar past that had the seeds of a glorious dream, that is, Arab power through unity and social revolution leading to leadership of a downtrodden Third World. This dream persists in favor of the creative task of facing current realities and problems with current possibilities and givens. It is a secret wish on the part of a schismatic Arab nation that fears a present strong, united, and dominant Egypt in favor of recognition of a past image that poses no current or future threat of changing, fearing any force leading or dominating the region and threatening the hegemony of the world powers or the regional elites, while paradoxically needing a moderately strong Egypt that protects them from each other and their own people. For example, while such regimes would support any forces that prevent the internal unity and strength of Egypt, they have no real wish to see Egypt crumble (or perhaps revive) through a mass revolution such as is threatened by the so-called Islamicists (so-called because all they represent is an unorganized, unideological alternative without a clear and rational strategy or vision).

Nevertheless, they find objective bases for the emotional appeal of Islamicism to Egyptian masses. On the one hand, it would undermine Egyptian nationalism, unity, strength, and development; on the other, it would perpetrate the schism that makes Egyptian allegiance shift from Cairo vis à vis Riyadh (via Mecca), Damascus, Baghdad, Tripoli, or even Tehran. It was a pathetic state of affairs when Arabs (specifically Libya and Syria) allied themselves with Iran against Iraq, which, despite its active role in condemning Egypt's peace initiative with Israel, received enthusiastic support from Egypt and Jordan. While Saudi Arabia, realizing its own inability to lead by culture, ideology, or military and economic (not financial) power, tried to keep a balance by secretly supporting and simultaneously undermining each of the parties. Because of its political poverty, Saudi

Arabia could have misgivings about Egypt's strength as well as Iraq's or Syria's. So, keeping them all in a well-balanced conflict of nonwinner and nonloser was the only strategy for maintaining a false and flimsy Saudi Arabian financial and pseudocultural imperialism. Better still was the paralysis of Iran and the certainty of American protection against Israeli aggression. In exchange America would contribute still further to the undermining of any real potential Arab power, starting with its active role in Egyptian–Israeli de jure peace, Syrian–Israeli de facto peace, and vicarious war in Lebanon between all parties, especially if based on religious, sectarian, tribal fanatic allegiances, at the expense of Arab national-ism. This sectarianism undermines a potentially powerful Arab union. Iran's Islamic revolution was a blessing for Western imperialism, since Muslims would destroy each other over a dubious ideology that posed no threat to a world political power game. Among the world's elite, religious and ideological differ-ences were transcended in favor of regional or multinational economic interests. What could be more cynical than a Europe that united former Nazis, Jews, Protestants, Catholics, as well as French, German, Scandinavian, and Southern Mediterranean (Italian, Spanish, and Greek) and now Eastern bloc Communist nations and Western bloc capitalist liberal democratic nations, while Arabs, and to a lesser extent Muslims, with all the potential of a major world power, con-tinued to fight? (Arab power almost became a reality for a few hours after the October 1973 war with Israel, but quickly evaporated.)

Nevertheless, Sadat had the strategic vision and the ability to transcend enmity based on race, religion, or even nationalism to make that giant step to Jerusalem which shook the world more than the giant step of the first American astronaut to the moon. Sadat's grave error was that he was too creative, or if you wish, erratic, capricious, unpredictable, or even mad, to make such a step on the basis of his own initiative and intuition. This was too dangerous for the calcula-tions of rational computerized manipulations of world politics. It was a threat to control, a threat of unpredictable changes in the calculated balances of power.

America, the West, and Israel itself were too much taken by surprise to consider not joining the process. For the whole crux of the Western game was that Israel wanted peace and it was the Arabs who rejected it. As Moshe Dayan put it when Rogers made his first peace initiative, there was no need for Israel to reject such an unwelcome settlement. Israel was quite happy with its victor-occupied status. The Arabs, Dayan said, would relieve Israel of the job and reject the Rogers plan.

Paradoxically, it was Sadat as Nasser's vice president in his temporary ab-sence who took the initiative of rejecting the Rogers peace proposal. Nasser, who had returned from a trip to the Soviet Union, quickly entertained the proposal, but Nasser did not have the adventurous, gambling posture for fully challenging Israel's willingness for peace. Moreover, he did not feel strong enough (although his confidence was partially restored by the 1967 defeat). Moreover, he was not trusting enough of Western support or mistrusting enough of Soviet nonsupport.

Sadat met more favorable circumstances: he lost faith openly in Soviet sup-port, took the brunt of displaced Arab vendetta against Nasser's former attempts to dominate them, gambled on the prospects, even without promises or deals, of American and Western support, and had the confidence gained by the 1973 victory (even if in military terms the outcome could be considered ambiguous—psychologically it was an unpredicted victory and was accepted as such from the first day regardless of any subsequent outcome). Finally he was who he was as a personality—a dramatist, a risk taker, and, without claiming it, a mystic who believed in what he said—"no more war." His genuineness came across effectively through the mass media and practically forced the politicians in Israel and the West to respond to their people's belief in Sadat's genuineness.

Again, all this was a threat to the rational, computer-determined Western orientation. Politics was a power game and there was no place for ideology and spiritualism. Like all spiritually motivated historical changes, the Caesars and worse still the volatile mobs, including the followers of their visionary leaders, had to crush and crucify their Christs, stone their Muhammads, and expel their Moses. Sadat had to die (and so did Faisal who also was an ascetic, an almost mystical visionary who supported and respected Sadat). Underdogs were to remain leashed and wild spirits were to be caged like animals.

Sadat was let down politically and economically by the united elites of the world, from Israel to the United States, and including the Arabs and his own proteges. He was to be cut down to size and portrayed as his unromantic enemies wanted: a traitor who took unilateral peace in exchange for a false, even harmful economic transition ("infitah" or open door); an exchange probably infected with a virulent virus that would kill Egypt's economic power while flooding it with useless paper money and consumable, gluttonous goods, further consolidating Egypt's economic dependence. Egypt has acquired debts, much of which are used to supplement two thirds of its basic food needs, and worse still, continuing to pay the growing interest and inflation of those very debts.

Furthermore, Sadat was denied his chance to speak out for a radical solution to the Middle East conflict, namely the Palestinian problem. Again, the West did not have to make any efforts to isolate Egypt from the Palestinians and Arabs; they did the job quite enthusiastically. Sadat was robbed of his soul and his idealism; he was robbed of his selflessness which was already scarred by his own mobs in the 1977 riots. Without ideals, without a soul, without the allegiance of his Arab colleagues, even of his own people, Sadat progressively became more enclosed in himself, imprisoned and blinded by his own paranoia. Killing him outright would have been an easy job for any mediocre secret intelligence agency, not even a CIA or KGB or a Mossad. Again, why dirty their hands since the mediocre ones would do the job on their own with even more enthusiasm, fanaticism, religious fervor, and martyrdom. Sadat was not allowed martyrdom. His soul first had to be drained. His selflessness had to be distorted into egocentric paranoia. Then, when his physical demise would be completed, there was the certainty that none of him would remain.

In a world still inflated with materialistic power, the revival of the soul was a threat. Sadat and his memory before him had to be buried. Yet the world is suffering from its materialism; and it is my hope that we may be feeling the birth pangs of a new spiritual revival.

The new religionism, including the new liberal Islam, is finding suitable soil in the Western world. There are more liberal Muslims who have bridges with Western religion in the West than there are among the billion-plus Muslims in the

Moslem world; and there, the greater concentration of that newer quality in Egypt which produced Sadat.

Egypt is the geographical and cultural bridge that can integrate East and West, North and South. Egypt produced and made Sadat; and though it still is unable to verbalize or acknowledge its ownership of Sadat, for fear of losing what seems to be a promise of Arab and Muslim leadership, it cannot rightly earn its place as leader of transition unless it reintegrates that part of its history which Sadat represented.

This is needed for Egypt's survival; indeed, a need for the region, including Israel, and a need for the Western world and the world as a whole. There must be *no more war*. Egypt said it, not just Sadat. Egypt's heritage of 7,000 years has had many more visionaries, some known and hence deliberately kept out of power, some unknown and within the realm of influence, occasionally being accepted in the power elite, and quickly rejected. It is in the world's interest to preserve this spiritual heritage. Not just Egypt's temples and dead remain, Egypt's culture and heritage must be rediscovered.

REFERENCES

Adler, B. (1977). *The wit and wisdom of Jimmy Carter*. Secaucus, NJ: Citadel Press.

Barber, J. D. (1977). *The presidential character: Predicting performance in the White House*. Englewood Cliffs, NJ: Prentice-Hall.

Bion, W. (1975). *Experiences in Groups*. New York: Ballantine Books.

Burns, J. M. (1978). *Leadership*. New York: Harper & Row.

Brzezinski, Z. (1983). *Power and principle: Memoirs of the national security advisor, 1977–1981*. New York: Farrar, Straus, Giroux.

Carter, J. (no date). Manuscript Annapolis diaries.

Carter, J. (no date). Manuscript health booklet.

Carter, J. (1976). *Why not the best?* New York: Bantam Books.

Carter, J. (1982). *Keeping faith: Memoirs of a president*. New York: Bantam Books.

Carter, J. (1985). *The blood of Abraham*. Boston: Houghton Mifflin.

Carter, J. & Carter, R. (1987). *Everything to gain: Making the most of the rest of your life*. New York: Random House.

Carter, R. (1984). *First Lady from Plains*. Boston: Houghton Mifflin.

Carter, L., & Spann, G. C. (1977). *Away from home: Letters to my family*. New York: Simon and Schuster.

Carter receives Liberty Medal. (1990). *New York Times*, July 5, p. B6.

Christopher, W., Carswell, R., Davis, R. J., Hoffman, J. E., Jr., Owen, R. B., Saunders, H. H., & Sick, G. (1985). *American hostages in Iran: The conduct of a crisis*. New Haven: Yale University Press.

DeFrank, T. M. (1990). A diminished Ron, A refurbished Jimmy. *Newsweek*, April 2, p. 36.

deMause, L. (1984). *Reagan's America*. New York: Creative Roots.

Elovitz, P. H. (1977). Three days in Plains. In L. deMause & H. Ebel (Eds.), *Jimmy Carter and American fantasy: Psychohistorical explorations* (pp. 33–57). New York: Two Continents Publishing Group.

Gwertzman, B. (1979). U.S. decision to admit the Shah: Key events in 8 months of debate. *New York Times*, November 18, pp. 1, 14.

Hargrove, E. C. (1988). *Jimmy Carter as President: Leadership and the politics of the public good*. Baton Rouge: Louisiana State University Press.

Heikel, M. (1983). *Autumn of fury: The Assassination of Sadat.* New York: Random House.

Hinnebusch, R. A. (1985). *Egyptian politics under Sadat: The post-populist development of an authoritarian-modernizing state.* Cambridge: Cambridge University Press.

Irving, W. (1911). *The Life of Mohomet.* London: Everyman's Library.

Jones, C. O. (1988). *The trusteeship presidency: Jimmy Carter and the United States Congress.* Baton Rouge: Louisiana State University Press.

Jordan, H. (1982). *Crisis: The last year of the Carter Presidency.* New York: G.P. Putnam.

Mazlish, B., & Diamond, E. (1979). *Jimmy Carter: An interpretive biography.* New York: Simon and Schuster.

McFadden, R. D., Treaster, J., & Carroll, M. (1981). *No hiding place.* New York: Times Books.

Moritz, C. (Ed.) (1984). Ted Koppel. In *Current biography,* pp. 216–220. New York: H.W. Wilson.

Muller, K., & Blaise, M. (1981). *Anwar Sadat: The last hundred days.* London: Thames & Hudson.

Pahlavi, M. R. (1980). *Answer to history.* Briarcliff Manor, NY: Scarborough House.

Powell, J. (1984). *The other side of the story.* New York: William Morrow.

Reagan, R. (1965). *Where's the rest of me?* New York: Dell.

Rozell, M. J. (1989). *The press and the Carter presidency.* Boulder, CO: Westview Press.

Rubin, B. (1980). *Paved with good intentions: The American experience and Iran.* New York: Oxford University Press.

Sadat, A. (1978). *In search of identity: An autobiography.* New York: Harper & Row.

Sadat, J. (1987). *A woman of Egypt.* New York: Simon and Schuster.

Salinger, P. (1981). *America held hostage: The secret negotiations.* Garden City, NY: Doubleday.

Sick, G. (1985). *All fall down: America's tragic encounter with Iran.* New York: Random House.

Smith, G. (1986). *Morality, reason and power: American diplomacy in the Carter years.* New York: Hill and Wang.

Turner, R. W. (Ed.) (1976). *"I'll never lie to you": Jimmy Carter in his own words.* New York: Ballantine Books.

III

A Global Village?
Childhood Roots, Reflections, and Hopes

What happens when you have committed your national identity to a war and the enemy resigns.

TODD GITLIN, *San Francisco Chronicle*, December 20, 1989

The enemy image is becoming a thing of the past. Ideological stereotypes are fading away. We have begun to understand each other's motives. As we are changing and becoming closer to each other, we have not ceased to be different. But it turns out that this is not so bad. Quite the opposite—it is useful. For diversity is a vital force of development.

I feel that we are now witnessing the emergence of a general idea which is conquering people's minds on the eve of the 21st century. It is the idea of unity. To make this idea a reality is a truly monumental challenge.

MIKHAIL GORBACHEV, *The New York Times*, June 1, 1990

In Part III, our collective voice becomes truly international. Here we examine childhood roots, hopefully to rediscover and clarify what was, so as not to repeat the past. In bridging East and West, a psychoanalyst from Czechoslovakia reflects on growing up in a totalitarian regime (Marlin). This is psychodynamically compared to McCarthyism in the United States (Smith). The "gentle revolution" in Eastern Europe could not have happened without some modification toward more humanitarian child-rearing practices. A new Soviet character will slowly emerge, as family parenting attitudes change (deMause). Finally, we look to the horror of Nazism, the architects of the Holocaust, and benefit from the clarity of vision of a psychoanalyst who grew up in Nazi Germany (Wundheiler).

175

10

The Gentle Revolution

The Childhood Origins of Soviet and East European Democratic Movements

Lloyd deMause

An eighteenth-century French visitor to Russia wrote the following description in his diary of a traditional baptism ceremony he had just attended:

> Melissino and I were present at an extraordinary ceremony [on the river Neva], then covered with five feet of ice.
> After the benediction of the waters, children were baptized by being plunged into a large hole which had been made in the ice. On the day on which I was present the priest happened to let one of the children slip through his hands.
> "Drugoi!" he cried. That is, "Give me another."
> But my surprise may be imagined when I saw that the father and mother of the child were in an ecstasy of joy; they were certain that the babe had been carried straight to heaven. (Machen, n.d., p. 511)

The incident was typical of Russian child-rearing practices until well into this century—practices that were still medieval compared to those of the West. Most Russian parents, for instance, believed that subjecting infants to extreme heat and cold properly "hardened" them and "weeded out the unfit." As one English visitor reported:

> The Muscovites [make] their children endure the extremities of heat and cold, hunger, thirst, and labour. They wash their new-born infants in cold water, and roll

LLOYD DE MAUSE • Director, The Institute for Psychohistory, New York, New York; editor, *Journal of Psychohistory*; author, *Foundations of Psychohistory* and *Reagan's America.*
Reprinted from *Journal of Psychohistory*, Vol. 17, No. 4 (Spring 1990), with permission of Lloyd deMause, editor and publisher.

Politics and Psychology: Contemporary Psychodynamic Perspectives, edited by Joan Offerman-Zuckerberg. Plenum Press, New York, 1991.

them upon ice, and amongst snow, which if they out-live not, their mothers think them not worth a tear. (Anonymous, 1744, p. 10)

Home baptism in ice water typically lasted for over an hour. Lomonosov described one he witnessed in 1883:

The large stone hall of the parent's house in which the baptism would occur was not heated for twenty-four hours [and] water was taken directly from the well . . . the child cried out furiously and did not cease screaming with his whole strength except for short spells of breathing after complete immersion . . . the child fell into an unconscious state [and] developed convulsions and fever. (Pokrovskii, 1888, p. 244)

It is not surprising that until recently child mortality in Russia was triple that of Western Europe, with well over half of all born dying during childhood (Dunn, 1974, p. 385; Ransel, 1978, p. 236).

In Western Europe, such severely abusive child-rearing practices had gone out of style centuries earlier. Ice water bathing, for instance, had been a standard practice in all of Europe, but began to be widely criticized during the eighteenth century. While earlier diaries had often reported that newborns had "died of being baptized" in ice water and doctors had recommended daily ice water baths for children, parents by the end of the eighteenth century began to consider such "hardening" practices unnecessarily severe (Earle, 1968; Floyer, 1702; Jones, 1579). As one wrote in 1797:

To see a little infant [washed] in cold water . . . itself in one continuous scream, and the fond mother covering her ears under the bed-clothes that she may not be distressed by its cries has ever struck me as a piece of unnecessary severity. (St. Marthe, 1797, p. 63)

In Russia, however, effective opposition to traditional abusive child-rearing practices did not begin until well into the twentieth century. This two-century delay in child-rearing reform is the origin, I believe, of the two-century delay in political reform in Russia compared to the West. Furthermore, the vast improvement in Soviet child rearing in recent decades has produced the changes in Russian mentality and laid the groundwork for the dramatic political changes that have been occurring in recent months.

CHILD REARING REFORM AND POLITICAL REFORM

The central theme of my psychohistorical studies during the past two decades has been that child-rearing reform has always preceded political reform. Russia provides a particularly dramatic test and proof of this thesis. The political nightmares of Czarist and Stalinist Russia were exact recreations of the nightmares of traditional Russian childhood. Widespread infanticide, severe beatings, and other physical abuse have been the models for the physical violence of the Kremlin, the KGB, and the Gulag. And what Nathan Leites (1953) calls the traditional Russian personality traits—their fears of independence, their mood swings, and their need for external controls—were all results of the long swaddling, emotional abandonment, and cold parenting that were widespread until recently. Just as infants who have been swaddled cry out for their bindings when they are unbound—so used to restraint have they become—so, too, adults who have been physically and emotionally swaddled as children cry out for totalitarian restraints in their political systems.

THE NIGHTMARES OF TRADITIONAL RUSSIAN CHILDHOOD

In many ways, traditional Russian child rearing has resembled that of India and other Eastern countries more than the West. Infanticide and child marriage, for instance, were widespread in Russia well into the nineteenth century (deMause, 1982; Ransel, 1988). Not only were most girls married and sexually initiated prior to puberty (Levin, 1990), but fathers often had intercourse with their sons' child brides. As one nineteenth-century traveler reported:

> Fathers marry their sons to some blooming girl in the village at a very early age, and then send the young men either to Moscow or St. Petersburg to seek employment.... At the expiration of some years, when the son returns to his cottage, he finds himself the nominal father of several children, the offspring of his own parent who had deemed it his duty thus to supply the place of a husband to the young wife. This is done all over Russia. (Porter, 1952, p. 327)

Lengthy, tight swaddling (consisting of tying up infants with layers of bandages) for up to the first year of the infant's life had continued in Russia until a few decades ago. In Western Europe the practice ended during the eighteenth and nineteenth centuries. Russian infants were tightly bound and turned into excrement-soaked sausages in order to "stop them from tearing their eyes out." The babies were then prevented from crying out by having their mouths constantly "plugged" with dirty pacifier bags, which often were drawn into their throats, suffocating them (Dunn, 1974a; Gorer and Rickman, 1949).

Beating little children with whips—called "the eradicator of evil and the cultivator of virtue" (Dunn, 1974a, p. 396)—was a normal practice even among the educated (Dunn, 1974a; Okenfuss, 1980). As the traditional family handbook, *Domostroi*, suggested, one must "inflict more wounds on him and you will rejoice afterward ... crush his ribs while he is not yet grown, or else he will harden and cease to obey you." Even daughters were often whipped unmercifully: "Unconditional obedience and crushing discipline was our father's motto," wrote one woman revolutionary (Engle, 1978, p. 47). The whip was so often used on children and wives that it was often presented to the husband as part of the wedding ceremony.

Parents who showed empathy toward their children were thought sinful. When one concerned mother took her sick infant from the nurse's breast and rocked her to sleep herself, a relative warned her that "such exaggerated love was a crime against God, and He would surely punish it" (Aksakov, 1924, p. 205). Those who did not whip their children but rather treated them kindly were considered odd. At the end of the nineteenth century, Grigorii Belinskii, who did not beat his children, was described as "the only father in the city who understood that in raising children it is not necessary to treat them like cattle" (Dunn, 1974b, p. 389).

Parents were usually cold and unempathic to their children's needs. Children of the nobility were usually sent to wet-nurse in peasant families for their early years and handed over to servants when they returned home. "Children kissed their parents' hands in the morning, thanked them for dinner and supper, and took leave of them before going to bed," one woman recalled (Engel, 1978, p. 48). Even when they were not being beaten, strict discipline was enforced. "We feared [father] worse than fire," another remembered. "One glance, cold and penetrating, was enough to set us trembling" (p. 48). Kostomarov summed up traditional Russian child rearing succinctly: "Between parents and children, there reigned a spirit of slavery . . . " (Dunn, 1974a, p. 390).

RECENT CHANGES IN SOVIET CHILD REARING

Although some efforts to change traditional child rearing practices were introduced after the 1917 revolution—especially by setting up crèches where physical abuse by parents was reduced—progress was slow until the 1930s, when childhood began more to resemble that of the rest of the modern world.

Tight swaddling was ended for children of the educated, whipping became unacceptable, and parental warmth began to melt the "spirit of slavery" that pervaded most childhoods until then (Benedict, 1949; Bronfenbrenner, 1970). Education for all expanded, even to girls—a sure sign of improving childhood. In fact, women by now make up a majority of soviet workers with higher education. In the past three decades, "family clubs" have become popular, as in the West during the nineteenth century, discussing how to best bring up children while protecting their freedom and individuality. Recently, feminist groups have even been organized who have fought for children's rights (Cole, 1986; Vishneva-Sarafanova, 1981, p. 116).

The changes in childrearing are reflected in the changing personality traits of Russian leaders. Lenin's mother, who herself had been subjected to traditional "hardening" practices such as regularly being put to bed wrapped in cold wet towels (Deutschen, 1970, p. 10), brought Lenin up "in a Spartan manner" (Possony, 1964, p. 77), including the usual swaddling and wet-nursing. He reportedly could not walk until almost three and was considered a "wild, unruly child" who was "often in a rage" (Payne, 1964, p. 50). As an adult, he was icy in his emotions, murderously violent toward enemies, possibly impotent, and little concerned with democratic freedoms (Mazlish, 1968, pp. 113–141).

Stalin, in turn, had an alcoholic father who used to give his wife and children "frightful beatings," kick them with his boots, and try to kill them. His mother used to beat him as well (Rancour-Laferriere, 1988, p. 36; Tucker, 1973, p. 72). Stalin also beat his own children. Predictably, as a leader, he was responsible for the deaths of millions of his countrymen.

In contrast, Gorbachev, born in 1931, had parents who treated him with respect and a childhood that one agemate remembers as being "very joyful" (Medvedev, 1986; Murarka, 1988; Remnick, 1989; Sheehy, 1990). Although hardly a crusading democrat, Gorbachev has personality traits that are quite different from those of his predecessors. Calm and even-tempered even as a child, able to be romantic toward women, including his wife, he can represent those in the Soviet Union who no longer need political swaddling and violence and who are able to tolerate democratic reform.

Leaders, after all, are only delegates of the people's wishes, and these take several decades to change after child rearing has changed. By the time Gorbachev came to power, it had been five decades since the nightmare of traditional Russian childhood had begun to disappear, so that many in the Soviet Union now find they no longer need totalitarian leaders, violent collectivizations, or Gulags.

Few observers have been able to explain the timing of the current democratic revolutions in the Soviet Union and Eastern Europe. In fact, the end of Communism was caused neither by economic decline (there actually was economic progress during most of the past decade) nor by the trillion-dollar buildup of American arms (as Ronald Reagan claimed). Nor has it "just got old and died," as one writer put it (Nelson, 1989, p. 1).

Unlike violent revolutions, peaceful revolutions are results of an earlier growth of love toward children. Rather than hate revolutions, they are love revolutions. Rather than *economic class* revolutions, they are *psychoclass* revolutions, revolutions of new kinds of historical personalities, revolutions that, to use the words of Camus, "come into the world as gently as doves . . . amid the uproar of empires and nations a faint flutter of wings, the gentle stirring of life and hope."

WILL DEMOCRACY PREVAIL?

Will Soviet democracy prevail, or will it collapse like the democratic experiment of the Duma in 1906? And will the democratic movements in Eastern European countries prevail, or will they, too, succumb to the need for authoritarian rule that has so often been the downfall of democracy in the past?

Unfortunately, child-rearing progress has been very uneven in the Soviet Union and Eastern Europe. Tight swaddling, regular whippings, and abusive parenting remains common in many of the Soviet Republics and in many areas of Eastern Europe even today (Hermann, 1972; Krimsky, 1976; Lewis & Bann, 1977; Puhar, 1982). Even in Germany—where as late as 1964 half the children were regularly beaten by their parents with sticks—there are many areas of child abuse that continue to be alarming, including a high rate of childhood sexual molestation, which one recent study found was reported by the majority of Berlin schoolchildren who were interviewed (Havernick, 1964, p. 49; see also Berentzen, 1989; Biermann, 1969).

What this lingering pattern of child abuse means is that the success of democracy in the Soviet Union and Eastern Europe is far from guaranteed. One way to see which countries might succeed is to examine the infant mortality rates in each of them—one measure of the comparative value each puts on their children (McFarland, 1990).

Of the nine countries experiencing recent political revolutions, the five with the lowest infant mortality rates per thousand have the best chance of achieving peaceful democratic reform: German Democratic Republic (9.6), Czechoslovakia (15.3), Bulgaria (15.4), Hungary (17.0), and Poland (18.5). The two countries with medium-range infant mortality rates are moving toward democratic reform but accompanied by more violence: Romania (23.4) and the Soviet Union (26.0). And the two countries with the highest infant mortality rates have so far been unable to produce successful democratic movements: Yugoslavia (28.8) and Albania (44.8). The correlation between child rearing as measured by infant mortality and recent political reform turns out to be perfect.

A PEACEFUL EUROPE?

Finally, can a democratic Europe be a peaceful Europe? In particular, will a reunified Germany likely be a threat to the peace of Europe?

If war, like other political violence, is also a reflection of child rearing, then the vast changes in childhood for the majority of people in Germany and Eastern Europe since World War II should make it unlikely that another European war will be possible. German childhood is changing so rapidly today that Germany is likely before long to be seen as the peacekeeper of Europe, rather than as the chief initiator of European wars.

Nations that have progressed from physical abuse of their children to more psychologically abusive methods do not go to war in their own territories—they find distant Falklands and Vietnams in which to sacrifice people. If this is so, then 1990, "the year of democracy," could lay the foundations for 2000, "the century of European peace"; that is, peace on the European continent, while engaging in military activity elsewhere, as the United States does.

I admit that pan-European peace seems a utopian expectation so soon after a century in which 100 million people died in European wars. But the more I study war as a psychohistorian, the more I am convinced that all wars are perverse sexual rituals whose purpose it is to relieve unbearable feelings of being unloved, feelings that are results of abusive child rearing practices. War, like lynching and political torture, solves inner tensions for those who have been starved for affection as children and trained to be guilty about their impulses. War's economic goals are, I believe, usually mere rationalizations.

If the nightmare of war originates in the nightmare of childhood, then it is possible that a new spirit of love and freedom in the family will change Europe from a perpetual slaughterhouse to a quarreling but peaceful continent, like North America.

If this vision should come true, then the "gentle revolution" will have fulfilled its promise.

REFERENCES

Aksakov, S. T. (1924). *Chronicles of a Russian family.* London: Routledge & Sons.

Anonymous (1944). *The common errors in the education of children and their consequences.* London: Private Printing.

Benedict, R. (1949). Child rearing in certain European countries. *American Journal of Orthopsychiatry, 19,* 340–356.

Berentzen, D. (1989). Personal communication on survey of Institut fuer Kindheit.

Bronfenbrenner, U. (1970). *The worlds of childhood: U.S. and U.S.S.R.* New York: Russell Sage Foundation.

Cole, S. (1986). Soviet family clubs and the Russian human potential movement. *Journal of Humanistic Psychology, 26,* 48–83.

deMause, L. (1982). *Foundations of psychohistory.* New York: Creative Roots.

Deutscher, I. (1970). *Lenin's childhood.* London: Oxford University Press.

Dunn, P. P. (1974a). That enemy is the baby: Childhood in imperial Russia. In L. deMause (Ed.), *The history of childhood* (pp. 381–405). New York: The Psychohistory Press.

Dunn, P. P. (1974b). Fathers and sons revisited: The childhood of Vissarion Belinskii *History of Childhood Quarterly, 1,* 389–407.

Earle, A. M. (1968). *Customs and fashions in old New England.* Detroit: Singing Tree Press.

Ende, A. (1980). Battering and neglect: Children in Germany, 1860–1978. *The Journal of Psychohistory, 7,* 249–279.

Engel, B. A. (1978). Mothers and daughters: Family patterns and the female intelligentsia. In D. Ransel (Ed.), *The Family in Imperial Russia* (pp. 40–50). Urbana: University of Illinois Press.

Floyer, J. (1702). *The ancient psychoroloysia Revived, or an essay to prove cold bathing safe and useful.* London: Sam Smith.

Geiger, H. K. (1968). *The family in Soviet Russia.* Cambridge: Harvard University Press.

Gorer, G. & Rickman, J. (1949). *The people of Great Russia: A psychological study.* London: The Cresset Press.

Havernick, W. (1964). *"Schlage" als strafe: Ein bestandteil der heutigen familiensitte in volkskundlicher sicht.* Hamburg: Museum fuer Hamburgische Geschichte.

Hermann, A. (1972). *Early child care in Hungary.* London: Gordon and Breach.

Jones, J. (1579). *The arts and science of preserving bodie and soule in healthe.* Ann Arbor: University Microfilms.

Krimsky, G. A. (1976). The Russian babushka: Absolute arbiter of all things baby. *Worcester Sunday Telegram,* July 18, p. D1.

Leites, N. (1953). *A study of bolshevism.* Glencoe, IL: Free Press.

Levin, E. (1990). *Sex and society in the world of the Orthodox slavs, 900–1700.* Ithaca: Cornell University Press.

Machen, A. (n.d.) *The memoirs of Jacques Casanova de Seingalt.* New York: G. P. Putnam.

McFarland, R. B. (1990). Infant mortality rates as a guide to how nations treat children. *The Journal of Psychohistory, 17,* 417–423.

Mazlish, B. (1968). *The revolutionary ascetic: Evolution of a political type.* New York: Basic Books.

Nelson, L. (1989). *Daily News* (New York), November 12, p. 1.

Okenfuss, M. J. (1980). *The discovery of childhood in Russia: The evidence of the slavic primer.* Newtonville, MA: Oriental Research Partners.

Payne, R. (1964). *The life and death of Lenin.* New York: Simon & Schuster.

Pokrovskii, E. A. (1888). *Pervonachal'noe fizicheskoi vospitanie detei.* Moscow: N.P.

Porter, R. K. (1952). Traveling sketches in Russia and Sweden, 1905–08 In P. Putnam (Ed.), *Seven Britons in imperial Russia, 1698–1812* (pp. 320–330). Princeton, NJ: Princeton University Press.

Possony, S. T. (1964). *Lenin: The compulsive revolutionary.* Chicago: Henry Regnery Co.

Puhar, A. (1982). *Prvotno besedilo zivljenja.* Zagreb: Globus.

Rancour-Laferriere, D. (1988). *The mind of Stalin: A psychoanalytic study.* Ann Arbor, MI: Ardes Publishers.

Ransel, D. L. (Ed.) (1978). *The family in imperial Russia: New lines of historical research.* Urbana: University of Illinois Press.

Ransel, D. L. (1988). *Mothers of misery: Child abandonment in Russia.* Princeton, NJ: Princeton University Press.

Remnick, D. (1989). The cultivation of young Gorbachev. *The Washington Post,* December 1, p. B1.

Sheehy, G. (1990). The man who changed the world. *Vanity Fair,* February, p. 118.

St. Marthe, S. de (1797). *Paedotrophia: Or, the art of nursing and rearing children.* London: John Nichols.

Tucker, R. C. (1973). *Stalin as revolutionary: 1879–1929—A study in history and personality.* New York: Norton.

Vishna-Sarafanova, N. (1981). *Soviet women: A portrait.* Moscow: Progress Publishers.

11

Growing Up in Nazi Germany
Lessons to Be Learned

Luitgard N. Wundheiler

We live in eventful times. As I am working on this chapter, in early March 1990, the two Germanys are rushing to unite. Many of us look askance and with dread at a newly powerful Germany. There are even rumors afoot according to which some Germans march through the streets shouting Nazi slogans. There are neo-Nazis in some other countries, including this country. That makes this chapter even more urgent. The Anti-Defamation League of B'nai B'rith (ADL) listed, in its special report for 1988, 67 hate groups in America (ADL, 1988). They all preach hatred against those who are different. The Identity Church Movement testified in a federal court that the ultimate goal of the organization was "the annihilation of the Jewish race" (ADL, 1988). Some of the others are the National Association for the Advancement of White People (NAAWP), the White Aryan Resistance, the Aryan Nation, and the Christian American Advocates. Of course, there is also the LaRouche political cult. The ADL is admirably active in exposing the hate groups in this country. Its *Security Handbook for Community Institutions* (1986) is prepared in cooperation with the crime prevention section of the New York City Police Department and provides practical guidance on security measures.

Important for this chapter is another publication which the ADL, together with the National PTA, put out in 1989. It is a flyer entitled *What to Tell Your Child about Prejudice and Discrimination*. It is, of course, laudable that the ADL offers to the public publications such as this. But even the ADL does not offer much more than homilies like the following:

LUITGARD N. WUNDHEILER, Ph.D. • Faculty and Supervisor, Brooklyn Institute for Psychotherapy and Psychoanalysis, Brooklyn, New York; Private Practice, 925 Union Street, Brooklyn, New York 11215.

Politics and Psychology: Contemporary Psychodynamic Perspectives, edited by Joan Offerman-Zuckerberg. Plenum Press, New York, 1991.

> Take appropriate action against prejudice and discrimination. For example, if other adults use bigoted language around you and your children, you should not ignore it. Your children need to know that such behavior is unacceptable even if it is from a familiar adult. A simple phrase will do: "Please don't talk that way around me or my children," or "I don't think that joke is funny." That should get your point across (ADL, 1989)

Unfortunately, such simple advice raises more questions than it answers. Children are thinkers because they want to understand the world they grow up in. They will want to know, at the very least, why "bigoted language" is used by some people but not others, and against some people but not others. Still, it is better to have a point of view than not, and it is better to speak up than remain silent.

The editor of this book, Joan Zuckerberg, asked me to write this chapter not because we are friends, but because I am German. Although I have lived more than half my life in the United States, and although my passport says that I am a citizen of the United States, I was born and raised in Germany, and that means that my personality was formed there. On January 30, 1933, when Hitler became Chancellor of Germany, I was a child, not quite 11 years old. That means that an important part of my personality development was, among other things, subject to influences exerted by the Nazis.

It is painful to be German. Not only do many people have negative notions about the Germans, but I have deep feelings of shame about being German.

In his book *The Drowned and the Saved* (1988), Primo Levi rewrites a passage he first wrote in *The Reawakening* (1965). In it he says something about shame that expresses exactly what I feel. This is the passage:

> They [the Russian soldiers facing our Lager packed with corpses and dying prisoners] did not greet us nor smile; they seemed oppressed, not only by pity, but also by a confused restraint which sealed their mouths, and kept their eyes fastened on the funereal scene. It was the same shame which we knew so well, which submerged us after the selections, and every time we had to witness or undergo an outrage: the shame that the Germans never knew, the shame which the just man experiences when confronted by a crime committed by another, and he feels remorse because of its existence, because of its having been irrevocably introduced into the world of existing things, and because his will has proven nonexisting or feeble and was incapable of putting up a good defense. (pp 72–73)

"The shame which the just man experiences when confronted by a crime committed by another . . . " are the crucial words. It is the shame we feel because we identify ourselves as human beings. The Nazis, too, were human beings and they committed unspeakable crimes. I must identify myself as a human being, and as a German, and therefore I feel ashamed. Primo Levi is wrong, of course, about the Germans. Many of them are ashamed, but it is in the nature of shame to hide. By definition, one does not, cannot speak about one's shame. As a human being, I feel ashamed when other human beings do something reprehensible and proud when someone does something wonderful and admirable. We say: "I am proud of you," or "I am ashamed of you," when we are in some way identified with the "you." Family members are sometimes proud or ashamed of each other. Similarly, members of the same nation or members of the same species may be proud or ashamed of each other. Parents, in particular, may be proud or ashamed of their children for they are, in part, responsible for what their children are like. I am who I am, in part because I am German, and I am, in part, responsible for what the Germans are like and for what they did and do. The feeling of shame and responsibility does not diminish with time, but it can be acknowledged and spoken about.

In an attempt to deal with the title of this chapter, I want to relate a few memories from my childhood and youth before writing about what lessons can be learned from my experiences.

The memories I will report go back to the years of my latency and adolescence: important years for personality development. They are excerpts from an as yet unpublished manuscript, *Growing up in Nazi Germany.*

*   *   *

The year was 1930 or perhaps 1928 or 1929. I was eight years old, perhaps a year or two younger. My family and I were vacationing near Berchtesgaden in the Bavarian Alps. We were staying in a small village that consisted of about ten half-timbered houses. We had rented a floor in one of these houses for the month of July. The village was quiet, the mountains above glowed in the sun, the meadow was covered with fragrant flowers, and—most important—Father was always in a good mood and approachable. Why was he so moody and difficult to live with in the city where he was a judge and I went to school? I did not like going to school, I did not like the crowds of noisy, rowdy children with their crude manners and rough behavior. I always felt an outsider among them. I *was* an outsider, certainly I felt that way. I was different somehow, although I did not know how or why. The other children did not like me either. Why did I always keep to myself? Why was I so quiet? Who did I think I was? Did I think I was better than they? Although I did not like the other children, it pained me to think that they did not like me. Father had once said something very consoling to me: "Don't worry that you are not popular; it is much easier to be independent if you are not. Just accept it." His words had pleased me, although I did not quite understand them. These words expressed Father's approval of me, and that was most consoling. I felt honored that Father thought even I, a little girl, could be independent. I was not sure what it meant to be independent, but I knew that Father considered it a virtue to think independently. How does one learn to do that? Did I not think, most of the time, in ways that I knew would please my parents and teachers? Father's words were puzzling. Did he really mean that I should stop trying to please *him* and think differently? And how would I get my thoughts if not from him?

On this particular day, as I was lying in the meadow smelling the flowers and talking out loud because there was nobody to listen, somebody came to disturb me. It was Henner, my older brother, shouting that Hitler—whoever that was— was going away on a trip, and that that was a big event we should not miss. So, let him go to . . . well, I did not know where he was going or who he was, this man called Hitler. Why should I be excited? I knew only one thing about him: that he had big German shepherd dogs who began barking as soon as anyone approached the house. Henner said a crowd was gathering near Hitler's house to see him off. Did that mean he was famous or important?

Henner insisted that we should go and watch. There would be other people present today, the dogs would behave themselves, and if not, the crowd of grownups would protect me. Grown-ups were not afraid of dogs. I was already rising from that secret spot in the meadow as I had known I would. I was always docile when my brother asked something of me. Was I dependent on him, too? Some time later, I would think about that tricky question. Right now, there seemed to be no time, for a crowd was already gathering near Hitler's house, and we would miss his departure if we did not hurry. Okay, we ran to join the crowd. It was a small crowd, perhaps 10 or 15 people, mostly men, and about three or four women. The women had come in their housedresses and aprons, and the men wore that uniform that Mother found so ugly. She refused to admit anyone wearing that uniform to our apartment in the city. I had not seen the uniform more than once or twice, and I rather agreed with Mother. The color was ugly, neither brown nor beige, it was the color of shit; dog shit, I thought. Was that the reason Mother disliked the uniform so much? Probably not. Mother did not usually refuse to see someone because of what he was wearing. What was it, then?

Henner and I joined the crowd. Everybody was waiting. Ten minutes, 20 minutes, one hour, several hours? I could not tell; it seemed like an eternity. I very much wanted to go back to my meadow. As the sun began to set, the colors would change, the mountains would glow more deeply, and slowly turn golden-pink—in that mysterious "Alpenglühen" that transported me into a state of bliss every time I saw it. The blue and white and rose of the flowers would darken and become intense in the glow of the setting sun; but here I stood in that small crowd of 15 people and did not leave, merely because they did not leave. (Was I dependent on them, too? What an absurd thought!) Yet, I kept waiting for no other reason than Henner had said that this was an important event, and because everyone else was waiting. Finally, a man appeared, relatively small, with dark hair brushed with effort to the side to reveal an undistinguished forehead, and with a black moustache that looked as if it were merely pasted on the upper lip to hide something—but what? I felt an urge to tear off this moustache; but of course, I did not—I was a well-brought-up girl. One does not simply give in to one's urges, especially when they lead to behavior that might hurt others. He wore the same uniform in the same shit color as the men who were there to see him off. He mounted a motor bike and everybody raised his or her arm; what did that mean? I had never seen anyone do that before. The man, called Hitler, also raised his arm, but in a different manner: he bent his arm sharply at his elbow, everybody else stretched out his arm straight. Everyone, including Hitler, shouted, "Heil!" Then his motorbike made a lot of noise and he sped away surrounded by a cloud of dust.

I was relieved, even happy, when everyone shouted "Heil!" "Heil" was a nice word, a word I knew well. When something broke, Mother usually said: "Das kann man wieder *heil* machen" (one can fix it again), and when I or one of my siblings hurt ourselves, Mother would often sing a little ditty: "*Heile, heile* Segen." "Segen" was something good, a blessing, and so was "heil." It had something to do with getting better and getting well. I liked that and so I cried "Heil!" with the others. It made me feel less lonely, not altogether left out. Henner was even raising his arm and looked very smart. I did not raise my arm, as I did not know what that meant, and I never said or did anything that I did not understand. I knew that to be a serious fault: in school, I was often reprimanded for it. I refused to say something merely because someone else, be it the teacher himself, said it was correct. Unless I understood it, I would not say it. My teacher called me stubborn for that reason. But I could not help it, although I knew it was a fault to be stubborn.

Well, the excitement of the day was finally over, Hitler had left, and Henner and I went home. We walked along the dusty road; we felt letdown without admitting it to each other. We walked in silence. After about 100 yards, a narrow path branched off to the left. It led through the meadow that I loved so much and on to the house where my family were staying. I hardly glanced at the meadow now; I sensed rather than saw the bluish shadows of early evening muting the vibrant colors of the flowers. Henner and I both went straight to the house and found the rooms our family occupied empty. I went outside to look for Mother. I found her lying in the hammock reading. The hammock was made of rope—straw-colored rope—the same kind of rope used to make Mother's shopping bags. All the women I knew had shopping bags made of rope. The rope was knotted into sturdy squares, well suited for carrying things; at the top the rope was crocheted into handles, just like the rope of the hammock was crocheted into large handles at both ends by which it was hung from the branches of two trees.

I felt guilty without knowing why when I saw Mother. She turned and looked at me in that singularly intense way that I have never seen in anyone else. She always knew what I felt and thought. It was no use trying to hide anything from her. I was dependent on her approval. Did I feel guilty because I had seen those men in the uniforms that Mother detested? I climbed into the hammock beside her and tried to avert my eyes. Mother asked in her soft, yet insistent voice: "Where have you been?" I tried to sound nonchalant: "We went to see Hitler off, he left for a trip." Mother looked serious. After a long pause, she said: "Please don't go near his house again, he is an evil man." ("Schlecht" was the word she used, not "böse," not "unfreundlich," but "schlecht.") Why? I wondered. What did he do? Mother hardly ever called anyone "schlecht," not even children who really did evil stuff, like calling bad words after old ladies, or playing practical jokes and awful tricks that frightened them. How evil must one be to be called "schlecht" by Mother? That was a word of moral condemnation.

* * *

In 1933, a few months before I turned 11, I came home from school one day to find Mother crying. She was all by herself, sitting in the living room near the window, crying. I was shocked. It was not the first time that I saw Mother cry. Not long ago, her brother, Uncle Carl Georg, had died rather suddenly, and Mother had cried bitterly. But I had never seen her sit by herself and cry, apparently unaware of whether she was alone or not. When Mother noticed me, she said: "Ach, Kind, das verstehst Du noch nicht" (oh, child, you don't understand that yet); "Hitler was made Chancellor of this nation, and that means there will be a war soon." I really did not understand. I knew something about war, though not much. Father had been severely wounded in the last war, and as a result, he had lost the use of his right arm and leg; but I had always thought that happened a long, long time ago, when people were still savages. In the world where I grew up, it was unthinkable that people would wound each other for life. People tried to be kind to each other. When they had serious differences, they would argue and fight with words, but shoot each other? I could not imagine that that would ever happen again.

Only children fought with their fists, and sometimes even with their feet. And children, including myself, were trying to become as well behaved as grown-ups. Anyhow, how could Mother *know* that there would be war? Or did she mean some other kind of war? Like arguments where people would fight with words? But that would not be a reason to cry so sadly. Even Mother herself sometimes had arguments with Father, and quite often with her children, but they never lasted very long, these arguments. In the evening, when Father came home, I could see that he, too, was worried, but by no means as distressed as Mother. He put his arm around her to calm her, and said something to the effect that it would not be as bad as she thought; *"we Germans are reasonable people"* (wir Deutsche sind doch vernünftige Menschen), he added.

* * *

The year was 1934 or 1935. My family was still living in an apartment in a very nice house with a sun clock painted on the front which really worked when the sun shone, which did not happen very often. As was true of most Germans—German Christians, that is—our economic condition had vastly improved during the first one or two years of the new regime, the Hitler regime. That was the reason Father was thinking of building a house for his family. Why did Mother continue to call Hitler evil? Why was a man evil who all but eliminated poverty and saw to it that millions of jobless, starving people had food on their tables and were employed again? I had learned in school that that was one of his accomplishments. Did he not do a lot of good? I did not understand Mother. Why did she continue to think Hitler evil, and why did she still dislike those uniforms so much? I myself could no longer think of a reason, except that they were ugly.

It was a wonderfully warm and sunny day, summer vacation had just started, and I was at home. Mother was sitting at her writing table, a beautiful old secretary, and was writing a letter to someone. Writing letters filled her intense private life—the life in which she was free to express herself, free from the constant pressures to be a good mother, a good wife, a good housekeeper, a good daughter, a good daughter-in-law, a good sister, and a good sister-in-law (so many relatives also lived in this city and constantly demanded that Mother meet all their expectations). These few morning hours were hers. Father was at work in court; nobody was allowed to disturb her. The bell rang. I felt a sting of resentment. Someone was coming to disturb Mother while I had been trying hard to stay out of the living room and not interfere with Mother's one or two free hours. I listened intently to recognize the voices at the front door. I was curious to know who came. There could be no doubt, it was Mrs. B., a neighbor. It was most unusual for Mrs. B. to come in the morning, when she, too, usually enjoyed a few free hours of privacy. Did something unfortunate happen? Did she want comfort and advice from Mother? I felt pangs of jealousy at the mere thought. I would like to be comforted by Mother. But what for? I was well and had no worries, except for some secret worries that I did not want Mother to know about.

And even if I had been ready to disclose those worries, I would not have known how to communicate them. And therefore, my worries had become *my* private life. Finally, I gave in to my curiosity and descended the stairs to join the two women in the living room. The living room was flooded with light. Its windows faced south, and at this hour, at about 11 o'clock in the morning, the sunlight flooded in through the open windows. The view from the living room was beautiful. One could see the southern part of town and the low mountain ranges and the mist-filled valley beyond. Although Mother was listening intently to Mrs. B., she noticed me and gave me a sign with her expressive face not to interrupt. I had no intention to interrupt. I stood behind Mrs. B. and gave no sign of my presence. Mrs. B. was talking about a man who had been released from a Nazi prison. I did not understand why he had been in prison. Mrs. B. said that he had been a Social Democrat. But that really did not explain anything. As Father was a judge, I knew something about prisons and why people are sent to prison. People were jailed when they had robbed or murdered or had done something else that was terribly wrong. But nobody had ever told me that it was *wrong* to be a Social Democrat. What did they do that was so terrible that they were sentenced to jail? This man, apparently a friend of the B.'s, had been tortured in prison, beaten with clubs, immersed in water so that he could not breathe and was afraid he would drown. Why? Suddenly I felt sick and then indignant. It was plainly wrong to torture this man. No matter what a man did, he should be treated decently. That much I had learned from Father. But this was really elementary; nobody had to *learn* that it was wrong to torture people. Mrs. B. went on talking for a long time, while tears were running down her rosy cheeks. It almost looked funny, or rather, it would have looked funny, if she had not been talking about such horrible things.

* * *

When he was only 14, Henner was already admired by everybody. He was very smart and had already read a lot of philosophy. He could even talk about the philosophical works he read and one could make sense of what he said. Henner joined the Hitler Youth. Although he was usually very articulate, he was not at all articulate about his reasons for joining. Could it be that he joined because most of his classmates had joined? But that was impossible, because it would mean that he was not nearly as independent as I thought him to be. I must believe that he had better reasons than that. If he did not, some of my beliefs would crumble. And if he was not independent, who was? And what was independence? Surely, if he was not independent, neither was I. And in that case, I would have to revise my self-image.

But then, one day, something happened that shook me up, although it re-established my faith in Henner as an independent person. Henner came home quite early from his Hitler Youth "Dienst" (service). That was the words they all used when they spent a few hours with the Hitler Youth, or the S.A., or some other Nazi organization. Whom or what did they serve? Hitler? Because they called themselves "Hitler Youth?" Well, when Henner came home that day unexpectedly early, he went straight to his room and stayed there the rest of the day. Once, I knocked on his door, but as there was no answer, I retreated.

After supper, I could not contain myself any longer. I went to his room and opened the door: there he sat, motionless, and stared out the window. I approached him. "What happened?" For some time, Henner did not answer.

Finally, he stirred and looked at me. Night had fallen, and I could hardly see him any more. His "Aryan" profile was sharply outlined against the dusky sky. "The ordered us to throw rocks into the windows of a Jewish store and curse the shopkeeper." Henner was speaking softly and quickly. It was hard to understand him. "They used all the worst and dirtiest words they could think of. I couldn't do it. So, I came home. That's all. I have been thinking about it ever since." "What have you been thinking?" I asked, "and what are you going to do?" "There is nothing much to think about," Henner said, "I will never do what they did today. I'm thinking about what I can do so that I will never be asked again to do something like that."

In this house, so far away from the city noises, the only sounds one could hear were inside the house or sounds that flowed in from the garden through the open window. Henner and I could hear Father's steps in the living room downstairs. From time to time, one could also hear a door open and close. Our younger brother and sister, "die Kleinen," as we referred to them, were going to bed. We could hear Mother, as she ascended the stairs and went to their rooms. Henner and I were silent for a long time. Finally, I asked: "Will you always just go away when they order you to throw rocks into people's windows and curse them? Perhaps, you can tell them what you think so that you won't be asked any more." Henner looked at me in surprise and asked me if I really thought things were so simple. Did I not know that the Hitler Youth leaders were not people like our family who honored other people's opinions and beliefs?

Suddenly, Henner got a hold of himself and said rapidly: "You don't know them, they think this is right. All I can do is refuse to do what they tell me when I think it is not right. They will continue to give orders like this one and even worse ones." Then, he was silent again. Suddenly, he switched the light on, and turned to look at me. "I know what I can do. I will write a letter and resign from the Hitler Youth." That seemed like a good idea. Of course, I would write the letter with him. We would compose it together, but then I would write it. Henner was so upset that he would not be able to write it. Besides, he seemed so superior that it seemed natural to me to serve as his secretary. I sat down at his desk, and Henner opened the drawer and took out some clean white sheets of writing paper. We were ready to start. The beginning was easy. We said that Henner would never join in inhuman and cruel actions and that, therefore, he wanted to resign. "Unmenschlich" (inhuman) and "grausam" (cruel) were the words we chose. It took us no time at all to decide that these were the words that best described what we wanted to say. The rest of the letter was far more difficult, for we wanted to *explain* our decision. We spent many hours writing it. We wrote and crossed out what we wrote. We rewrote words, sentences, paragraphs. We wanted to say far more than that Henner would never do what he thought was wrong. We wanted to justify his right to refuse to do so. We used all the philosophy we had read to make our point. We also wanted to influence the recipient of this letter, Henner's Hitler Youth leader. We wanted to make him think. We wanted him to understand that each human being had a right and obligation to think for him/herself and make truly moral choices. When we were finally finished, we read it again; we each read it out loud to the other to make sure it was clearly expressed.

We thought that Henner's leader who was a couple of years older than us, was intelligent enough to understand what we understood. We did not consider the possibility that we understood because we *wanted* to understand and that Henner's leader did not have that wish. We did not consider the possibility that he wished to show Henner that he was wrong, that his thoughts were antagonistic to the thinking of the German people, that they were "volksfremd"—a word that was used more frequently every day and applied to everything that did not please the stupid masses. Were the masses really so united? Henner and I were snobs, and we knew it.

Finally, well past midnight, Henner and I were finished. We looked at each other silently. We felt proud, but also afraid. For a fraction of a second, we knew that we were about to do something dangerous. While we were engrossed in writing the letter, that seemed the hardest task to complete that night. We did not foresee the difficulty of actually mailing it. We put it in an envelope and sealed it. We suddenly felt like conspirators. A feeling that holds some pleasure, especially for young adolescents. We agreed to mail the letter that night. We knew that we would not mail it if we waited until the next day. We tiptoed downstairs through the house, which was silent at that late hour. We walked quickly to the letter box. We ran down the steps through the garden and then down the familiar path, called "Bucergäßchen," which we walked down several times each day, when we went to school, when we went to our various lessons music, art—or when we went to visit someone. We knew every cobblestone, and we knew where we could run and where we had to watch our steps. We passed the lamppost that stood about halfway between our house and the main street at the bottom of the "Bucergäßchen." Finally, we reached the letter box. It took us no more than three minutes to get there, but that night, three minutes seemed like a long time indeed. Our hearts were heavy and we were very afraid, but neither of us admitted it. Strangely enough, I even felt guilty. I had experienced that before. Something like guilt, when one does something that is right, but not generally approved. Probably, one should not call it "guilt," although it *feels* like guilt to many people. I thought a hundred times while running beside Henner: "It is not yet too late, we can return without mailing this letter." And feel safe again. What a good feeling: safe. We stood by the letter box, silently, and looked at each other. Finally, I raised the lid, and Henner dropped the letter into the box. The deed was done. Was I responsible because I raised the lid, thereby encouraging Henner to drop the letter into the box? What would be the consequences? Neither Henner nor I knew. Actions like this one did not have foreseeable consequences. People who wanted their actions to have predictable consequences had better act like everyone else. To act according to one's own judgment makes one feel afraid—and perhaps even guilty. And very alone. We need the approval of others when we are 13 or 14 years old. The approval of others is a protection against guilt feelings. Supposedly, it demonstrates a higher stage of moral development to be able to form one's judgments according to one's own set of principles, independently of the opinions of others. But when we *act*, we want and need the approval of others. Without it, we may feel in the wrong.

* * *

Nineteen thirty-six was a difficult year, a hard year. Father got a letter from a superior who was of high rank in the National Socialist Party. There was an enclosure that Father was asked to sign. Signing it was tantamount to a loyalty oath to the Nazi ideology and Hitler. Father raised us to think independently. This was the year to put his teaching to the test and to put his actions where his mouth was.

Father discussed the content of the statement he had been asked to sign with those family members he thought old enough to think independently. That included Mother and me—and, of course, Henner. The two "little ones," my younger sister and brother, were not considered old enough to have an opinion on such difficult matters. I was asked to come to my father's study, by myself. Father was a judge and he knew how easily people are influenced by others, particularly by others they love. He knew how easily I was influenced by Henner who I loved so much. That was the reason he asked me to come to his study alone.

Father's study was in the southeast corner of the house. It had two windows, one faced east and the other south. When I entered, Father sat at his desk in the center of the room. I sat down on the sofa from which I could see the larch tree outside the east window. Father handed me the statement he was asked to sign. He said nothing, but looked worried and very small, although he really was a tall person. I glanced at him and then read the statement carefully. It was written in stilted, bureaucratic language, but its meaning was clear. The major premises of the Nazi ideology were stated, the premises that were extraordinarily familiar to every German in those days, including myself. They were about the superiority and goodness of the Germanic race and culture, about the duty of every German to proselytize—convince as many others as possible of the superiority of the Germans and the inferiority of others, particularly the Jews. The Jews, as every German was told innumerable times, were fiendish, devilish people who were trying to control everything, not only in Germany, but everywhere in the world. Every patriotic German was therefore dutybound to defeat them. At the end of this statement, there were the inevitable words: "Heil Hitler!" and a space for Father's signature.

I read the statement slowly in order to give myself time to think. I did not know what Father would ask me. But I was very afraid, I sensed how momentous the occasion was. Finally, I looked up and asked Father: What are you going to do? Father spoke haltingly: "I haven't made up my mind yet. But I want to know what you think. No matter what I do, the consequences will be felt by all of you." He explained that signing this statement was equivalent to lying. But also that we would be allowed to live in relative comfort, as we had until then, if he signed. If, on the other hand, he would return the statement unsigned, the consequences would be unpredictable. Perhaps, nothing at all would happen, but that was unlikely; perhaps he would lose his job, perhaps *they* (I knew who *they* were) would take him away, and we might never see each other again. I interrupted him and said: "You cannot lie, you never lied in your life." Father said very slowly:

"Yes, I've always tried to be truthful." According to Father, to be truthful was as important as independence. Even today, more than 50 years after the event described and almost 20 years after his death, I cannot recall a single instance when Father lied. If he ever had, I would have lost all respect for him. Children and adolescents are like that: unforgiving, absolute in their thinking. Father dismissed me. I left his study with a heavy heart. I had not said outright that he should not sign the statement he had been asked to sign, but probably Father sensed that my love and admiration of him were contingent on my belief in his absolute truthfulness. And that was enough. There was no point in expecting me to say more. That same day, Mother talked with him. It seemed that he was pretty much decided, and that Mother, although very scared, stood by him.

I was relieved, and probably looked proud and radiant. I had no real idea of the sinister consequences a man might have to face who still thought and acted according to his own judgment. I had been told about some of these consequences, but they were not at all real to me. People were punished for doing what I had been taught was right? They were thrown into prison because they thought on their own? They were beaten until they gave in? They lost their jobs? Their families were ostracized? This made no sense at all. How could it? I lived in a family who considered it a virtue to think and act independently. How could I think that the country we lived in was different? I was a child—14 years old—but a child nevertheless. That day, I was happy because I did not lose my father. He did not lie, and I could continue to love him. That was all that mattered. I could not and did not think about the following day. I wanted my father. That was all. I did not think about the future. I was a child, my father's child.

When I came home from school the next day, a look at Mother's face sufficed to tell me that Father had sent back that statement unsigned. Nothing was said, but Mother's serious face told all, even before Father came home. I was no longer happy. I sensed fear in my parents. My parents had been afraid before, but it had never been like this. They could not give each other any comfort, they could not relieve each other's fear. I began to doubt that my words of the previous day had been brave and honest. They had been rash and selfish and thoughtless words.

As it turned out, the worst did not happen. Father did not even lose his job, but he had little work to do in Marburg. He was sent quite often to small, out-of-the-way places where he had to do lowly jobs, usually done by a beginner or a law clerk. He felt humiliated, and as he had to travel much, his lame leg gave him a great deal of pain. Naturally, he was too proud to complain openly, but he let Mother know that he suffered.

This was the second time that our family was spared terrible consequences of brave and honest actions. Nothing much had happened to Henner when he had resigned from the Hitler Youth. His leader had asked him for an interview and tried to persuade him to stay on and try, together with him, his leader, to "humanize" (menschlich machen) the Hitler Youth. Henner had declined and his leader, Karl Seehausen, had had no choice but to let him go.

* * *

It was the day after Kristallnacht, November 10, 1938. On that day everything seemed different, although it was just an ordinary school day. Many children, boys too, were running in the direction of our school, the girls' high school. Not a sound could be heard, so that I could not guess why they were running there. As my sister, Hella, and I were approaching our school, I noticed a large crowd just across the street from our school, where the synagogue was. When we came closer, we saw that the crowd was standing around a pile of smoldering ashes. The synagogue had been whole only yesterday. I looked repeatedly in order to convince myself that today it was in ruins. It was before Word War II, and we had never seen buildings destroyed in one brief night, and did not yet know that it was possible. We still thought of buildings as something permanent. It was true: where the whole synagogue had been only yesterday, there were ruins and smoldering ashes today. Some SA men in their brown uniforms and some SS men in their black uniforms stood between the crowd and the smoldering ashes. It looked as if they were guarding the ashes and the ruins of the synagogue. I shivered.

The crowd was completely silent. People did not look each other in the eye. Were they shocked at what they saw? But why had they not been ashamed during the night when the destruction was committed? They had been silent, then, as our parents had been. Did *they* know what had happened? Soon, the crowd began to disperse, the SS and SA men sped them on.

I entered the school building together with the other girls and went to the art room for the first lesson of the day. From the windows, one could see the ruins of the synagogue. The girls crowded near the windows and spoke in hushed voices. The teacher, Miss Weber, a woman with a clear mind and a courageous voice, told us that as far as she knew, all synagogues in Germany had been destroyed during the night from November 9 to November 10. The destruction had been ordered, and people did as they were told. She also said that even the most beautiful synagogue, the synagogue in Worms, had been destroyed. The artist in her was speaking, I felt. She seemed to feel more sorrow for the synagogue in Worms than for the others. And more sorrow for the beauty of the synagogue than for the people who worshipped in it. I realized suddenly that the children who had been forbidden to attend German schools because they were Jewish could no longer go to their synagogues for instruction either. More than 900 synagogues had been destroyed in Germany.

After that realization, I was in deep thought. I was aware that I did not know how a synagogue looked inside. I had never been inside one. Presumably, the reason was respect and reverence. One does not visit holy places out of curiosity. But was that really the reason? Definitely not. When my family went on trips, we visited cathedrals and churches to admire the art work inside, out of curiosity, I assumed. Why had we never visited a synagogue?

When I returned home from school that day, there were no tender welcoming kisses and embraces as on other days; instead, there was Mother's sad, stern face. Why did she look so sad and stern? As if somebody had done something wrong? Stupid girl! A lot of people had indeed done something very wrong! It was time to grow up indeed! How childish and self-centered of me to think that Mother's sad, stern face was necessarily meant for one of her children! As if there was nothing else to worry about in the world!

*   *   *

I think it was during the same year, in 1938, that another event occurred which is etched even more deeply into my memory. I had a religion teacher who was Jewish. Miss Janow was, of course, a converted Jew. If she had been Jewish by religion, she would not have taught religion to Christian girls. But that made no difference to the Nazis. Her parents had practiced the Jewish faith, and hence, Miss Janow was judged Jewish. I am not sure when she had been dismissed from her teaching position, perhaps in 1935, when the Nuremberg laws had become the laws of the land.

One rainy fall day, I walked along a street I knew very well. It was a street in the center of the town and was called "Barfüßerstraße." It was named after a monastic order that had established itself in Marburg in the late Middle Ages. When going from my parents' house to the marketplace or to my favorite book-store, I had to walk along Barfüßerstraße. Just before reaching the Markt, the square in front of town hall—an imposing and rather beautiful structure erected during the Renaissance—a steep and narrow *Gasse* joined Barfüßerstraße from the left.

On that day, as I was walking along Barfüßerstraße, I suddenly spotted Miss Janow, my ex-teacher. Miss Janow was wearing the Jewish star on her coat, as Jews were supposed to do, and she was not watching her step (as she should have, considering the unevenness of the cobble stones) but rather the people in the street. Suddenly, our eyes met, very briefly, for a fraction of a second. Miss Janow, whose face was very stern, immediately averted her gaze. I, however, greeted her with exquisite, almost exaggerated politeness and smiled. In addition, I did something very unusual, something only little girls did in Germany in those days, I bent my knees a little, as I smiled; in short, I curtsied, *knickste*. At my advanced age of 16, girls no longer used that form of greeting, particularly not in those days when one was supposed to raise one's arm and say: "Heil Hitler!" when greeting someone. For many years thereafter, if someone had asked me why I greeted Miss Janow in that childlike manner, I would have been flustered and not been able to give a reason. But I never told anyone of that brief encounter, and therefore nobody ever asked. As I said before, Miss Janow's facial expression was stern and forbidding and she looked very proud. I knew that she had had that facial expression before our eyes met, I therefore knew that it was not directed at me.

Why, then, did I feel ashamed? I think one part of the answer is clear. I was a decent girl, and it is painful for decent people to watch someone who is totally unprotected and fair game for anybody, without the ability to help. Perhaps I had additional reasons to feel ashamed. Realistically, Miss Janow was far more vul-nerable than I was. Yet, it was she, not I, who had the presence of mind to protect herself as well as me. By not acknowledging my greeting, she had made it impossible for anyone to know whom I had greeted. I had committed the crime of being decent to a Jewish woman. It was forbidden for Jewish and Christian Germans to have polite, let alone friendly, relations with each other. A person weaker than myself had protected us both. Probably I felt ashamed also because that event brought home to me the awareness that *I* now belonged to the priv-ileged class of the "master race," while Miss Janow, my revered teacher, had to suffer dehumanizing contempt and persecution. The teacher–pupil relationship of years past was of no importance. I realized that Miss Janow was Jewish at the wrong time of history. It was not my doing, but nevertheless I felt ashamed. It was shameful to belong to a relatively invulnerable group of people when there were others who were acutely vulnerable. My father had taught me that justice has no meaning at all unless it has the same meaning for everybody. To be forced into a position where one cannot act according to one's principles must provoke shame.

A contrasting feeling perhaps also contributed to my sense of shame: I was not like other Germans. I was unable to ignore Miss Janow or even feel hostile to her. Why was I so "un-German?" Why was I different? Why could I not do the "German" thing, surely the right thing, and look at Miss Janow and feel contempt? I did not feel any contempt for her; what was wrong with me? I felt tortured also because no matter what I felt and did, I was always wrong. I was unable to feel secure in the knowledge that I was German and I was totally unable to feel superior, and I also could not identify with Miss Janow. I felt the pain of ambivalence.

*   *   *

When I was about 16 or 17 years old, I had a Latin teacher who was a Nazi. All our Latin lessons deteriorated into lessons on Nazi ideology. With this teacher, Mr. Hädrich, I had many fights. I tried to confront him with everything that lacked logic in his ideological sermons and told him that I thought his thoughts were immoral. On the other hand, Mr. Hädrich thought himself to be a good German and felt that my ideas were despicable.

He threatened repeatedly to send me to a "reeducation camp" (I knew that that was a name for concentration camps). Incidentally, the expression "K.Z." (konzentrations-lager) was used freely in everyday language. As teachers and parents used to threaten children with the bogeyman and witches (der schwarze Mann und Hexen) in the past, they now took to threatening them with the K.Z. "Wenn Du Dich nicht benimmst, kommst Du ins K.Z." (Unless you behave you'll go to the K.Z.) children were told. Nothing was ever said about what happened in the K.Z., but the tone with which the threat was made indicated that it was as terrible as hell. The implications for German child-rearing methods are obviously disastrous. Obviously, everybody knew about concentration camps, postwar denials notwithstanding.

To return to the arguments I had with my Latin teacher: he often called me a "liberal Jewess," the worst curse words he could think of. To be called "liberal" meant that he considered me subversive, and that he called me "Jüdin" meant that he thought me as un-German and "artfremd" (foreign to the German race) as only a Jew could be. He regularly expressed surprise that these words did not rile me. Since I considered neither of them a curse word, but felt pleased that I had so much power over him that I could provoke him to use them, he became even more enraged. There were several occasions when the vehemence of his anger frightened me.

I had the tacit, and sometimes explicit, support of at least three of my classmates. This was of great importance to me for it meant that even with my subversive remarks I did not run the risk of being completely ostracized. On the contrary, some of my classmates admired and supported me. Also, I realized that my arguments with Mr. Hädrich had become the talk of the town. That knowl-

edge, of course, spurred me on to ever more daring behavior. I felt protected by
the citizens of Marburg. Sometimes, I sensed that Mr. Hädrich had become the
laughingstock of the entire town. I think this is an important facet of my story, for
it means that Marburg had become a city in which some impotent dissidence was
rampant. It also meant that I did have as much support as an adolescent needs to
form an identity. Yet, in retrospect, I must add that the tacit approval of my
behavior by the citizens of Marburg simply meant that they believed in authoritarian values. They probably thought: Who ever heard of a mere teenager defeating a teacher in an argument? Such a teacher deserves to be the laughingstock
of the town.

One day, something happened that put an end to all this. It was the custom
then that every class in every German school had a "classbook." It was the duty
of every teacher to enter in this book the theme of the lesson he or she had taught.
Mr. Hädrich's entries were always the same. He would write: Tacitus or Livius
or whatever else might be the case, and then some arbitrary chapter headings.
One day, the entire class period was spent on an argument about the Semitic
linguistic form of the ten commandments: "Thou shalt not . . . " Mr. Hädrich
claimed that the negative was typical of the Semitic spirit. The Jews, he said, were
nihilists, hence "Thou shalt *not* . . . " The Germanic peoples are life-affirming, he
claimed, and therefore express their commandments in the positive mode. "But,
where are they?" I asked. "Did anyone write them down? Perhaps, the Germanic
peoples did not know how to write in the days when the Jews carved their
commandments in stone?" When the lesson had ended, I checked the classbook
and saw that Mr. Hädrich's entry was as false as ever. This was too blatant and
too much. I took my pen and wrote plainly beside his entry: "Du sollst die
Wahrheit sagen" (thou shalt speak the truth), a positively stated and, hence,
Germanic commandment. I was fully aware that the principal and every teacher
in the school would soon know what had happened.

In the course of the next few days, not only the teachers, but all parents
learned exactly what had happened. I could not help but notice that my parents
were pleased, perhaps even proud of me. There was not a word of reproach from
them, both smiled at me approvingly, albeit secretly. They did not want
anyone else to know that they approved of my behavior. This meant to me that
they were afraid. I understood their fears. I put into practice what they had taught
me: I spoke my mind and insisted on truthfulness. Were they worried about how
I would survive with such unpopular values? Should they have raised me differently? Did they not endanger their children by supporting such unpopular and
unrealizable values? To live with such values meant to endanger our physical
lives to live without these values, or in accordance with popular values, meant to
endanger our spiritual survival.

Although my parents had discussed so much with us, or if not with us,
certainly in our presence, they never discussed their worries about us, their
children, in our presence. The matter with Mr. Hädrich was as good as forgotten
in a few days. I realized that I had been admired not because of my courage, but
because of a profound misunderstanding. I had given expression to the wishes of
many members of the school community. Many parents felt that this nincompoop

of a teacher who wasted his time arguing with a mere adolescent should be replaced by a competent teacher. By acting as I did, I had exposed Mr. Hädrich's incompetence.

* * *

Wolfgang was Henner's closest friend. He was shy and seemed preoccupied with thoughts he did not share with anybody. For some time, he and I were good friends because he was a close friend of Henner's. I did not think about my feelings for Wolfgang, or his feelings for me. Of course, we were friends; whoever Henner was friends with, was also my friend. In 1938, when I was 16 and Wolfgang 18, our friendship blossomed into love. We loved each other with tenderness and respect which transformed our lives, and pleased Henner greatly.

Wolfgang's family had come to Marburg in the mid 1930s from Jena. Rumor had it that Wolfgang's father, a professor of economics, had provoked the displeasure of his colleagues and superiors with his subversive opinions until they had him transferred to a small university, like Marburg, where he could not influence such large numbers of students. A few other professors had been transferred to Marburg for the same reason, among them Reidemeister, the mathematician, from the University of Königsberg. The University of Marburg was thus becoming a center for politically undesirable professors who were not "criminal" or subversive enough to be put away without causing indignation among the population. During those years, the Nazis were relatively polite, when that suited their purposes, and tried to foresee public opinion.

I spent much of my free time in Wolfgang's house and met both his parents, his older sister, Maria, and his older brother, Jürgen. Although I liked being there, I did not feel at ease there, the atmosphere was cold, almost forbidding compared with my own parental home. But although I did not have tender feelings for him, I respected Wolfgang's father. He was extremely intelligent and extraordinarily courageous. He made no bones about his highly critical political stance.

Like my father, he loved debating, but did so more skillfully, and often engaged his family in discussing political issues with him. He was a passionate patriot; he loved Germany more than himself or even his family, and for that reason he condemned and hated the Nazis. He thought them a disgrace and terrible blemish on his beloved Germany. He had nothing but contempt for stupid people and he thought the Nazis and their followers singularly stupid. He did not understand how anyone could fail to see that Hitler would sooner or later bring about Germany's downfall. Therefore, he felt the Germans must rid themselves of this idiotic Satan. He soon revealed to me that he was secretly working, together with some other courageous men, for Hitler's assassination. How, he did not reveal, nor did he reveal any names. I felt that even under great pressure, he would not do so. That he liked me was obvious to anybody.

Wolfgang and I shared our worries and thoughts—philosophical thoughts, political thoughts, religious thoughts. Philosophically, we were both ardent rationalists, and discussed Kant for days on end. Politically, we had not adopted a system of any kind: we were entirely preoccupied with the immorality of the Nazi system of government. Nothing else about the Nazi regime concerned us. As Wolfgang was drafted into the German Army in the early winter of 1939, our discussions were, most of the time, confined to letters. Needless to say, Wolfgang had to be in the army if he did not want to be executed. Much of our political thinking started with this experience. We asked ourselves: Was it morally just for a nation to force young men to kill, even when it was against their consciences? Another question followed: Was it morally right for a country to force its citizens to act against their consciences? I do not think we knew that the number of Germans who felt "forced" was very small. But I do remember that we both believed that many Germans could be made to see that they were fighting for a morally wrong cause.

We knew that our letters were censored. We did not think that by writing about complicated ethical, philosophical questions we endangered ourselves. And it appeared that we were right about that. But we used a code for political anti-Nazi statements. The German people were informed that mail to German soldiers was censored. It was censored on the grounds that soldiers should only read what supported their morale. The censor supposedly could decide that better than the soldiers' families and closest friends and sweethearts. I was puzzled by the two expressions "morale" and "moral." Could one support the "morale" of anyone by supporting their immoral actions?

* * *

I remember one incident, when I was ashamed to be with Wolfgang. It was winter, and Wolfgang and I were going for a walk. He was wearing his lieutenant's uniform. Since he did not become a lieutenant until 1942, it must have been in the winter of 1942–43. Perhaps I was home for the Christmas recess and Wolfgang was on leave for the last time before being flown to Stalingrad. We met another couple, a soldier in the uniform of the German army and his girlfriend. We passed each other silently, and eyed each other curiously. Suddenly, after we had passed each other, Wolfgang stopped, let go of me, and yelled at the young soldier for not having greeted him. According to army rules and regulations, a private should greet his superiors. The soldier's girl and I exchanged timid sisterly glances, we were both embarrassed, but were trying to communicate with our eyes and without words that we did not understand these silly, preposterous rules and could not understand why men took them so seriously. Throughout Wolfgang's yelling, the poor private stood at attention and said a few times: "Jawohl, Herr Leutnant." When Wolfgang was done, we resumed our walk. We were both embarrassed. We were too embarrassed to talk. We ended our walk silently and far sooner than intended. This whole incident had been so unlike Wolfgang as I knew him that for the first time I had doubts concerning the security of our relationship. Neither of us spoke. Wolfgang said nothing to explain or apologize, and I did not know what to say.

Something occurred at about the time of which I knew nothing until a couple of years ago. It might explain what I just reported. Heidi, Wolfgang's third wife, told me that Wolfgang had died a few months earlier, in the summer of 1987, and she initiated our meeting. Heidi told me that Maria, Wolfgang's sister, had told her that late in 1942, before he joined the 5th Army near Stalingrad, Wolfgang was about to be drafted into an "Einsatzkommando," and that for several days and nights, he and his sister, Maria, had tried to think of a way of avoiding that horrifying assignment. Neither he nor Maria could think of a way out that would not lead to Wolfgang's court-martial and execution. In the end, Wolfgang found somebody who changed places with him in return for several pounds of sugar, which Wolfgang promised to get for him. Sugar was severely rationed at that time, and a lot of people were willing to commit illegal actions for sugar.

The fellow who was willing to change places with Wolfgang was apparently willing to become a murderer for sugar. To be the kind of murderer an Einsatzkommando wanted was not only legal; the Army High Command made SS men who killed Jews and other "undesirables" believe that they were heroes. Obviously, this story has unanswered questions. The most apparent ones are: How could Wolfgang change places with anybody without changing his official identity? Who was the other fellow with whom he made the deal?

Wolfgang apparently knew what he would have to do in the Einsatzkommando, or else he would not have tried so strenuously to avoid it. Why did he tell only Maria about it, but not his father and not me? I knew that there had been times when Henner would confide in no one, but *his* sister, namely myself. Sisters can be more trustworthy than mothers and fathers. Sisters can be comrades-in-arms. No mother can be that. Brothers and sisters grow up together, they share a lot, and often act in unison. The shared past—especially if brother and sister are close in age, as Wolfgang and Maria were—may lead to absolute loyalty.

In any case, Wolfgang's having gotten out of his assignment to the Einsatzkommando might explain his behavior toward the couple we met when going for a walk near Marburg. Wolfgang would have had good reason, in that case, to be very careful. It is not farfetched at all to assume that he was spied on day and night. The young soldier who did not greet Wolfgang might have been a stooge. The very person the Nazis would designate as a spy might have been asked to first seduce Wolfgang to commit the behavior for which they intended to denounce him. Wolfgang would have had good reason to watch what he was doing and assume what the Nazis considered "good behavior."

When Heidi told me this, I felt deep compassion for Wolfgang, although Wolfgang was no longer alive and despite the decades that had passed since. My capacity to feel compassion with Germans was reawakened. Who knows the inner tortures some members of my generation had to endure when we were young? And how could we remain true to ourselves and shape our identities?

Wolfgang was severely wounded in the Battle of Stalingrad, just in time to be flown out; that is, just before the Russians were victorious and took all surviving German soldiers and officers prisoner. Wolfgang was first hospitalized in Katowice, then Kattowitz.

*   *   *

In the summer of 1944, Wolfgang was in Marburg and staying with his parents. I do not remember the reason. But whatever it was, during the events I am about to report, Wolfgang was definitely present. His father seemed worried during that summer. One day, Wolfgang told me why. An attempt on Hitler's life was planned again. Other assassination attempts in the past had failed, but he thought that this one could not fail, it was so carefully planned. On July 20, we all sat around the radio, listening closely to the BBC. We all expected to hear the news of Hitler's death momentarily. We expected the BBC to broadcast the news perhaps a little earlier than the German radio station. Hitler was expected to give a speech; Stauffenberg, a member of the German nobility, which had always loathed Hitler as an upstart, was to carry a bomb in his briefcase and have it explode near Hitler. We all felt that it could not fail to come off this time. Stauffenberg had the necessary papers to be allowed in Hitler's immediate vicinity. It was clear exactly where and when Hitler would deliver—or screech—his speech. Yet, Wolfgang's father was worried and skeptical. And when I asked him why, he said it was too late, too many terrible things had happened, Germany had lost her reputation as a trustworthy partner in any negotiations in any case. As the hours of the afternoon passed one by one, his skepticism deepened into gloom. Finally, an announcement was broadcast: a "criminal attempt" had been made on Hitler's life, but naturally, it had failed again, as repeatedly in the past, because divine Providence, "die Vorsehung" Hitler referred to in many of his speeches, had saved him again.

At this, Wolfgang's father became very pale. I had never seen him look frightened before. He was not only frightened for his friends, associates of Stauffenberg, but he was also frightened for himself. And with good reason: he was in the know. We sat around the radio a little longer. We were completely silent. Wolfgang's mother was close to tears. She had lost one of her sons. Jürgen, Wolfgang's older brother, had been killed early in the war, Wolfgang had been severely wounded and almost died, and now she feared for the life of her husband. We waited, thinking that we would learn something of the reasons for the failure of the attempt on Hitler's life. But there was no more news that shed any light on it. Wolfgang took me home. While we walked through the narrow, familiar streets, we fantasized aloud how the world would have looked, how the course of history would have changed, if this assassination attempt would have succeeded. We were careless. We talked as we would have if we had been alone. We talked as if everyone agreed with us. But very soon, we were brought up short to reality. We ran into the grocer with whom Wolfgangs' mother did most of the family's shopping. He was obviously excited. "Did you hear?" he said, "some crooks tried to kill the Führer, but they didn't get him." As he continued to tell us what we already knew, his joy at the outcome was apparent. We were once again confirmed in what we knew and usually were mindful of: that we were alone and that nobody could be trusted. We had to pretend to share most people's feelings. I felt very close to Wolfgang. Did many people think as the grocer did? Did he not realize that this had been Germany's last chance to be recognized as a halfway reliable partner among other nations? Did he not realize that the final and total defeat would come very soon, and that the failure of this assassination attempt would mean that the killing and the cruelty would continue, although Germany's defeat was in sight?

* * *

In the preceding pages I have revealed a great deal about myself. It is not customary to do so in scientific papers or chapters of books. But the title of this chapter is, Growing Up in Nazi Germany: Lessons to be Learned. I can hardly do that without being very personal.

There are many lessons to be learned, but they can all be summarized under two headings. Briefly, and banally stated, they are: (1) shame, by its very nature, and almost by definition, is something one cannot talk about. But if there were groups of people with feelings of shame and if they would meet for that reason, then perhaps they could open up to each other and talk about their shame. Perhaps they would learn from each other and transform their sense of shame into something more constructive. The sense of shame is paralyzing rather than constructive. (2) In the years when we grow up, we need to feel protected and secure in our relationships with people we believe to be good, like our parents and other elders, so that we can identify with them and feel safe from relationships to evil people.

Let me elaborate on these two "lessons." Although I quoted Primo Levi, who does not distinguish between shame and guilt, I want to insist that shame and guilt differ. Helen Block Lewis (1958), who worked more deeply on this issue than anyone else, has this to say:

> Since shame is about the *self*, while guilt is about *something*, the position of the self with reference to events is very different in the two states. In particular, the relation of the self to the internalized "other" is different. In shame, the "other" is personified, while in guilt the "other" is not apparent as the instigator and may or may not be apparent as the object to whom guilt refers. (p. 87)

The Mitscherlichs (1975) also say something that I find very important:

> The ego-ideal, while closely related to the super-ego, aims at fulfilling the parents' internalized values and wishes rather than their moral demands. Failure to live up to the ego-ideal produces shame, and fear of rejection and abandonment, while falling short of the demands of the super-ego evokes feelings of guilt and fear of punishment. (p. 201)

Helen Block Lewis makes it clear, it seems to me, why shame is usually even more painful than guilt. Since the internalized other is *personified* in shame, not living up to its standards, that is, the ego-ideals, is excruciatingly painful. So painful that the most common defense against it is denial. We know and were furious at the Germans who they did not show any shame. But since denial is the defense against this very common affect, it is hardly surprising that they did not show shame. My considerations also explain why shame is such an unconstructive affect. One does not learn anything from something that must be denied. But if there are others who protect the person who is ashamed from the pain of it, because they know from their own experience how painful shame is, the person who hides shame might open up and talk about her or his shame.

I find it interesting that Erikson (1950) connected shame to the ability to stand on one's own feet. We know that the most frequent German response after the Holocaust was the excuse: "I only followed orders." In other words, they had not stood on their own two feet. It is, or was, part of German child rearing, certainly at that time, to prevent the child from standing on his own feet. It is to the great credit of my parents that I was expected and helped to stand on my own feet. That younger Germans can acknowledge shame is perhaps not only due to the fact that many years have past since the Holocaust so that acknowledging shame is less painful, but also to changes in German child-rearing methods. Perhaps the generations that were born after 1945 were allowed and helped to stand on their own feet. The majority of my generation of Germans and those older were raised to believe that it is bad and dangerous to stand on one's own feet, and that the autonomy necessary to do so must be broken, eliminated, done away with. We have learned from Erikson that autonomy and shame and doubt develop early in life; so too do defense mechanisms, including denial. If a person learns early in life that autonomy is something bad, that one ought to be ashamed of it, one also experiences early in life that denying shame is an effective defense against feeling it. And what one learns early in life is hard to change.

The other lesson has been stated so many times that I almost blush when restating is, but I will restate it anyhow. Relationships in childhood to parents and other elders must be very close and strong, because only close and loving relationships help us learn and grow from ambivalence. We all feel hate as well as love toward parents and idealized others because they all let us down sometimes. If love is strong enough in these relationships, the relationships will not only survive the hate, but because we feel loved, we can remain in the ambivalent relationship without the fear that our hate will lead to rejection and abandonment or some other terrible disaster. Unresolved ambivalence is a great enemy of human relations, for the unresolved and un-understood hatred may be acted out suddenly and without warning against the unsuspecting other person. I am afraid that not only this country, but many other countries are against close parent–child relationships. Presumably, close parent–child relationships make people dependent on those they love. As a result, we see pseudoindependence in young people and even adults. Psuedoindependence not only hides dependency needs, but ungratified longing for the perfect parent. Lack of closeness means that one is full of ambivalence that may be acted out, as it was in Germany against the Jews, in the United States against blacks and Indians, and in many other countries against others. South Africa and Ireland are only the best known but not at all the only examples.

I have assumed that we agree on what is morally good, that we agree that empathy and tolerance of others are high moral values. But I know that human beings do not agree on what is morally good. It is apparently one of those issues that is unresolvable. Nobody seems to be able to *prove* that some moral principles are binding for everybody. Yet, we know that moral principles are important to us, and that they impel us to act. Even those who do evil by our standards do so by invoking our conscience and by claiming that they do good. Certainly, the Nazis are a case in point. As Lifton (1986) reminded us, "Himmler is said to have referred to the 'Karma' of the 'Germanic world as a whole,' for which 'a man has to sacrifice himself; he oughtn't to think of himself'" (p. 435). Sacrifice for evil? Perhaps that is what got the Germans to be Nazis? Do we not usually think of sacrificing for something good: do we not usually think of sacrifice itself as something good? This would really be a reversal of values.

In conclusion, I began this chapter by referring to the many hate groups in the United States. Then, after reporting some of my own experiences in Nazi Germany, I state two lessons to be learned: that shame must be acknowledged to become constructive, and that we need strong, positive relationships to parents and other loved elders to become independent.

REFERENCES

Anti-Defamation League of B'nai B'rith. (1988) *An ADL special report: Hate groups in America. A record of bigotry and violence.* New York: Anti-Defamation League of B'nai B'rith.

Anti-Defamation League of B'nai B'rith. (1986) *Security handbook for community institutions.* ADL, rev. ed. New York: Anti-Defamation League of B'nai B'rith.

Erikson, E. H. (1950). *Childhood and society.* New York: Norton.

Levi, P. (1965). *The reawakening.* Boston: Little, Brown.

Levi, P. (1988). *The drowned and the saved.* New York: Simon & Schuster.

Lewis, H. B. (1958). *Shame and guilt in neurosis.* New York: International Universities Press.

Lifton, R. J. (1986). *The Nazi doctors.* New York: Basic Books.

Lynd, H. M. (1958). *On shame and the search for identity.* New York: Harcourt, Brace and World.

Mitscherlich, A., and Mitscherlich, M. (1975). *The inability to mourn.* New York: Grove Press.

The National PTA and Anti-Defamation League of B'nai B'rith. (1989) *What to tell your child about prejudice and discrimination.* New York: Anti-Defamation League of B'nai B'rith.

12

Bridging East and West

Splitting and Integration

Olga Marlin and Nancy Smith

This chapter begins with a psychological analysis of the totalitarian system that is based on Marlin's experience of growing up in Czechoslovakia, "behind the Iron Curtain." This is followed by analysis of reasons why democracy again has a chance in Czechoslovakia after the Velvet Revolution of 1989. The second section is a discussion of the cause and effects of McCarthyism in America, an era that began in 1950 when Smith was 21; Smith gratefully acknowledges Marlin's psychoanalytic comments on material in this section. Change in the United States, in response to change in the Soviet Union and Eastern Europe, was an emerging story as this chapter was being written.

BEHIND THE IRON CURTAIN (Marlin)

From Stettin in the Baltic to Trieste in the Adriatic, an iron curtain has descended across the Continent. Behind that line lie all the capitals of the ancient states of central and eastern Europe. Warsaw, Berlin, Prague, Vienna, Budapest, Belgrade,

OLGA MARLIN, Ph.D. • Supervisor, William Alanson White Institute, New York, New York; Faculty, Postgraduate Center for Mental Health, New York, New York; Faculty, Brooklyn Institute for Psychotherapy and Psychoanalysis, Brooklyn, New York; Private Practice, 110 East End Avenue, New York, New York 10028. NANCY SMITH • Author, 271 East 78th Street, New York, New York 10021. Biographical note: One of us grew up behind the Iron Curtain, the other, in the United States. Separately, we researched the material this chapter draws on, feeling a need to learn the truth about formative political history. After sharing our experiences informally, we developed a more integrated view of and deeper understanding of the dynamics of political choice in both the East and the West.

Politics and Psychology: Contemporary Psychodynamic Perspectives, edited by Joan Offerman-Zuckerberg. Plenum Press, New York, 1991.

Bucharest and Sofia, all these famous cities and the populations around them lie
in what I might call the Soviet sphere. (From Churchill's Iron Curtain Speech, 1946,
cited in Harbutt, p. 183)

Growing up in Czechoslovakia, in the years it was occupied by Nazi Germany and then submerged in the Communist totalitarian system, I lived out the helplessness of my people, overtaken by arrogant ideological powers. In 1938 we were betrayed at Munich, and my people mourned lost hope, dignity, and freedom. On March 15, 1939, the German army occupied Czechoslovakia. Hitler declared a protectorate over the western provinces of Bohemia and Moravia, and Slovakia became a German puppet state. Our universities were closed, our schools were Germanized, our native culture was suppressed. Humiliated, brought to our knees, we had to greet the Führer.

Despite the loving protection of my family, I sensed my parents' fear and the black terror around me, thinly masked by the appearance of daily life. Playing with my cousins in grandmother's comfortable house and her beautiful garden, I pretended to live in a world that was peaceful and free. I imagined this world from my parents' stories about the first republic and from their memories about the Western countries they had visited.

At the end of the war we were freed by the Soviet army, to the dismay of many of us. (Two divisions of the American army under the command of General Patton liberated Pilsen and stopped there.) Nevertheless, we again became hopeful about a future democratic state. Then in 1948, the Czechoslovak Communist Party, backed by the Soviet Union, seized power and instituted a totalitarian state. Our democratic institutions were again destroyed. Our political leaders were jailed, executed, or forced to flee. We became part of the Soviet sphere. The "aggressor" now was internal as well as external; insidiously, they joined forces.

Western democracies spoke against the loss of freedom and democracy in Czechoslovakia, but again they did not intervene. Repeatedly abandoned and betrayed by our friends and powerful allies, we became a nation divided from within. Continuity with our history and tradition was repeatedly disrupted, as we became prisoners of an arrogant power meshed with suppressive ideology. However, the intended focus of this section, is not a historical or political study of these events. Rather, this description serves as a background to a psychological analysis of the totalitarian system.

In my article "Group Psychology in the Totalitarian System: A Psychoanalytic View," my thesis was that regressive group psychology played a central role in totalitarian ideology. We were organized in political and interest groups espousing Communist ideology from childhood on: ideologically, "group membership was valued above any other type of relationship, and the illusion was maintained that all persons are equal. Everyone was expected to identify with the socialistic ideal and work for it" (Marlin, 1990, p. 46). In this insidious process of manipulation we were to lose our individuality and become submerged in the "omnipotent group." Opposition or deviation was punished by execution, imprisonment, or social ostracism, and economic deprivation. We were deprived of our civil rights. Communist ideology, like a fog, infiltrated our lives. We could no longer express our thoughts and opinions publicly.

As members of the omnipotent groups, we had to obey our leaders who were idealized saviors of mankind; they were to show us the way to solve all our problems through the socialist, and later the Communist state. This utopian state was to bring all-encompassing equality and fulfillment of our needs. Portraits of our leaders became icons in the new church. They were all-powerful, all-knowing, and protective of all of us—archaic, godlike symbols of parents. They were to either accept us or punish us, depending on our behavior. We were expected to believe everything they said; their pronouncements were sacrosanct. Stalin was raised to the position of semireligious leader, all-knowing, a symbolic father of his people. He was often called "our light, our good father, our sun, our savior." Although in Czechoslovakia his cult was not as widely popular as in the Soviet Union, there were many who followed this line. A gigantic statue of Stalin towered over Prague.

I remember regularly scheduled political demonstrations where we had to proclaim our eternal love and friendship for the Soviet Union and the Communist party. Participation was compulsory; nonparticipation meant creating problems for oneself and one's family, such as losing the opportunity for higher education or a good job. In the 1950s, during the Stalinist period, the only possible protest was to march silently. Nevertheless, in these mass spectacles, framed by red flowers and smiling leaders, with loudspeakers yelling slogans, all of us had to appear cheerful and enthusiastic, showing support for our Communist leaders. We also had to show hatred for enemies—people outside our group. American imperialists were the worst, plotting our destruction. In the totalitarian system, aggression was projected mainly outside the group, to other groups, individuals, or systems.

This paranoid, split view of the world was promoted in education and in the public sphere. Our system was always good. The capitalistic system was destructive, inhumane, totally bad. There were no shades of gray. Growing up in this situation, I always felt divided, guilty, and ashamed. Outwardly I maintained a facade of conformity. Inside I opposed it. I learned from my parents the truth about our past, and I knew of their criticism of the regime. My mother grew up in a well-to-do Czech family, and lived abroad before the war. She dismissed Communist propaganda as lies. My father, a Russian émigré who fought the Bolsheviks as a young man, explained to me many important facts about the Russian Revolution and what followed. The picture of history I learned from my parents, older friends, and grandparents was complex, multifaceted, conflicting. It was very different from the false ideological picture with its absolute abstract notions, simplistic good and bad dualities, and stereotypes, devoid of uncertainty and realistic conflict, promoting regression to childlike thinking, dependency, denial, and splitting of thoughts, emotions, and experiences.

Having lived in a totalitarian system and seeing that many people either worked to create it or willingly participated in it, I searched for a long time to understand its underlying dynamics and to answer the question: How and why were so many people susceptible to the Communist ideology? I eventually concluded that regressive individual and group psychology played a central role in the ideological process of manipulation, a conclusion based on the psychoanalytic concepts of Freud, Bion, and Fromm. I summarize here the theoretical section of my previously cited paper.

Freud's original contribution to exploration of group psychology comes mainly from his work, *Group Psychology and the Analysis of the Ego* (1921). The main thesis states that libidinal ties (love relationships) constitute the essence of the group mind, ties based on unconscious processes in the ego. In the course of the analysis of two societal groups, the church and the army, Freud found that both groups are held together by the illusion that the leader loves all individuals in the group equally, as a substitute father. He says:

> It is not without a deep reason that the similarity between the Christian community and a family is invoked, and that believers call themselves brothers in Christ, that is, brothers through the love which Christ has for them. There is no doubt that the tie between each individual with Christ is also the cause of the tie which unites them with one another. The like holds good for the army. The Commander-in-Chief is a father who loves all soldiers equally and for that reason, they are comrades among themselves. (Freud, p. 26)

An individual's lack of freedom in a group is caused by simultaneous ties to the leader and to other members of the group; these ties bind an individual and lead to alterations and limitations in his or her personality. Group ties are based on identifications that are the earliest and original forms of emotional ties derived from the child's relationship to his or her parents. Freud described identification as the wish "to be like another" distinguished from object love or "the wish to have another." Identification is the original form of emotional tie with an object; secondly, when an object is lost or given up, the subject may regress to introjecting it. A third, later form of identification arises with "any new perception of a common quality shared with some other person who is not an object of sexual instinct. The more important this common quality is, the more successful may this partial identification become, and it thus represent a beginning of a new tie" (Freud, p. 40). The mutual tie between the members of a group is such an identification, based upon an important common emotional quality.

Freud sees the ego divided into ego and ego-ideal—which encompasses self-observation, moral conscience, and censorship (later this concept was developed in his theory of superego). For many people this differentiation within the ego is incomplete and poorly developed, which opens up a way for regression to childlike feelings and actions. This tendency is magnified in groups by way of emotional identification with others and by the tie to the leader, who becomes a symbolic father. "A primary group is a number of individuals who have put one and the same object in the place of their ego-ideal and have consequently identified themselves with one another in their ego" (Freud, p. 48).

In the primary group the individual, according to Freud, gives up his ideal and substitutes for it the group ideal as embodied in the leader. The leader is idealized and members of the group have to be equal; they have to give up their rivalry in order to be loved equally by the leader. They are ruled by the leader who is superior to them.

I found that the psychology of the totalitarian system reflected many of the regressive dynamics pointed out by Freud as typical for primary groups. As I have described (Marlin, 1990), idealized political leaders were put forward as symbolic fathers for all, who were told that they were equal and must accept unquestioningly the group's socialistic ideal. The Communist party leaders functioned as would-be semireligious leaders, and also as would-be commanders in the army. Ideologically based groups proliferated and people were officially valued primarily as members of the group. Outsiders were ostracized and punished as heretics or traitors. Equalization was further promoted by state ownership of formerly private property, which enforced the illusion that all got the same share.

Two other psychoanalytic thinkers, Wilfred Bion in the British object relations school and Erich Fromm in the American cultural school, further developed Freud's theory of group processes. Bion supplemented Freud's view by applying Kleinian theory of early development to group dynamics, in both small and large groups. His contention was that:

> The more the group is disturbed, the more central to its dynamics are activation of psychotic (infantile annihilation) anxiety, and defenses against it. Groups, he believes, are peculiarly prone to the activation of the primitive mechanisms described by Klein as characteristic of paranoid–schizoid and depressive positions. He calls these modes of behavior and feeling in groups "basic assumptions." Bion's central concept is that in every group "two groups" are present: "the work group" and "the basic assumption group"; these are two aspects of the functioning of the group process. Basic assumptions are regressive emotional states in groups derived from irrational, unconscious aspects of personality which have to do with defending against early overwhelming anxieties. According to Bion they are present, in varying degrees, in all groups. These are the basic assumptions of (1) increased dependency, (2) fight–flight behavior, and (3) intimate pairing. If these basic assumptions prevail in the group, it resists change and it does not learn and adapt to reality. (Marlin, 1990, p. 48)

The "work group," on the other hand, is analogous to the functions of the conscious ego in the Freudian sense. It deals with realistic tasks in a rational manner, being capable of self-reflection, critical thinking, and learning.

According to Bion, basic assumptions are usually channeled into societal institutions such as the church and the army (or aristocracy) so as not to interfere with the work-group function of the main group. Bion points out, however, that the more a group is disturbed, the more its basic assumptions prevail—and they all include fantasy of the leader. Furthermore, there is a mutually dependent relationship between leader and group. The power of the leader lies in his or her ability to respond to and articulate the group's powerful basic assumptions and to merge with them, becoming omnipotent, godlike. The paranoid leader appropriate for the fight–flight mentality will recognize enemies, mobilize the group for attack, or lead the group in flight. Preservation of the group is paramount in this process, disregarding the individual and his interests. This was indeed the case in the totalitarian system where individuals were expendable in the service of ideology and where the "enemy" was constantly invoked (fight–flight mentality). I have found that many other processes Bion described as typical of pathological basic assumptions—primitive impulsive feelings/actions, dogmatic thinking, fantasy, splitting perceptions into good and bad polarities, and a "pairing" mentality (utopian, messianic fantasies)—were sustained by the ideology. I concluded that totalitarian ideology represented the influence of regressive basic assumptions mentality, while work group functions were also present, allowing for some development and progress. As I wrote in my paper on totalitarian psychology,

> Group dynamics described by Bion helped to explain, in my opinion, how a society can be swept or manipulated into the state of regression. Since primitive, unconscious processes exist in all people—as potentials for regression—and since they are especially stimulated in groups, they become dangerous possibilities that could be (under certain conditions) actualized in political movements or religious cults. They can be manipulated and used by leaders who fit particular "basic assumptions" for their objectives. (Marlin, 1990, p. 50)

To explain why regression occurs more readily and pervasively in some groups and cultures, I analyzed Fromm's writings, exploring the mutual interplay between culture and individual psychology in its conscious and unconscious dimensions. Fromm sees man's central psychological problem as one of solving the conflict between self-reliance on one hand and feelings of loneliness on the other. This is even more true for modern man, who is more alone and isolated than those living in previous epochs, who had a defined place in their social groups. Fromm points out that if human beings are unable to individuate and find positive freedom in productive, integrated love and work, they may try to escape and fall back on an archaic, symbiotic way of relating, trying to merge with someone or something outside themselves, in order to undo their separation or isolation:

> [They] attempt to become a part of a bigger and more powerful whole outside of oneself, to submerge and participate in it. This power can be a person, an institution, God, the nation, Conscience, or a psychic compulsion. By becoming part of a power which is felt as unshakably strong, eternal, and glamorous, one participates in its strength and glory. (Fromm, 1941, p. 177)

Fromm calls the ways in which men try to escape the problem of individuation "mechanisms of escape." These are regressive tendencies, potential driving forces in all people, and a group can easily become a path of escape. Irrational methods of relating back to the group are sadomasochism, destructiveness, and automaton-like conformity. A dialectic relationship exists between individual neurotic tendencies and cultural patterns—another important idea of Fromm's. If an individual finds cultural patterns that satisfy masochistic strivings—for example, submission to the leader in fascistic or totalitarian ideology—he gains illusory security by uniting himself with others who share his feelings. This process was apparent in the communist totalitarian system where the interests of the group/party/nation/system or leader were always stressed over individual choice. A favorite slogan of the state communist propaganda was "One for all and all for one."

Fromm points out that a culture with predominantly destructive patterns can promote the development of certain characteristics which, in turn, become the basis for destructive social and political systems. This was an ongoing process in the Soviet Union, I found, and it also existed in Czechoslovakia for the last forty years. That is, ideology promoted dependence on leaders and on the group, which severely restricted initiative and personal responsibility. Aggressive confrontation in absolute terms and projection of blame was promoted, a regressive, split, black-and-white view of people and the world. This process further deepened disintegration of personal responsibility and individual integrity. Furthermore, individuals, as part of their social role, had to disguise their thoughts, offering false opinions and the responses demanded by the ideology, which led to further internal splits. A sense of shame and guilt often resulted, as well as loss of self-respect, which led to an increased sense of powerlessness. In other instances, cynicism led to an increase in opportunism—many people cooperated with the regime to gain personal advantage, even by becoming informants. These traits could be seen as part of the "social character" that Fromm defined as "the essential nucleus of the character structure of most members of a group which has developed as the result of the basic experiences and mode of life common to that group" (p. 305). Fromm describes as an example of social character an "authoritarian character"—simultaneously possessing sadistic and masochistic traits— typical of the lower middle-class in Germany that became the psychological basis for fascism. Typically, "an authoritarian character admires authority and tends to submit to it. At the same time, however, he wants to be an authority and have others submit to him" (Fromm, 1941, p. 186). The most important features of an authoritarian character is not only a craving for submission to a higher power but also a conviction that life is not determined by one's wishes and interests. Finally, if people with an authoritarian character do rebel, the longing for submission unconsciously remains. This is why such people can suddenly change from extreme radicalism to extreme authoritarianism.

I concluded that Fromm's analysis of the authoritarian character could be applied to an understanding of the common social character in Russia, and in Czechoslovakia, where it became the psychological basis for communist totalitarian systems.

Perhaps in Czechoslovakia authoritarian and utopian trends became more prominent in some groups in the postwar climate after betrayal at Munich in 1938, and then after occupation by the Nazis, which was experienced as a national trauma. This worked to the political advantage of the Czech Communist Party. In 1946 this party received thirty-eight percent of the vote (except in Slovakia, where the democratic party was much stronger) (Korbel, 1959, p. 153). Historically, the party was working overtly through ideological manipulation and covertly by violent means to seize power, which happened in 1948. On the other hand, there were other historic and cultural forces opposing this trend—a historical-spiritual connection with European developments, the pluralistic ideal of the nineteenth century—the history of cultural and political links with western democracies. T. G. Masaryk, the internationally known first president of the Czechoslovak Republic (1918), led and organized the struggle for the country's independence from the Austro-Hungarian Empire with the aid of leaders in England and France, and with the aid of America's President Woodrow Wilson. Masaryk was a prominent philosopher of democratic humanitarianism, who based his politics on ethical and religious principles opposing Marxism (Capek, 1936). In my opinion, the moral force of Havel's work and of ideals expressed in the Velvet Revolution represent the continuation of this humanitarian tradition. During the Velvet Revolution portraits of Masaryk and Havel were displayed together in Prague with the inscription "Truth Wins!" (personal observation).

Iron Curtain Dismantled: What Does the Future Hold?
Czechoslovakia's Velvet Revolution

> Above all, any existential revolution should provide hope of a moral reconstitution
> of society, which means a radical renewal of the relationships of human beings to
> what I call the "human order," which no political order can replace. A new
> experience of being, a renewed rootedness in the universe, a newly grasped sense
> of "higher responsibility," a new-found inner relationship to other people and to
> the human community—these factors clearly indicate the direction in which we
> must go. (Havel, 1980, pp. 117–118)

Havel wrote these words in a significant essay of 1978, "The Power of the
Powerless," 11 years before the Velvet Revolution took place. He also condemned
the Czech posttotalitarian system (after 1970) as a bureaucratic structure per-
meated by hypocrisy, lies, and demands for conformity:

> The inner aim of the post-totalitarian system is not mere preservation of power in
> the hands of a ruling clique, as appears to be the case at first sight. Rather, the social
> phenomenon of self-preservation is subordinated to something higher, to a kind of
> blind automatism which drives the system. No matter what position individuals
> hold in the hierarchy of power, they are not considered by the system to be worth
> anything in themselves, but only as things intended to fuel and serve this auto-
> matism. (p. 44)

For this world of appearances to exist, Havel stressed that people must live
within a lie:

> Ideology, in creating a bridge of excuses between the system and the individual,
> spans the abyss between the aims of the system and the aims of life. It pretends that
> the requirements of the system derive from the requirements of life. It is a world
> of appearances trying to pass for reality. (p. 44)

People are both victims and supporters of this system which is a complex
mixture of manipulation, alienation, and utilitarianism. Although individuals do
not often believe the mystification of the system, they must behave as if they do
or tolerate it in silence, living within a lie, accepting ritual and appearance for
reality: playing by the rules of the game. No genuine political action is possible.
However, when people claim their identity and express themselves genuinely
and truthfully, not in ideological terms, they oppose and challenge the system. All
who participate in the independent life of society—dissidents, writers, scientists,
artists and clergymen carrying on their activities privately and in unofficial
groups—oppose the alienating pressure of the regime and "live within the truth"
as Havel expresses it. It is this activity, which is opposed to violence and concerned with human values in the here and now, that can promote change. In this
"second culture"—unofficial, uncensored culture—the authentic needs of people
were expressed and developed. Without an understanding of the hidden independent life of the society and the strength of the second culture, we cannot
understand the roots of the Velvet Revolution.

Czech writer Klima pointed out in his speech, "The Unexpected Merits of
Oppression," at the conference on Czech literature and culture (New York University, March 1990) that almost the entire body of important contemporary
Czech literature was practically forbidden because most writers refused to cooperate with the regime. Also, in order to work in this abnormal situation, writers

organized reading groups where they read their work in progress; unofficial publications included works by important writers, as well as translations from world literature. Psychologically, the second culture represented preservation not only of memory but of creativity. Klima said in his speech:

> In a seeming paradox, prohibition of publication brought for many a liberation—the liberation from all secondary influences and interests, from the self-censorship which they had been practicing in the hope they might cheat the vigilant supervisors (and made them free from interests of the market as well). The writer continued to work only because he or she felt it as an existential necessity.

Unofficial scientist and artist groups similar to writers' groups were also formed. All these groups, in my opinion, can be viewed as work groups (Bion's concept) that developed in response to the need for learning and progress in an atmosphere devoid of stimulation and free expression. Thus, learning and development continued despite harassment (police surveillance and arrests) and censorship.

Historically, Czechoslovakia was a democratic republic before the war, with a flourishing culture linked to Western development. In 1968, a democratic movement surfaced within the system, led by writers and intellectuals. The Communist party could not really promote or lead radical change, however. (The historical irony is that Dubcek's "Socialism with a human face" was crushed by the "fraternal" Soviet army together with armies of Warsaw Pact countries.) Later, with Gorbachev's era of glasnost, the threat of Soviet aggression ended and the country was again ripe for change. Except for the initial violence of the police against student demonstrators, it was a *nonviolent movement*. Czechoslovakia's "Velvet Revolution" was not a revolution by the usual definition. With the help of mass demonstrations, the government was brought down within 14 days. Seen from the West, it looked rather miraculous; dissidents became ministers; people recently jailed took government posts. Victims and jailers exchanged places, as if in the theater of the absurd. However, this situation becomes clearer if we know previous historical and social development. As Peter Pithart (1990), former leading independent politician and currently Prime Minister of the Czech region, states:

> It was not a revolution; the old regime collapsed too easily for a revolutionary process to occur. When some students' blood was shed, the demand for change was irresistible. Opinion in Czechoslovakia was already impatient for innovation. Unlike some neighboring countries such as East Germany, we never passively adopted Communist models. In dissident groups we were already working on alternatives. Now the search for new national equilibrium is suddenly able to proceed in political liberty. (p. 18)

Discontent was first expressed openly in demonstrations in August 1988. These continued in 1989 and were severely suppressed. A very large peaceful student demonstration took place on November 17, 1989 to commemorate the death of a student killed by the Nazis. Demonstrators were trapped in the main street by cordons of police and a terrorist squad of Red Berets. Witnesses described police brutality against young people and others who joined them; women and old people were attacked as well, and many were seriously injured. Before this happened, students tried to open a dialogue with the police. They handed flowers to the police and said, "You should protect us." The juxtaposition of peaceful acts of young people and the brutal attacks of the police underscored opposite forces in the nation and brought the conflict into the open, shocking the nation and igniting mass demonstrations. Czech writer Pechar expressed to me his opinion that through these events, the national trauma of loss and humiliation was recalled and reexperienced. I agreed, but offered the proposition that now the national traumas (Munich, World War II, postwar developments that brought Czechoslovakia into the Soviet sphere, and the failed reform movement of 1968) could finally be mastered. Students, actors, scientists, and workers became connected in this process of national reunion, which led to change. Change was also promoted by an atmosphere of lowered international tension, since the threat of Soviet aggression was no longer present.

Students who organized the protest strike were in the forefront of the movement. They established the Coordinating Committee of Prague to connect the separate campuses. According to the personal account of a student active in the committee, they organized spontaneously and effectively, working 22 hours a day. They printed newsletters and broadcasted the news. They went to factories (in the beginning some were arrested) and to other parts of the country to explain about their political goals. Soon actors joined them. Theaters were closed and lively discussion forums were held. When workers of major factories joined in, the battle was won. (In the beginning there had been a period of danger and uncertainty—the People's Militia were prepared to take action. Fortunately a compromise was reached, thanks to more liberal members of the party.)

Civic Forum was created as an umbrella organization of civic and political groups, it was led by Havel and other members of Charter 77. Many of these people had been collaborators and friends for a long time. This made it possible to organize quickly and effectively.

All those I interviewed in Prague (December 1989 to January 1990) stressed the orderly process and the caring people expressed toward each other during mass demonstrations. Cooperation prevailed: for example, food and money were brought to striking students by many people. Students organized watch groups to maintain order and prevent violence. It seemed that people believed civilized order and good humor would carry them through as they were bringing down the hated regime. Continuity with political history was reestablished as Dubcek and Havel addressed rallies in Prague. The favorite song of President Masaryk was sung by thousands with much emotion. Banned artists and singers reappeared, some coming from exile, welcomed and cheered by hundreds of thousands. Popular singer Marta Kubisova, not allowed to perform for the last 20 years, sang her famous song, "Prayer for My Country," in a voice trembling with joy. The national anthem was sung solemnly in the main square with its statue of beloved Czech King St. Vaclav protecting his people. In New York, watching on the television screen the huge crowds shouting "Svobodu! Svobodu!" (Freedom! Freedom!), I was with my people too, shouting, singing, and crying! The miracle we waited for so long had finally happened.

After the Velvet Revolution was won and Havel was elected president of Czechoslovakia, I conducted a series of interviews for a pilot study concerning attitudes and values of the younger generation in Czechoslovakia. Altogether, I interviewed 15 people, 8 of a younger group and 7 of an older group. (In the younger group, one was 14 years old, two were between 18 and 20, three were in their early 20s, and the rest were in their mid-20s.) Interviews were open-ended, of 1 to 3 hours' duration, and psychoanalytically based.

The main question of the study was: How did young people, who grew up in the totalitarian system, develop the humanistic values and ideals, the democratic attitudes, so characteristic of change in Czechoslovakia? Analysis of the interviews revealed six main themes reflecting significant conditions that influenced development in the young generation.

1. Transmission of democratic tradition and values in families, or in relationships with significant adults;
2. transmission through unofficial culture (literature, art, religion);
3. influence of negative (traumatic) experience with the totalitarian regime;
4. development of nonviolent opposition against the regime in the young ("We're not like them"), based on the moral influence of Charter 77 and the ideas of Havel and Gandhi;
5. travel abroad; and
6. the flight of East Germans to the West through Prague.

The following excerpts from interviews illustrate these themes.

PAULA, 14 (high school student): [Describing a demonstration commemorating November 17 massacre] We all carried many candles. People cried and sang national songs . . . I thought of how terrible it was on the 17th of November. I never would want it to happen again. How many were terribly injured. They will never be able to walk again. They will have to be in a wheelchair. How many people disappeared and nobody knows what happened to them? How could they [the police] do it? Did they ever think about their parents? If they could only see themselves on the other side, how would they be able to do such a thing?

[Reflection about the most joyous experience of the revolution] I was happy when Havel was elected President. I had wished for that. He spoke well and also I knew what he lived through. He was jailed and persecuted. Before, they offered him money to leave the country. He could have lived very well with his family if he had taken it, but he didn't. He stayed here although his works could not be published and his plays could not be performed. I think that now we can have a real democracy. Before, they called it a democracy, but we could not really say what we thought at all. If we said what we really thought, we would be severely punished. [themes 3, 4]

GEORGE, 22 (student at a teachers college): [Reflecting upon his experience during the students' strike] When the student movement started, I had to overcome fear and decide what I should do. For the first time in my life I stood before a real choice to participate or not; before this happened, we didn't have an opportunity or responsibility to make a real choice. I had to decide for myself whether to strike or not. I had to think through the meaning of the demands of the students, I had to take a risk. Also, I thought that it made sense to strike because many of my classmates in college whom I respected were among them.

What influenced me most were negative sides of the regime, for example, the bad health care situation. My father died because he didn't get proper treatment. And I was shocked to find that they didn't tell parents whose children were dying in the hospital that they could be helped by medication from abroad.

Also, for many years we couldn't travel. Later, when it became a little easier to travel, I could compare the situation at home with that in the Western countries I visited. [themes 3, 5]

DAVID, 24 (economist): We heard the truth only in our homes or from some other people [neighbors, friends]. In school, information was falsified. I knew a great deal from my family and also about national history as it was expressed in the lives of my parents and grandparents. Also, I think our nation was so democratic. We have it in our blood. We knew about the first republic and later, when we could travel, we could compare our situation with Western countries. We knew that there was a better world that was more free. We felt it very strongly, and when we came back we realized how unfree we were. My strongest experience was in 1985 in London, at an international professional conference. I could see how people from free countries were much stronger individuals. They were much more as-sertive. They have their life in their own hands. I saw this incredible contrast between our world and theirs. Although I knew it before, I understood even more the difference between our system and theirs, and I knew that there was no possible future in our system. We knew that we could not really live in that situation. There were only two solutions: either to leave the country, or to change the country. It was understandable that the young had a major role because this was the first generation which was not frustrated or disappointed in 1968. They felt they didn't have much to lose. They were really fighting for the future. The older generation was frustrated and disappointed by what happened in 1968.

[Regarding nonviolent character of the movement] The film about Gandhi, shown two years ago, was important. The tradition of Charter 77 was in the spirit of Gandhi's work. No one wanted violence. Young people made sure that any violence was suppressed right away. *We didn't want to be like them.* We did not want revenge, only fair punishment. Lawlessness cannot be punished through law-lessness. We wanted a free republic in a free Europe and we knew that we could not become integrated with Europe through violent means [because violence breeds violence]. We knew as Masaryk stressed, that in order to be successful a small nation has to do politics in the context of world politics. In our tradition we always valued common sense, finding a way around obstacles to achieve our goals—dialogue rather than aggression, convincing and winning by intelligent dialogue, rather than fighting against the opponent. I think it is in our nature. We also feel now very strongly that we don't want to spoil the beautiful nonviolent spirit of our revolution. [themes 1, 2, 4, 5]

IVAN, 26 (economist): My whole family suffered because of the Communist take-over. My mother's family owned a factory that was nationalized after 1948. After that, no one in the family could get a higher education. My mother had to do factory work. As I grew up, my parents criticized many negative practices of the regime, for example, the unbearable elections. They also talked about the first republic, what life was like then . . .

My mother used to reminisce about the famous Liprt's delicatessen in Prague, how nice and rich it was. . . . Also, my parents were members of the Scout group and I was influenced by these values too. I knew about events in 1968 mostly from my parents since I was a young child then and couldn't understand much about what happened. We had newspapers from 1968 at home and later I read them. Also, I was influenced in my youth by books that described strong individuality, for example, *The Count of Monte Cristo*, and cowboy stories. My family often talked about how the nation had been brought to its knees in the seventies. We, the younger generation, felt that we couldn't be this way anymore. We did not want to have two faces. We wanted to have only one face, our own! We could not live this way anymore! Also, there was the moral influence of Havel and Charter 77. What we felt, vaguely, Havel said very clearly—that men should stand for truth and say the truth. We should have an authentic identity and one face. We also had our historical democratic tradition and tradition of cultural productivity, skillfulness and diplomacy. I value Charles IV [Czech king and German and Roman emperor who established Prague University in 1348] more than J. Zizka [leader of the Hussites in the fifteenth century]. [themes 1, 2, 3, 4]

PETER, 26 (medical student): I developed my basic worldview in the family. We always discussed what was going on. I was also influenced strongly in my youth by the work of the writers Simecka and by Havel. Reading the letter to Dr. Husak by Havel when I was 16 was for me an incredible intellectual experience. First I studied journalism, but soon I understood that in that field I would have to subscribe to ideology and to solve this conflict, I decided to study medicine. There I could be in a more neutral field. During the revolution and at present I am again expressing my journalistic interest through work for the students' radio. How did change occur so quickly? I think that change in the international situation was important, and also many people were influenced by the flight of East Germans to the West through Prague. They could identify with their expressed desire for freedom, and the realization of it. . . .

Before, in families, we all felt social schizophrenia. For example, parents said one thing in the family and something else outside and for young people this was more and more unbearable.

The ideology was empty. There was no conviction behind it. It broke like a bubble. I think that the young people in leading roles were from families where the parents talked to them and informed them, so that they knew where they stood. People who looked for information could find it. Books were published in samizdat and also abroad. Also, Havel became more known, paradoxically, through his persecution by the Communist government. People had to sign a petition condemning Charter 77, although they could not read what was in it. Propaganda against Charter 77 and Havel had the opposite effect. He was respected for his moral stand, going to jail for his principles. In Bohemia, the intellectual movement has a long tradition in politics. In Slovakia, where religious influence is stronger, unofficial opposition developed through the church.

In the system in which we lived, we had to make concessions against ourselves. People lost joy from life because of this two-faced way we had to live. In my opinion, people stopped liking themselves and became indifferent to others. As a result, society stopped functioning because people stopped being themselves. People knew they could not really be involved in civic affairs, so they turned to materialism and escapism. They became *homo apoliticus*. But in the parallel culture, in dissident groups, the national tradition of political reflection continued. [themes 1, 2, 3, 4, 6]

In summary, Czechoslovakia's Velvet Revolution was a democratic movement led by students, intellectuals, and other activists who were supported by the majority of the population. The totalitarian system was rejected. Continuity with the past was reestablished, especially with Masaryk's humanitarianism and ideals of democracy. My study showed that despite repression these ideals had been kept alive in the society, transmitted through families and the "second culture," politically expressed in the civil rights movement of Charter 77. Young people of the generation born too late to be affected by suppression of the 1968 reform movement were in the forefront of the demand for change. They showed ingenuity, courage, and devotion to democratic ideals. The experience of national trauma, I believe, was reexperienced and then mastered in the process of national reunion during the Velvet Revolution.

THE OTHER SIDE OF THE IRON CURTAIN (Smith)

Soon after Roosevelt became president in 1933, my parents became New Deal Democrats. Because of that political heritage, I believed I had the right, in the early McCarthy era, to sign the Stockholm Peace Petition (a friend advised against it—possibly FBI files do contain my maiden name!). But after liberal Democrat Adlai Stevenson (labeled "egghead" by his Republican opponents) lost the 1952 presidential election, my interest in politics and "important news" atrophied. For example, I viewed the reaction of a friend to the Cuban missile crisis of 1962 as hysterical. In 1982 two events woke me up: Jonathan Schell's *The Fate of the Earth*, and the huge United Nations nuclear disarmament rally. Then by chance I found a book (*The New Priesthood*, Lapp, 1965) that summarized milestones in the development of early U.S. nuclear weapons policy. I began to research and write, adding in significant cold war events, attempting to understand my past. McCarthyism, of course, was one of those significant events.

Not long after World War II, the Truman administration developed a policy that exaggerated Churchill's stark vision of a divided world, embodied in his "Iron Curtain" speech (briefly excerpted in the previous section; President Truman was a prominent member of the audience). It is the thesis of Harbutt (1986) that Churchill's views a few months prior to that speech had an influence on the Truman administration; I speculate that in fact the administration overreacted, taking a good-versus-evil stance. For example, Truman's Secretary of State Byrnes, probably thinking about his actions on behalf of Iran in the United Nations early in 1946, concluded in an April 1946 memo:

> If, as may occur, the United Nations breaks down under the test of opposition to Soviet aggression, it will have served the purpose of clarifying before American and world public opinion, and thus make easier, whatever future steps may be required by the U.S. and other like-minded nations in the face of a new threat of world aggression. (Harbutt, 1986, p. 257)

Hearings by the Congressional House Un-American Activities Committee (HUAC) preceded McCarthyism by over three years. Due to Senator McCarthy, similar hearings took place in the Senate in the years 1951–1954. These hearings targeted intellectuals (members of the teaching profession, writers, and ministers) and individuals in the movie industry, in government, and in labor unions. Many careers were destroyed; those who did not desire martyrdom became silent; that is, self-censorship ensued (see below). Thus, in about seven years the United States was whipped into shape for action against what most perceived as ruthless Soviet aggression.

As mentioned in the previous section, in any society there is a potential for regression in groups. In his 1965 essay, "The Paranoid Style in American Politics," Hofstadter analyzed right-wing phenomena in postwar America, namely, the 1964 presidential campaign and McCarthyism. Of particular interest, however, is his general description:

The recurrence of the paranoid style over a long span of time and in different places suggests that a mentality disposed to see the world in the paranoid's way may always be present in some considerable minority of the population. But the fact that movements employing the paranoid style are not constant but come in successive episodic waves suggests that the paranoid disposition is mobilized into action chiefly by social conflicts that involve ultimate schemes of values and that bring fundamental fears and hatreds, rather than negotiable interests, into political action. (p. 39)

Hofstadter then says that "catastrophe or the fear of catastrophe is most likely to elicit the syndrome of paranoid rhetoric" (p. 39). He does not speculate about the "catastrophe" in post-World War II America; I speculate that it was fear of losing atomic monopoly (related to fear of the weapon itself), particularly after a Canadian-based British atomic physicist pleaded guilty early in 1946 to wartime spying for the Soviets. It seemed the "secret" could be stolen (leading to much tighter control of U.S. nuclear research), although scientists who were campaigning for international control of atomic weapons said there was no "secret." (The scientists' organization would be labeled a Communist front in 1947 by an alarmist author; Burnham, 1947, p. 72).

During the scientists' campaign, "ultimate schemes of values," nonnegotiable interests, began to emerge. The U.S. Baruch Plan, presented to UN delegates in June 1946, appeared to be a generous offer to control an impending nuclear arms race. Embedded in the plan, however, was distrust of Soviet Russia and the plan faded away. The same distrust led Truman to authorize the hydrogen bomb program shortly after Russia tested its first atomic bomb in 1949. The result in each case was a victory for those who feared Russia. The nuclear arms race has rarely been amenable to rational discussion.

In the paranoid-group view "what is at stake is always a conflict between absolute good and absolute evil" (Hofstadter, 1965, p. 31), but the group often mirrors the evil enemy. Hofstadter quoted the author of a study of antisubversive groups in pre-Civil War America:

Though [they] generally agreed that the worst evil of subversives [Freemasons, Catholics, Mormons] was their subordination of means to ends, they themselves recommended the most radical means to purge the nation of troublesome groups and to enforce unquestioned loyalty to the state (pp. 33–34)

It appears that there is first a perceived "catastrophe" triggering deep-seated fears; then the group may accept that the end justifies the means, and dissent becomes disloyalty. Marlin notes that from the psychoanalytic point of view, this process can be seen as a regressive "fight–flight" response in the group (Bion's concept). The group has to preserve itself from the "enemy," who is not seen realistically. Another facet, I suggest, of ends justifying means is indifference to destructive consequences; an example will be given to illustrate this thesis.

FEAR OF DISSENT

Dissent is the essence of the right of free speech. The nature of those who dislike dissent, and the ultimate responsibility attached to this right, are features of Einstein's May 1953 reply (in Nathan & Norden, 1960, p. 346) to a letter from a New York City public school teacher who was subpoenaed by a Senate committee:

> Reactionary politicians have managed to instill suspicion of all intellectual efforts into the public by dangling before their eyes a danger from without. Having succeeded so far, they are now proceeding to suppress the freedom of teaching and to deprive of their positions all those who do not prove submissive, i.e., to starve them out. . . . Frankly, I can only see the revolutionary way of non cooperation in the sense of Gandhi's. Every intellectual who is called . . . ought to refuse to testify. He must be prepared for jail and economic ruin, for the sacrifice of his personal welfare in the interest of the cultural welfare of his country.

Einstein added a postscript: "this letter need not be considered confidential." The letter was published in the *New York Times* on June 12, 1953, and because of negative press response nationwide, British philosopher Bertrand Russell wrote the *New York Times* toward the end of June. Einstein thanked Russell, and concluded:

> All the intellectuals in this country, down to the youngest student, have become completely intimidated. Virtually no one of "prominence" besides yourself has actually challenged these absurdities in which the politicians have become engaged. Because they have succeeded in convincing the masses that the Russians and the American Communists endanger the safety of the country, these politicians consider themselves so powerful. The cruder the tales they spread, the more assured they feel of their re-election by the misguided population. (in Nathan & Norden, p. 550)

The Emergency Civil Liberties Committee, organized to aid suddenly unemployed academics, asked Einstein to respond to written questions for a March 1954 symposium. Among his statements: "Those who endeavor to lead us toward an authoritarian government are particularly anxious to intimidate and silence the intellectual" (in Nathan & Norden, 1960, p. 552). And also, "[Conditions have been created] which people consider a threat to their economic security. Consequently, more and more people avoid expressing their opinion freely, *even in their private social life*" (underlining added; in Nathan & Norden, p. 551). (This mirrors Ivan, who spoke of "two faces.")

The 1953–1954 case of J. Robert Oppenheimer, "father of the atomic bomb," was clearly one where dissent was construed as disloyalty (McMillan, 1990, pp. 130–134; Lapp, 1965, p. 125). It had its roots in 1949 when, as chairman of the president's science advisory committee, Oppenheimer (and all other committee members) opposed "high-priority" development of the hydrogen bomb because of its technical nature (it could not be "proof-tested" in a laboratory), and because of its questionable military value: "It has generally been estimated that the weapon . . . [would devastate] hundreds of square miles," with corresponding radiation (York, 1976, pp. 154–155). In 1952, in the course of a routine reappointment check by the FBI, Edward Teller ("father of the H-bomb") expressed distrust of Oppenheimer because he was sure that Oppenheimer had actively obstructed the first phase of developing the H-bomb. Oppenheimer was not reappointed.

A friend of Teller's became chairman of the U.S. Atomic Energy Commission (AEC) in July 1953; also that month, *Foreign Affairs* published Oppenheimer's article "Atomic Weapons and American Policy," which was critical of that policy. A new FBI check on Oppenheimer was ordered which resulted in a list of charges consisting of those dismissed in 1943 (membership in Communist-front groups), as well as Teller's 1952 statements. After an AEC hearing in April 1954, Oppenheimer lost his security clearance and the small community of counsellors to the U.S. nuclear weapons program lost a wise voice. Nearly all AEC members—and their successors—preferred to listen to Edward Teller, promoter of the hydrogen bomb and later of the neutron bomb, Star Wars, and of ideas that helped to destroy the chance for a comprehensive test ban treaty in 1963 (the Limited Test Ban Treaty was written and ratified instead). Of historical interest, in January 1990, it was reported that Teller himself unwittingly obstructed development of the H-bomb, by insisting for several months on an unworkable approach (Hirsch and Mathews, 1990, p. 26).

McCarthyism ended in mid-1954, after McCarthy made a bad showing in the televised Army–McCarthy hearings. In many ways, however, FBI director Hoover was his spiritual successor. FBI surveillance was as prominent a feature of the 1960s civil rights movement as was Martin Luther King, Jr.'s use of Gandhi's nonviolent dissent, at first because there was evidence that King's key adviser once handled finances of the American Communist party. Then, disappointed that Communist influence on King's movement could not be proved, Director Hoover authorized collection and dissemination of material on King's extramarital activity (the media refused to publish it). Garrow (1981) noted that Hoover had been part of a law enforcement team during an earlier McCarthy-like era, the "Red Scare" of 1919–1920, and then commented:

> Within the Bureau, "Communism" came increasingly to be not a label for any specific organization or adherence to a certain doctrine, but simply a catchall term of opprobrium to be applied to anyone whose political beliefs and cultural values were at odds with those of mainstream America and the men of the FBI. (p. 212)

King's widow later remarked, "The FBI treated the civil rights movement as if it were an alien enemy attack on the United States" (Garrow, 1981, p. 212).

Marlin finds evidence here of an undifferentiated paranoidlike reaction to a controversial, stressful sociopolitical issue, leading to regressive projection of unconscious, split-off images. Internal fears in such situations resonate and blur with external conditions to exaggerate and "mystify" the threat. She notes that politicians can manipulate such feelings and develop policies based on them. However, in a country with democratic structures, and in a period of lowered international tension such as existed after resolution of the Cuban missile crisis of 1962, which strengthened the United States abroad and at home, such politicians do not arise. In the end, the FBI did not prevail. Presidents Kennedy and Johnson successfully urged Congress to enact civil rights legislation. Nevertheless, regressive tendencies in the culture led to King's assassination.

Until recently, one accomplishment of the McCarthy era had not been abolished: the McCarran Act of 1952 excluded foreigners with unacceptable views. In one case, unsuccessfully litigated by the New York Civil Liberties Union in 1982, visas were denied to Japanese delegates invited to speak at the June 1982 UN nuclear disarmament session. The New York Civil Liberties Union director commented at the time that because Japan was the only nation to experience the effects of atomic warfare, the government's intent perhaps was to "stifle debate on issues of nuclear disarmament," which might "signal a new determination by the Administration to rely on the discredited but still existing legal framework of the McCarthy era to chill debate and dissent" (Samuels, 1982, p. 10). Prial (1990) recently reported a study by the Lawyers Committee for Human Rights. There may be as many as 350,000 persons previously excluded for ideological reasons; however, President Bush signed legislation in February 1990 to end exclusion based on belief in "anarchy, communism or totalitarianism."

INDIFFERENCE TO DESTRUCTIVE CONSEQUENCES

Indifference to destructive consequences may follow an irrational, paranoid response to a perceived threat or catastrophe. Objective criticism and feedback is curtailed or disallowed. As one example, administrators of nuclear weapons programs followed a policy, for nearly 45 years (it ended in 1990), that mandated suppression of records documenting radiation cancer risk or injury to U.S. citizens and military personnel (the initiation of this policy was described by Honicker in 1989). Almost 1.5 million have been at risk (Schneider, 1989), and many have died, perhaps 79% if the death rate of plaintiffs in a 1980s class action suit against the government is used as a measure, 19 out of 24. The remaining five plaintiffs represented nearly 1,500 other victims living downwind of the Nevada test site in the years of atmospheric testing, 1952–1963. One plaintiff produced a 1955 pamphlet, *Atomic Effects in the Nevada Test Site Region*, that said "your best action is not to be worried about fallout" (Schmidt, 1982). Although the judge ruled in the downwinders' favor, a superior court reversed that decision, concluding that the government had "discretionary authority" to pursue its nuclear weapons programs free of liability for future claims. (Taylor, 1988). (The *New York Times*, December 14, 1989, reported that two congressmen have proposed legislation to compensate these citizens.) The same chilling indifference existed in the Soviet Union, of course. In 1989 the Soviet government acknowledged that a weapons plant accident in 1957 killed "hundreds." Residents of 30 villages in the area were evacuated and the villages disappeared from the map (Clines, 1989).

Military spending has been responsible for other consequences. Economist Seymour Melman (1989) stated that from 1947 to 1987, $7.6 trillion went to the military (documented in a report published by the federal government), and that this would have been enough to "rebuild nearly everything that is manmade in the United States."

IRON CURTAIN DISMANTLED; WHAT DOES THE FUTURE HOLD? DEBATE ABOUT THE U.S. PEACE DIVIDEND

Senator Boren, Democrat of Oklahoma, in a *New York Times* op-ed essay (January 2, 1990) wrote about an emerging issue, the peace dividend:

Savings [from the military budget] can and must be used ... to rebuild the decaying infrastructure, improve education and develop human resources ... We cannot be a world leader if we allow an underclass to develop at home, plagued with the waste of human talent that comes from school drop-out rates that are tragically high, and explosive increases in drug addiction.

The following partial summary of "Legacy of Shame" by Ralph Nader and Mark Green (1990)—a scorecard of what the Reagan years accomplished and a forecast of George Bush's policies—is background to debate about the peace dividend. Two issues they presented relate to the indifference phenomenon.

Infants and Children

The study used by Nader and Green ranked the United States as 19th in infant mortality (p. 444). A recent U.S. Census Bureau study reported by the *New York Times* (March 19, 1990) compared the United States to Australia, Britain, Canada, France, Hungary, Italy, Japan, Norway, the Soviet Union, Sweden, and West Germany; only the Soviet Union had a higher infant death rate than the United States. That study also noted that U.S. children were more likely than those in the other ten countries to live in poverty (17%; the Nader–Green figure is 20%). Teenage pregnancy was the highest (10%).

In a letter to the *New York Times* (Sloan, February 22, 1990), a physician first noted that only the United States and South Africa, among industrialized nations, lack a comprehensive health care plan and that "Ronald Reagan succeeded in cutting Medicare funds in favor of Stealth bombers and 'Star Wars'" (p. A18). He then stated that reduction in assistance to children and pregnant women (women and infant care, or WIC) translates to the fact that by 1989 WIC aid was reaching 60% fewer women and children.

Maintaining the Infrastructure and Cleaning Up the Environment versus Military Spending

The General Accounting Office of Congress estimated in 1988 that $500 billion is needed to renovate bridges and the interstate highway system (Nader & Green, p. 444). According to Oregon State Governor Goldschmidt (p. A35), "billions for infrastructure are bottled up in Federal trust funds," but the funds will not be used "because each dollar spent from the trust fund would increase the deficit by $1—a political taboo in the Reagan–Bush era." Bush, it should be noted, has asked the states to repair the system. Goldschmidt points out that because "the efficient flow of people and products between states was critical to our nation ... [lawmakers] explicitly protected the Federal interest in interstate commerce in the Constitution."

Nader and Green note environmental emergencies—toxic waste and contaminated nuclear weapons sites—and estimate that $250 billion is needed for cleanup (p. 444). Military spending in 1990 is about $300 billion, a figure essentially unchanged since 1985, ranging from a low of $300 to a high, in 1987, of $319.3 billion (Kaufmann, 1990, p. 37).

The peace dividend story was still breaking as this chapter was being written, but the news was not hopeful. Rosenbaum reported in the *New York Times* (March 25, 1990) that the Bush administration had not assigned anyone to examine the issue and, according to New York State Governor Cuomo, the reason is politics: "Why should [Bush] fool with the peace dividend now, when he can save it till 1991 just before the election?" Furthermore, according to Senator Rudman (Rep., Vermont), there is "deep concern that advocates of every social program [that] people have been scheming about, from child care to health benefits" would claim the peace dividend (p. A32). What is the estimated size of the peace dividend? According to Rosenbaum's report, over a period of ten years it would amount to about $500 billion. That sum was mentioned as the amount needed to repair bridges and highways.

On a broader note, it is disturbing, inasmuch as it has been a trend since the McCarthy era, that denigration of the word "liberal" ("the L-word") is such a successful tactic of right-wing politicians. Perhaps this represents denial, a refusal to face real problems, permitting emotional simplification of substantive issues such as abortion (emotionality instead of discussion). For the long term, however, there is reason for hope. Liberal activists come forward to lead the many thousands to protest on specific issues. This happened during the war in Vietnam and when President Reagan expressed militant nuclear-tinged opposition to "the evil empire." His sentiments revolved 180 degrees by the end of his presidency and I believe the Nuclear Freeze movement can take the credit. There are other reasons for hope. For example, in the United States, unlike Communist countries, although important truths may be hidden from public view, there are whistle blowers in addition to dissenters; also, archives eventually become accessible. Most important of all, the sound democratic structure of the legal system offers a means of achieving societal change, if people use it.

Finally, dissent as an American right has been a focus of this section, and therefore it is encouraging that on June 21, 1990, the House of Representatives voted against a Constitutional amendment that would prohibit burning or destroying the American flag in political protest. Democratic Speaker of the House Foley successfully counseled that every country has a flag, but only America has a Bill of Rights.

U.S. foreign policy has not been a focus of this section, but it seems, from reading the daily papers, that after an initial cautious approach by the Bush administration concerning change in Eastern Europe, and events in Lithuania (acquired by the Soviet Union in the secret portion of the 1939 Nazi–Soviet pact), President Bush is attempting to work with Soviet President Gorbachev, despite opposition to that policy by the Republican right wing. (The daily papers also report that Gorbachev is having trouble with right-wingers in his country.)

CONCLUSION

The main thing is, it seems to me, that these revolutionary changes will enable us to escape from the rather antiquated straitjacket of this bipolar view of the world, and to enter at last into an era of multipolarity; that is, into an era in which all of

us, large and small, former slaves and former masters, will be able to create what
your great President Lincoln called the family of man. (Havel to the U.S. Congress,
February 21, 1990)

We are happy to cite Havel in 1990, miraculous proof that the world Churchill described in 1946 no longer exists, to our surprise. We each spent many
years, due to our experience of growing up in a divided cold war world, research-
ing aspects of that phenomenon. In sharing our knowledge we corrected blind
spots, distortions, and idealizations, developing a more integrated view of our
own and world history. In particular, Marlin learned from Smith not to idealize
America, and Smith learned from Marlin that America is generally a viable and
hopeful society.

Our conclusion is that both the totalitarian system and paranoid trends in the
United States typify regression in the face of perceived overwhelming loss, threat,
or catastrophe. Regressive individual and group psychology plays a central role
in this process and some individuals seem especially prone to become members
or leaders of such trends, which societies and cultures can reinforce, providing the
basis for oppressive political regimes.

Totalitarianism does not seem to sustain itself because it severely restricts
freedom, a basic condition for growth and integration. The recent movement
away from Communism in the Soviet Union and almost all countries behind the
former Iron Curtain seems irreversible, despite the many problems these nations
face in the process of change. In the United States, reaction to change in Eastern
Europe and the Soviet Union was still an emerging story as this chapter was being
written, but it appears that official policy is to cooperate with Soviet President
Gorbachev and leaders in Eastern Europe.

Psychoanalytic theory asserts that unconsciously we are always vulnerable
to the wish to merge with others, vulnerable to idealization of authorities, and
prone to acting out and projection of aggression, as well as to splitting of our
perceptions and emotions, especially in overwhelmingly threatening situations.
This tendency is greatly magnified in groups and can be manipulated by political
leaders. This vulnerability, stemming from inadequate integration of our early
childhood experiences, is at the root of our continuous struggle to establish and
maintain our separate, uncertain, responsible existence.

REFERENCES

Boren, D. (January 2, 1990). New decade, new world, new strategy. *New York Times*, p. A19.
Burnham, J. (1947). *The struggle for the world.* Chicago: John Day.
Capek, K. (1936). *President Masaryk tells his story.* London: Allen & Unwin.
Clines, F. X. (June 18, 1989). Soviets now admit '57 nuclear blast. *New York Times.* p. A1.
Donovan, R. (1977). *Conflict and crisis: The presidency of Harry S. Truman 1945-1948.* New York:
    Norton.
Freud, S. (1959). *Group psychology and the analysis of the ego.* New York: Norton. (Original work
    published 1921)
Fromm, E. (1941). *Escape from freedom.* New York: Holt, Rinehart & Winston.
Garrow, D. J. (1981). *The FBI and Martin Luther King, Jr.* New York: Norton.
Goldschmidt, N. (March 25, 1991). As highways crumble, Bush stumbles. *New York Times*, p. A35.

Harbutt, F. J. (1986). *The Iron Curtain: Churchill, America, and the origins of the Cold War*. New York: Oxford University Press.

Havel, V. (1980). The power of the powerless. In J. Vladislav (Ed.), *Living in truth* (pp. 36–122). London: Faber & Faber.

Hirsch, D., & Mathews, W. G. (1990). The H-bomb: Who really gave away the secret? *Bulletin of the Atomic Scientists*, January/February, p. 26.

Hofstadter, R. (1965). *The paranoid style in American politics*. New York: Knopf.

Honicker, C. T. (1989). The hidden files. *New York Times Sunday Magazine*, November 19, p. 39.

Kaufman, W. W. (1990) A plan to cut military spending in half. *Bulletin of the Atomic Scientists*, March, pp. 35–39.

Klima, I. (1990). *The unexpected merits of oppression*. Paper presented at the Symposium of Czech Literature and Culture from Fin de Siecle to Fin de Siecle. New York University, New York, March 17–22, 1990.

Korbel, J. (1959). *The communist subversion of Czechoslovakia, 1938-1948—The failure of coexistence*. Princeton, NJ: Princeton University Press.

Lapp, R. E. (1965). *The new priesthood*. New York: Harper & Row.

Marlin, O. (1990). Group psychology in the totalitarian system: A psychoanalytic view. *Group*, Spring, pp. 44–58.

McMillan, P. J. (1990). Book review of Edward Teller biography. *Scientific American*, May, pp. 130–134.

Melman, S. (December 17, 1989). What to do with the Cold War money. *New York Times*, p. F3.

Nader, R., & Green, M. (April 2, 1990). Passing on the legacy of shame. *The Nation*, pp. 444–446.

Nathan, O., & Norden, H. (Eds.) (1960). *Einstein on peace*. New York: Simon and Schuster.

New York Times. (December 14, 1989). Atomic testings' legacy of grief. p. B14.

New York Times. (March 19, 1990). U.S. found lagging in children's well-being. p. A20.

Oppenheimer, J. R. (July, 1953). Atomic weapons and American policy. *Foreign Affairs*, pp. 525–535.

Pithart, P. (February 26, 1990). An interview. *International Herald Tribune*, p. 18.

Prial, F. J. (June 23, 1990). Big growth disclosed in list of barred alients. *New York Times*, p. 24.

Rosenbaum, D. E. (March 25, 1990). No long-term plan on military saving. *New York Times*, pp. A1, A32.

Samuels, D. (1982). *NYCLU Newsletter*, September, p. 10.

Schell, J. (1982). *The fate of the earth*. New York, NY: Knopf.

Schmidt, W. E. (September 14, 1982). Trial to open today in lawsuit over nuclear fallout. *New York Times*, p. A16.

Schneider, K. (December 3, 1989). Opening the record on nuclear risk. *New York Times*, p. E6.

Sloan, D. (February 22, 1990). Health care suffered in "Reagan Boom." *New York Times*, p. A18.

Taylor, S. (January 12, 1988). Ups and downs on federal liability. *New York Times*, p. A20.

York, H. (1976). *The advisors—Oppenheimer, Teller, and the superbomb*. San Diego, CA: Freeman.

IV

Making War, Making Peace

We know from our psychoanalytic work that changes we wish to make in the outside world must be borne by changes in ourselves.

A. LADAN , *The Wish for War*
(International Review of Psychoanalysis, 16 (3), 331–337, 1989)

We must learn how to place morality and responsibility ahead of politics, science and economy.

VACLAV HAVEL, speech to the U.S. Congress

In Part IV, we probe into the possible ingredients that go into making war and making peace. The roots of altruism (Oliner) are counterbalanced with a new look at the death drive (Rubin). Even in this warmer climate, a hoped-for "world without walls," the psychological fallout of the nuclear threat is something that continues to require attention, perhaps even anxiety (Wangh, J. Offerman-Zuckerberg). And, we know that in order to survive in this world, we must reach out as one toward common security—"our only way out" (Rogers).

13

Common Security
The Only Way

Rita R. Rogers

Common security is a concept that is much in use currently in the field of international relations. Although it is applied primarily to U.S.–Soviet relations and to Europe, common security is a profoundly psychological concept that is validly applicable to conflicted relationships both between nations and between individuals. Indeed, introducing the concept of common security into a conflicted relationship helps to create an atmosphere of cooperation that can extend across international, national, familial, and personal levels of experience.

In essence, the concept of common security emphasizes *cooperative pursuit based on self-interests*. It imposes mutual responsibility for security on nations that are in conflict with each other. Karkoszka (1987) has rightly described the creation of common security in Europe as an ongoing *process* rather than as a short-term task. It is a process that hinges on an understanding and valuation of the interrelatedness of all concerned parties. Karkoszka states that such understanding and valuation enable one side to perceive its security as enhanced while the security of the other side is not diminished in relation to their own frames of reference.

BACKGROUND OF THE COMMON SECURITY CONCEPT

The evolving concept of common security in Europe has proceeded from three basic assumptions: (1) that any armed conflict in Europe may involve

RITA R. ROGERS, M.D. • Clinical Professor of Psychiatry, University of California at Los Angeles, Los Angeles, California 90024; Private Practice, 36 Malaga Cove, Suite 203, Palos Verdes Estates, California 90274.

Politics and Psychology: Contemporary Psychodynamic Perspectives, edited by Joan Offerman-Zuckerberg. Plenum Press, New York, 1991.

nuclear weapons; (2) that if nuclear weapons are used, there would be unacceptable risk of escalation; and (3) that a nuclear war is not winnable.

The concepts of national, collective, and alliance security continue to dominate political thinking. Ironically, in the name of these concepts (which are actually firmly held beliefs), numerous wars have been fought. At the present time, there are two main conceptions of how yet another war may arise. One view contends that European security is primarily threatened by the possibility that nations may "stumble" into a war they do not want. Political and military circumstances may produce a series of incremental moves that bring nations to the brink of war.

The second view contends that premeditated attack will ignite a war. There is a growing concern that some states or groups of states are deliberately reinforcing their military forces in order to prevail at a given opportune moment.

The policy of nuclear deterrence has instilled a measure of cautiousness on both sides of the East–West divide. Not only have the major powers shown restraint on the European scene, but since 1945 they have also avoided involvement with their own forces in any conflict threatening confrontation. While causality is difficult to demonstrate at the macrolevel of history, in this particular respect the contention that nuclear deterrence has helped to prevent war between East and West in the period after World War II cannot easily be dismissed.

However, it also must be noted that by enhancing enmities and creating fear, nuclear deterrence influences domestic politics and international relations in ways which also increase the danger of war. The concept of nuclear deterrence nurtures perceptions of adversaries who are inhuman and aggressive and who merit total extinction as far as nuclear preparations are concerned. Furthermore, the concept inhibits proper understanding of the variety and complexity that inevitably characterize the concerns and interests on the other side; and it encourages and legitimizes military confrontation rather than political cooperation. Since the dawn of the nuclear age, arms buildup has been the twin brother of deterrence. At times, the overriding significance attached to military policies has threatened to reduce the management of East–West relations to "nuclear accountancy."

Ironically, deterrence attempts to combine the prevention of war with the preparation for it in a way that resembles the old prescription, *si vis parcem, para bellum* (if you want peace, prepare for war). However, there is considerable historical evidence to disprove this proposition. Statistical data on the history of crises and wars strongly suggest that a crisis is more likely to lead to war if it has been preceded by an arms race.

Because fear of nuclear war has nudged the superpowers toward assuming mutual responsibility for global security, they must take into consideration the security perceptions of potential adversaries. Because of this far-reaching reality, the common security process cannot be dismissed as a mere utopian dream of cooperation; its emphasis is clearly on pragmatic concerns and common interests rather than on an idealized notion of cooperation.

An emphasis on common interests implies a rethinking of relationships in psychological terms: it implies a familiarization with long-range goals of the other side (one's counterpart); and it implies an assessment of one's own perceptions of threat, as well as the perceptions of threat held by the opponent.

PSYCHOLOGICAL OBSTACLES TO APPLYING THE CONCEPT OF COMMON SECURITY

While the benefits of considering the security, or insecurity, perceptions of one's counterpart are self-evident, the act of doing so meets with obstacles. These obstacles must be met with psychological maturity because it is difficult, in anger, to focus on cooperation rather than on confrontation. Anger blinds one's ability to view oneself from the perspective of the opponent. Anger fixates one's focus on the perceived enemy, narrows the breadth of the perspective, and shortens reaction time, so that short-term goals gain supremacy over long-term goals. Destruction of the enemy becomes a much more coveted goal than the goals of self-interest. The cancellation of U.S. participation in the Olympic Games after the Soviet Union's invasion of Afghanistan is a case in point.

The Bind of Dependency

As individuals, we struggle throughout our lives with the tension inherent in a desire for dependence (security) that is counterpointed by a drive for independence (an assertion of freedom to decide one's destiny). This struggle also occurs on national and international planes of experience. In any kind of important relationship, be it personal, social, or political, the qualities of dependence and independence must be served simultaneously. Strength and self-reliance must be fostered even while dependency needs are being fulfilled. For without the growthful movement toward self-sufficiency, dependency is perpetuated, and anger and resentment become the guaranteed concomitant.

In order to be able to consider the security needs and perceptions of threat to one's counterpart, a nation, group, or individual needs to feel a certain degree of mastery over its destiny. As far as Europeans are concerned, they not only have a glorious common cultural heritage, but also a history of striving and struggling, of national hatreds and rivalries, and recent memories of two bitter world wars during which they lost their men, their dignity, and their status. They vividly remember their dependency on those who later became the superpowers.

Indeed, European anger and resentment have simmered for years over the status of dependency on the superpowers. Europeans fear that, once again, their countries will become the arena for the most deadly confrontation of the two nuclear giants; and they feel a loss of control over events and issues of vital importance to them. For example, they were shocked that at Reykjavik, "forty years of alliance strategy were undercut with nary a breath of consultation."

Both superpowers, in their different styles and world views, are attempting to maintain a hegemony in decision making that was established in a past time and in accordance with the unique circumstances of that time. The volatile gyrations in East–West relations that result from this struggle for hegemony have served to increase frustrations and resentment in Europeans over their dependence and have mobilized their yearnings for independence. The accompanying feelings are those of anger and fear: anger against their powerful ally, and an increased fear of their perceived enemy. These feelings alienate Europeans from their superpower allies while failing to foster a stronger sense of self-reliance.

Another sobering concern is the cycle of victimization that arises out of the binds of dependency. When Europeans feel victimized by their dependency on the superpowers they, like all individuals, react to the victimization by victimizing others: be it their neighbors for whom they harbor simmering hatreds of *terra irredenta* (Hungary–Romania); or be it toward their foreign workers, immigrants, and foreign students (now catalyzed by a fear of the AIDS epidemic).

The ambiguity of European dependence on the United States and their vulnerability in case of a conflict between the superpowers has created tension in the NATO alliance. In Eastern Europe, while Staar (1984) emphasizes that the military alliance is strong among the Warsaw Pact nations, he warns that among the population, there is an increase in nationalistic sentiments and a concomitant feeling of indifference toward the State. The Warsaw Pact nations need to consider the possibility that their citizens might succumb to the regressive tendencies of a nationalistic mentality due to their perceptions of their own weakness, helplessness, and impotency in contributing to decision-making aspects of their destinies. Ultimately, the current goals and necessity of Eastern Europeans for economic growth, stability, and progress can be reached only by their perception that they are, to some extent, masters of their own fate.

In conflicted parent–child relationships, a youngster's perception that he has no input in the family decision-making process can lead to a caricaturing of decision-making behaviors through delinquent activities or through a withdrawal from any kind of self-initiated endeavors. A similar pattern of behavior can be discerned in the aggressive nationalism one encounters when one talks to people in the streets of Riga and Tallinn (also in Moscow in the organization Pamyat). One can feel the palpable rise in nationalism, which contrasts sharply with the ursine-patriotism of the Russian people. This is a nationalism that accentuates the "we–they" schism, and which is creating strain in both alliances and in the respective superpowers.

Mistrust of Superpowers

Insecurity in Europe can be traced to mutual fears (some old, some new) that exist between the two superpowers. Elimination (or even reduction) of this attitude of fear and distrust could yield an essential shift toward a sense of security in Europe—even without alterations in any of the other major contributing variables (militaristic, political, technological, and economic).

Europeans would find it easier to cultivate an enhanced feeling of security, self-reliance, and self-improvement if the two superpowers would move away from their fixation on each other, cease to project their intentions onto one another, and decrease their reliance on the preoccupation with their nuclear arsenals.

THE REPERCUSSIONS OF MISPERCEPTIONS

Misperceptions between countries and superpowers ignite old wounds and cast further obstacles onto the pathway of common security. For example, when NATO was being formed in 1949, it appeared imperative that the United States maintain sizable ground and air forces in Europe. It was widely believed that the Soviet Union might, at any moment, unleash its army against the West; in such an event, Soviet troops could invade the English Channel before the U.S. Strategic Air Command could be effectively deployed (Ulam, 1983). NATO's strategy is thus based upon the perception or *misperception* that the Soviet Union hopes to extend its political hegemony across the European continent. Alterman (1985) states that a clear study of the Soviet Union's military doctrine reveals that Moscow is primarily concerned with its own defense.

Here we encounter a perception or misperception from four decades ago that is still influencing current-day strategy and decision making. From a psychiatric perspective, this displacement of perceptions is a familiar phenomenon. Psychotherapy is a process that consists of correcting early misperceptions and of translating them into here-and-now realities. As psychotherapists, we explain to our patients how they are confusing present-day situations with earlier, emotionally charged experiences from their formative years. In essence, we attempt to help them heal themselves of earlier misconceptions by emphasizing that today's reality is separate and different from their previous experiences.

In an analogous fashion, a group or nation will enshrine with bitterness the memory of a hurtful event that occurred at a crucial time of its development. For example, the Western powers' attempt to topple the fledgling Soviet government in 1917 (Rogers, 1986) was a memory that became enmeshed with the trauma of Hitler's attack on the Soviet Union in 1941, while he had a nonaggression pact with the Soviet Union.

A current-day example of the power of old hurts and unhealed wounds and their impact on current events can be found in Shiite Moslem history. Two scholars, Ajami and Lewis, trace the wrath of Shiite Moslems to the 680 AD death of Aliibrali Talib's son, Hussein, in battle on the desert at Karbala in what is now Iraq. According to these scholars, this death crystallized a schism between the followers of Abn Bakr (who became Caliph) and the Shia (partisans of Ali), and gave the Shiites their emphasis on suffering and martyrdom.

For we who live in the twentieth century, it is indeed a powerful and frightening lesson to witness how rigidified anger of 14 centuries ago can be unleashed in our times to threaten the present international order. The manifestation of the Shiite wrath is convincing testimony that a group's anger or frustration cannot and should not be ignored, even when it has lain dormant for centuries. This potent and volatile human element deserves attention and consideration in all security arrangements.

West, East, and Central Europeans possibly could reset their perceptual memories simultaneously: West Europeans do not want to hear about how the Marshall Plan saved them from starvation, and East Europeans do not want to be reminded about the invasion of the Soviet Union in 1941. These reactions are similar to young people whose parents (on whom they depend financially) continually tell them how hard they have worked and how bitter their life was when they were children. Europeans want a new global approach in which powerful allies recognize and accept political, economic, and social change. But all Europeans from the East and West crave that their historical and cultural identity as Europeans be respected and appreciated.

ACKNOWLEDGING "OTHERNESS" AS THE BASIS OF COMMON SECURITY

In order to accept the realistic limitations that accompany the process of decision making on both individual and national levels, there is a psychological need for understanding, accepting, and acknowledging "otherness." Acceptance of otherness is an essential ingredient for international cooperation in the establishment of a common security in Europe. Such acceptance depends on the nonjudgmental perception of geopolitical, sociocultural, and historical differences among nations and peoples. The sociocultural realities of a homogeneous nation cannot be compared with those of a heterogeneous or multiethnic group or nation.

Accepting otherness demands maturity and necessitates the acceptance rather than the projection of one's own, or one's nation's identity. We need to avoid projecting or transplanting our realities, our systems, our styles, and even our preoccupations onto others. For example, Americans are tempted to categorize Soviet decision makers into "hawks" and "doves," thus projecting onto them. One hears the American expression of fear that President Gorbachev's attempts at reform will be squashed by the "hawks" in the Soviet Union. The Soviet political decision-making body is quite different from that of the United States. Recognition, acknowledgment, and acceptance of this difference or "otherness" is much more likely to lead to cooperation and negotiation. "Otherness" means accepting limitations, for instance, placed on glasnost, as well as the calculated use of glasnost. It also demands that we do not idealize our own system as foolproof and perfect, and that we simultaneously attempt to understand the reasons that our counterpart embraces a different system.

An acceptance of otherness is further contingent on an acceptance of change. Nations, like individuals, need to sort out their past from their present. The Europe of 1989 is not the Europe of 1945. The Germanys, West and East, of the 1980s are not Hitler's *Herrenvolk* (master nation); they are, rather, *zwei Volker* (two nations), and their ambitions and aims are quite different than were German ambitions of 1941. In today's multicultural framework of international interactions, however, mass media messages about foreign interventions elsewhere (for instance, Afghanistan, Nicaragua, etc.) make this task of acceptance of change increasingly difficult, frequently rekindle fears of interventionism of one's own country, and further skew old and new fears. This reaction pattern to mass media messages then constellates further obstacles to the acceptance of otherness on a global level.

CONCLUSIONS

The ability to acknowledge change within oneself (one's group, country, or system) requires flexibility and imagination. One needs a "double dose" of these ingredients in order to perceive and accept change in others. Each society plays a crucial role in either facilitating or inhibiting such a willingness. Einstein wrote[1]:

> One cannot fathom that a Society could develop to a higher level without the participation of individuals who think and judge in an independent way, just as it is inconceivable to imagine the development of an individual without the nurturance of his Society.

Einstein's thoughts can be applied to the human factors involved in achieving European society. Europe cannot evolve toward its fullest human potential and develop cooperation instead of confrontation without participation of individuals and countries who think and judge in an independent manner. At the same time, Europeans and the individual countries of Europe need the nurturance and support of their European heritage, history, and sociocultural roots. Einstein understood that the global progress of society could occur only through the mutual efforts of individuals and their societies. Beyond change in policy or strategies, it is the human factor that holds the key to enduring social and political transformation. For it is only through changes in personal and societal attitudes and beliefs that individuals and nations will be able to transcend parochial frames of reference and to accept and embrace the broader, multifaceted "otherness" of global society.

NOTE

1. Informal communication with the curator of the Einstein House in Bern, Switzerland, shared with author.

REFERENCES

Alterman, E. R. (1985). Misperceived threats and unforeseen dangers. *World Policy Journal, 2*(4), 681–709.
Karkoszka, A. (1987). Towards a more secure Europe. *Pugwash Newsletter, 24*(3), 68–71.
Pugwash Working Group II. (1987). Report of working group II. *Pugwash Newsletter, 24*(3), 73–75.
Rogers, R. R. (1986). Psychological aspects of diplomatic contacts in a multicultural setting. *Coexistence, 23*, 283–300.
Staar, R. F. (1984). Soviet relations with East Europe. *Current History, 83*(495), 354–356, 386–387.
Ulam, A. B. (1983). Europe in Soviet eyes. *Problems of Communism, 32*(3), 22–30.

14

Growing Up in a Nuclear Age
Yesterday, Today, and Tomorrow

Joan Offerman-Zuckerberg

Is nuclear age anxiety an anachronistic concept, given this temporarily warmer global climate?* I do not think so. As a psychoanalyst, I understand the painstakingly slow pace by which real change takes place. Political lip service can be given to disclosure and sharing, to verifiability and mutuality, but genuine trust must have time to grow. It is just the beginning and we need to resist being seduced into a premature feeling of complacency and cooperation. Since the advent of nuclear weapons, tribal mentality has not changed significantly. The creation of nuclear arms has transformed our potential for destruction from village, state, and country to the world. However, we remain tribal in our instincts, anxiously paranoid in our thinking, readily given to projection, splitting into good and bad, chronically dependent on externalization processes such as "it's the enemy out there." Though nuclear age anxiety is not necessarily easy to articulate, nevertheless, it is a constant piece of our socio-cultural climate, and in that sense permeates, albeit insidiously, our consciousness (see Escalona, 1982; Mack, 1982). To ignore annihilation anxiety is to deny a psychological fact, a given of the twentieth–twenty-first century.

With regard to this, adolescents have much to say that is truthful and from the heart. Sociologically speaking, they are facing the real world for the first time

*This chapter was written in the early months of 1990. Some editorial comments were added later.

JOAN OFFERMAN-ZUCKERBERG, Ph.D. • Member, Psychoanalytic Society of the Post-doctoral Program, Inc., New York, New York; Faculty and Supervisor, Brooklyn Institute for Psychotherapy and Psychoanalysis, Brooklyn, New York; Supervisor, Yeshiva University Clinical Program and National Institute for the Psychotherapies, New York, New York 10033.

Politics and Psychology: Contemporary Psychodynamic Perspectives, edited by Joan Offerman-Zuckerberg. Plenum Press, New York, 1991.

as participant–observers. And, developmentally they parallel the angst of transition seen today all over the world. Their vision is emotional, critical, demanding, hungry, and idealizing. What they see is often a product of their intrapsychic world, their wishes, conflicts, hopes, but there is also a more conscious conflict-free sphere of perception, reaction, and feeling that is fresh and realistic. This chapter deals for the most part with these voices, together with the voice of the writer and a close colleague who lived in Nazi Germany during her childhood and adolescence. Her thoughts echo and affirm the spirit of what is being said here and adds yet another dimension: the horror that can be if we do not listen to and understand *what has been*. Throughout this chapter, time's passage, from 1984 to 1990, is noted, to indicate the evolution of perception, its sameness and change.

The voices of the adolescents are heard from four sources: (1) A workshop with young adolescents on nuclear age anxiety; (2) the essays of adolescents written for a course on adolescent psychology; (3) the essay of one young adolescent, entitled "The Human Brain: For Better or For Worse"; and (4) the writings of my colleague who lived in Nazi Germany *during* her adolescence.

The following material comes from a journal I kept during and following the workshop I gave on nuclear age anxiety at a private school in New York. The year was 1984. Contained in these notes were preliminary thoughts, reflections, and reactions to questions asked during the workshop, and to the experience as a whole. In order to retain the spontaneity of these reactions, I have kept to this structure.

The primary experience that triggered my concern about nuclear threat and anxiety had to do with a day at my son's school. It was 1984. They were having a nuclear awareness day and I was asked to run a parent–older adolescent group. There was the experience of parents coming in expecting this to be an interesting academic exercise, learning about "nuclear age anxiety." My notes follow.

> The feeling was something quite different. The kids were really agitated, concerned, anxious about their future, anxious about the continuity of the human race. I felt that our generation had betrayed them. We haven't provided a safe future: one's own sense of identity, à la Erikson, rests on some minimal belief that life will continue into the future. That's been shaken. I wondered about the influence of this anxiety on this so-called narcissistic age. I wondered about the effects of that shaken sense of identity and sense of future. What will all that mean? I wondered whether these changes contribute to being more self-involved, more impulse-ridden, more involved in direct stimulation, etc. I had a feeling, substantiated by some of the papers I received from adolescents in 1983 [included in this chapter], that they are despairing and pessimistic. Now, one might be cynical about the tone of these papers and say, "Well, isn't that part and parcel of the adolescent experience? Whatever is going on in the contemporary world will be used to support the problematic adolescent character." I don't think so; these papers really went beyond that. Even the healthiest, most integrated students spoke of despair! Nuclear anxiety was not just being used as a displacement for adolescent turmoil, it went beyond individual differences. It was a general mood. As a clinician, this concerned me.

The description of the workshop that I outlined to myself captured some of the issues that I wanted to think about then (and now). It read to the parents and kids: "Nuclear Age Anxiety: What's Your Reaction?" The workshop would deal with an exploration into the possible psychological repercussions of living in a nuclear age. In the discussion I wanted to listen and focus on issues related to annihilation, death, and separation anxiety. Is this a real psychological syndrome or verifiable phenomenon? Does this exist in increasing intensity in our children and adolescents today? How do we recognize and cope with this phenomenon as it may appear in ourselves, our patients, and our children? What ensued after the workshop was a conviction that the nuclear threat is much more profound and much more pervasive than I had thought.

> I started to experience my own denial. I had, as many adults do, successfully prevented myself from experiencing this, and there's good reason for it. As psychologists we know that anxiety is very painful, particularly free-floating anxiety, and as psychological beings, we don't allow it to go on for very long. What we do with free-floating anxiety eventually is to bind it. How is an individual matter. Some people somatize it, convert it into a headache or an ulcer. Some people intellectualize; some people deny; some people depersonalize. Anxiety can become externalized, "out there," "the enemy," separate from the self. Sometimes there's an isolation of affect, the feeling gets separated from the idea. We have all kinds of defenses to protect us from the pain of anxiety. *My view is that the human tendency to deal with anxiety through denial is as frightening a fact as the possible reality that we will blow each other up.* I don't think that this is going to happen. I'm optimistic enough to think that the human race will go on.
>
> What's more frightening to me is that children today and young people, young adults, have lived with the kind of anxiety that derives from nuclear threat and *are* living with it, but we don't know it. We're not confronting it. We're not talking about it. Parents don't know how to handle it. That in itself, I think, has its own psychological repercussions. Understanding this psychological reality is, to me, more important than talking about the intricacies of nuclear technology. I think that it's critical to have the language and psychological equipment to talk.
>
> On this issue of communication, near the time of the workshop, the program "The Day After" was viewed on television by many students. I recall the panel discussion that followed "The Day After." It was very limited in scope, highly intellectual, lots of talk about the details of technology. I think the only one who really went beyond technical terms was Eli Weisel who spoke humanly and with great feeling of the Holocaust. I treat a number of Holocaust survivors and their children. They represent one population which has lived with disaster. They have an experience of having been caught up in insanity, a cultural psychosis—where there is no sense of rational thought, where the *unthinkable is thought*, where the world is no longer safe. Some become numb emotionally. This psychic numbing, or closing off (a term initially used by Lifton) is a defense mechanism used against incredible pain, massive death, and overwhelming anxiety.* When the system is so flooded that there is nowhere to go, you shut off, become immune.
>
> In a very active way, you become anesthetized, like the drug addict, actually any addictive type; you are searching for that numbed state, a state of nonbeing. Some Holocaust survivors have described their childhood in the camps as having been spent behind a camera—it was as though they were just taking pictures. That is an expression of an attempt to remove oneself from feeling the pain and horror of what one is seeing, to "distance" oneself. That is a form of psychic numbing. I

*Lifton used this term to refer to the emotional state of survivors after the Hiroshima bombing (Lifton, 1982a).

have had a number of patients who have been abused in childhood. They can tell you, "It was at that time when my mother came down with that knife that I stopped feeling." It's a final act of protection, turning to stone. Children in play therapy will draw pictures of themselves as living in locked caves, protected inside balloons; superheroes with super defenses.

Parents and adolescents alike ask, the question: "How do we counteract denial, numbing, and projection? Consider the psychology of the average Soviet citizen. They may be a lot more afraid than we are. They have experienced terrible wars, a very troubled history, a weak economy, and they have every right to feel phobic. If we can understand that, understand that *we are all afraid* instead of merely "reacting" to each other's aggressive acts, that would become a humanizing experience.*

In raising two sons, I find similar situations. The other week [summer 1984] we went up to our place in the country. We have a pond there. My 8-year-old said, "I don't want to go in that water. I don't know what is in there—those creatures!" "Well," I said, "they are more afraid than you are. You know you're bigger. I think we can live together—you, the creatures, and the frogs can all have a good time in the pond." He struggled with that, and after a while, it worked. He was playing with the frogs and looking for creatures. He said, "This is a lot more fun than Uncle Michael's swimming pool where there are no creatures." I began to believe it, too!

We must try to stop thinking in terms of "me" versus "them," "us" versus "the enemy," "winners" and "losers."

Remember living through Vietnam and watching those numbers on the television screen every night: after a while, what did they mean? Those numbers didn't have any reality to us. We couldn't relate to it. This is another important concept, a kind of depersonalization, a dehumanization. It's not real, I'm not real. It is a very powerful phenomenon. I can barely imagine *one* bomb, much less the total number which we have. I'm sure nobody can, not even the guys who make them. Did they know what they were dropping on Hiroshima? That's part of the phenomena of depersonalization, dehumanization, and denial.

Our intellectual capacity and our ability to create technologically is far more developed than our emotional sophistication, our emotional depth. *We have gone beyond ourselves; we can't imagine the consequences of what we have created.*

Some workshop members asked, "How do we begin to resolve our conflicts in a different way?" I really feel hopeful, I think that this election coming up has opened up a possibility which may be realized in another 10 to 20 years. My own clinical observations on early bonding help me to understand the complex equipment that is called upon and cultivated daily in the average woman who becomes a mother—what you have to learn very quickly to be a mother. A mother must learn to be empathically attuned to the emotional life of a nonverbal child and to deal with "conflict resolution" day in and day out. There's always the question: Who's more capable? Are there differences between men and women? I do think, and am probably sexist in saying this, that women have been historically trained to deal with conflicts and emotional life in a way that is a little bit different than the average male. I think that there are gender differences with regard to that particular variable. The average nursery school teacher will substantiate that. It's not that females are not aggressive. History can attest to that, but I do think that their morality and general responsiveness is of an interpersonal nature, rather than suffused with rigid absolutes that can dictate highly defensive responses.

The discussion goes to the election of 1984. People are responding to hope again. I wonder how strong hope is as a political force. I think that there is

*Perhaps now, a renewed effort can be made at creative diplomacy in the Middle East.

something in idealism and hopefulness that has been terribly missed. We lost it all in Nixon. A vote for Carter was a vote for purification. Political figures are really screens that we project on to. We don't know these guys so we project certain feelings and ideas on to them.

Newness engenders both hope and anxiety in the human being. But, as much as we reach out for the new we are also very resistant to change, and cling to the familiar, to "father figures," to old symbols. There's got to be the right balance. We talk about it politically, what the right balance between old and new is. The numbing and hopelessness that come with becoming entrenched in this nuclear buildup is related to the anxious wish to find some new way of dealing with this dilemma in a productive manner. It's a matter of survival.

The polls indicate that there are a lot of people who may like Reagan, but are very concerned about his policies toward nuclear disarmament, his ways of dealing with other superpowers.

The parents are saying at this point, what direction do we take? In the best of all possible worlds, we're going to have a planet that recognizes that man can develop in different ways, different directions, have different political ideologies, etc. Differences don't necessarily have to be attacked, differences don't necessarily kill. I don't think we're ever going to be all the same, we can give up that hope. A benign symbiosis is not going to happen. Assuming that we'll all be different, there's got to be a way of dealing with that which is not belligerent and which can even be looked upon as interesting and as providing a new mode of thinking. It's quite possible.

From my own observation of children and their methods of dealing with conflict, I don't think that humans are naturally destructive. I think that our survival instinct is far greater than our destructive instinct. There's a powerful need to communicate, to get along, to love, to touch, to have affection. If there weren't, civilization could not have gone on the way it has. Sometimes, when I'm sitting on a subway in 90 degree heat I ask myself why there isn't *more* breakdown? The reason is that there are powerful mending or healing mechanics in the average person, survival mechanisms which are far greater than the destructive one.

The problem with technology is that man has outgrown himself. Let's say that we agree that our survival instincts are greater. It doesn't matter any more. It's out of control. *We've created weapons that don't rest on our good human nature; they have a life of their own.* There can be an accident.

Given this, we must minimize the possibility of accidents. There are instances in which technology is beyond our control and, at that point, man's creation truly becomes a monster. It will be that monster that kills us, not the one out there, but the monster we created. That's the essence of the nightmare. When it's out of your control, when the guy at the other end is saying, 'Wait a minute, I did't mean it!' and it's already too late, that's a nightmare. We're living with some of that now. Sometimes it feels like it is too late, it's gone too far.

What's difficult is that we are talking about both resistance to change and resistance to feeling—defending against anxiety. One of the reasons that this is so difficult is because the nuclear age confronts us with the task of *knowing the unknowable, of believing in the unbelievable, of picturing destruction and annihilation to the extent that it penetrates our narcissistic shell.* I'm not thinking about "narcissism" as excessive self-involvement. I'm thinking about "primary narcissism," the fact that we live in this body and this self, that has basic integrity and wholeness. We wake up every day, and we think we're going to be okay. When we try to imagine annihilation, it wounds our very core. We don't want to think that; we don't want to feel that. But children have dreams of being reduced to dust, of waking up and not seeing; there is only darkness. Children are much more open than we are, clearer at times, and less defended. *Annihilation anxiety has to be recognized in order to really know what the potential is behind those weapons.*

The other thing that concerns me is how can we create something without ever using it? I hope I'm wrong but the possibility is always there. It is so powerfully there! Are we big enough—I hope we are—and brave enough, do we have enough humanness, and are we principled enough to say, "I made a mistake. This is wrong. Let's get rid of or at least reduce nuclear weapons?" That willingness to reconsider requires a big person! All that money, all that time, all that energy, all the politics that have gone into the creation of this technology, all the taxpayers' dollars. Someone's going to have to say, "Wait, slow down, we've made a mistake!"

We turn now to 1983, a similar time but the age range of students is now approximately 18–19 years. The statements that follow were in response to an assignment given in a college course on adolescent psychology. The question approximated something like this: "Talk about nuclear age anxiety in your life." The adolescents speak. (Several themes appear in italics.)

I feel as if I am aging a year with each passing day. After reading the paper, I often wonder how many more years will I live? Who are these men who take chances with our lives? My life should be the one thing that I have the most *control* of (with full knowledge that I will eventually die—hopefully, of natural causes), yet I feel as if the future of the human race is being determined and jeopardized by a small number of "men." There is so much destruction and so many killings that I often wish that I wasn't alive to witness such wide-scale inhumanity. I wonder how many people are killed each day in Lebanon, Afghanistan, South Africa, El Salvador, etc.? I mentally count the dead and the children who have only known death and destruction all their lives. I often find myself saying within the context of a seemingly uncomplicated and trivial conversation, "Oh, why should I even bother? *I probably won't live to be forty*" and then I laugh in an attempt to conceal the anxiety.

An 18-year-old speaks of *loss of control, hopelessness,* and anxiety about the future.

Every party is merely looking out for the interests of its own people—but we are all human beings who share this planet. It should be a cooperative effort, not merely for the betterment of the Russians or the Americans, but for the benefit of the human race. It is difficult for me at times to be optimistic about the future of mankind. *I know that it is up to those belonging to my generation to make the world livable again*—for future generations. The earth should be a place where we want to remain, not escape from.

Here an 18-year-old speaks of *cooperation, responsibility,* and *collective security* as the only response. The following is from an older student in the class who interviewed several adolescents:

After listening to the adolescents speak about their thoughts on nuclear war, one thing was very clear: that they believe that it is a very real possibility. In addition, some of them had the feeling that the threat of nuclear war was running their lives. More precisely, they felt that if there was going to be a nuclear war, they may as well not go to college because they felt that they might not get a chance to reap the benefits. The underlying feeling I got from these children was to enjoy life to the fullest while they are still around. Jill, my 14-year-old cousin, said, "Why should I study so hard if I might not even be here to go to college?" Eric, another adolescent interviewed, said, "Sometimes I wonder if I am even going to be here tomorrow." The youngest adolescent that I interviewed, Mark, had the same pessimistic feelings about being around tomorrow. He said, *"I better hurry up and become a man, or I'll never know what it's like."*

A 19-year-old observes the *pressure* on adolescents to enjoy the moment and simultaneously the pressure to grow up, for there may not be a tomorrow.

The horrors felt today are ever so much stronger and more real than in my parents' generation. On the other hand, the Holocaust of World War II was actually a reality for them. Their parents, in turn, lived through both World Wars I and II. We are lucky that a prevention of war lasted many more decades than ever before. Ironically, this is thanks to nuclear advancement which has acted as a deterrent. However, we have a sense of the horrifying imminence of a nuclear war, particularly the younger generation. As has been shown, *they often times look toward their future with despair and uncertainty, hence, the question is, which is the more fearful: uncertainty, or actual devastation?* Obviously the latter. In the midst of fear *we can have hope.* In addition, not everyone, including adolescents, is so struck with apprehension.

A 16-year-old speaks of a future of *uncertainty, fear,* and *hope.*

Why are we expected to accept the threat of nuclear destruction? It's part of our growing-up experience. Who is looking for a life, with death looking over your shoulder? I find myself in a trance, dreaming about my future, and then cutting it off and saying, "That's ridiculous."

What we are being faced with today is clearly not the same as the 1950s situation. We are confronting something more final; we are facing the possibility that the entire human race will be destroyed. There are many who have avoided the issue as a result of feeling helpless. *The ever-popular passive mode is certainly not the answer to understanding and/or preventing a nuclear holocaust.* Unless the adult educators initiate programs for children to cope with the world they are growing up in (and be "trained," so to say, in nuclear age decision making), there is that frightening possibility that tomorrow's world may never come to pass.

The focus here is on turning *passivity* to action and toward creative coping.

However, it is up to the adults in society to take on the responsibility of nuclear education to ward off nuclear fears. In Iowa City, an eighth grader recently polled 370 children her own age and found 75% think about nuclear war often or always, 66% are scared because of it, and 57% feel helpless to do anything about it. One eighth grader wrote, "We're up the creek without a paddle and I'll be blown away before I'm 30 years old." There is a fine line to be drawn between depicting a realistic picture of the nuclear age and not a horrifying one. Perhaps the theory of living one day at a time and enjoying ourselves is the result of an undertone of nuclear fears that we as adults choose to keep in our minds subconsciously. We have control over the nuclear age if we face the fact that it will not disappear. It is here to stay and must be kept under control by our government. *Educating our children to face the possibilities of the devastation of nuclear war will stimulate tomorrow's adults to keep the nuclear age under control.*

The emphasis here is *education*, because of a full and deep acknowledgment of the danger of denial.

A friend just told me we can't eat the snow any more because of something called "acid rain." I wonder about acid rain. Does it drop from the sky in hot oozing droplets, smelling of rusted tin? Is its color a golden-orange or a silver-black? When it hits the ground, does it sizzle like water in a frying pan, disappearing into the sidewalk and pavement? If I pulled a piece of the pavement up, would I find gobs of accumulated acid dripping underneath . . . does someone come and scrape it off and bring it to a secret place, or does it just go away? As much as I want to escape from nuclear power and war, it haunts me. Last summer, I had a horrible dream about a nuclear or some kind of war. I don't remember it that well, but I think it was the Russians against us. There were a lot of little tents around with people shoved tightly in them. The guards told us we could crawl to a large shower room to bathe, but we had to be back quickly before "it" happened. I couldn't make it in time and I knew I was going to be killed. I woke up so frightened—it seemed so real.

A 17-year-old reports *nightmares.*

While it is interesting to look back and try to recall how I used to view war (nuclear or conventional), it seems futile. I say futile because of the problem of anxiety that I am faced with now (as many other people my age, as well as younger and older, face) is very crucial, very frustrating, and all encompassing. I do not think people who are informed, intelligent, and sensitive to our existing dilemma know how to express their feelings, or knew where and to whom their thoughts should be expressed. This feeling I am describing is one of helplessness—of *not having any control.* I think we all give thought one time or another to the possibility of nuclear war, but like many other subjects we cannot or do not know how to handle, we dismiss it from our consciousness.

An excellent explanation is given to *denial,* as a defense against the terror of feeling out of control.

"I always sort of had the feeling that if the world was going to end, it would be in my lifetime," I said with Jackie's head bobbing up and down in affirmation. "I mean, I try to picture myself with kids, with a husband, and a career and all, and I just can't do it. It's as if I can picture my existence only up to a certain point, and then—nothing. There'll be no more world tomorrow. I don't really *believe* that, but *I believe it,* you know," I said.

Trust in tomorrow. Of course, no one needed to argue the feasibility of this nuclear deterrence plan. We all recognized it for what it was—a way to think about the unthinkable (without really thinking about it)—and we appreciated it.

These two excerpts express thoughts on the thin line that separates belief from disbelief.

The topic of nuclear armament and war has always been a controversial subject in my life. Growing up in a family where the breadwinner was the vice president of a major defense company created an atmosphere in which I could hear or think about the possibility of a nuclear war and the necessity for nuclear arms. Like the adolescents that I interviewed, I, too, was told by my father that remaining strong militarily was not a catalyst for war but was instead a deterrent. He claimed that it was only through a strong defense system that we could counter the threat of invasion and war. Having also been very idealistic as an adolescent, I could not relate to my father's type of thinking. I found it very difficult to understand that so much of our national income could be poured into arms just so that they would never have to be used. Not only did this seem illogical to me, but I also saw so many others in need of food and shelter that I could not accept what seemed to be such blatant waste.

It was only after seeing a film about Hiroshima that I came to understand the awful possibility of a nuclear war truly happening. I can remember spending hours afterward in my room, thinking of ways that I could prevent this type of disaster. *Recurring nightmares that I was the sole survivor of a nuclear explosion haunted me through my early years in high school. Constant debates with my father only seemed to make matters worse because of my inability to accept that the construction of anything as dangerous as a nuclear bomb would be in any way beneficial to the world.*

What concerns me here in these powerful words and feelings are the consistent themes of anxious hopelessness, passivity, and helplessness, with regard to the future, together with the clear and powerful wish for change, cooperation, peace, and for a future. The anxiety and uncertainty enter our subconscious and permeate our dreams. It becomes a dynamic force in the unconscious.

This is a dream reported on April 14, 1986, by a 19-year-old college student, which occurred several days before.*

I was with three of my closest friends. I was staying in a house in a country area upstate. There was a view of New York City that is the same as that from Route 17 south going home; we were looking outside New York City and it was attacked. Nuclear attack—after the attack we went outside—we saw three more missiles go directly overhead and explode behind us. That was it. The explosives were fiery orange and yellow. I felt shocked.

We now turn to the year 1990. Over six years have gone by since the workshop and course. Perhaps nuclear age anxiety more than ever is being acknowledged in today's world. Let's turn to a young student, Benjamin, aged 13, and his thoughts on "The Human Brain: For Better or Worse."

In the present time human beings rule the planet known as Earth. Humans have, with their great intellect, traveled to distant points in the solar system, and have accomplished many great tasks and deeds. Humans have created the law-making justice systems and have constructed a law-enforcing system to make sure those laws are carried out to their fullest extent. The human mind is the center of all these great accomplishments, and is what gives mankind the honored title of being the most intelligent species on the planet. But, along with great intellect and passion comes an even greater stupidity.

With our understanding intelligence we are capable of anger, frustration, malice, deceit, and greed. Some humans have squandered their precious gift of intelligence, and instead of working to kindle the light of life, have tried unrelentingly to extinguish that very same light. *Thus, while we are the most intelligent species on earth, we are also the most dangerous.* Even the ferocious bear does not have the power to destroy a world which contains life, happiness, and liberty. There are individuals who have superior intelligence, and have worked a lifetime trying and in some cases succeeding to make this world a better place, yet there are others who take the ideas of these men and women and corrupt them. Thus comes the idea of world threat, domination, and nuclear destruction.

In the oppressed society that I live in today there is always a strong feeling of anger and tension. This anger and tension, in part, come from the unyielding threat of

---

*The student's dream—reported to me by Paul Elovitz, Ph.D.—is a chilling reminder of the SCUD missile attacks on Saudi Arabia and Israel.

world destruction and death. Our leaders and scientists have made the very tool that could end all life as we know it, the nuclear missile. Some people are proud of this mighty weapon and some people deny its existence. What has the human race come to when there are some people bent on the destruction of mankind? *With our vast intelligence why must we destroy instead of giving the most wanted gift, life?* Also, what happens to the innocent people and animals? Must they share our cruel and unjust fate?

War is the outcome of the need for power and the lack of will to understand each other. Nothing fruitful and good can come from war. For some the gruesome memories of war will never disappear. There will always be the horrible guilt and pain of war. For some were forced to kill their own kind, and they will never forget the horrible experience of pumping a bullet into the body of another human being and watching the person's limp body fall to the ground. War can destroy a person's life mentally, or end it physically.

It is our choice. Will the future be filled with light, life, happiness, liberty, and justice? Or instead, will it be replaced with blackness, death, destruction, greed, pain, and chaos? It is our choice, fellow humans, it is our choice.

This 13-year-old's thoughts are suffused with choice. The defense of denial, isolation, hopelessness, and despair, so much a part of the students in the early 1980s, have perhaps been transformed into a greater sense of hope, warning, and choice. Now we turn to a different time but a similar "place" (psychologically).

The following are excerpts written by a psychoanalyst, a friend and close colleague. The material appears in her unpublished autobiography on growing up in Nazi Germany. It relates in parallel fashion to the possible advent of another holocaust, and contains lessons to be learned (see Chapter 11, this volume).

The year is *1939*.* It is a time of *early adolescence*. I met Alex. Alex was a Jew from Warsaw in Poland. He was in Switzerland because he wanted to get the only remaining members of his family out of Poland. His brother, Rafael, Rafael's wife, and Stefan, his infant son. When the Germans invaded Poland, Alex himself had been in New York attending a mathematical conference. Perhaps he could have or should have foreseen the political events that were about to happen when he went to New York in the summer of 1939. *People in Europe and the rest of the world should have foreseen so many things in those days, but we did not.* First of all, as always, a person was a student of philosophy or mathematics, or a writer, or a judge, or a carpenter, or a musician, or a plumber, or an office worker, who pursued his or her daily activities or rounds of duty as usual. In our spare time, we thought about the political situation, and read and argued—but then, suddenly, we had no spare time left in which to do anything at all. *The Nazis had become so powerful, the country had become a dictatorship and we were helpless. Who could foretell that the political events would engulf everything, so that not an ounce of a person's life was left untouched? The person was raped, consent was never asked.* I sometimes thought: What if I refused to consent to the war, the policy of extermination my government was pursuing, the Nuremburg laws, the crimes of the Kristallnacht? What if I would refuse to consent and say so? What if I said: "*Ich habe meine Zustimmung nicht gegeben.*" [I have not given my consent]? Of course, I know that *they* would just laugh in my face. Perhaps they would say something to the effect: "We couldn't care less," perhaps not even that; they would probably simply shoot me. *And like so many millions of others, I said nothing.*

It was at times like that when I had such thoughts that I realized how much I wanted to stay alive, how much I wanted to survive the war. Alex, too, wanted

*Italics are the editor's.

to stay alive and he wanted his brother and his family to stay alive. It was for that reason that he had returned from New York to Europe, not to Poland, of course. Poland was in German hands, or under German boots, and atrocious reports (or rumors?) about the fate of the Jews had begun to leak out. Alex had been in Switzerland for approximately ten to twelve months when we met. *He was alarmed, but in spite of the reports he heard, he could not believe that Germany, whose science and music he so admired, also produced people capable of bestiality.* As a result, he did what all too many people did. *He waited too long.*

He did not succeed in his attempts to rescue his brother and his brother's family. Alex learned later, after the war, that Rafael committed suicide just before or during a transport to a death camp, that his wife managed to flee and went to South America, and that their infant son was rescued by their Gentile maid who pretended that he was her son. Alex also had an older brother who had lived in the U.S.A. for several years. His parents had died some years before the war. Both had died a "natural death," a death that was soon to become virtually unattainable for Jews.

Many Jews and Germans and nationals of other countries could not believe, could not realize, or concretely imagine that the reports they heard were true. What is one to do when the horror of reality exceeds the imagination? When the unimaginable is real? Is that not the reversal of what the human mind has learned to do? Does the imagination not usually exceed reality? How can one blame those who would not believe what they heard? In particular, how can one blame someone for not having been realistic? Is it realistic to believe the unimaginable? There was no model for the horrors that were committed. Nothing in anyone's experience enabled anyone to believe what was happening. Did not mothers, after reading gruesome fairy-tales to their children, calm them by saying, "It is not true, it is only a fairy-tale?" How should those same mothers suddenly believe that reality was a hundred times more gruesome than the most terrifying fairy tales? *Television and even some sci-fi have influenced the human mind so that many people can now imagine what once was unimaginable. But I'm writing about events which happened decades ago before our imaginations had become influenced by the media.*

Anyhow, Alex and I met that day in the hospitable home of the Red Cross officer. We soon fell in love and trusted each other. Sometimes we threw caution to the winds and went out together where German eyes might see us. Since German–Jewish relations of any kind were forbidden, and Switzerland was full of German spies, what we were doing was dangerous. We took long hikes together on the shores of Lac Leman [Geneva]. If a German had seen me and denounced me, I might have been publicly humiliated and killed. But I found that I lacked the capacity to be afraid of human beings for extended periods of time. I had grown up in a family where people helped each other and relied on each other. That had resulted in a feeling of trust with the world.

Some years elapsed, and the author continues:

I had experienced other losses, losses I could not mention to anybody because they did not count. *I had lost the belief that human beings are essentially good, that life has a degree of permanence, that people can be trusted to help each other, rather than fear each other to pieces. Also, compassion is limited: my compassion was with the six million Jews "we" had killed, with the twenty million Russians "we" had killed, not to mention the millions of others, whose numbers I know less clearly.* When I began to talk about it with anybody, the usual answer was: Yes, that is a lot and it is terrible, but "we" [Germans] also lost ten million. I was incapable of compassion with "us." I did not quite know why I was part of "us" or "we," and since I usually first thought of the Jews, the Russians, the Poles, my compassion was usually exhausted before I got around to even thinking of "us," the Germans. Besides, I found it is difficult to have compassion with both sides. It took a special effort of the imagination and of thought to have compassion with Germans. I had to recognize (re-cognize) that most young Germans (like me) were caught up in something that was not their doing. It was not difficult to have compassion with Wolfgang [her brother's closest friend]; I did not consider him a "German" although, of course, he was as German as I was. But we were not part of the "we" and "us" that so many people kept talking about, were we?

We are comparing here what could be, that is, nuclear holocaust, the reality of evil unleashed, with what was, genocide. Differences notwithstanding, the underlying psychological mechanisms remain the same—helplessness, passivity, hopelessness, denial—the failure of imagination.

In psychology, anxiety is defined as a warning signal that the psychic system is, in certain ways, being threatened, overwhelmed, and in conflict. Free-floating anxiety is normally attended by a feeling of being "out of control"—of not knowing or being able to label the feelings, their source, boundaries, or their beginning and end. As psychologists, when confronted by our patients' anxiety, we try to direct energy to the source: by giving verbal expression to what is translating itself, somatically or otherwise, we take a step toward understanding ourselves.

Can we talk of an age of anxiety, a generation of anxiety, a century-to-come of anxiety? Interviews have indicated that children are, indeed, uneasy about their future and fear the nuclear threat. To the question, "What does the word 'nuclear' bring to mind," a teenager responded: "Big gray clouds, red warning lights, dead wildlife and humans, unnecessary deaths and bodies." Another student's associations included danger, death, sadness, corruption, cancer, waste, bombs, pollution, perhaps terrible, terrible devaluing of human life. Though generally reported as decreasing in intensity, children today still remain anxious and preoccupied. The adolescents speaking out in 1983 and 1984 are the young adults of today, the parents of today, tending to an anxiety that they cannot readily allay—no Band-aid for this wound. Have we fulfilled our responsibility to provide a future of hope and certainty? Perhaps there is renewed hope, and perhaps the anxiety of yesterday, the Holocaust of yesterday, served a useful function, that is, as an alarm, a signal that the world is in terrible distress, that terrible, terrible things can happen. Perhaps the young adult of 1990, the former anxious students of the early 1980s, helped shape the hope of today. So we ask, what can we do further and how can we educate? The Nazi Holocaust was fed in part by denial—a powerful denial and passivity on the part of Jews and non-Jews alike. All nationalities participated to some extent in a massive conspiracy of silence.

What lesson can we extract from this monstrous piece of history; how do we counteract denial, dissociation, passivity, victimization, psychic numbing, and feelings of helplessness? To begin by exposure, remembering together, talking together, thinking together, we counter psychic numbing. By exposure, we counter pessimism about the future and we build toward faith and trust in the fundamental structures of human existence. What we are up against here is so massive, so large, so seemingly beyond our control that we do feel, at times, helpless and "shut down" psychologically. We dehumanize the enemy; we cannot imagine the repercussions so we do not think. The anxiety becomes disguised and covered up.

If suppressed too long, it can grow into apathy, depression, and despair, an inability even to mourn fully.

Anxiety, though, is crucial, for it signals that we are responsive, alive, and stirred; that we refuse to deaden ourselves to this fact, that we will forever be living in a nuclear age, that we refuse to become cynical, intellectual, and casual about it. To me, as a professional psychologist, as a mother of two sons, as a person living today, I fear less and less the end of life on earth. Somehow, the human race will prevail and that slowly, very slowly iron curtains will continue to rise and Berlin walls will collapse. What I do fear is the absence of appropriate fear, and premature trust. What I am concerned about is our numbing ourselves to the notion of the "inevitable confrontation" and/or inevitable peace. At the same time, what I do fear is fear itself, a persistent, pervasive, and insidious anxiety, in our children and in ourselves—the knowledge that we live with a kind of fear perhaps unknown to man before and one that we feel limited in handling and unwilling at times to recognize.

It is the juxtaposition of this insidious anxiety, camouflaged by the media-drowned White House, together with our limited access to substantive issues and leaders who have to develop far more creative and constructive responses to change, that is, at best, disquieting. This, together with the "unbelievable" power to destroy the world at any given moment, *is particularly frightening*. It is the juxtaposition of limited mentalities (i.e., not unintelligent, just limited), together with nuclear power increasingly in the hands of countries that we have trouble understanding, *that is particularly overwhelming*.

When we listen to 13- to 19-year-olds yesterday and today, and to a German psychoanalyst who grew up in Nazi Germany, we realize that this climate of violence and potential annihilation exacts a high price. The cost is that a whole generation is growing up without a solid sense of safety—without an expectation of future, without basic trust that life itself on this planet will continue. This reality is more troubling to me than the actual possibility of planetary suicide. There is renewed hope that we will go on, but how and what manner of human being are we to become remains an open question.

REFERENCES

Escalona, S. K. (1982). Growing up with the threat of nuclear war. *American Journal of Orthopsychiatry, 52*, 600–607.

Escalona, S. K. (1982). In R. Rogers *et al.* (Eds.), *Psychosocial Aspects of Nuclear Developments*, pp. 64–93. Task Force Report #20. Washington, DC: American Psychiatric Association.

Lifton, R. J. (1964). In G. H. Grosner, H. Wechsler & M. Guerblatt (Eds.), *Psychological Effects of the Atomic Bomb in Hiroshima: The Theme of Death in the Threat of Impending Disaster*, pp. 152–193. Cambridge, MA: MIT Press.

Lifton, R. J. (1982a). Beyond psychic numbing: A call to awareness. *American Journal of Orthopsychiatry, 52*, 619–629.

Lifton, R. J. (1982b). *Death in Life*, 2nd ed. New York: Basic Books.

Mack, J. E. (1982). The perception of U.S.–Soviet intentions and other psychological dimensions of the nuclear arms race. *American Journal of Orthopsychiatry, 52*(4).

15

The Relevance of the Death Drive to the Nuclear Age

Lowell J. Rubin

INTRODUCTION

As the twentieth century draws to a close we are forced to conclude, as we look around us, that we have important limitations as individuals and societies. These limitations are not just external, but involve forces within us that are hard to control. They now threaten us in a way that was not possible before.

We have wonderous capabilities and possibilities, individually and collectively. But something within us, and within the group process that occurs when we band together, seems to endanger our good ideas, good intentions, and good work, again and again.

This observation is not new. These internal forces were, in one way or another, always recognized as potentially harmful to society. In fact, they are the basis for one of mankind's oldest institutions: religion. Religion has concerned itself with our limits as human beings: limits in our capacity to be alone, limits in the time that we have, limits as to what we can do as individuals, and limits to our ability to be and do good.

Good and evil, life and death, these are indeed among the oldest concerns of the introspective man. Historically they are the domain of our oldest organized intellectual endeavors: along with religion we would include here philosophy and literature.

LOWELL J. RUBIN, M.D. • Faculty, The Boston Psychoanalytic Institute, Boston, Massachusetts; Assistant Clinical Professor of Psychiatry, Brown University, Providence, Rhode Island 02912.

Politics and Psychology: Contemporary Psychodynamic Perspectives, edited by Joan Offerman-Zuckerberg. Plenum Press, New York, 1991.

We do not seem to escape our limitations. At the end of the twentieth century we are struck by the same old paradox. With all of our great creativity, with all that we have made, with all the possibility of making a more wonderful world, we are still, maybe even more than ever, confronted with our limitations. Everything that is potentially good seems to have potential for evil. And evil seems to follow irresistibly from good.

So much are we aware of our limitations at this point that many of us wonder if we will end up fouling our own nest and destroying ourselves. Will we poison our land, our sea, and our air? Will we blow each other up and maybe even the world that we inhabit? Is the force of life somehow doomed to create death and destruction?

As we think about this we remember some of the lessons that literature, philosophy, and religion have taught us. But we also might wonder what some of the newer disciplines, like psychology and psychiatry, have to contribute to our understanding of human limitations and what are we to do about them if we do not want to perish altogether as a species.

One example of such an endeavor comes from a branch of psychiatry and psychology associated with the name of Sigmund Freud: psychoanalysis. In the early part of this century, Freudian psychoanalysis identified a force of death and destruction thought to be inherent in human nature.

Although others had planted the seeds, the "death instinct" concept curiously was most forcefully introduced into psychoanalysis by a young woman who had had a nervous breakdown in her youth, but who went on after treatment to become a doctor, a psychiatrist, and eventually a psychoanalyst. This woman, Sabina Spielrein, a patient, then mistress and student of Carl Gustav Jung, left Zurich to join Freud's circle briefly in Vienna in 1911. Her first presentation before the Vienna Psychoanalytic Society, at Freud's apartment, was on a subject she had thought about for a number of years, the "Destructive Component of the Sexual Drive" (Spielrein, 1911). Two weeks before her presentation, Wilhelm Reik had presented a paper to the group, "On Death and Sexuality" (Kerr, 1988). The idea of a destructive force of death separate from sexuality was later introduced by Freud in 1920 (Freud, 1920). In its final form, this concept generalized the idea of a negative drive that opposed and complemented his earlier idea of the more positive drive, Eros.

Even in his earliest psychoanalytic work, Freud (Breuer & Freud, 1893–1895) saw the mind in conflict. This is what caused symptoms and what was at the heart of his "dynamic" view of human psychology. Throughout his working life, his ideas evolved as to how the conflict was to be understood and what forces were in conflict. The death drive (or "instinct," as it was translated into English) was a final summing up of this force in opposition to life and love, a force that he thought lay at the root of such illnesses as depression, masochism, self-destructive behavior, suicide, as well as sadism, homicide, and war. It even caused interference with therapy in the form of the "negative therapeutic reaction." Because he came to appreciate the great power of this force in human life, Freud was seen as a pessimist (Gifford, 1988). Indeed, Freud was no simple child of the Enlightenment, or of nineteenth-century optimism. Freud, who lived well into the twentieth century (he died in September 1939), was a true twentieth-century thinker. He had seen war and destruction on a mass scale during World War I. He even came to understand the very real possibility of total world destruction, paradoxically "created" by man with tools that his brain could fashion.

This chapter will endeavor to review critically the concept of a death drive proposed by certain psychoanalysts. It will show that despite caveats, limitations, and criticisms, the idea of a death drive can be a useful and stimulating concept. I will suggest that it is possible that in order for Eros, the life force and love drive, to survive, Thanatos, the death drive, has to be contended with.

Beginning with some of the earliest notions in political and social theory, there were contrasting views of human nature. They can be summed up by the positions of Hobbes (1651) and Rousseau (1762). For Hobbes, the human animal was competitive, warring, and destructive. Man's instincts and drives were base and needed to be controlled. The establishment of control over the destructive forces within us, in the form of social organization, was a basic necessity for man in Hobbes's view. In opposition to this were the views of Rousseau, best stated in his "Discourse on Inequality." For him, man was a "noble savage," inclined by nature to be good and to do good. Social organization was often only an impediment to the natural constructive outflow from the springs of goodness in all men.

From one perspective, man was inherently evil and social organization was good and necessary. From the other position, man was basically good and social organization was destructive and an obstacle to his true flowering.

Where did Freud's ideas fit in? We would have to conclude that his point of view was more complex and inclusive of both perspectives. First his work primarily focused on the individual, although he did venture into the study of and speculation about group behavior. His position on the individual clearly was that he was both good and evil. In Freud's view man was driven by two forces: Eros (the life force and the force of love—creation, joining, synthesis, etc.) and Thanatos, a term not used by Freud (the death drive—a force of destruction, annihilation, and entropy).

In terms of our concerns in this chapter, it is important to note that Freud located a drive or force of death, destruction, and annihilation of life within human beings, not outside them. At the same time, he recognized that while the group had potential for curbing and controlling this force, it might also expand, extend, and unleash it (Freud, 1921). He made attempts in his essays on aggression and on war (Freud 1915a, 1933) to point out that there were contervailing forces within that could bring an end to war and save the world from complete destruction. He recognized the power of human intelligence and the life force. Unfortunately, we know that intelligence is fought over, like a beautiful woman, by both drives, the one toward life and the other toward death.

As it turned out, the death drive concept was not met with much enthusiasm by most of Freud's followers, with a few notable exceptions. The reasons for this we will explore shortly. Freud himself held fast to the idea to the end of his life and tried to work out its ramifications and consequences (Freud, 1923, 1924, 1930, 1933, 1938–1940).

The fate of this concept for most of his followers has been quite different. It was basically stripped of a number of its elements and has lived on as the concept of the aggressive drive. But the questions still remain: What is the nature of this aggressive drive? How does it come into being? What is it made of? What are its vicissitudes? Moreover, how does it figure in the problems of war and social destructiveness?

I will argue that when it comes to considering man as a social animal, the concept of the death drive is relevant and helpful. We are certainly more than ever aware, at the end of the twentieth century, of the extent of man's folly. We know that not only as individuals, but as groups, we are and can be destructive on any scale imaginable. With more and better tools constantly at our disposal, now we have to ask if anything can save us from our propensities for evil, death, and destruction.

It is the main thesis of this chapter that by taking the idea of a death drive seriously, we can work at countering it with the help of the countervailing forces: reason, the life force, and love.

A BRIEF HISTORY OF THE IDEA OF A "DEATH DRIVE" AND ITS FATE IN PSYCHOANALYTIC THINKING

While the idea of the death drive is usually attributed to Sigmund Freud, some of the credit for this concept seems to belong to a young Russian psycho-analyst, Dr. Sabina Spielrein. The idea of a death instinct related to the sexual drive and in some kind of opposition to it appears to have been a preoccupation of hers that occurred after her own mental breakdown (Carotenuto, 1982), which Jung diagnosed as a hysterical psychosis. The basis for her original ideas on this subject might have had to do with the kind of world destruction fantasies (Carotenuto, 1982) that Freud described in the case of Shreber, where a sense of impending doom and disorganization is projected onto the world.

Dr. Spielrein had developed a number of mental symptoms by the age of 14. Eventually, at the age of 19, she was brought by her wealthy parents from Russia to Zurich for treatment at the Burgholzli Sanitorium. There, during the year 1904–1905, she became one of the first patients of Dr. Carl Gustav Jung. She was probably the first patient upon whom he used the new psychoanalytic method pioneered by Freud. Jung treated her in the hospital, and when she improved he continued to see her as an outpatient for many years. He apparently fell in love with her. At this time, before transference and countertransference were well understood, Jung violated the therapeutic relationship and she became his mistress while still his patient (Carotenuto, 1982). She and Jung discussed many ideas together during a formative period in the working out of his own theories. She considered that she had made important contributions to his thinking (Spielrein, 1982). Jung found her quite intelligent and encouraged her to take up medical studies, which she did, eventually qualifying in psychiatry and psychoanalysis.

When her parents learned of the affair, they pressured Jung to break off the treatment. Jung apparently sought Freud's advice as to what to do. Freud advised that the treatment be ended. This interlude probably was one source of the developing split between Freud and Jung.

It was during her analysis with Jung that she sketched out her ideas of a death "instinct." Soon after she broke off her treatment and affair with Jung, she moved to Vienna for about a year, where she was able to join the meetings of the Wednesday Evening Society, eventually the Vienna Psychoanalytic Society. In Vienna, only a month after her introduction to Freud, the 26-year-old Dr. Sabina Spielrein, in the presence of 18 august members of this pioneer psychoanalytic group, which included Freud, Fenichel, and Tausk, presented a report to illustrate her ideas on a "death instinct." This was published a year later, in 1912 (Kerr, 1988), in the *Jahrbuch fur Psycho-analyze*. Freud wrote years later, "I remember my own defensive attitude when the idea of an instinct of destruction first emerged in the psychoanalytic literature, and how long it took before I became receptive to it" (Freud, 1930, p. 120). Freud was not alone. When he himself offered his hypothesis in *Beyond the Pleasure Principle* (1920), it was not well received by most psychoanalysts, although Freud himself became more attached to the idea as time went on. It was taken up again ten years later in one of his major works on social theory, *Civilization and its Discontents* (1930), and its importance was reiterated by Freud in several publications up to his death in 1939.

Although this concept, as has been noted, is not widely accepted in its original form in psychoanalytic circles today, the presence of the nuclear threat and other behavior of large groups that appears to threaten everyone, provides compelling reasons for a reexamination of this concept. Can it provide any insight into why we seem propelled in one form or another toward our own destruction and that of our environment in defiance of reason? Can the concept of the death drive offer us any insight at all as to how we might move away from this self-destructive course?

A few analysts, in fact, in the years immediately following the introduction of the death drive theory did show some interest in it. Paul Federn (1932), for example, who had been part of the original group in Vienna before he came to the United States in 1938, was one of those who supported the idea. His paper, "The Reality of the Death Instinct," published in 1932, stated that, "the drive towards death can be observed in its purest form in the melancholias" (Rosenfeld, 1987, p. 126). His analysand and pupil, Edoardo Weiss (1935), who became the first psychoanalyst in Italy, proposed in a paper that narcissism involved not only libido turned toward the self, but also aggression, or as he termed it "destrudo," a form of the death drive (p. 126).

On the other hand, Karl Abraham, a close collaborator of Freud's before his untimely death, who was an important psychoanalytic investigator of aggression, narcissism, and depression, did not take up this idea of a death drive (Heiman, 1955). For example, four years after the publication of Freud's *Beyond the Pleasure Principle*, Abraham (1924) published a paper, "The Development of the Libido," where he spoke of a "pre-ambivalent" oral stage. His most well-known analysand, Melanie Klein, however, did not agree. She saw the earliest stages of life suffused with the death drive. As Money-Kyrle (1955) points out, she went even further than Freud, eventually, to make the death drive in fact the cornerstone of her theories. "She not only accepts the Death Instinct but believes the fear of death to be at the root of persecutory and so indirectly, all anxiety" (Money-Kyrle, 1955, p. 50).

It was Klein's work and that of her followers that showed how the notion of a death drive could be widely applied clinically to the individual and to the group. On this account her work is of particular interest in the context of this chapter, but also, I believe, in general, in its applications to social theory.

Before we return to a consideration of some of the more useful aspects of the death drive concept, what were some of the problems that the critics found in the concept? The way Freud used it, the death drive seemed to be at the root of a number of thorny clinical problems as well as a major one in the social sphere: war.

One of the important critiques of the death drive was put forward by Otto Fenichel (1935) in his paper, "Critique of the Death Instinct." He contrasts the earlier dual instinct theory—sexual instinct versus ego instinct—which seemed more consistent with biology than the final theory of Eros versus Thanatos.

As he makes clear, the purpose of an instinct theory is solely heuristic, that is, to create a stimulating explanatory concept. Fenichel felt the death instinct did relate the body to the mind, which was an important dictum of psychoanalysis. But he felt that the death instinct theory had a number of drawbacks. He found that the idea of reduction of tension would be no more appropriate to the Nirvana principle than the sexual instinct. As for fusion and defusion, he pointed out that logically in a state of regression, where there is supposedly defusion of instincts, there should be as much Eros as Thanatos. This contradicts the observation that in regression Thanatos seems to predominate. Fenichel also agrees with Wilhelm Reich's criticism of the death instinct that one of the problems of such an anthropomorphic view of instincts used as an explanation of conditions such as masochism or depression is that it makes it too easy to put everything down to an overabundance of the death instinct.

Many of the critics have felt that the concept was either too biological or not biological enough. Those who felt it was not really biological at all, like Fenichel, thought the death drive was incompatible with the drive toward survival so basic to Darwin's widely accepted observations of the animal kingdom. Moreover, it did not seem to relate to something observable, but rather to be an abstract notion.

For those who saw the idea as too biological, Freud was seen as leaving the realm of psychological explanation and returning to some sort of primitive biological force to explain everything. To them, the death drive seemed crudely reductionistic, a kind of deus ex machina that could be invoked to explain everything, but which did not seem to really clarify or explain anything. Or, on the other hand, some felt like Wilhelm Reich (Fenichel, 1953) that such a use of the death drive would eliminate consideration of the psychological and social factors from the etiology of the neurosis.

Other critics looked at the idea in terms of the development of Freud's ideas. The death drive concept seemed to contradict Freud's view that the idea of death did not appear in the unconscious (Fenichel, 1935).

Another kind of critique of the death drive concept has been made by La Planche (1976) on more purely logical grounds. In his book, *Life and Death in Psychoanalysis*, he does a careful etymological and philosophical dissection of the theory. He is concerned about the many different meanings attached to the death drive concept: reduction of tension, the inorganic state, death, destruction, hate, aggression, and so forth. He feels that there is all kinds of slippage of logic, poor organization of ideas, confusion of different levels of meaning, and different systems that are invoked, which results in confusion from the interchangeable meaning of the terms. La Planche sides with those who look for a more personal inspiration that compelled Freud to move in La Planche's terms, from "meta-physical reverie [to] dogma" (La Planche, 1976, p. 110).

The definitive revision within psychoanalysis of the idea of the death drive was carried out by Hartmann (1948) in his paper, "Comments on the Psycho-analytic Theory of Instinctual Drives." He proposed that the death drive be left behind as a kind of "biological speculation" and abstract theorizing in favor of a more clinically useful and observable drive, the aggressive drive (also see Hart-mann et al., 1949). It seemed too big a jump from some underlying death drive to those manifestations that occurred clinically in more muted forms.

Yet there remained those who found the concept useful. Karl Menninger thought the notion was salient. He wrote a book, *Man Against Himself* (1938), in which he detailed the various ways in which the death drive made itself manifest in self-destructive behavior. Hermann Nunberg (1926) also supported the useful-ness of the idea in his paper "The Sense of Guilt and the Need for Punishment." Ernst Simmel (1944), too, wrote about "Self-Preservation and the Death Instinct." But, as we have noted previously, one analyst above all made the death drive the cornerstone of her understanding of human development and psychopathology, Melanie Klein. It was on this account, I believe, that despite other analysts' criticisms of her revisions of some of Freud's ideas, Mrs. Klein saw herself as the true heir of Freud. Her great contribution in terms of social theory and the study of war was her focus on the pervasiveness of aggression, which she saw as emanating from the death drive.

FREUD'S CONCEPT OF THE DEATH DRIVE AND HIS DEVELOPMENT OF THIS IDEA

Freud, in his efforts to understand hysteria and later other "neuroses," came to the conclusion that beneath the physical or psychological symptoms, there was a psychological conflict. It is striking how his model of the formation of symptoms parallels the German philosopher Hegel's scheme of the development of world historical ideas. The ideas of Hegel, who wrote and taught in the early 1800's prior to Freud's birth (1856), had great impact on the German-speaking world. The basic Hegelian system (Hegel, 1807) was a dialectical one. The formula for the development of ideas that he proposed was: thesis, antithesis, and synthesis. Freud's idea of the development of symptoms conformed to this basic model.

First there was the wish that was unacceptable (the libidinal wish). This was countered by the censor (ego). Since the instinctual wish was unacceptable to the superego, it was repressed, but not necessarily altogether. Some kind of compromise formation resulted from this struggle, which was the symptom. In this compromise formation, something of the wish was expressed, but it was altered, transformed, and defended against (Freud, 1923).

This dynamic, dialectical view of mental life remained a cornerstone of Freud's outlook. Basically it was a theory of conflict. There was always one force in conflict with another, or one part of the mind in conflict with another. However, in attempting to refine and adjust the theory, to explain new and more mental phenomena, the idea of what was in conflict with what underwent several changes.

After his and Breuer's initial momentous discovery of the importance of sexuality in the pathogenesis of the neurosis (Breuer & Freud, 1893–95), Freud proposed that the basis for neurotic conflict was the opposition between the uninhibited sexual drive and wishes and the prohibitions of the external world represented by another part of the mind. This was originally described as the opposition between the conscious and the unconscious. The agency causing the repression of the wish, partial or total, was the "censor." At this point the sexual instinct was understood to be in conflict with the self-preservative instinct. The self-preservative or ego instinct was thought to be conscious, while the sexual instinct was buried in the unconscious.

In the course of trying to work out the explanation of narcissism, Freud (1914, 1916) found that the previous theoretical construct had a problem in that it now seemed that both the sexual and the ego instincts had a libidinal instinctual basis. So at this point Freud proposed that the basis of conflict was what the aim of the drive was. At this point he saw the "ego" libido in conflict with an "object" libido. But this conceptualization did not then really provide the basic duality of instinctual forces in opposition that Freud thought was essential to explain dynamic conflict.

It was during this time that he gradually developed a greater understanding and appreciation of aggression. Originally he thought of aggression as only part of the libidinal drive, but eventually he separated it out and categorized it with a "nonlibidinal component" of the ego instinct (Freud, 1915b).

In his further clinical investigations of traumatic neuroses, as previously with dreams, Freud came up against the "repetition compulsion." If seeking pleasure was at the bottom of everything, as he thought, than why were there situations when it seemed as though pain and displeasure were sought over and over again (Freud, 1920).

Also, as precursors to the idea of the death drive in the *Project for a Scientific Psychology* (Freud, 1950), which he sketched out hurriedly in 1895 to try to link the current knowledge of neuroanatomy and physiology to psychological disorders, Freud had thought about the nervous system as basically resisting stimuli and seeking to return to a state of rest and lack of tension. This was consistent with the biological principle of homeostasis and the ideas in physics of the third law of thermodynamics—that energy was constantly being lost in any system—or the idea of entropy. Freud came back to this in 1920 as one of the components of the death drive. It was clearly appealing to Freud that there should be a force concerned with breakdown, destruction, and death to counterbalance the force that he formulated that had to do with multiplying and building up—Eros.

It is also important in terms of his developing theoretical ideas that as early as the *Case of a Phobia in a Five-Year-Old Child* (Freud, 1909), commonly known as the case of "Little Hans," Freud began to address the issue of aggression to which his competitive colleague in Vienna, Alfred Adler, had given more emphasis in his explanations of neurotic behavior (Selesnick, 1966). Freud traced Hans's phobia to suppressed sadism and death wishes toward his father. Freud remarked about the "propensity towards cruelty and violence, which is a constituent of human nature" (Freud, 1909, p. 112).

Adler had joined the Wednesday Evening Society as one of the original members in 1902. His work at that time centered on psychological theories based on biology. He was particularly interested in the concept of a person's need to overcome feelings of inferiority and weakness. He proposed that they did this by "overcompensation," which had biological analogies. According to Adler, the "aggressive instinct" was the biological anlage or source of psychic energy utilized by the individual to overcome their "organic" inferiorities through overcompensation (Selesnick, 1966).

By 1908, Adler had departed from Freud by stressing the importance of both aggression and sexuality, but particularly aggression. He further proposed that if there is a "confluence of drives," for example if the sexual and aggressive drives occur together, aggression is always sublimated to the sexual drive. Freud borrowed the phrase "confluence of drives" or "fusion of drives" from Adler and acknowledged him as the source.

When, in 1920 and 1923, Freud placed the aggressive drive within the death drive concept, Adler sarcastically remarked that he was "glad to have made a present to Freud of the aggressive drive" (Selesnick, 1966, p. 80). By this time Adler himself was no longer concerned with the "instincts," according to Selesnick. He considered that the aggressive drive was really a "mode of striving" to accomplish adaptation.

When in the case of "Little Hans," Freud noted that he "considered that the boy's hostile and aggressive feelings were manifestations of aggressive propensities, he agreed this did" seem a most striking confirmation of Adler's views (Freud, 1909, p. 140). At this time and even later, Freud believed that all drives have the power of becoming aggressive, hence there was no need, he thought originally, to include it as a separate drive or give it as much emphasis as Adler had.

So it would appear that one factor that delayed Freud's appreciation of aggression was his rivalry with Adler. At the same time, it is only fair to point out that of course Freud was working from his own perspective. His interest from the outset had been on understanding the complexity of the role of sexuality, which he had discovered (influenced by many other people from this period) played such a large part in neurotic conflict.

Freud always emphasized that the attempt to work out certain clinical problems drew him toward the death drive. Yet I find it convincing, considering what has happened in our own times and the impact it has had on all of us, to consider that historical and personal considerations may also have been at work.

Freud's concerns about death increased after he reached the age of 60 in 1916. No doubt this was enhanced by the threat to the lives of his sons who were both in World War I. The war, with its great loss of life, untold suffering, and privations, even on the home front, made clear the quantity of man's aggressive tendencies.

With amazing perspicacity, Freud (1930) seems to have prophetically seen and understood the arrival of the nuclear age, when in *Civilization and its Discontents*, he wrote:

> The fateful question for the human species seems to me to be whether and to what extent their cultural development will succeed in mastering the disturbance of their communal life by the human instinct of aggression and self-destruction . . . Men have gained control over the forces of nature to such an extent that with their help they would have no difficulty in exterminating one another to the last man. (p. 145)

Those of us who have entered the nuclear age can only be more impressed by mankind's potential for destruction. Certainly awareness of the degree to which aggression and destructiveness are a part of our psyche, together with our need to deny or project this, is a major cause for alarm.

The inescapable fact of our warring tendencies and the clear danger of our abandon in wasting resources, or poisoning our environment, may cause us to feel that the death drive idea makes some kind of intuitive sense, that it has a resonance with the reality of human behavior, and that it needs to be explored more seriously.

Yet as Freud himself pointed out (Jones, 1957), his thoughts about aggression and a death drive antedated the war, or the death of his daughter, or threats to the lives of his sons.

Freud stressed his involvement in the clinical problems of depression, masochism, self-destructive behavior, traumatic neuroses, transference, negative therapeutic reaction, and particularly the ubiquity of the "repetition compulsion" as the sources for his growing recognition of what he called a death drive. All these clinical conditions seemed to go against the idea of the dominance of the pleasure principle as the main motive for behavior or mental activity, hence the title of the book, *Beyond the Pleasure Principle*. He was led to conclude from his study of these conditions that another powerful force was at work beside the progressive libido: a regressive force of destruction and decay. He concluded that this newly recognized force existed in every cell of the body, although finding a source for aggression unlike the sexual drive was to raise other problems.

As Freud (1920) conceptualized it, the death drive operated internally and silently against the shelf. In order not to self-destruct, Eros had to turn this drive outward in the form of aggression and destruction toward others. Under certain circumstances it was either not able to be focused outward or it became redirected toward the inside, which caused a variety of masochistic or self-destructive phenomena.

Freud did not believe that this biological death drive was expressed directly, but only through mental representations. He also observed that it did not appear in pure form, but in almost all cases was fused with libido. Whatever its limitations, this was clearly a powerful explanatory tool.

Perhaps it is important to point out that a lot of mischief was done when Thanatos and Todestreib were translated into English as death instinct. Freud did not use the term "instinkt" in German, which in biology has other connotations, but rather "drive" (Bettleheim, 1983; Hartmann et al. 1949). For Freud the drives had their origins in the body, but they were manifest only indirectly as elaborations of the mind.

HOW THE DEATH INSTINCT WAS KEPT ALIVE: THE CONTRIBUTION OF MELANIE KLEIN

As noted by Greenberg and Mitchell (1983), Melanie Klein combined a very strict bias toward "instinct theory" (with particular emphasis on the death instinct) together with a "relational," or object relations approach. It was her emphasis on hate, aggression, the death instinct, envy, and so forth that distinguished her contribution. Her work made up for what Freud later in his life had confessed to, the lag in his own and psychoanalysis's appreciation of aggression.

Mrs. Klein recognized the psychosexual developmental scheme, but she gave equal or more weight to "innate" aggression, which she called the death instinct. It was in fact only the use of the primitive defense of projection and the basic sense of the distinction between inside and outside that prevented the internal aggression from destroying the self. Only later the internalization of love protected both the self and the object from the destructiveness of the death instinct.

Like Freud, Klein "assumed the instincts themselves to be acting on a biological level, but having representatives in mental life (Phantasies) by which they were known" (Frosch, 1987, p. 114). Both love and hate in her view were operative from the beginning of life. As she described it, the death instinct operating from within created an overwhelming feeling of death, which had to be projected out to preserve the infant from annihilation or overwhelming depression. The death instinct was the basis for anxiety and a major force to be dealt with from the outset. In her metaphorical way she described how the early ego of the child copes with the threat of internalized aggression by deflecting it outward onto the breast as a "part object" representing the mother.

In the next step the projected aggression becomes the "persecuting object" as the aggression is experienced now outside the self and threatening it. The main anxiety during this period is that the object will get inside the ego and overwhelm it (Frosch, 1987).

As Mrs. Klein summed up her thinking:

> I hold that anxiety arises from the operation of the Death Instinct within the child, is felt as a fear of annihilation (death) and takes the form of fear of persecution. The fear of the destructive impulse seems to attach itself at once to an object—or rather is experienced as the fear of an uncontrollable, overpowering object. (1946, p. 4)

It is not difficult to see how this would lead to ideas like that of Volkan (1985), Stein (1982), and others about the "need to have enemies" in order to deal with our own overwhelming aggression.

As with Lacan, there is for Klein no clear distinction between the external and the internal world, "Phantasy is not merely an escape from reality, but a constant and unavoidable accompaniment of real experiences, constantly interacting with them" (Segal, 1981).

Klein felt that there were inborn, biological variations in the force of the instincts, following Freud:

> In speaking of the innate conflict between love and hate, I am implying that the capacity both for love and for destructive impulses is, to some extent, constitutional, though varying individually in strength and interacting from the beginning with external conditions. (Klein, 1957, p. 176)

The relationship of the individual to society is not immediately apparent in Klein's work. It can be extrapolated from the way in which the object modifies and shapes the instincts, at best providing a good experience to offset and contain the internal aggression and destructiveness. Freud was much more explicit about the relationship of the individual to society. He saw them in a dialectic of mutual struggle. The price for harnessing the instinctual drives, which allowed for social peace and progress, was an internalization of controls and repression of the forces causing conflict. This led inevitably to guilt, self-destructive tendencies (masochism), and neuroses. Tension between the individual and society remained always ready to break out in some subversive or destructive fashion unless channeled and controlled.

Returning to the basic dichotomy established in the introduction, represented by Rousseau and Hobbes, Klein was more of a Hobbesian, seeing the drives, particularly aggression, as innate and in need of external control. Freud perhaps had a position that combined in this sense both Hobbes and Rousseau. While he emphasized the innate nature of the drives, first of Eros and later of a death drive, he also saw the child as partially pure, subjected to trauma. In the end, there was a combination of bad stuff inside and bad stuff outside that led to problems.

THE IMPLICATIONS OF THE DEATH DRIVE CONCEPT
AND WHY IT IS IMPORTANT

The concept of a death drive provided Freud not only with a force worthy of being set against sexuality and the life drive, but it seemed also to put him in touch with something as stubborn and insistent as sexuality. This force was as diffuse and rooted in life as the sexual drive, and finally it went even beyond life, to return to the inorganic sphere. The death drive rounded out the very cycle of life from dust to dust. If it was followed, its roots spread into the whole multitude of phenomena of mental life inextricably linked with Eros, but a danger when it was not so well joined with it. Just as earlier in the evolution of Freud's thought the emphasis was on development and every road seemed to lead to or from sexuality, toward the end of his life, hope and optimism gave way to a realism if not pessimism about the limits of life and change. He became more fully aware of repetition and regression. There was not only a force that breathed life into nonliving matter, but a force that drained life away returning to stasis and the inanimate state.

Freud became fascinated with trying to discover how this newly recognized force played itself out. In his own chosen realm, the goal was to understand how biological and social forces played themselves out in the mind. He had an inkling of disaster ahead when the demonic and regressive forces were enhanced by man's capacity for making extensions of himself—machines. With the great insight that he had, the possibility of the ultimate death machines could be imagined along with the hope for new life machines that had so caught the imagination of Western man. The death machines were only the extension of another aspect of the human being that had to be recognized and accepted more fully.

If the force of evil, as it were, were not only powerful but innate and implacable, it requires the utmost seriousness and all our reason and energy to bring it under some kind of control. Psychoanalysis predicted and demonstrated how man would want to deny and forget this conclusion. Freud's hope was that reason and the "binding force of love" (Jacobs, 1988) might overcome the treachery of the powerful force of death within us. If I understand him correctly, there was following World War I a postmodern turn in Freud's thought. He moved away from an earlier form of optimism, away from the hope of change and progress toward a powerful sense of limits. Perhaps it was ingrained in his personality, but if so this strain was encouraged by advancing age and by the recognition of what did not yield. In relation to the times he was not alone. One of the great advocates of the life force and sexuality, Wilhelm Reich (1928), showed at the height of his own thinking a profound appreciation for repetition and resistance. He called it character armor. Character analysis, defense analysis, and ego psychology were some of the offshoots of the greater recognition of this "stickiness," which became of more interest during the period of the 1920s and 1930s.

It would seem that throughout psychoanalysis's brief history, those analysts with social concern, particularly those who took up the problem of man's warring, showed a greater interest in the death drive idea. Reich was something of an exception, although as has been shown he was influenced by some of the thinking connected with the death drive. Others, like Money-Kyrle (1955), Glover (1933), Menninger (1938), as well as Segal (1988), Gifford (1988), and Wangh (1986) demonstrate this correlation.

THE EFFECT OF GROUP PROCESS ON THE DEATH DRIVE

Freud's (1921) basic conclusion about group process was that it caused regression in certain functions among the individual members of the group. More developed, higher-level functions, such as the moral functions, got diluted or lost in the group. The group returned the individuals within it to the most basic levels of concern about security and the struggle against external threats. These conclusions were corroborated in the later work of Bion (1955). To put it another way, this is a primary function of human groups and the main reason people band together in groups. In this sense the group is a stabilizing force but not a creative one. New ideas within the group necessitate the formation of a new group or subgroups that will either convert the larger, previous group, or split off to form an opposing group.

The group is primarily concerned with basic needs and drives (Bion 1955). Sexuality must be sublimated to reinforce the bond between members of the group. Heterosexuality must be controlled and repressed while homosexuality is utilized and strengthened, even if it is not acknowledged. As for aggression, it has to be projected outward or the group will end up destroying itself or its leaders.

At first the group is a threat to an individual and the new member a threat to the group. This is dealt with by various rites of initiation. In the next phase the group is a form of help and security for the individual. Eventually the group must deal with rivalry and envy among the group members. This is handled in the first instance by obsessional defenses leading to hierarchy and rules. When this fails, basic group defense mechanisms come into play: denial, splitting, and projection. Finally at a later stage, group member must be retired from the group and fears of the older group members' anger over loss and expulsion dealt with by the rest of the group.

We could expect the death drive to impact on the group process in a number of ways. On the one hand, it would bolster and support weakness and loss of power in the individual. On the other hand, it could divert aggression away from those who were depended on and needed. Just as Klein described the process of dealing with the death drive in the individual, the group provides mechanisms for using and discharging this drive.

We should note that a few serious problems result from the death drive's interaction with the group process. Group processes extend and prolong the life of the individual, but at the price of trying to harness individual energy and eliminate individual uniqueness. Also in the process of the individual becoming part of the group, rivalries are stimulated that must be worked out. This is done primarily by extrusion and projection of fears and angers to other individuals or groups. On a small scale this occurs in intergroup rivalries between competing groups, for example, in the economic sphere. But most ubiquitously in our societies we see these tensions worked out in the area of sports competition. When this does not suffice, which is often the case ultimately, within any large group the projection must occur outside of the larger group to an enemy "across the border" or far away.

In the end, the group process has the danger of multiplying the internal threat as well as organizing the ability of the group to deal a death blow to the "enemy." As Pogo says in Carl Schulz's cartoon, "I have seen the enemy—and it is us." Now that we have reached the point where there is no place to project the anger of any group that will not threaten or destroy all groups, there is a great and very serious danger. A new repository for these forces will have to be found.

HOW WE CAN NOW UNDERSTAND AND UTILIZE
THE DEATH DRIVE THEORY

Despite many conceptual difficulties, which make it easy to dismiss, I believe the idea of a death drive resonates with our experience and the growing evidence in our times with respect to the worldwide dilemma of uncontrollable power. The death drive concept contains a number of crucial insights.

To begin with, we are still only beginning to understand that aggression is a much more serious problem than was supposed, or is easily accepted. We rather think of ourselves as loving instead of hating, as cooperative rather than competitive in a lethal way. This kind of denial, this way of thinking no longer is adequate to the degree of the threat posed by nuclear bombs and other technological "advances." By fully accepting and beginning with aggression, paradoxically we may be on safer ground.

Next, the death drive theory emphasizes the powerful innate tendencies toward aggression and destruction. In this view it is not just a response to frustration, unless one thinks of the frustration of life in general along the lines of Rank's birth trauma idea. As Arnold Cooper and Otto Kernberg concurred at a recent symposium on human aggression,* whether we think of it as a response to frustration or simply innate, there is overwhelming evidence that aggression is universal in human experience, so it is moot to argue whether or not it was there from the beginning, or if it is merely due to frustration since frustration is ubiquitous and inevitable in human development. The innateness of aggression is also explained by Downey (1984) in an important discussion of basic infantile aggression. If it is there more or less from the beginning, if it is in a certain sense fixed and implacable, it is not something that can be forgotten or overlooked. This is an essential point of view if we are to deal with the danger our technological advances have pushed us to. This view forces us to look for the manifestations of aggression more carefully. Even more important, it suggests that some permanent structures and processes have to be put in place in order to counter the tendencies toward external and internal destruction if life is to be nurtured and continued.

By beginning with the acceptance of such a powerful enemy within, a more sober optimism can be maintained in terms of the struggle to overcome this powerful force, not outside us, but within us.

The question of course finally becomes if from a theoretical point of view we can substitute some better, more realistic idea of inevitable if not innate human aggression for a complex and possibly confused notion of a death drive. But as Stephen Frosch (1987), the English psychologist, points out, the Kleinians, by their acceptance of the death drive,

> Confront the painful phenomenon of destructiveness and examine what can be made of it, how gratitude and other positive feelings can be constructed, how social relations can be maintained in the face of envy and greed ... it reaches out to social ways this might be overcome. (p. 120)

---

*Symposium on aggression sponsored by the Columbia Center for Psychoanalytic Training and Research to honor Aaron Karush, M.D., October 1989.

Such an approach, based on an acceptance of a negative drive and its manifestations such as hatred, envy, greed, and destructiveness toward others forces us to look for the ways of amelioration. It places emphasis on the needs for control and the expression of reparative urges as well as the work required to bring out the positive role of relationship.

Expressed in more purely psychological clinical terms in the way Hanna Segal (1986) does, the death drive concept is more readily acceptable. However, as I note, some of the power of this idea comes from the notion of its biological underpinning in the way that it was originally conceived.

The challenge the death drive concept appears to present is whether and how some of what it explains in relation to our present behavior might be explained in better or alternate ways. If it is as compelling as I believe it is this would be a useful piece of work. In the meantime, the death drive theory seems to have considerable heuristic usefulness in directing us toward vitally needed social concern.

REFERENCES

Abraham, K. (1949). Development of the libido. In *Selected Papers of Karl Abraham*. London: Hogarth. (Original work published 1924)

Bettleheim, B. (1983). *Freud and man's soul*. New York: Knopf.

Bion, W. (1955). Group dynamics: A review. In M. Klein, P. Heiman, & R. Money-Kyrle (Eds.), *New directions in psychoanalysis*. New York: Basic Books.

Breuer, J., & Freud, S. (1961). *Studies in hysteria. Standard edition of the works of Sigmund Freud* (Vol 2). London: Hogarth. (Original work published 1893–95)

Carotenuto, A. (Ed.). (1982). *A secret symmetry*. New York: Pantheon.

Downey, T. W. (1984). Within the pleasure principle: Child analytic perspectives on aggression. In A. Solnit, R. Eissler, & P. Neubauer (Eds.), *The psychoanalytic study of the child* (Vol. 39, pp. 101–136).

Federn, P. (1932). The reality of the death instinct especially in melancholia. *Psychoanalytic Review, 19*, 129–151.

Fenichel, O. (1935). Critique of the death instinct. *Imago, 21*, 458–466.

Freud, S. (1961). A phobia in a five-year-old child. In *Standard edition of the works of Sigmund Freud* (Vol. 10, pp. 3–141). London: Hogarth. (Original work published 1909)

Freud, S. (1961). On narcissism: An introduction. In *Standard edition of the works of Sigmund Freud* (Vol. 14, pp. 73–102). London: Hogarth. (Original work published 1914)

Freud, S. (1961). Thoughts on a time of war. In *Standard edition of the works of Sigmund Freud* (Vol. 14, pp. 273–300). London: Hogarth. (Original work published 1915)

Freud, S. (1961). Instincts and their vicissitudes. In *Standard edition of the works of Sigmund Freud* (Vol. 14, pp. 111–140). London: Hogarth. (Original work published 1915)

Freud, S. (1961). Introductory lectures on psychoanalysis, lecture 26: The libido theory and narcissism. In *Standard edition of the works of Sigmund Freud* (Vol. 16, pp. 412–430). London: Hogarth. (Original work published 1916)

Freud, S. (1961). Beyond the pleasure principle. In *Standard edition of the works of Sigmund Freud* (Vol. 18, pp. 3–64). London: Hogarth. (Original work published 1920)

Freud, S. (1961). Group psychology and the analysis of the ego. In *Standard edition of the works of Sigmund Freud* (Vol. 18, pp. 69–143). London: Hogarth. (Original work published 1921)

Freud, S. (1961). The ego and the id. In *Standard edition of the works of Sigmund Freud* (Vol. 19, pp. 3–66). London: Hogarth. (Original work published 1923)

Freud, S. (1961). The economic problems of masochism. In *Standard edition of the works of Sigmund Freud* (Vol. 19, pp. 159–170). London: Hogarth. (Original work published 1924)

Freud, S. (1961). Civilization and its discontents. In *Standard edition of the works of Sigmund Freud* (Vol. 21, pp. 64–143). London: Hogarth. (Original work published 1930)

Freud, S. (1961). Why war? In *Standard edition of the works of Sigmund Freud* (Vol. 22, pp. 199–215). London: Hogarth. (Original work published 1933)

Freud, S. (1961). Outline of psychoanalysis. In *Standard edition of the works of Sigmund Freud* (Vol. 23, pp. 144–207). London: Hogarth. (Original work published 1938–40)

Freud, S. (1961). Project for a scientific psychology. In *Standard edition of the works of Sigmund Freud* (Vol. 1, pp. 295–387). London: Hogarth. (Original work published 1950)

Frosch, S. (1987). *The politics of psychoanalysis: An introduction to Freudian and post-Freudian theory.* London: Macmillan.

Gifford, S. (1988). Freud's fearful symmetry. In H. Levine, D. Jacobs, & L. Rubin (Eds.), *Psychoanalysis and the nuclear threat* (pp. 15–34). Hillsdale, NJ: Analytic Press.

Glover, E. (1933). *War, sadism and pacifism.* London: Allen & Unwin.

Grosskurth, P. (1986). *Melanie Klein, her world and her work.* New York: Knopf.

Greenberg, J., & Mitchell, S. (1983). *Object relations in psychoanalytic theory.* Cambridge: Harvard University Press.

Hartmann, H. (1949). Comments on the psychoanalytic theory of the instinctual drives. *Psychoanalytic Quarterly, 17,* 368–388.

Hartmann, H., Kris, E., & Lowenstein, R. (1949). Notes on the theory of aggression. *Psychoanalytic Study of the Child, 3*(4), 9–36.

Hegel, G. W. F. (1966). *Phenomenology of the spirit.* Garden City, NY: Anchor Books. (Original work published 1807)

Hobbes, T. *Leviathan.* London: Everyman Library. (Original work published 1651)

Jacobs, D. (1988). Love, work and survival psychoanalysis in the nuclear age. In H. Levine, D. Jacobs, & and L. Rubin (Eds.), *Psychoanalysis and the nuclear threat* (pp. 173–187). Hillsdale, NJ: Analytic Press.

Jones, E. (1957). *Life and work of Sigmund Freud* (Vol. III, pp. 266–280). New York: Basic Books.

Kerr, J. (1988). Beyond the pleasure principle and back again: Freud, Jung and Sabina Spielrein. In P. Stepansky (Ed.), *Freud: Appraisals and reappraisals, Freud studies* (Vol. 3, pp. 3–79). Hillsdale, NJ: Analytic Press.

Klein, M. (1988). *Envy and gratitude and other works.* London: Virago Press. (Original work published 1957)

La Planche, J. (1976). *Life and death in psychoanalysis.* Baltimore: Johns Hopkins Press.

Menninger, K. (1938). *Man against himself.* New York: Harcourt Brace.

Money-Kyrle, R. E. (1955). An inconclusive contribution to the theory of the death instinct. In M. Klein, P. Heiman, & R. E. Money-Kyrle (Eds.), *New directions in psychoanalysis* (pp. 499–509). New York: Basic Books.

Nunberg, H. (1926). The sense of guilt and the need for punishment. *International Journal of Psycho-Analysis, 7,* 420–433.

Reich, W. (1945). *Character analysis* (Theodore P. Wolfe, Trans.). New York: Orgone Press. (Original work published 1928)

Rosenfeld, H. (1987). Destructive narcissism and the death instinct. In *Impasse and interpretation* (pp. 105–132). London: Tavistock Publications.

Rousseau, J. J. (1964). Discourse on inequality. In R. Masters (Ed.), *The first and second discourses* (pp. 101–181). New York: St. Martin's Press. (Original work published 1755)

Segal, H. (1981). *Melanie Klein.* Harmondsworth: Penguin.

Segal, H. (1986). *On the clinical usefulness of the concept of the death instinct.* Scientific Meeting of the Boston Psychoanalytic Institute, March 26.

Segal, H. (1988). Silence is the real crime. In H. Levine, D. Jacobs, & L. Rubin (Eds.), *Psychoanalysis and the nuclear threat* (pp. 35–59). Hillsdale, NJ: Analytic Press.

Selesnick, S. (1966). Alfred Adler. In F. Alexander, S. Eisenstein, & M. Grotjahn (Eds.), *Psychoanalytic pioneers* (pp. 78–87). New York: Basic Books.

Simmel, E. (1944). Self-preservation and the death instinct. *Psychoanalytic Quarterly, 13,* 160–185.

Spielrein, S. (1982). Diary and letters. In A. Carotenuto (Ed.), *A secret symmetry* (pp. 3–127). New York: Pantheon. (Original work published 1911)

Stein, H. (1982). Adversary symbiosis and complementary group dissociation: An analysis of the U.S./U.S.S.R. conflict. *International Journal of Intercultural Relations, 6,* 55–83.

Volkan, V. (1985). The need to have enemies and allies: A developmental approach. *Political Psychology, 6,* 219–247.

Wangh, M. (1986). The nuclear threat: Its impact on psychoanalytic conceptualizations. *Psychoanalytic Inquiries, 6,* 251–266.

16

Further Clinical Considerations of the Psychological Fallout of the Nuclear Threat

Martin Wangh

The title of my chapter, "Further Clinical Considerations of the Psychological Fallout of the Nuclear Threat," necessitates that I summarize what I have published in earlier papers on this matter (Wangh, 1972, 1981, 1982). I will add at the end some practical proposals for further explorations of what drives us on in the nuclear arms race.

My most comprehensive paper on the subject, "The Nuclear Threat: Its Impact on Psychoanalytic Conceptualizations," was published in a special number of the *Psychoanalytic Inquiry* on aggression (Wangh, 1986). The purpose of this paper was—it might seem strange to have to say this—to give *psychoanalysts access* to the issue of the urgency of the nuclear bomb danger under which we all live. I felt it was necessary to find a way to raise their awareness to the fact that they, too, like the rest of the citizens of the world, are tempted to shy away from an affective appreciation of the nuclear threat, to deny its actuality, and to avoid its recognition in the treatment room. They fail to discern how much of the anxiety and the defensive reactions of their patients are fed by a general underlying anxiety about the potential eventuality of human self-erasure.

MARTIN WANGH, M.D.   •   Training and Supervising Analyst, New York, New York; Professor Emeritus, Clinical Psychiatry, Albert Einstein College of Medicine, Bronx, New York 10461; Training Analyst, Israel Psychoanalytical Institute, Jerusalem, Israel; Scholar, Freud Center, Hebrew University of Jerusalem, Jerusalem 91905, Israel.

Politics and Psychology: Contemporary Psychodynamic Perspectives, edited by Joan Offerman-Zuckerberg. Plenum Press, New York, 1991.

My paper at the beginning calls attention to a painting by Francisco Goya y Lucientes, which hangs in an underground room, a quasi-shelter, in the Prado Museum in Madrid. It depicts two giants going at each other with huge clubs in their hands while their legs stand in a foggy bottom pulling them apparently deeper and deeper into its obscurity. Its title is "The Cudgel Fight." Goya could not have illustrated our present world situation more succinctly.

We have to ask ourselves: How has it come about that humanity has brought itself to the point where total mutual destruction seems not only thinkable but possible? And what does this fact do to us who are living under this continuous threat? As usual in medicine, we learn from the pathological about what is also present but less detectable in the so-called *normal*. So, under extreme danger to life, there is a reduction in differentiation, realization, and altruism. For example, Terence des Pres (1977) describes the behavior of man in extreme situations in his book *The Survivor: An Anatomy of Life in the Deathcamps*. He concludes: "The purpose of actions in extremity is to keep life going; the multiplicity of motives which gives civilized behavior its depth and complexity, is lost" (p. 183). The official diary of the Lodz ghetto notes that "a constantly increasing indifference to each other's fate" is taking place among the unfortunates compressed more and more in the trap of the Lodz ghetto (Dobroski, 1984).

I have transposed these observations into a wider social context. I published these reflections in a paper (in German, Italian, and Spanish) called "Narcissism in our Time" (Wangh, 1983a–c). I propose that presently widespread withdrawal is a shadow of the experience of concentration camp and ghetto inmates. Narcissistic withdrawal is the most widespread means to deny the overwhelming nuclear danger. "I can't think of these matters of nuclear threat, let the government worry about it" was the most common answer in an informal, unpublished survey of ordinary people undertaken in collaboration with the Yankelovitch organization. It is also interesting to note that the heightened narcissistic behavior of the population coincides with the psychologist's theoretical preoccupation with the concept of self. Self-psychology has become a whole new branch in present-day psychoanalytic theoretical thinking.

The Jews of Warsaw, although forewarned by the murder of thousands of Jews in Vilna, a town not even 500 kilometers away from them, still maintained that this could not happen to them. They made themselves believe that "only Communists were murdered by the Nazis in Vilna" (Laqueur, 1982, p. 127).

I called this denial to the attention of psychoanalysts together with the "splitting" mechanisms that we employ when too much anxiety besets us, to evade the recognition of actual danger. Dehumanization of the victims and even of themselves, the perpetrators of the mass murders, was employed methodically by the Nazis in order to keep a semblance of sanity in their own ranks (Lifton, 1982).

From such general, sociological observations, I proceeded in my papers to clinical observations of the psychological fallout of the nuclear threat. I interviewed several well-known child psychoanalysts, asking them what did the children, whom they had under treatment while they were exposed to atom bomb shelter exercises in schools and in kindergartens, report to them in their psychotherapeutic sessions. To my own and their astonishment, none of them could recall remarks, behaviors, and affects related to fears aroused in the children by the widely publicized surface nuclear explosions and the school shelter drills.

One of these child psychoanalysts, Berta Bornstein, commented in self-wonderment: "Maybe I, myself, did not want to hear anything about that." Hardly any one of the 3,000 psychiatrists and psychoanalysts to whom I had sent my paper on the student rebellion together with a questionnaire, in 1972, could report that discussion on nuclear fears took place in their one-to-one treatment sessions with their patients at the time of these drills.

I then tested this matter out in group sessions and in face-to-face interviews with young adults who had grown up in the two decades after World War II. They all recalled their anxiety during the bomb drills and they recalled the recommendation to build shelters in their own backyards. But it was also noticeable how in each instance the single interviewees or the group members became more and more uncomfortable and began to employ various methods, prominent among them sardonic hilarity, in order to evade the seriousness of the discussion and the anxiety reevoked by these recollections.

Finally, in the first-mentioned paper (Wangh, 1986) published in the *Psychoanalytic Inquiry*, I cited two psychoanalytic cases where the psychoanalytic situation was at least temporarily broken off in relation to the imaged or imagined nuclear bomb attack threat. In the one instance, the patient removed herself and her family entirely from New York City during the week of the so-called Cuban missile crisis. She and the whole clan assembled in the far-away mountains, where they had a large shelter. The other patient had to sit up and face me in silence for quite a while after he had told me in the previous session of a dream that led to the recollection of his anxiety in kindergarten during atom bombshelter drills.

The fact that in these two psychoanalytic cases the issue of the nuclear threat came so clearly to the surface, in the treatment situation, may in part have been idiosyncratic, as in both instances the father's profession dealt closely with the use of nuclear power. It may also be ascribed to the fact that by that time I had begun to pay attention to such contents in the productions of my patients.

What became clear to me, in an overall manner, was the extent to which the post-World War II generation, who had experienced the agitation around shelter exercises and shelter building and had seen powerful television films on atom explosion tests, was deeply affectively sensitized by the threat of surface nuclear testing. (Since the research of Sybill Escalona [1963] and my own on these matters, many other clinical observations may have been published. I wish to call special attention to Mack [1988] and Parens [1988].)

It seems that the next generation, which grew up after the surface nuclear test ban in 1963, was less sensitized. Intellectually these age groups are fully aware of the menace, but they are less emotionally involved or involvable, at least in the United States. These young men and women of the 1970s and 1980s are quite unlike those of the 1960s. Of course the actuality of the Vietnam War did not face them. (This discussion of generationally differing childhood imprinting is often neglected when considering the arousability of political constituencies.)

I would like to add here that it might be worthwhile to examine closely to which generation those persons belong who prepare the initial position papers for nuclear arms reduction negotiations.

To come back to the reactions of my analytic patients, I noted their with-drawal from me, the analyst, as an object. The patient, the one who sat up, staring at me in silence, obviously trying to regain the image of the object by studying me intently. The other patient, who came back after her absence during the Cuban missile crisis, became defensively aggressive after I questioned her about her absence. She came at me with the angry remark: "You analysts live in the clouds." I believe that her anger was in part an expression of her guilt for having "aban-doned" me in time of danger without even warning me of it. Because of her father's position she had, she believed, more than ordinary information. But I have to ask myself, why did I not pursue her anger more assiduously in the subsequent analysis. Was I, myself, not too intimidated and did not want to become fully aware of the degree of my own apprehensions during this time? Had I been able to pursue the matter, would I not have learned more about her and my own neurotic contributions to our respective "real" anxieties? I might have learned more about the earlier feelings of my patient to the nuclear threat, that is, about her childhood perception of the threat. (It has been fairly recently revealed by Dean Rusk, John Kennedy's Secretary of State, that Kennedy had been ready for further concessions to the Russians had they become necessary in order to avert the threat [*New York Times Index*, 1987].)

One of the young women whom I interviewed directly about her recollection of surface nuclear tests told me: "I sat with my parents in front of the TV screen and we watched what I believe was the test at Yucca Flats. I was eleven years old. No affiliation was going on." Another analytic patient recalled the "crawl-under-the-table exercise in kindergarten; it was weird, everyone was so intent and serious." Both thus noted the alienation among those present.

All this returns us to the sense of isolation and the sole concentration on one's own physical survival in prisoners under extreme conditions, of which I first spoke. To maintain life at all costs was the primary aim. Could the life drive withstand the pull of the death drive? This was the ultimate question.

Freud's (1961) formulation that our existence is fueled by two opposing forces, Eros and Thanatos, though reductionistic, offers the most plausible ex-planation of what propels mankind under stress.

When in 1931, Einstein put before Freud his apprehension that mankind was approaching a state of mutual destruction and asked for his advice, Freud pes-simistically answered that the only hope lay in reinforcing Eros to counteract the pull of Thanatos. Many of our colleagues have therefore suggested that we must find a new kind of morality; or according to the American Catholic Bishops' Conference, a renewal of our trust in God is needed. A new religion? Our ex-perience is that under the guise of new religions the bloodiest wars have been fought. As I see it, we psychologists are in a paradoxical situation, knowing that anxiety produces nefarious defensive reactions, we must recommend facing our fears, demonstrating the danger that arouses them, in order to react with realistic planning toward them. Anxiety in measure alerts us to meet realistic danger realistically. We must acknowledge that man is indeed endowed with an impulse toward self-erasure, toward a state of entropy, as Freud (1961) pointed out in *Beyond the pleasure principle*. In its admixture with a degree of libido, this thanatic tendency is most often rationalized as a paranoidal stance of self-defense. In its name we have by now accumulated more than 50,000 nuclear warheads, when 5,000 nuclear bombs are quite sufficient to bring about a "nuclear winter," which would spell the end of human existence on this planet together with much of the biosphere (Sagan, 1983). This totalistic estimate has recently been questioned. But nevertheless, the continuance of such surplus accumulation is a sign of "drive." It is impossible to rationalize it as self-defense.

The *awareness* of the enormity of these facts (and not their immorality) by a generation who early in its life was sensitized by the familial concern about home shelter building (recommended by Governor Rockefeller in New York State), by the impressions of atomic explosions from the television screen, and by the shelter exercises from kindergarten on may help humanity to steel itself against the prevailing of Thanatos. We witness now that even some of the older political leaders, for whom war still had a heroic, phallic character, are pressed by these new generations to seek control over the thanatic propulsion.

Yet let us not forget that counter to this increase in awareness runs a denying mystical current. It is contained in numerous millenary and fundamentalist notions that indulge in apocalyptic visions in which only *the evil* will perish while *the just* will be revived to live forever. While the thinking of these groups, in measure, tends to rectify the isolating, narcissistic tendencies of which I spoke earlier, their accompanying demonization of the "other" and the glorification of martyrdom pander to the promotion of Thanatos.

In casting around how best to illustrate this willingness to embrace death, I came upon the myth of the sacrifice of Isaac, which is so central to Jewish, Christian, and Moslem lore (Wangh, 1989). Isaac, a young man by the time Abraham takes him to be sacrificed, only meekly asks (Genesis 22:7, 8), "Where is the lamb?" He is easily quieted by his father's reply, "God will provide," and then lets himself be bound and laid upon the pyre. According to Jewish legend, he even boasted to his brother Ishmael of his willingness to become a sacrifice, should God demand that of him (Ginsberg, 1955). We cannot but conclude that Isaac stands in for all those young men who have volunteered for war service ever since their clans, nations, or religions have called upon them to do so. We also must conclude that their willingness, often eagerness to do this, is a manifestation of a drive toward self-erasure. Though there has always been a promise that went with it, it asserts itself through the explicit promise that the self-sacrifice would bring some sort of eternal life to the self-sacrificer, or at least to his stirps. Death and rebirth rituals were always linked.

Yet, in an atomic war these heroic conceptions will be futile. There will not be any singers who praise their valor nor any audience to hear it. Do we know of any analogies of such a self-erasing drive in species other than man? We are puzzled by the behavior of whales, who beach themselves, and that of lemmings, who drown themselves. Once we recognize that such a striving for self-erasure may exist in man, we are challenged to investigate it with all our intellectual strength and urgency, and from all sides. Psychologists, biologists, and ethologists from all civilized nations should be mobilized to join in such an investigation. An international forum should be created with the specific task of fathoming man's primary masochism, as Freud has also named this death drive, which drives us on toward *catastrophe*, and not *apocalypse*, as those who still wish to indulge in fantasies of eternal survival would like to call it.

REFERENCES

Escalona, S. (1963). Children's responses to the nuclear war threat. In *Children*. Washington, DC: U.S. Dept. of Health and Welfare, U.S. Govt. Printing Office.
des Pres, T. (1977). *The Survivor: An Anatomy of Life in Death Camps*. New York: Pocket Books.
Dobroski, L. (1984). The chronicles of the Lodz ghetto. *New York Times Magazine*, July 29.
Freud, S. (1961). *Standard edition of the Works of Sigmund Freud* (Vol. 18). London: Hogarth.
Ginsberg, L. (1955). *Legends of the Bible*. Philadelphia: Jewish Publication Society of America.
Laqueur, W. (1982). *The Terrible Secret*. New York: Penguin.
Lifton, R. (1982). Beyond psychic numbing. In *Preparing for nuclear war: The psychological effects*, pp. 61–62. Physicians for Social Responsibility.
Mack, J. E. (1988). The threat of nuclear war in clinical work. Dynamic and theoretical considerations. In H. B. Levine *et al.* (Eds.), *Psychoanalysis and the Nuclear Threat*, pp. 189–214. Hillsdale, NJ: Analytic Press.
New York Times Index (1987). August 6, p. 24.
Parens, H. (1988). Psychoanalytic explorations of the impact of nuclear disaster on the young. In H. B. Levine *et al.* (Eds.), *Psychoanalysis and the Nuclear Threat*, pp. 189–214. Hillsdale, NJ: Analytic Press.
Sagan, C. (1983). The nuclear winter. *Boston Sunday Globe*, October 30.
Wangh, M. (1972). Some unconscious factors in the psychogenesis of recent student uprisings. *Psychoanalytic Quarterly, 41*, 207–223.
Wangh, M. (1981). On aggression: The psychological fallout of surface nuclear testing. *American Imago, 36*, 305–322.
Wangh, M. (1982). Psychologische Folgen der Atombomben Tests (1945–1963). *Psyche, 35*, 401–415.
Wangh, M. (1983a). Narzissmus in unserer Zeit (Narcissism in our time). *Psyche, 37*, 16–40.
Wangh, M. (1983b). Narcismo Nella Nostra Epoca. *Revista de Psicoanalisi, 29*, 352–380.
Wangh, M. (1983c). Narcisimo en Nuestro Tiempo. *Revista de Psycoanalisis, 40*, 339–351.
Wangh, M. (1986). The nuclear threat: Its impact on psychoanalytic conceptualizations. *Psychoanalytic Inquiry, 5*(2), 251–266.
Wangh, M. (1989). Psychoanalysis and the Visual Arts: The Sacrifice of Issac. Paper given June 1989 in Jerusalem: Conference on Psychoanalysis and Visual Art organized by Sigmund Freud Center, Hebrew University of Jerusalem.

17

Altruism

Antidote to War and Human Antagonism

Samuel P. Oliner

Few will dispute that war is the most persistent plague on humanity. Some say that with the exception of certain rodents no other vertebrate habitually destroys members of its own species. No other animal takes pleasure in exercising cruelty upon another of its own kind (Storr, 1968). Why are war and human antagonism so prevalent? There have been numerous attempts to explain human aggression over the past several hundred years, so many in fact that it is impossible to even summarize them. We shall instead outline a few major causes of war and human antagonism. In this chapter, besides sketching the causes of war and violence, we shall devote the major section to the attainment of human consensus and antidotes to war, stressing the role of global education, global government, moral courage, and altruism in achieving peace. Special attention will be given to altruistic behavior during the Nazi occupation of Europe, which is based on our recent research of rescuers of Jews.

War is defined by Webster's dictionary as open, armed conflict between nations or states, or between parties in the same state; contentiousness; a state of hostility. Quincy Wright (1943) defines war as a condition that prevails while groups are contending by arms; Clausewitz (1968) asserts that war is organized violence, and that war is not an independent phenomenon, but rather a continuation of policy by different means. Finally, Cicero maintained that there are only

SAMUEL P. OLINER, Ph.D. • Professor of Sociology; Project Director, Altruistic Personality and Prosocial Behavior Institute, Humboldt State University, Arcata, California 95521.

Politics and Psychology: Contemporary Psychodynamic Perspectives, edited by Joan Offerman-Zuckerberg. Plenum Press, New York, 1991.

two kinds of contests: by discussion and force. The latter is war. It is obvious that conflict in the form of disagreement will always exist, but why does it lead to war and mass violence?

WHY WAR?

Humankind has fought hundreds of wars, killing uncountable millions of people. During this century alone, approximately 100 million people have lost their lives during dozens of wars. There is of course no simple answer, and scholars have long looked for multicausal explanations, some of which include: (1) sociocultural; (2) economic; (3) political and psychological, especially the role of leaders, their ideology of superiority and dreams of dominating the world; and finally (4) biological, that is, innate aggression embedded in the genetic structure of all living species, including human beings.

Sociocultural Perspective and War

Culture and Ethnocentrism

Many social scientists agree that conflict is embedded in culture and that ethnocentrism is a divisive social process. Ethnocentrism, defined as loyalty to an in-group and hostility to an out-group, has been seen by many as an important explanation for group conflict within and between societies. Various theories proffered about the role of ethnocentrism include frustration and aggression, which may be exacerbated by ethnocentrism; reference group theory, which examines group-based judgments about social injustice; and relative deprivation, which posits that relative deprivation and rising expectations lead to frustration and consequent displacement of aggression against the outsider group, forming a "group enemy" image.

Based on these theories, one can speculate why ethnocentrism is so universal. Probably it can be attributed to the isolation of groups and the development of culture intended to foster group survival and group identity, which functions to instill values, norms, customs, and habits. Ethnocentrism serves to establish group solidarity and adherence to the dominant values and ideology of the group. Culture helps determine whether a person becomes cooperative or aggressive, the type of political society a group will adopt. It fosters a collectivistic or individualistic society; socialism or capitalism. Within the cultural setting, members are taught a certain understanding of the world, perceptions of what is right and what is wrong, and to what "ism" they owe their allegiance. Sociocultural explanations appear to be powerful nurturers of values and personality and help people, through socialization, propaganda, and persuasion, to define who the "enemy" is, to identify who is on the wrong side and who is on the right side. For example, over the last 40 years we have developed a diabolic image of the Communist enemy said to be behind all the evil and unrest in the world. This trend began with the cold war in 1946 and continued until the arrival of Gorbachev in 1985, with his glasnost and perestroika. Researchers suggest conflicts can be resolved through information, which would reduce strong ethnocentrism as well as help develop a realistic and empathic understanding of the outsider group, resulting in a reduction of stereotypes and distorted images of others.

Religion, whose primary function is to explain the origin and meaning of life and foster the altruistic education of unselfish love, is an integral and important part of culture. However, religions have been and continue to be associated with ethnocentrism and numerous bloody wars. With the exception of Islam, no religion has provided as much war in the short run of a few centuries as has Christianity. Specific wars have been and are still being fought for religious reasons because of an ethnocentric attitude of contempt for any doctrine or belief but their own "true faith." Sociologists and anthropologists inform us that a basic tenet of all the major world religions is that unselfishness is a primary virtue and that selfishness lies at the root of the world's ills. If the world's religions did a better job of upholding this primary tenet, and if they integrated their teachings with their actions, perhaps they would have a greater effect on bringing about peace on earth.

The Conservative Perspective on Causes of War

Two cultural perspectives, the conservative and the liberal, are associated with war. The conservative ideology, according to Nelson and Olin (1979), begins with a bold assertion that there is a social reality and a social good that is prior to and greater than privately determined individual rights and individual good. Edmund Burke (1961), criticizing the French Revolution, said that the individual does not exist apart from the group. He rejected the desirability, even the possibility, of an autonomous individual, a concept so central to the liberal perspective. Burke's sense of the individual's connectedness to the network of social obligations binding men together is the theme that, for us, represents the conservative perspective. According to Burke, society is a partnership, but it is a partnership "not only between those who are living, but those who are dead, and those who are yet to be born" (p. 110). Thus it is not love, fraternity, or self-esteem, but rather deference, awe, and respect for this great primeval and eternal contract between the past, the present, and the future that cements the partnership of humanity. Alexis de Tocqueville (1945) expresses basically conservative sentiments that echo a number of political theorists of the nineteenth century who believed that values and norms, and institutions and relationships ought to be preserved unchanged. Dismayed at the changes taking place, he wrote, "In our days men see constituted power crumbling down every side; they see all ancient authority dying out, . . . and the judgment of the wisest is troubled at the sight" (p. 333). Another major conservative principle is hierarchy based on differential status: conservatives hold that leaders are wisest and better fit to rule than the people, who may challenge and topple the established authority.

The conservative perspective considers the causes of war to be the introduction of foreign ideologies, such as Marxism, which threaten the destruction of established values upholding the social order and its authority, leading to a world of unrestrained individual passion and disobedience. Individuals such as Thomas Hobbes (1909), who upheld the necessity for strong government, saw humanity as leaning toward disaster: when norms, constraint, and values break down, institutions crumble and chaos sets in.

The Liberal Perspective on the Causes of War

The liberal perspective maintains that human beings are potentially rational and self-reliant, that they desire to be free and to exercise their capabilities, and that they long for equality as well as social mobility. The liberal perspective opposes all forms of power that might impair or thwart the individual aspirations and holds that people fight wars in the name of freedom: political, economic, and religious freedom, democracy, and decolonization. The German Enlightenment philosopher, Immanuel Kant (1914), who rejected the pessimistic belief that war can never be eliminated, gave impetus to the liberal perspective. In his work, *Eternal Peace*, he made a fervent plea for universal peace and predicted that peace could be accomplished through a voluntary world federation of republics. According to Kant, the strength of any nation-state derives from the amount of liberty enjoyed by its subjects. In order to survive competition among nation-states, rulers would be forced to grant greater liberty to their subjects until finally the republican form of government would become the pattern for the entire world, leading to enduring peace. This viewpoint was also held by Woodrow Wilson, who believed strongly that national self-determination and self-government under law were essential preconditions for international peace. Thus, in the liberal view, in order to prevent war it is necessary to give people more and more freedom.

Economics and War

Many sociologists and social psychologists offer the explanation that intergroup violence is caused by class struggle, that is, by a group's perception of being oppressed and subjected to social, economic, and political injustice. James C. Davies (1962), comparing collective violence in the United States and Russia in his famous "J-curve" hypothesis, explains that major revolutions come about as a result of rising expectations and reversal of gained economic and social desirables of life.

In the nineteenth century, Claude-Henri de Saint-Simon maintained that world peace cannot be guaranteed unless there is a positive relationship between industrial growth and the owners of the means of production, who must become conscious of their social responsibility to their workers. Progress and mass production will uplift the status and economic conditions of people, but unless it is carefully balanced it can lead to a highly stratified world of haves and have-nots. When people are economically desperate, they go to war. The Russian Revolution, the Cuban Revolution, as well as World War II, are examples of conflict resulting from miserable economic conditions. In the past, European nations went to war in order to acquire colonies and enlarge their empires, others fought because they needed markets and new materials. Inflation, unemployment, and economic inequity have led to frustration and many recent wars and riots in Eastern Europe, South Africa, Asia, and Latin America.

Political and Psychological Factors

Hadley Cantril (1950), Kenneth Boulding (1959), and Leon Festinger (1957) have placed blame for war and violence on such factors as distorted images, stereotypes, and cognitive dissonance. This notion has been elaborated by Ralph White (1984) in *Fearful Warriors*, in which he maintains that war-promoting motives and war-promoting perceptions of the enemy frequently lead to war. White says that among nations that go to war there are five war-promoting misconceptions, with almost identical images: (1) the diabolical enemy image, (2) the moral-self image, (3) the "pro-us" illusion, (4) overconfidence and worst-case thinking, and (5) overlapping territorial images.

The diabolical enemy image is exemplified by the characterization, promoted in the United States until very recently, of the Soviet Union as the "Evil Empire"; the perception was encouraged by stereotypes, caricatures, and distortions that Soviet troops are waiting to conquer the world. In 1989, General Manuel Noriega of Panama was the recipient of the title of diabolical enemy, which was followed by an invasion of Panama by U.S. troops.

The moral self-image is a self-deception, which says that "we" are a peaceful society and "they" are not; that, for example, we Americans would never start a war—forgetting, of course, that we have fought over 30 wars since 1945, including the recent invasion of Panama.

The "pro-us" illusion, much less recognized than the others, is a tendency to perceive ourselves as more friendly, less hostile, and more reasonable than our enemies, and to feel that the world is on our side and that our allies approve of what we are doing. This "pro-us" illusion takes several forms, including underestimating the chance that potential opponents will become actual opponents, thus initiating a war in the spirit of overconfidence, as occurred in the Bay of Pigs invasion of Cuba. There, the "pro-us" illusion contributed to the mistaken belief that the Cubans would welcome the nationalists and rise against our hated enemy Castro. As an extension of this illusion, nations tend to underestimate the insurrectionary possibilities in countries whose governments they regard as allies, as the United States did in Vietnam and Iran, and the Soviet Union in Afghanistan.

Overconfidence and the worst-case scenario is explained thus: Overconfident nations feel that they have enough power, unity, and esprit de corps to fight and win—and if things do not go well, they always have the atom bomb. Thus, the enemy will not fight because they know the inevitable result.

Overlapping territorial self-images occur in places throughout the world where two nations or ethnic groups feel that they have a justifiable claim to the same territory. For instance, areas where such disputes have led to violence include the West Bank, the Polish Corridor, South Korea, the Sino-Indian and Sino-Russian borders, and the Falkland Islands.

White (1984) also discusses the problems created by exaggerated fear and the "Freudian" anxiety that nations have about each other. For instance, he suggests America's policy in Vietnam was based mainly on fear of the domino effect: that first, Southeast Asia and then the other Third World countries would fall into Communist hands. The Soviet intervention in Afghanistan led to the fear that the Soviets would soon dominate the Middle East. "Macho pride" is another suggested factor—the need to remain the most powerful nation. A 1976 Gallup national survey found that Americans believed that the United States should retain, at all costs, its dominant position as the world's most powerful nation, even going to the brink of war if necessary.

Another factor White associates with war is hate and anger. Examples would be the mood of Americans after Pearl Harbor, the mood of the French after they lost the war of 1870 against the Germans, the reaction of most Americans to Soviet intervention in Afghanistan, the fears of the Arabs about Zionist expansion, or the reaction of the Irish about the British occupation of Northern Ireland.

Finally, there is something that White calls "selective inattention," a kind of subconscious denial by "sweeping things under the carpet." For instance, very frequently nations do not pay attention to situations and places where the "pot is beginning to boil," such as the United States not paying attention to Iran during the reign of the Shah, Israel not paying attention to the West Bank for 26 years, South Africa not paying attention to the various black townships and Bantustans. Such negligence frequently leads to violence.

Alliances and Nationalism

To the above causes of war must be added the defense alliances that nations make with each other and are then forced to come to each other's defense. For example, Germany had to defend Austria, which resulted in World War I. The growth and development of nationalism, as well as deep aspirations for national sovereignty, leads to war. Some say vengeance, redressing past humiliations, and restoring national pride are factors contributing to contention by arms. Others claim that technological advances are correlates of war.

Because of alliances such as NATO, the Warsaw Pact, and other political and military arrangements since World War II, the two superpowers have come into existence; both, having large quantities of nuclear weapons, now find themselves in the role of world policemen, especially since the older European powers have lost their colonies and declined in military and economic power. The superpowers need to protect their interests and expand their spheres of influence by using various kinds of techniques including alliances, subversion, proxy-wars, propaganda, and even active participation in overthrowing governments. Technologically advanced countries are sometimes more likely to feel overconfident and are therefore ready to become adventurous and try to redress real or perceived historical grievances by "getting even" with the enemy. Until very recently, when perestroika came on the scene, the global strategy of keeping each other off balance has had national, public support in both the United States and the Soviet Union.

Leaders and Conflict Management

Leadership plays a vital role in war and peace. A competent leader and statesman can manage, foresee, and resolve crises that might otherwise lead to war. The leader could use various conflict resolution approaches, including third-party mediation, arbitration by international courts, and so forth. For example, the Jimmy Carter Center is currently involved in conflict resolution, producing some results in Ethiopia where violence has raged for a period of 28 years between the Marxist government of Ethiopia and the Eritrean People's Liberation Front (King, 1989). Psychohistorians who examined the personalities of world leaders, such as Hitler, Lyndon Johnson, and others, claim that the destructiveness of some world leaders begins in the sandbox. The kind of socialization and life experience that the leaders gain as children determines their personality and their actions. Some leaders view war as a glorious and regenerative experience. Some even suggest that war is good for the human character, that it makes "courageous men" out of nations that fight, and a new breed of better human beings. The German general Helmuth von Moltke (Neson & Olin, 1979), who was involved in winning the Franco-Prussian war, claimed, "War fosters the noblest virtues of man, courage, self-denial, obedience to duty, and in the spirit of sacrifice; the soldier gives his life. Without war, the world would stagnate and sink into materialism" (p. 25). The Swiss historian Jacob Burckhardt (1943) held that, "lasting peace only leads to a fear-ridden, distrustful life among people, or a useless clinging to life. War, he claimed, restores real ability to a place of honor. As for these precarious existences, war may at least reduce them to silence" (p. 261).

Theodore Roosevelt (1926) complained about the fact that the activities of money-grubbing American fat cats were "producing a flabby, timid type of character which eats away the great fighting qualities of our race" (p. 66). He added,

> There are higher things in life than the soft and easy enjoyment of material comfort. It is through conflict or the readiness for conflict that a nation will win greatness. . . . A rich nation which is slothful, timid, or unwieldy is an easy prey for any people which still retain those most valuable of qualities, martial virtues. (p. 67)

The view has been advanced that male leaders are inherently prone to be warlike, aggressive, and competitive. Some feel women can do better. In this regard, what is required is to accentuate and bring to the forefront the wisdom of the female spirit. After all, women are givers of life, and therefore they should have more to say about when and why they should sacrifice their sons and daughters. They should be involved in the decision making about life and death, war and peace. The power of women, if organized and unified, could help bring about human harmony on this earth.

Some scholars maintain that there is a desperate need for better international crisis management. It is not only necessary to monitor potential conflict, but to prevent it before it begins, through the moral and political leadership of the major nations that carry influence. Professor Irving L. Janis (1972) informs us that one of the main reasons chief executives make wrong decisions is that they are poorly advised and informed or do not have enough time to make the proper decisions. Many leader are surrounded by advisors who practice groupthink; that is, they tend to agree with the chief executive so that they will be perceived as "team players." Moral leadership could include an end to the manufacture and distribution of arms. The superpowers and the major manufacturers of arms must refrain from supplying arms to contending power.

Biological Basis of Aggression

This perspective asserts that human animals are born to be aggressive, and social institutions must develop some kind of outlet for the aggressive instinct. According to Sigmund Freud, Konrad Lorenz (1966), and Robert Ardrey (1966), there exists some primitive, innate force in man urging him to fight. Aggression appears to be a basic, animal impulse that frequently overrides rational self-interest. To this explanation must be added the emotional element of fear. Lorenz has suggested that excitation is built into each instinctive center within the nervous system and is dissipated when the instinctual act of aggression is performed. Among animals, fighting can arise as a result of competition for dominance, food, sexual partners, or territory. This, for the ethologist, attests to the aggressive nature of animals. The aggressive activities in the cases above are a reaction to some perceived obstacle to the attainment of desirable goals.

Today, however, most social scientists give little credence to the ethological explanation for war, emphasizing rather the sociocultural–psychological explanations. Aggression, violence, and war are much more likely to be found in highly competitive societies, where violence and competitiveness begin in the playpen or sandbox. Numerous studies indicate that violent individuals come from violent homes, and that warlike countries are made up of ambitious, individualistic men. It is not the most "primitive" man that is the most violent one, however. Erich Fromm (1965) has pointed out that often the most "civilized" man is the most warlike, and it is civilization that breeds aggression. Conflict is a learned form of social behavior, acquired in the same manner as other types of behavior and influenced by many of the same social, situational, and environmental factors. Tahitian society values the avoidance of conflict and favors peaceful relations between individuals. This and other peaceful cultures illustrate that it is possible to inculcate peaceful values into a society and its members. For example, studies including the altruistic personality research (Oliner & Oliner, 1988), support the assertion that generosity results from identification with warm and nurturing significant others. Mussen and Eisenberg-Berg (1977) found that generous nursery school boys saw their fathers as more friendly, warm, and nurturing than less generous boys did. In the balance of this chapter we shall address several factors that we consider antidotes to the causes of antagonism and war.

PEACE AND ITS CORRELATES:
THE ATTAINMENT OF HUMAN CONSENSUS

Just as there is no single explanation for war and human antagonism, there is no single factor that will lead to a world without war. It has been said numerous times before that the world is ready to settle down to peace and human cooperation: Indicators around the globe today demonstrate that people are beginning to recognize their common humanity and to agree that war is no longer an option for solving conflict. Perhaps this realization is, as Victor Hugo said years ago, that "one thing stronger than all the armies in the world . . . is an idea whose time has come" (Ferencz & Keyes, 1988, p. 74). But before the idea of peace can be realized, specific action by humankind must be taken. Much has been tried to attain a harmonious world. None, in our view, are more likely to produce peace than (1) global education, (2) attainment of global government, (3) the teaching of moral courage, and (4) the role of altruism.

Global Education

Reardon (1988) feels that in order to maintain peace, we have to educate for and about peace. The field of global education for peace is now favorably received. It is no longer thought of as leftist or "Marxist," but rather considered as necessary, like reading, writing, and arithmetic. Such education must include a series of various processes. Peace educators themselves must engage in a transformational process, envisioning the values to be sought and imagining the educational process for which a model curriculum might be developed. Global peace education involves a linkage between all human beings and how we are bound together on this earth as well as ecological and planetary education. Peace must go beyond people not using weapons against each other: it must include sharing of resources, so that the basis for conflict no longer exists. Such education has to be seen as part of a developmental process: the development of the individual, of humanity as a species, and of the human species in relation to other species on the planet. This involves at least three components: concern, care, and commitment. Concern is that which propels the learner to become knowledgeable about the issues or problems. Effective commitment to democratic citizenship is important because it demonstrates the commitment to the well-being of all. Hence commitment, a synthesis of knowledge and values, is evidence of both the capacity for, and the sense of, urgency on the part of the citizen learner. Peace education ought to also be directed to all classes, cultures, and living communities. There has to be a convergence between individual transformation and institutional transformation. With the establishment of degree programs in peace studies in many colleges and universities, and the introduction of nuclear age education and peace education into literally hundreds of schools, as well as the appearance of numerous books and articles on peace education, the climate is now favorable to push forward and influence significant changes in our curriculum and educational practices.

An introduction into the curriculum of a nonviolent pacifistic philosophy can also contribute to the reduction of violence. Pacifism involves humanitarian, global, and nonviolent community building—a philosophy that is in harmony with the needs of our times. Pacifism advocates civil disobedience, questioning unjust laws, and standing up against absolutist rule. It includes the concept introduced by Gandhi, of satyagraha, or overcoming evil by good, anger by love, and lies by truth. Peace requires an orientation that is other-directed, and as

Schopenhauer asserted, in order to have a moral society we have to feel the kindred spirit among human beings.

Global Government

Global government and regional integration have been advocated by many people: Mazrui (1975), the Misches (1977), Sakamoto (1975), Staub (1989), Bok (1989), Reardon (1988), and Harman (1988). Some even suggest that the United Nations could serve as a basis upon which a stronger and constitutionally empowered world government could be built. Among the great men and women who have supported global federation, Einstein said,

> With all my heart I believe that the world's present system of sovereign nations can only lead to barbarism, war and inhumanity . . . and that there is no solution for civilization or even the human race other than the creation of the world government. (Ferencz & Keyes, 1988, p. 26)

Jawaharlal Nehru, the Indian Prime Minister, said, "I have long believed the only way peace can be achieved is through world government" (p. 49).

Peter Ustinov, the renowned actor, said,

> World government is not only possible, it is inevitable; and when it comes, it will appeal to patriotism in its truest, in its only sense, but patriotism will be for men to love their national heritage as deeply as they wish to preserve safety for the common good. (p. 143)

Norman Cousins, late president of the World Federalist Association, maintained that the only security for Americans today, or for any people, is the creation of a system of world order that enables nations to retain sovereignty over their own culture and institutions, but that creates a workable authority for regulating the behavior of nations in their relationships with one another (Ferencz & Keyes, 1988).

Philosopher Bertrand Russell maintained that, "Science has made unrestricted national sovereignty incompatible with human survival. The only possibilities are now world government or death" (Ferencz & Keyes, 1988, p. 52).

Golda Meir, Prime Minister of Israel, said, "Internationalism does not mean the end of individual nations. Orchestras don't mean the end of violins" (p. 44).

Ali Mazrui (1975) also advocates the need for a world culture as well as a world government. However, he feels that we might be able to achieve a world culture sooner than a world government. International communication and contacts in every field including the arts, sciences, business, and popular culture have developed close relations between the inhabitants of the "global village." Global socialization will foster and encourage global citizenship and global patriotism rather than narrow, nationalistic patriotism. Visits and travel among nations are important because face-to-face interaction helps reduce tension and shatter stereotypes. A world culture must not be simply Eurocentric, however; it has to include the Third World and their values, because they are also rich and beautiful.

The teaching of multilingualism is also necessary because it increases understanding and reduces suspicion among people. In the midst of a genocidal massacre of 347 Vietnamese on March 16, 1968, Harry Stanley, a black American soldier, refused to obey Lieutenant William Calley and murder innocent civilians. One of the main reasons he gave for not shooting the Vietnamese was that he had learned their language and found more reason to treat the Vietnamese as human beings. There are presently five languages that are spoken by over 200 million people each; these are English, Russian, Chinese, French, and Arabic. While these ought to remain the five major world languages, it is also necessary that regional languages as well as communal languages be taught. This can only come about when we accept a world culture and a world government. A world government must be democratic and have equal representation for all cultures and all regions. Minimally, by democracy we mean guaranteeing people freedom from hunger and political and religious oppression. Currently the North dominates the South, and a great economic disparity prevails. The technology of the West is not shared equally, which creates polarization between nations.

A world constitution would provide for settlement of regional disputes, secure autonomy and self-reliance for groups, help with regional integration, and establish free markets such as the current free trade markets between Canada and the United States. The forthcoming integration of Western Europe will secure each nation's autonomy and freedom, justice on all levels of society, and will help formulate common goals to cope with common concerns, including environmental problems.

On the domestic level there must be full participation by the people, commitment to the principles of equality, and a balance between central authority and decentralized structure for the purposes of decision making. In the area of economics, in order to have a more peaceful world, we have to change our model from growth based to need based, and therefore appropriate technologies must be introduced and used. While we are advocating global integration and global government for the purposes of peace and stability, local political units have to have autonomy and self-governance. These must be encouraged and nurtured. This approach can succeed, though it will take time and, above all, the good will of leaders who can lead, as well as an informed populace.

The author agrees that there ought to be: (1) world economic and social councils, (2) a general assembly that would be part of a world parliament, (3) a council of world jurists, and (4) a world commission of human rights, ever vigilant against human and civil rights violations.

There are currently some examples of regional integration that could serve as stepping stones toward global integration; for example, the Organization of American States, the Arab League, NATO, the Warsaw Pact, SEATO, and the EEC (European Economic Community). Gerald and Patricia Mische (1977) suggest that nations give up national sovereignty and adopt a world citizenship. As a first step, there has to be discussions and debates on (1) why a global community is needed, (2) what are the reasons for it, (3) what kind of world do we want, and (4) how can we attain it. We have common global problems such as poor housing, malnutrition and suffering, inadequate health care and a neglect of the elderly, fear of walking the streets, and racial and ethnic polarization; we must now begin to reverse these conditions. We need to catalyze people and form multiissue coalitions because the problems are similar and global.

No single country can carry the world-order movement by itself. Leadership must come from both developed and developing nations. The world-order model has to include scholars, social and political experts, and institutions that will network and lobby on behalf of that plan. The Misches (1977) remind us that there are a minimum of 17 global issues that are in need of immediate, common solutions: (1) hunger, (2) housing, (3) health care, (4) education, (5) employment, (6) environment, (7) war prevention, (8) crime prevention, (9) prevention of alienation and addiction, (10) care for the aged, (11) racial justice, (12) women's rights, (13) religious freedom, (14) penal reform, (15) urban planning, (16) population control, and (17) democratic participation. Multiissue coalitions with common concerns have much to do, and by working together they can help solve the problems. Global education can play an important role in that it will help us to realize that we can no longer deal with single-issue regional problems; rather, countries are linked to one another and therefore global solutions are required.

Other networks already in existence are the religious networks. These institutions circle the globe, and have common goals and concerns in the areas of justice and compassion. During international conferences these bodies can push for solidarity of the human family, reverence for life, love, and cooperation to enhance human well-being. Similarly, educational networks can and must play a role.

The many national and international professional conferences of engineers, educators, physicians, social scientists, and others can provide opportunities for international dialogue between thousands of persons who share common concerns about particular issues. These networks can provide a central vehicle for the multiissue coalitions for world order. In addition, theories of harmonious intergroup relations tell us that when people are involved in solving common problems, intergroup prejudice and polarization diminishes substantially and mutual understanding and respect increases.

Teaching Moral Courage

Courage should not be confused with rashness, bravado, or brutal physical prowess; rather, courage is the foundation that underlies all other virtues such as love, fidelity, caring, compassion, and trust. All of these involve risk. To trust, to love, to be open, to be compassionate, to be faithful involve risk, and that is why it is courageous. The term "courage" itself comes from the French world "coeur" meaning "the heart." Just like the human heart, which by pumping blood throughout the body enables all the other organs to function, so too courage makes all the psychological virtues possible. Without courage, says Rollo May (1975), other values will wither away into a mere facsimile of virtue. Rescuers had such courage. For them it was not just a matter of admiring courage. They acted on it by standing up to Nazi murders of innocent people, saving lives, as we shall elaborate later.

Rollo May (1975) and writers such as Camus, Nietzsche, and Kierkegaard have proclaimed that courage is not the opposite of despair: it is rather the capacity to move ahead in spite of despair. Courage requires centeredness, without which a person is a vacuum, a kind of emptiness within corresponding to outward apathy. In the long run, apathy becomes cowardice and indifference. Daisaku Ikeda (1989) says that the requisite of courage is a heart-to-heart understanding, necessary to forge peace among nations that are at odds.

Sissela Bok (1989), in her book, *A Strategy for Peace*, says that states will have to submit freely to moral law and that the federation of states will have to act only according to the maxim whereby one can at the same time will that it should become a universal law. Furthermore, she says that cooperation among nations, as well as stress on morality, compassion, concern, and justice, would reduce war. A universal moral framework is required, not only in the public arena, but also in the private arena. In particular, governments have to become more moral than they currently are. She cites as a recent immoral action the French sinking of The Rainbow Warrior in 1985 in a New Zealand harbor because they were annoyed by the Greenpeace ship's interference with French atomic testing. Bok maintains there are at least four moral constraints on peace that have to be overcome: violence, deceit, betrayal, and excessive secrecy. These correspond to four moral principles: nonviolence, veracity, fidelity, and publicity. A moral society requires more than four moral principles, of course, but they are a good beginning. In addition to these moral principles for a peaceful and altruistic world, we ought to pay attention to the ten commandments and to Confucian ethics, to lend an ear to Micah and to ask humanity to act justly. Finally, we need to listen to Kant's and Sorokin's insistence that human beings owe one another love and respect, empathy, and mutual benevolence.

Along with Kant, Gandhi, Buber, Sorokin, and others, Bok warns that nations must live up to their moral principles or nothing will work. They have to distinguish between what is moral and what is immoral and do what is right and not what is expedient. There should be no appeasement of terrorism, there should be no abuse of human civil rights; governments and leaders must give people confidence and hope that there is a way to achieve a moral, fair, kind, and just future.

In order to eliminate mistrust and reduce risks, a functioning hot line should be established between leaders of the major powers, as well as smaller powers. Military budgets need to be reduced, and there needs to be diplomacy rather than pressure and coercion. Exchange of intelligence, technological help, and commercial and cultural activities among nations would go far to reduce mistrust. Openness and publicity should be adhered to at all costs so that the people will know what governments are doing, and so that they will not be betrayed and dragged into wars through manipulation in secrecy.

By their actions, people of great moral courage such as Gandhi, Martin Luther King, Buber, Solzhenitsyn, and Tolstoy stood up against the establishment by protesting the cruel and unjust treatment of their people. They stood up against war and the dehumanization of others. The rescuers in Nazi-occupied Europe scored significantly higher than bystanders on the scale of empathy and social responsibility for diverse other groups.

Unfortunately, one of the most prevalent statements in our world today is "I don't want to get involved." May (1975) calls this masking or hiding cowardice. We would rather say that it indicates a lack of commitment to others. The opposite of apathy is involvement with the community and humanity, what May called social courage. It is the courage to include other human beings and to relate to them as human beings. It is the capacity to risk one's self in the hope of achieving meaningful intimacy and close the gap between self and others.

Courage to risk may result in solidarity with others and lead to harmony. But solidarity with others must always be questioned to be sure that it is not just "the we syndrome," the dichotomization between we and they. We should question whether commitment to some cause excludes others and their causes, that it is not ethnocentric or exclusionary. We must ask whether it is motivated by a sense of justice and care for all. Asking these questions will help to guard against developing the kind of destructive "solidarity" of insider groups such as the Nazis.

Kenneth Lieberman (1986), in his article "The Tibetan Cultural Praxis: Bodhicitta Thought Training," describes a Tibetan cultural praxis that consists of the ethical training of people in their responsibility for all others, including their enemies. This exercise includes thought training, which entails including one's friends as well as one's enemies in one's circles, care, and how to control against anger, which is considered destructive. This philosophy involves treating others with loving kindness, holding one's enemies in one's heart as though they were precious jewels. In their daily practices, Tibetans visualize in front of them their worst enemy, as well as any person to whom they have had unkind thoughts during the previous day. They contemplate each person until they are able to regard them with genuine affection. In addition, through an equalizing practice, they endeavor to show such parties the same regard they have for their friends and strangers so that friends and strangers are equally treated.

This secular logic of altruism was offered recently to a contemporary audience by the Dalai Lama when he spoke in Washington, D.C. He said, "Just as I myself have the right to obtain happiness and the right to get rid of suffering, so others equally have the same feelings and the same rights" (Lieberman, 1986, p. 117). The Tibetan people have developed a kind of cultural practice of altruism for generations that operates on a mass scale and is based on sound philosophical logic. In the Tibetan system of Bodhicitta thought training, epistemology interacts with ethical practices: the method and the wisdom mutually affect each other. Just as one is said to be incapable of achieving enlightenment through altruistic action alone, it is held to be impossible to obtain Buddha nature with only wisdom. Compassion and wisdom are mutually influential consciousness. The Sermon on the Mount, according to James G. Williams (1986), is another example of altruism and love. It advocates the love of one's enemy because that kind of love requires sacrifice and risk and offers satisfaction to the self and redemption of life, which may also be instrumental in avoiding violence. For the religious and nonreligious altruist, it is a matter of nonseparation between self and other. Williams informs us that it is necessary to distinguish between love and forgiveness. The latter may be impossible if one party refuses the necessary condition for reconciliation. The Sermon asks people not to retaliate but to love their enemies. It calls for creative moral action.

To argue, for example, about forgiving genocidal murderers keeps everyone involved, going around fruitlessly in circles. However, if forgiveness is seen as a way of starting a new universal community of being, then other possibilities arise.

One possibility would be to tell descendants of the murderers the story of the genocide with the hope of offering reconciliation with the living.

Altruism and Peace

Thus far we have given an overview of a number of suggestions made by a variety of different scholars about the causes and correlates of peace. In the balance of this chapter we will stress the importance of altruism in peacemaking. Altruism is defined as helping others who are in need and who will benefit from such help; such help must involve high risk and high cost, while the helper (the altruist/rescuer) does not expect any external reward. There are some who question the existence of altruism, arguing that altruism may be only self-aggrandizement; some have even gone so far as to suggest that those people who performed heroic and risky acts on behalf of strangers, such as rescuers of Jews in Nazi-occupied Europe, were only looking for "medals" or wanted to see a movie made of their life story. We maintain that altruism exists and that it is a process that is measurable and teachable.

Recently, we concluded a study of rescuers and bystanders titled, "The Altruistic Personality: Rescuers of Jews in Nazi Europe" (Oliner & Oliner, 1988). We interviewed three groups of people for our study: (1) bona fide rescuers (people who were recognized by the institution of Yad Vashem in Israel, and who had received medals for their heroic deeds), (2) bystanders (people who did not rescue, but who served as a comparison/control group), and (3) a small sample of rescued survivors. The latter group was interviewed because we felt that they had a profound insight into the reasons the rescuers risked their lives for them. What follows is a brief summary of the study and an attempt to draw a profile of the altruist and the implications of our study for peace.

We interviewed rescuers in Poland, Germany, France, Holland, Italy, Denmark, Belgium, and Norway, as well as rescuers who reside in the United States and Canada. We sought answers to three key questions: (1) Was rescue primarily a matter of opportunity, that is, a question of external circumstances? (2) Was rescue a matter of character, that is, personal attributes and values? And finally, (3) were those attributes and values learned, and if so how, when and where?

From this sample of over 700 interviews we concluded that rescue was not a matter of opportunity. Rescuers and nonrescuers had similar knowledge of the plight of the Jews, as well as the same physical circumstances and resources for hiding Jews. Our findings strongly suggest that values are heavily associated with rescue, because rescue opportunities did not simply happen. Rather, a number of rescuers actually sought out individuals to help, recognizing the urgent need, while bystanders did not. Some rescuers said they did it for religious reasons or from a sense of anger about the injustice perpetrated upon the Jews. One rescuer, giving the reasons for helping, said,

> The reason is that every man is equal. We all have the right to live. It was plain murder, and I couldn't stand that. I would help a Mohammedan just as well as a Jew. We have got to live as human beings and not as beasts. They were worse than beasts.

> These people just had the right to live like other people . . . much as Christian people. Jewish people are the same . . . all people are the same. (Oliner & Oliner, 1988, p. 166)

Some rescuers acted out of compassion and pity toward specific people. Pity, compassion, concern, and affection were a feeling reported by 76 percent of rescuers.

> When you see a need you have to help. Our religion was part of us. We are our brother's keepers. (p. 168)
>
> We have to give our help to these people in order to save them. Not because they were Jewish, but because persecuted human beings need some help. (p. 169)

Caring was another important factor that motivated people to act. It meant not just giving lip service to caring but assuming active responsibility. They felt that failure to act would be consenting to the deaths of those victims. One rescuer said, "I could not stand idly by and observe the daily misery that was occurring" (p. 168). Another said, "I knew they were taking them and they wouldn't come back. I didn't think I could live with that knowing that I could have done something" (p. 168). Yet another said, "When I saw what was happening to them I knew I had to act because if I didn't this would get in my way for the rest of my life" (p. 168).

Rescuers experienced an urgent need to act, and many of them said that there was no other choice but to help. One rescuer, while being picked up at the airport, was asked by a curious reporter why he rescued and risked his life. He asked this question of the reporter: "Was there any other way to behave?"

Our research findings point to values of compassion, caring, justice, and social responsibility as the major factors that motivated rescuers to risk their lives to rescue Jews. How, then, were these values acquired?

Parental Influences

Parents played a paramount role for both rescuers and nonrescuers as they were growing up. Their personality and worldview developed at home as they were growing from children to adults. Rescuers' parents modeled not only kindness, compassion, justice, peace, social responsibility, and benevolence but also caring. Close family ties that promote social responsibility and caring for others are conducive to peace and altruism. Empathy toward groups and cultures also contribute to human solidarity and peace. A number of rescuers expressed abhorrence of war. Of importance, too, was the nurturance and connectedness to family and others, as well as a sense of obligation to all human beings.

One rescuer said, "I learned from my parents generosity, to be open, to help people" (Oliner & Oliner, 1988, p. 164). Another rescuer said, "I learned to be good to one's neighbors, honesty, scruples . . . to be responsible . . . concern. To work and to work hard, but also to help . . . to the point of leaving one's work to help one's neighbor" (p. 164).

Thus helping, caring, and compassion were not simply confined to one's own group but extended to diverse others. For rescuers, helping and caring was not simply a spectator sport; it was a matter of getting involved personally. Approximately 87 percent of rescuers cited at least one ethical reason for helping. The ethics cited included justice, fairness, and the belief that persecution of the innocent could not be justified. But the ethic that mattered most was the ethic of care and compassion. For most rescuers, helping was rooted in the need to assume personal responsibility, to relieve other people's suffering and pain. While rescuers felt a special responsibility toward friends or schoolmates, they also felt an obligation to others generally, including people they did not know. More than 90 percent said that they actually helped at least one stranger as well as a friend. Compassion and concern for others are further illustrated by these statements made by rescuers.

> It was unfair that I was safe simply because I was born as a Protestant. That was the main reason for me. What I did was a question of justice, it was a very humble thing. (Oliner & Oliner, 1988, p. 166)

> I could not stand by idly and observe the daily misery that was occurring. (p. 168)

> I was just sorry for them. (p. 168)

> They were good friends and I liked them very much. (p. 168)

> I did it out of a feeling of compassion for those who were weaker and needed help. (p. 168)

> When you see a need you have to help. (p. 168)

> We had to give our help to those people in order to save them. Not because they were Jews but because they were persecuted human beings who needed help. (p. 169)

The values that rescuers remember learning from their parents also differ significantly from nonrescuers. Significantly more rescuers made a point that their parents had taught them that they owed an ethical obligation to all people: "They taught me to respect all human beings" (p. 165); "I learned logical reasoning. I also learned to be tolerant . . . not to discriminate against people because of their belief or social class" (p. 165).

Furthermore, significantly more rescuers than nonrescuers emphasized learning the value of helping from their parents helping others in the spirit of generosity without concern for getting something in return: "I have learned from my parents' generosity to be open to people" (p. 164); "My parents taught me the discipline of tolerance, serving other people when they needed something. It was a general feeling. If someone was ill or in need, my parents would always help. We were taught to help in whatever way we could. Consideration and tolerance were very important in our family. My mother and father both trusted those feelings. My father could not judge people who lived or felt differently than he did. That point was made to us" (p. 220).

Rescuers were disciplined by parents as they were growing up, as were nonrescuers. But what differentiated them from nonrescuers were the types of discipline used in the home. Rescuers' parents talked to them and explained how it was wrong to hurt somebody, while bystanders' parents were more likely to spank, kick, punch, or verbally abuse, rather than reason with them.

Rescuers and nonrescuers thus emerged from their parental homes grounded in certain basic attitudes toward the world and themselves. They had a sense of who they were and how they should regard other human beings, including outsiders, and what kind of relationships they ought to have. In sum, the core of their personalities was largely formed early in their lives.

More rescuers felt a sense of responsibility toward others, feeling an obligation to help even when nothing could be gained from such help. On the other hand, significantly more nonrescuers felt exempt from such obligations, and depended on others to assume responsibilities. Nonrescuers were more detached and less emotionally receptive to helping others.

Significantly more rescuers felt themselves similar to other human beings, including Jews. A greater number of rescuers had friends from diverse, different ethnic groups, including Jews, Gypsies, and so forth.

Concern to Action

While we can see common attributes that predisposed significantly more rescuers to help Jews, the picture is not that simple. Not all rescuers possessed similar qualities in equal amounts. We therefore divided our rescuers into three groups.

Approximately 52 percent of rescuers fall into the normocentric category. By normocentric we mean the rescuers felt obliged to obey the norms and expectations of the group with which they identified. For example, a number of rescuers of this sort both in Holland and Germany felt that their churches and their ministers wanted them to help because it was the Christian thing to do. Such influence illustrates the important role communities and institutions can play to encourage moral behavior. One rescuer said, "It was not a personal individual activity . . . I had orders from the organization. To help people, I was helping myself. Since I was weakening the Germans, it was an act of cooperation, military cooperation" (Oliner & Oliner, 1988, p. 200).

The second group of rescuers, labeled empathically oriented rescuers, represent approximately 37 percent of our sample. In this group, helping Jews had to do less with any authoritative order than with some event that aroused their empathy and pity. In many such cases it was a direct face-to-face encounter with stress. The following example will illustrate the motivation of empathic rescuers:

> In 1942, I was on my way home from town and was near home when Mr. M. came out of the bushes. I looked at him in striped clothing, his head bare, shod in clogs. He might have been about 30–32 years old. And he begged me, his hands joined like in prayer . . . he had escaped from Maidanek and could I help him? He knelt down in front of me and said "You are like the Virgin Mary. (It still makes me cry.) If I get through and reach Warsaw I will never forget you." Well, how could one not help such a man. So I took him home and fed him because he was hungry. (p. 187)

She gave him clothes and bathed him.

The third group of rescuers, called autonomously principled rescuers, represent approximately 11 percent of our total sample. They acted out of largely independently derived, overarching principles; that is, beliefs they arrived at as a result of their own thinking and largely without reference to what others might say or do. Yet one cannot help thinking that those rescuers, too, were emulating some moral role model.

Profile of a Rescuer

Briefly, rescuers were much more likely to extend their concern and commitment to diverse other people. Rescuers were attached to their family of origin, felt loved and approved of, and as a result of that attachment and approval were able to commit themselves to others as well as to social institutions. Rescuers did differ from nonrescuers with respect to their attachment to persons, that is, with respect to their interpersonal connectedness and relationships.

Our data indicate that rescuers, more often than nonrescuers, perceived their roles in such relationships as bestowers of care rather than as receivers; they were more likely to perceive themselves as obligated to assume responsibility for others. This broader obligation for others we call extensivity. Extensivity consists of two elements. The first is the propensity to attach oneself in a committed interpersonal relationship to one's own group, as well as to other groups including total strangers. The second is the assumption of social responsibility and caring for all others. Rescuers exemplify this tendency. This is the profile of the rescuer:

1. Rescuers are more likely to feel psychologically closer to their families of origin, parents, and siblings than nonrescuers.
2. Rescuers are more likely to have been taught and to have internalized the ethical obligation to care for all human beings.
3. Rescuers are more likely to accept social responsibility in their relationships with other people.
4. Rescuers are more likely to be empathic toward other people's pain.
5. Rescuers are more likely to advocate peace and pluralistic democratic values.
6. Rescuers are more likely to reject bigotry, ethnocentrism, and stereotypes.
7. They are more likely to have had friends of different social groups including different religious groups, such as Jews, while they were growing up.
8. Rescuers are more likely to feel psychologically similar to a great variety of people from different social groups—ethnic, national, and religious.
9. They are more likely to feel an internal locus of control; that is, they feel that they themselves are responsible for their behavior and are not easily influenced by others.
10. They are more likely to feel that they have personal integrity; that is, they are more likely to perceive themselves as honest, helpful, able to take responsibility, and willing to stand up for their beliefs.

11. They are less likely to value obedience to authority, especially blind obedience to malevolent authority.
12. Rescuers, when disciplined for their misdeeds as they were growing up, were spoken to and the consequences of their behavior explained rather than being slapped, beaten, kicked, or verbally abused as bystanders tended to be.
13. Rescuers now feel better about themselves; that is, they still help in the community, they are still involved with the world, and their children are proud of them.
14. Rescuers have moral courage, which is the opposite of apathy and despair.

In contrast, nonrescuers considered the world as peripheral and were more concerned with themselves and their own survival. They paid scant attention to other people's troubles and at best their sense of obligation extended to a small circle from which others may have been excluded.

In sum, in order to have a more peaceful world, the virtues of care and compassion can serve as a foundation for good will, justice, and equity. We believe that altruism can sustain and buttress all other virtues, ending the cycles of estrangement, alienation, and war.

The Implications for Peace

Just as bigotry, prejudice, discrimination, racism, violence and war, anti-semitism, and sexism are taught, so we believe altruism and the consequences of a polarized world can be taught. The Thomas Theorem says that when one defines a situation as "real," it becomes real in consequences. If we define the situation in Machiavellian and Hobbsean terms, as some do, then we might reap the fruits of such a definition. On the other hand, if we define human beings as compassionate, concerned, and caring, that, too, will bear fruit. If we want to have a world without war, we have to teach and inculate in people that all human beings are spiritually, and in every other way, brothers and sisters; and to borrow a phrase, that none are children of a lesser god. The rescuers, in our view, have spoken by their deeds that all human beings deserve to live in peace and include others in their universe of responsibility. For rescuers, the idea of altruism was not simply a matter of paying lip service to an ideal, but of getting involved by risking their lives. Acts of heroism are not the exclusive province of larger-than-life figures. On the contrary, rescuers were simply ordinary people whose moral courage grew out of the routine ways they lived their daily lives—their characteristic ways of feeling, their perceptions of who should be obeyed, their attitudes toward war and peace, and the rules and examples of conduct they learned from parents and friends, religious groups, and significant others.

Acting altruistically was nourished and nurtured in their relationships at home, but although the importance of parental influence cannot be overemphasized, we also cannot place the entire load on parents alone. If we are to empower people to actively intervene in the presence of destructive social impulses, if they are to resist war and genocide, then other social institutions, such as the schools, the churches, and the workplace, need to assume this obligation as well. It must be remembered that one third of people's lives are spent on the job; and more humane workplaces, which exhibit compassion, concern, and social responsibility, will go a long way to change the image of humanity and improve it.

All of the great world religions teach the idea of common humanity. They teach morality and peace, as well as helping the unfortunate and the stranger. They must become more successful at it. It is not enough to simply talk about how one ought to be altruistic, peaceful, include all others as brothers and sisters, and resist violence. Recently, sociologist Joseph Faulkner (Bord & Faulkner, 1983) reported that 70 percent of sermons from the pulpit are totally devoid of social concerns, such as race relations, peace, and justice. It is much more important that these institutions act on it and model it. They must become more caring, and all of them need to be linked to a larger community. All institutions need to take a larger role in the dissemination of information about environmental, political, economic, and moral concerns. No single group or institution can accomplish the goal of peace by itself.

It appears to us that the time for global peace has come. Gallup polls published in January 1990 showed that 68 percent of the people believe that peace between nations will increase substantially. Even the U.S. military has ordered that anti-Soviet posters be removed from all military bases. People everywhere are craving peace, justice, and human cooperation. This is the time to mold altruistic and virtuous behavior in people. That means actions such as helping the poor and homeless, writing letters to politicians and world leaders about the abiding longing for a peaceful world. Leaders from different walks of life, including the media, business, the arts, literature, music, the scholarly fields, and others, have to speak out against antagonism, to interact with their colleagues on behalf of peace. For most people, moral behavior is the consequence of strong attachment to moral communities. The leaders have to exhibit attachment to moral communities that are universally binding. Because the power of the media is great, it ought to be used as a tool to encourage international understanding, harmony, and the consequences of bystander behavior. Should our social institutions fail to teach and advocate peace and altruism now, they may also fail to empower ordinary people in the spirit of altruism, the spirit of peace, and the great benefits of a world without war. Emil Durkheim (1961) expressed the sentiment more than a century ago when he said, "rather than agreeable ornaments to social life, altruism is essential for the survival of any society" (p. 78). What Durkheim failed to emphasize, however, and what the research of our rescuers demonstrates, is that the virtue of altruism accrued not only to society as a whole, but also to the individuals who participate in it. Reaching out to others is healthy for people: it empowers the helpers and the care givers and gives them a feeling of potency, it encourages people, and, above all, it fosters caring skills and their humanity.

CONCLUDING REMARKS

We have suggested several approaches that may enhance peace, but for us altruism is the most important and fundamental process. The rescuers in our study served as moral, caring, and compassionate role models, living the kind of life that great philosophers and theologians wrote about. The German philosopher Carl Friedrich von Weizsacker (1988) concluded that we need to emulate great moral men and women such as Zoroaster, Buddha, Gandhi, Buber, Martin Luther King, Schweitzer, Mother Teresa, and others. We would add that we need to emulate the courage and morality of the rescuers. They all taught us that what the world needs is love, charity, and justice. This is the most important moral force that can help us transform humankind. This is the most urgent item on today's agenda. Without moral transformation in altruistic directions, neither new world wars nor other catastrophes can be prevented. Just as love is important in the survival of newborn babies, so it is necessary for the survival of the planet. In the words of Fyodor Dostoyevski, should we fight evil with force or humble love? Humble love, as he concludes, is the most powerful, unequaled by any other force in the world. Altruism, putting the welfare of others alongside our own, may save humankind.

REFERENCES

Allen, J. (1971). In W. B. Franklin & W. R. Webb, (Eds.), *As a man thinketh: James Allen's greatest inspirational essays.* Kansas City: Hallmark Crown Editions.

Altmeyer, B. (1988). *Enemies of freedom.* San Francisco: Jossey-Bass.

Ardrey, R. (1966). *The Territorial imperative.* New York: Atheneum.

Bok, Sissela. (1989). *A strategy for peace.* New York: Pantheon Books.

Bord, R. J., & Faulkner, J. E. (1983). *The Catholic charismatics.* University Park & London: Pennsylvania State University.

Boulding, K. E. (1959). National images and international systems. *Journal of Conflict Resolution,* 3, 120–131.

Bulletin of Peace Proposals. (1989). 20(3).

Burke, E. (1961). *Reflections on the revolution in France. [Bound with Thomas Paine,* The rights of man.] New York: Dolphin Books.

Burckhardt, J. (1943). *Force and freedom: Reflections on history.* New York: Pantheon Books.

Cantril, H. (Ed.) (1950). *Tensions that cause war.* Urbana: University of Illinois Press.

Clausewitz, C. von. (1968). *Clausewitz on war.* Anatol Rapoport (Ed.). Baltimore: Penguin Books.

Davies, J. C. (1962). Toward a theory of revolution. *American Sociological Review.* February 27, pp. 5–19.

Durkheim, E. (1961). *Moral education.* New York: Free Press.

Ferencz, B. B., & Keyes, K., Jr. (1988) *Planethood.* Coos Bay, Vision Books.

Festinger, L. (1957). *A theory of cognitive dissonance.* New York: Harper & Row.

Freud, S. (1968). Why war? In L. Bramson & G. W. Goethals (Eds.), *War* (pp. 71–80). New York: Basic Books.

Fromm, E. (1965). *Escape from freedom.* New York: Avon Books.

Harman, W. W. (1988). The quest for security viewed as a whole-system problem. R. Thakurd (Ed.), *International Conflict Resolution* (pp. 261–280). Boulder, CO: Westview Press.

Hobbes, T. (1909). *Leviathan.* Oxford: Clarendon Press.

Ikeda, D. (1989). Toward a new globalism. *Bulletin of Peace Proposals, 20,* 229–237.

International Journal on World Peace. (1988). *5*(4).

Janis, I. L. (1972). *Victims of groupthink.* Boston: Houghlin Mifflin.

Journal of Peace Research. (1989). *26*(1).

King, W. (1989). Carter redux. *New York Times Magazine,* December 10, p. 38.

Lieberman, K. (1986). The Tibetan cultural praxis: Bodhicitta thought training. *Humboldt Journal of Social Relations, 13*(1,2), p 113–126.

Lorenz, K. (1966). *On aggression.* New York: Bantam.

May, R. (1975). *The courage to create.* New York: Bantam.

Mazrui, A. A. (1975). World culture and the search for human consensus. In Saul H. Mendlovitz (Ed.), *On the Creation of a Just World Order: Preferred Worlds for the 1990's* (pp. 1–37). New York: Free Press.

Mische, G., & Mische, P. (1977). *Toward a human world order.* New York: Paulist Press.

Moltke, H. von. (1979). In K. L. Nelson & S. C. Olin, Jr. (Eds.), *Why War?: Ideology, theory and history.* Berkeley: University of California Press.

Mussen, P., & Eisenberg-Berg, N. (1977). *Roots of caring, sharing and helping: The development of prosocial behavior in children.* San Francisco: W. H. Freeman.

Nelson, K. L., & Olin, S. C., Jr. (1979). *Why war? Ideology, theory and history.* Berkeley: University of California Press.

Oliner, S. P., & Oliner, P. (1988). *The altruistic personality: Rescuers of Jews in Nazi Europe.* New York: Free Press.

Plato. (1961). The symposium. In E. Hamilton and H. Cairns (Eds.), *The collected dialogues of Plato* (pp. 526–574). Princeton, NJ: Princeton University Press.

Reardon, B. (1988). *Educating for global responsibility: Teacher designed curricular for peace education, K–12.* New York: Teacher's College Press.

Roosevelt, T. (1926). *Works,* vol. 18, pp. 66–67. New York: Charles Scribner's Sons.

Sakamoto, Y. (1975). Toward global identity. In S. H. Mendlovitz (Ed.), *On the Creation of a just world order: Preferred Worlds for the 1990's* (pp. 187–210). New York: Free Press.

Staub, E. (1989). *The roots of evil.* Cambridge: Cambridge University Press.

Storr, A. (1968). *Human aggression.* New York: Atheneum.

Tocqueville, A. de. (1945). *Democracy in America;* 2 volumes. New York: Vintage Books.

Weizsacker, C. F. von. (1988). Justice, peace and the preservation of nature. In R. Thakur (Ed)., *International Conflict Resolution* (pp. 231–260). Boulder: Westview Press.

White, R. K. (1984). *Fearful warriors, a psychological profile of U.S.-Soviet relations.* New York: Free Press.

Wright, Q. (1943). *A study of war.* Chicago: University of Chicago Press.

Wright, Q. (1980). The nature of conflict. In R. A. Falk & S. S. Kim (Eds.), *The War System: An Interdisciplinary Approach,* pp. . Boulder, CO: Westview Press.

ADDITIONAL READINGS

Barnet, R. J. (1990). Reflections (after the cold war). *The New Yorker,* January 1, pp. 65–76.

Becker, E. (1975). *Escape from evil.* New York: Free Press.

Becker, E. (1986). *When the war was over: The voices of Cambodia's revolution and its people.* New York: Simon & Schuster.

Blainey, G. (1973). *The causes of war.* New York: Free Press.

Boulding, K. E. (1956). *The image.* Ann Arbor: University of Michigan Press.

Boulding, K. E. (1963). The economic implications of warlessness. In A. Larson (Ed.), *A Warless World* (pp. 59–74). New York: McGraw-Hill.

Boulding, K. E. (1980). National images and international systems. In R. A. Falk & S. S. Kim (Eds.), *The War System: An Interdisciplinary Approach* (pp. 536–550). Boulder, CO: Westview Press.

Campbell, D. T. (1965). Ethnocentric and other altruistic motives. In D. Levine (Ed.), *Nebraska Symposium on Motivation* (pp. 283–311). Lincoln: University of Nebraska Press.

Charny, I. W. (1982). *Genocide: The human cancer.* Boulder, CO: Westview Press.

Corson, W. H., (Ed.) (1989). *Citizen's guide to sustainable development.* Washington, DC: Global Tomorrow Coalition.

Deutsch, M. (1973). *The resolution of conflict: Constructive and destructive processes.* New Haven: Yale University Press.

Eisler, R. (1987). *The chalice and the blade.* New York: Harper & Row.

Erikson, E. H. (1950). *Childhood and society.* New York: Norton.

Erikson, E. H. (1969). *Gandhi's truth.* New York: Norton.

Eron, L. D. (1982). Parent–child interaction, television violence, and aggression of children. *American Psychologist, 37,* 197–211.

Feller, G., Schwenninger, S. R., & Singerman, D. (Eds.) (1980). *Peace and World Order Studies.* Transnational Academic Program. New York: Institute for World Order.

Fried, M. (1968). In M. Harris & R. Murphy (Eds.), *War: The anthropology of armed conflict and aggression.* Garden City, NY: The Natural History Press.

Freud, S. (1953–1974). *The standard edition of the complete psychological works of Sigmund Freud,* (vols. 14 and 22). London: Hogarth.

Fromm, E. (1973). *The anatomy of human destructiveness.* New York: Holt, Rinehart & Winston.

Gallup poll. (1990).

Gewirtz, J. L., & Kurtines, W. M. (Eds.) (1984?). *Morality, moral behavior and moral development.* New York: Wiley-Interscience.

Gilligan, C. (1982). *In a different voice: Psychological theory and women's development.* Cambridge: Harvard University Press.

Gorbachev, M. (1987). *Perestroika: New thinking for our country and the world.* New York: Harper & Row.

Groeber, J., & Hinde, R. A. (1989). *Aggression and war: Their biological and social bases.* New York: Cambridge University Press.

Gurr, T. (1970). *Why men rebel.* Princeton, NJ: Princeton University Press.

Gurr, T. (1980). Psychological factors in civil violence. In R. A. Falk & S. S. Kim (Eds.), *The war system: An interdisciplinary approach,* pp. . Boulder, CO: Westview Press.

Hanh, T. N. (1976). *The miracle of mindfulness: A manual on meditation.* M. Warren (Trans.) Boston: Beacon Press.

Hey, R. P. (1988). How the faces of voluntarism are changing in America. *The Christian Science Monitor,* December 5, p. 17.

Hobbes, T. (1909). *Leviathan.* Oxford: Clarendon Press.

Hollins, H. B., Powers, A. L., & Sommer, M. (1989). *The Conquest of War.* Boulder, CO: Westview Press.

Kriesberg, L. (1982). *Social conflicts.* Englewood Cliffs, NJ: Prentice-Hall.

Latane, B., & Darley, J. (1970). *The unresponsive bystander: Why doesn't he help?* New York: Appleton-Crofts.

Link, A. S. (1954). *Woodrow Wilson and the Progressive Era, 1910–1917.* New York: Harper & Row.

Mazrui, A. A. (1988). The moral paradigms of the superpowers: A Third World perspective. In R. Thakur (Ed.), *International Conflict Resolution* (pp. 197–210). Boulder, CO: Westview Press.

Melko, M. (1969). *52 peaceful societies.* Oakville, Ontario: Canadian Peace Research Institute Press.

Mendlovitz, S. H. (1975). *On the creation of a just world order.* New York: Free Press.

Milgram, S. (1974). *Obedience to authority: an experimental view.* New York: Harper & Row.

Niebuhr, R. (1960). *Moral man and immoral society: A study in ethics and politics.* New York: Charles Scribner's Sons.

Niffenegger, S. (1989). Why we all love to hate. *Newsweek,* August 28, pp. 62–64.

Pilgrim, P. (1983). *Peace Pilgrim: Her life and work in her own words.* Santa Fe: Ocean Tree Books.

Schell, J. (1982). *The fate of the earth.* New York: Knopf.

Sharp, G. (1970). *Exploring nonviolent alternatives.* Boston: Porter Sargent Publisher.

Silverstein, B., & Holt, R. R. (1989). Research on enemy images: Present status and future prospects. *Journal on Social Issues, 45*(2), 159–175.

Staub, E. (1988). The evolution of caring and nonaggressive persons and societies. *Journal of Social Issues, 44*(2), 81–100.

Stoessinger, J. G. (1982). *Why nations go to war.* New York: St. Martin's Press.

Toth, K. (1988). Role of the church in conflict resolution. In R. Thakur (Ed.), *International Conflict Resolution* (pp. 211–222). Boulder, CO: Westview Press.

Wasserstrom, R. A. (1970). *War and morality.* Belmont, CA: Wadsworth Publishing.

Wiesel, E. (1989). Are we afraid of peace? *Parade Magazine*, March 19, pp. 12.

Wilson, E. O. (1975). *Sociobiology, the new synthesis.* Cambridge: Belknap Press of Harvard University.

Williams, J. G. (1986). The sermon on the mount as a Christian basis of altruism. *Humboldt Journal of Social Relations, 13*(1,2), 89–112.

Wolman, N. (Ed.) (1985). *Working for peace.* San Luis Obispo: Impact Publishers.

Overview

It is June 1990, a time of transition throughout the globe, a time of confusion, of rekindled fears, of old prejudices, and renewed hope. Change, even for the better, has a way of kicking up the past: the unconscious does not let go readily.

In sculpting this book and in kneading its contents, a common theme emerged. Though we collude, albeit sometimes unconsciously, in preserving illusion, in leaning too heavily on our infantile wishes for protection, security, and easy solutions, simultaneously we do strive for better reality. We powerfully wish for peace, for a safer world: we are capable of altruism, of mutuality of purpose, of interdependence. In creating a bolder, new global vision, one safeguarding common securities, we will struggle as well with our individual and collective resistance, a resistance to change itself. We will struggle with humanity's primary masochism, its drive to self-destruct, its malevolence, greed, and narcissism.

The challenge ahead is formidable, for it is psychologically easier to project and displace, to deny and repress, than to confront, accept, negotiate, and work through. We have become quite skillful at polarizing the world (and others) into good–bad and strong–weak. Clearly, a better world will depend on our achieving a higher level of psychological integration as a species. As in psychoanalysis, the ultimate success, in this struggle toward growth, is dependent largely on one's motivation. On the global scale, I suppose survival serves well as a motive base, for it seems clear what the alternative is.

Index